Legal Issues in S

Legal Issues in Special Education provides teachers and school administrators with a clearly written, well-organized, and understandable guide from the perspective of the practitioner without formal legal training.

Even though over 50 percent of students with disabilities are now educated in general education classes, most teachers are not required to complete coursework in special education law and can unwittingly expose themselves and their schools to liability for violating the rights of students with disabilities. This practitioner's guide explicitly addresses the major issues and legal complexities educators inevitably face when dealing with special education legal and policy issues.

Using case-based learning to synthesize important legal concepts and principles from leading special education legal cases, this text guides educators, administrators, and parents alike toward a thorough understanding of, and the ability to navigate, many of the current and pressing legal concerns in special education.

Kevin P. Brady, Ph.D. is Associate Professor and Program Director, University Council of Educational Administration (UCEA) Program Center for the Study of Leadership and the Law at the University of Arkansas, USA.

Charles J. Russo, J.D., Ed.D. is Joseph Panzer Chair in Education, Director of the Ph.D. Program, and Research Professor of Law at the University of Dayton, USA.

Cynthia A. Dieterich, Ph.D. is Professor of Special Education at Baldwin Wallace University, USA.

Allan G. Osborne, Jr., Ed.D. is the former principal of the Snug Harbor Community School in Quincy, Massachusetts, and former visiting Associate Professor at Bridgewater State College, USA.

Nicole D. Snyder, J.D. is a shareholder at Latsha Davis & McKenna, P.C. and represents numerous schools in special education law, education law, and charter school law matters.

Legal Issues in Special Education

Principles, Policies, and Practices

Kevin P. Brady, Charles J. Russo, Cynthia A.
Dieterich and Allan G. Osborne, Jr.
with Nicole D. Snyder

NEW YORK AND LONDON

First published 2020
by Routledge
52 Vanderbilt Avenue, New York, NY 10017

and by Routledge
2 Park Square, Milton Park, Abingdon, Oxon, OX14 4RN

Routledge is an imprint of the Taylor & Francis Group, an informa business

© 2020 Taylor & Francis

The right of Kevin P. Brady, Charles J. Russo, Cynthia A. Dieterich, and Allan G. Osborne, Jr. to be identified as authors of this work has been asserted by them in accordance with sections 77 and 78 of the Copyright, Designs and Patents Act 1988.

Library of Congress Cataloging-in-Publication Data
A catalog record for this book has been requested

ISBN: 978-1-138-32329-2 (hbk)
ISBN: 978-1-138-32330-8 (pbk)
ISBN: 978-0-429-45149-2 (ebk)

Typeset in Minion
by Apex CoVantage, LLC
Printed and bound by CPI Group (UK) Ltd, Croydon CR0 4YY

To my mother, Eileen Brady, whose struggles and strength of living with a disability taught me the importance of educational access for everyone. K.P.B.

To students with disabilities and their families who live the law every day. And my dad who instilled the importance of education and lifelong learning. C.A.D.

To Debbie and Debbie with all our love, now, always, and forever C.J.R. A.G.O

Contents

Illustrations

Figures

Tables

Acknowledgements

Writing a book such as this without the encouragement, support, and assistance of many family, friends, and colleagues would not have been possible. Thus, while it is impossible to acknowledge everyone who influenced us in some way or contributed to this book, the authors would, at a minimum, like to extend our sincere gratitude to those who have had the greatest impact in our personal and professional lives. All of us are extremely fortunate to work with professionals who understand and genuinely value our work and provide us with the necessary resources to continue our research.

At the University of Arkansas, I (Kevin P. Brady) would like to express my sincere thanks to my colleagues in the Educational Leadership Program, including Drs. Ed Bengtson, John Pijanowski, and Kara Lasater. My professional colleagues are each caring and supportive individuals who genuinely care about their students and developing quality school leadership in Arkansas as well as the rest of the country. I am also fortunate to have an amazingly supportive and loving family. Since meeting my wife Zuzia, she has improved my life in innumerable ways. This still holds true after nearly two decades of marriage. My two sons, Luca and Nic, are wonderful people, who bring me immeasurable joy and happiness. While baseball and the New York Yankees are still my favorite sport and professional team, I have embraced the world of soccer based on both my sons' pure love of this game.

I (Charlie J. Russo) extend a special note of thanks and appreciation to our two wonderful children, David Peter and Emily Rebecca. These two bright and inquisitive children that my wife Debbie and I have raised have grown to be wonderful young adults who provide me with a constant source of inspiration and love. Finally, thank you to my wife, Debbie, my best friend who shows great patience as I ramble on endlessly about litigation in special education.

I (Cynthia A. Dieterich) would like to extend a warm thank you to all the professionals that have contributed to my understanding of special education law, particularly to colleagues I have encountered in my decades as a member of the Education Law Association. Thank you to Marija Karic, Baldwin Wallace University student assistant, who masterfully searched for case law. My friends and colleagues across the institutions of higher education that I have served as a faculty member for supporting my journey as a researcher and educator. Particular thanks to Dr. Christine Villani for the many years of our collaborative work in education law. To all my family and friends who have provided unconditional support. Thanks to my husband for keeping the home fires burning in Virginia during my academic pursuits in Ohio. To my daughter who inspired me to strive and take on challenges to make me a stronger mom.

I (Allan G. Osborne, Jr.) would like to thank my former colleagues at the Quincy Public Schools for their decades of inspiration and support. I also wish to thank my friend and former doctoral mentor, Dr. Phil DiMattia of Boston College, for first encouraging me to investigate many of the issues contained in this book and for continuing to challenge my thinking. Finally, I would like to thank my wife Debbie who has been the major influence in my life and professional career.

About the Authors

First Author

Kevin P. Brady, Ph.D., is Associate Professor in the Department of Curriculum and Instruction in the College of Education and Health Professions at the University of Arkansas in Fayetteville, Arkansas. He is also an adjunct associate professor at Teachers College, Columbia University, where he teaches a course in school law and ethics in the Summer Principals Academy (SPA). His primary research areas are legal issues in special education, Fourth Amendment issues in schools, and equity issues involving school finance.

He is currently the Program Director of the University Council of Educational Administration (UCEA) Center for the Study of Leadership and the Law. He is a former member of the Board of Directors of the Education Law Association (ELA) and is on the editorial board of several journals, including *Education and Urban Society*, *Journal of Disability Policy Studies*, and *West's Education Law Reporter*. His scholarship appears in a wide array of educational leadership, law, and policy journals.

Second Author

Charles J. Russo, J.D., Ed.D., is the Joseph Panzer Chair in Education in the School of Education and Health Sciences, Director of its Ph.D. Program, and Research Professor of Law in the School of Law at the University of Dayton. The 1998–99 President of the Education Law Association and 2002 recipient of its McGhehey (Achievement) Award, he authored or coauthored more than 300 articles in peer-reviewed journals; authored, coauthored, edited, or co-edited 68 books, and has more than 1,100 publications. Also, Dr. Russo has spoken extensively on issues in Education Law in the 34 States and 30 nations outside of the U.S. on all six inhabited continents.

His is currently a visiting professor in the College of Education and Capital Normal University and Notre Dame University of Australia, Faculty of Law Sydney Campus, and has served in this capacity at Queensland University of Technology in Brisbane and the University of Newcastle, Australia; the University of Sarajevo, Bosnia and Herzegovina; South East European University, Macedonia; the Potchefstroom and Mafeking Campuses of Northwest University, South Africa; the University of Malaya in Kuala Lumpur, Malaysia; the University of Sao Paulo, Brazil; Yeditepe University, Istanbul Turkey; Inner Mongolia University for the Nationalities, Tongliao, Inner Mongolia; and Peking University in Beijing, China.

Third Author

Cynthia A. Dieterich, Ph.D. is a professor of special education in the School of Education at Baldwin Wallace University in Cleveland, Ohio. Her research has included the use of quantitative, qualitative, and legal analysis with publications in medical, legal, and educational journals. She has addressed issues related to special education law, teacher education, functional behavioral assessment, young children with hearing impairments, young children with hemangiomas, and health-related services in special education.

Her work is cited in journals beyond education including law, pediatrics, psychology, psychiatry, dermatology, plastic surgery, psychology, communication disorders, and otolaryngology journals in over a dozen countries. She frequently presents her research at national conferences of the Education Law Association, Council for Exceptional Children, American Educational Research Association, and Council for Learning Disabilities.

Prior to her position at Baldwin Wallace University, she was an Assistant Professor of special education at the Isabelle Farrington College of Education at Sacred Heart University in Fairfield, Connecticut and an Associate Professor of special education at Cleveland State University, Cleveland, Ohio. She completed her doctoral degree at Kent State University in special education with an emphasis in early intervention and psychometrics.

Dr. Dieterich began her career as an educator at the early elementary level in inclusive settings; a teacher for students in K–8 with learning disabilities; and a teacher/counselor for students who were emotionally disturbed. Her focus as a classroom educator was on the importance of family in the life of a child with a disability and the understanding that family plays a major role in the child's education.

Fourth Author

Allan G. Osborne, Jr., Ed.D., is the former principal of the Snug Harbor Community School in Quincy, Massachusetts, and a former visiting associate professor at Bridgewater State College. He received his doctorate in educational leadership from Boston College. Dr. Osborne has authored or coauthored numerous articles, monographs, textbooks, and textbook chapters on special education law, along with textbooks on other aspects of special education.

A past president of the Education Law Association (ELA), he has been a frequent presenter at ELA conferences and writes the "Students with Disabilities" chapter of the *Yearbook of Education Law*, which is published by ELA. Dr. Osborne is on the Editorial Advisory Committee of *West's Education Law Reporter* and is coeditor of the "Education Law Into Practice" section of that journal. He also serves as an editorial consultant for many other publications in education law and special education.

Contributor

Nicole D. Snyder, J.D. is a member of the Education and Litigation Practice Group and Chair of Special Education Practice at the law firm of McKenna Snyder LLC. Ms. Snyder represents numerous schools in special education law, education law and charter school law matters. She routinely advises and represents schools in cases arising under IDEA and Section 504 and regularly conducts trainings for school personnel and school boards. Ms. Snyder is a member of PBI's Legal Services for Exceptional Children's Committee, the Education Law Association, Alliance of Public Charter School Attorneys, and the Pennsylvania Bar Association. She has lectured and presented published articles at various seminars on special education law, education law and attorney ethics, including: PBI's Exceptional Children's Conferences, Lehigh University's Education Law Symposium, iNACOL, and ELA. She is a registered lobbyist who testified on behalf of charter schools for equitable special education funding.

She has been admitted to practice before the Supreme Court of Pennsylvania, the United States Court of Appeals for the Third Circuit, United States District Court for the Eastern District of Pennsylvania, the United States District Court for the Middle District of Pennsylvania, the United States District Court for the Western District of Pennsylvania, the Supreme Court of Ohio, the Supreme Court of New Jersey, and the United States District Court for the District of New Jersey.

She received her J.D. from Villanova University School of Law and her B.A. in English *magna cum laude* from Villanova University. Prior to joining private practice, Ms. Snyder served as a judicial law clerk for the Honorable Bonnie Brigance Leadbetter of the Commonwealth Court and served as a judicial intern for the Honorable Juan R. Sánchez when he presided over matters for the Chester County Court of Common Pleas.

Preface

Thank you for selecting our book as one of your sources of legal information involving the myriad of legal issues affecting today's students with disabilities enrolled in pre-elementary through secondary schools nationwide. Back in 1975, Congress enacted monumental legislation known as the Education For All Handicapped Children Act (EFAHC) mandating a free appropriate public education (FAPE) in the least restrictive environment (LRE) for all eligible students with disabilities, tailored to their unique needs in their individualized education programs (IEPs). Most recently reauthorized in 2004, this comprehensive federal law, now known as the Individuals with Disabilities Education Improvement Act (IDEIA) serves as the nation's leading federal legislation addressing the educational and behavioral needs of students with a wide variety as well as levels of severity of disabilities. In this book, we will refer to the present Individuals with Disabilities Education Improvement Act (IDEIA) as the IDEA 2004.

This book begins by tracing the need for improved special education legal literacy among those individuals who work closely with students with disabilities in school settings. A review of existing research literature provides compelling evidence that many current educators and school leaders who work closely with students with disabilities are either uninformed or misinformed concerning legal issues involving special education. Using a case-based learning (CBL) model approach, this book explores in detail many of the difficult and contentious areas associated with of the IDEA 2004 as well as its two accompanying federal antidiscrimination laws, Section 504 of the Rehabilitation Act of 1973 (Section 504) and the Americans with Disabilities Act (ADA). The authors synthesize important legal concepts and principles from important special education legal cases and provide excerpts from selected legal decisions to assist educators and parents alike how to better understand and more easily navigate many of the current and pressing legal issues and concerns in special education. Readers will find assistance in examining many legal issues impacting students with disabilities in school settings, including:

1. Identification, evaluation, and eligibility of students with disabilities
2. Free Appropriate Public Education (FAPE)
3. Least Restrictive Environment (LRE)
4. Related services, assistive technology, and student transition services
5. Disciplinary issues impacting students with disabilities
6. Parental legal rights in the special education process
7. Dispute resolution options in the special education process
8. Available legal remedies
9. Federal antidiscrimination laws that prohibit discrimination and improve the access of students with disabilities to educational facilities

While the current IDEA 2004 statute and its regulations are designed to be comprehensive in addressing the needs and legal rights of students with disabilities, this federal law and its accompanying regulations have generated more litigation than any other educational law in American legal history. Insofar as we live in a litigious society where parents are fully aware of their rights and those of their children, and are willing to seek judicial recourse, it should not come as a surprise that these conflicts would lead to litigation, a small portion of which is excerpted in this book. Aware of the complexity of the IDEA 2004, its regulations, and the many legal cases that these federal laws have generated, this book is designed to provide educators, whether in pre-service programs preparing to become teachers, administrators, school counselors or a variety of other positions in schools, or professionals already serving in these capacities, with wide-ranging information on legal issues pertaining to special education.

Using a case-based learning approach (CBL) to positively influence learning about critical special education-related legal information, concepts, principles, and practices, this book combines a narrative approach with carefully chosen legal cases involving students with disabilities that illuminate how both federal and state courts have interpreted the IDEA and its regulations, addressing the delivery of special education and related services to students with disabilities. As such, one of the primary goals of this book is to offer a comprehensive yet readable discussion of the leading principles, policies, and practices impacting the legally required delivery of special education and related services to eligible students with disabilities. Therefore, we believe that this book can serve as a primary text in courses on legal issues and special education or as a supplementary text in general educational law courses. As a book that uses actual legal cases to illustrate certain concepts and principles, this book examines both the substantive and procedural requirements associated with the IDEA 2004, its regulations, and the impact litigation has on educators and school leaders.

For Whom Is This Book Designed?

This book is designed to provide educators, whether in pre-service programs preparing to become teachers, building level administrators, counselors, or a variety of other positions in schools, or professionals already serving in these capacities, with wide-ranging information on the law of special education. Additionally, the authors believe this book can facilitate training or professional development initiatives aimed at school employees currently working closely with students with disabilities. This book is designed to assist in making educators and other school employees aware of the many requirements governing the law regarding special education, in the hope that this increased special education legal literacy will put them in a better position to implement quality and legally compliant special education and related services to eligible students as they work collaboratively with the parents and/or legal guardians. In light of the detail that the book provides, we also believe that it can serve as a current and concise desk reference for practicing educators ranging from building or district-level administrators to classroom teachers of all kinds as well as resource specialists in special education and related fields, such as counseling, social work, or health-related fields in schools.

This book is divided into three distinct parts. Part I, Addressing and Maintaining Special Education Legal Literacy, addresses the diverse literature on special education legal literacy, including but not limited to historical, legal, and educational perspectives on the journey of students with disabilities' exclusion and eventual access to schools across the country. Chapter 1 addresses the existing literature on special education legal literacy, especially the alarming number of individuals who are either uninformed or misinformed about important special education legal issues in school systems. Chapter 2 examines the historical development of laws impacting students with disabilities. Chapter 3 assists readers in finding special education legal information online. Part II of the book, IDEA 2004: A Legal Primer, comprises a sizable portion of the text's content. Chapter 4 describes the basic structures and major principles of the IDEA 2004. Chapter 5 addresses the multitude of legal issues surrounding the identification, evaluation, and eligibility of students under the IDEA 2004. Chapter 6 provides a detailed discussion of the individualized education program, or IEP, the so-called "legal blueprint" of special education and related services for eligible students under the IDEA 2004. Chapter 7 addresses two necessary and critical provisions of the IDEA 2004: free appropriate public education (FAPE) in the least restrictive environment (LRE) for eligible students. Chapter 8 discusses a variety of important special education provisions under the IDEA 2004, including related services, assistive technology (AT), and student transition services. Chapter 9 confronts the controversial legal topic(s) associated with disciplining students with disabilities under the IDEA 2004. Chapter 10 discusses alternatives to litigation through the various IDEA 2004's dispute resolution processes. Chapter 11 discusses the major legal remedies available when school officials are alleged to have violated the free appropriate public education (FAPE) provision of the IDEA 2004 for eligible students. Chapter 12 acknowledges the invaluable role of parents in the special education decision-making process. Part III of the book yields with the two federal antidiscrimination statutes impacting students with disabilities. The book's final chapter, Chapter 13, discusses the relevance of both Section 504 of the Rehabilitation Protection Act of 1973 and the Americans with Disabilities Act in educational facilities.

Again, we thank you for purchasing our book. All of the authors welcome your thoughts concerning how the book can be improved to better inform and maintain your own special education legal literacy.

Sincerely,
Kevin P. Brady
Charles J. Russo
Cynthia A. Dieterich
Allan G. Osborne, Jr.
Nicole D. Snyder

I
Addressing and Maintaining Special Education Legal Literacy

1
Introduction
Making the Case for Special Education Legal Literacy

Key Concepts and Terms in This Chapter

- Ignorance of the law is not always an excuse to liability
- Special education legal literacy
- Case-based learning (CBL) model
- Exhaustion of administrative remedies rule

Ignorantia Juris Non Excusat

The Latin maxim "ignorantia juris non excusat" is roughly translated to "ignorance of the law is no excuse" and represents a fairly long-standing U.S. legal tradition that individuals claiming they are unaware of a particular law(s) or principle(s) may not escape legal liability by simply indicating that they are either unaware or not knowledgeable of the law's content (Ballentine, 1916). According to Littleton (2008), the increasing "legalization of the educational environment" combined with educators' overall lack of knowledge related to legal concerns and issues taking place in schools is a major problem that needs to be addressed (p. 76). Presently, considerable research evidence suggests that today's educators and school administrators are either improperly prepared or not trained at all to effectively handle a majority of the legal situations they encounter on a regular basis in school environments (Bull & McCarthy, 1995; Imber, 2008; McCarthy, 2008; Pazey & Cole, 2013; Zirkel, 2006). One potential benefit of the "ignorantia juris non excusat" principle is that it provides an incentive and opportunity for individuals to educate themselves and become more knowledgeable about the law. As stated by Davies (1998)

> Citizens are compelled either to know the law or to proceed in ignorance at their own peril. While sometimes harsh, the gains secured by the maxim—a better educated and more law-abiding citizenry, and the avoidance of pervasive mistake of law claims—are thought to outweigh any individual injustice resulting from its application.
>
> (p. 343)

Given the ongoing, worldwide expansion, reliance, and accessibility to online sources for our daily information, it is often much easier and less costly today for people to better educate themselves about the law and its implications. Significant technological developments in the ability to access online, digitalized legal information, including legal information related to children and youth with disabilities has the real possibility to "dramatically change the nature of legal information from an economy of scarcity to one that is abundant with information and accessible to a wide audience" (Brady & Bathon, 2012, p. 589). As will be discussed in more detail in Chapter 3, there is a current, ongoing movement to make online digitalized legal information, including legal cases, documents, and specialized legal commentary related to education much more accessible to everyone for viewing and sharing with others at little to no cost (Brady & Bathon, 2012). A clear social justice and equity-centered benefit of improved online access to special education legal information is increased access, especially to those individuals, groups/organizations, or school systems without the appropriate financial resources to pay for accurate, quality, computer-assisted legal information and research (Pazey & Cole, 2013). Thus, improving and maintaining one's special education legal literacy through an awareness of available online special education-related legal resources is "likely to find a sizable receptive audience in the diverse education law community" (Brady & Bathon, 2012, p. 596). As will become apparent quite quickly, special education law uses many acronyms. Table 1.1 depicts many of the most common acronyms used in special education law.

Table 1.1 Common Acronyms Used in Special Education Law, Practices, and Procedures

Acronym	Term
AAC	Augmentative and Alternative Communication
ADA	Americans with Disabilities Act
ADD	Attention Deficit Disorder
ADHD	Attention Deficit Hyperactivity Disorder
ASD	Autism Spectrum Disorder
AT	Assistive Technology
BD	Behavior Disorder
BIP	Behavior Intervention Plan
CAP	Corrective Action Plan
CCEIS	Comprehensive Coordinated Early Intervening Services
C.F.R.	Code of Federal Regulations
DD	Developmental Disabilities; Developmental Delay
EC	Early Childhood
ED	Emotional Disturbance
EDGAR	Education Department General Administrative Regulations
EIS	Early Intervening Services
ESA	Educational Service Agency
ESY	Extended School Year
FAPE	Free Appropriate Public Education
FBA	Functional Behavioral Assessment
FERPA	Family Educational Rights and Privacy Act
FR	Federal Register
IAES	Interim Alternative Educational Setting
ID	Intellectual Disability
IDEA	Individuals with Disabilities Education Act
IEE	Independent Educational Evaluation
IEP	Individualized Education Program
IFSP	Individualized Family Services Plan
ILC	Independent Living Center
ISP	Individualized Service Plan
LD	Learning Disability
LEA	Local Educational Agency (e.g., school district)
LEP	Limited English Proficiency
LRE	Least Restrictive Environment
MDR	Manifestation Determination Review

Acronym	Term
MTSS	Multi-Tiered System of Support
NCLB	No Child Left Behind
OCR	Office of Civil Rights, U.S. Department of Education
OHI	Other Health Impairment
OSEP	Office of Special Education Programs, U.S. Department of Education
OSERS	Office of Special Education and Rehabilitative Services, U.S. Department of Education
OT	Occupational Therapy
PBS	Positive Behavioral Supports
PWN	Prior Written Notice
SEA	State Educational Agency
Section 504	Section 504 of the Rehabilitation Act of 1973
SPP	State Performance Plan
TA	Technical Assistance
U.S.C.	United States Code
VI	Visual Impairment

Current State of Special Education Legal Illiteracy in Our Schools

Based on a review of the research literature, legal and educational researchers stress the need to improve the current state of legal literacy among today's educators and building and district-level administrators, as well as the many individuals employed within school settings (Decker & Brady, 2016; Davidson & Algozzine, 2002; DiPaola & Walther-Thomas, 2003; Pazey & Cole, 2013; Painter, 2001; Powell, 2010; Osterman & Hafner, 2009; Zirkel & Lupini, 2003). The current state of insufficient legal awareness and knowledge among educators, school and district-level leadership, and school employees appears to be particularly acute in the area of special education (Bineham, 2014; Davidson & Algozzine, 2002; Decker & Pazey, 2017; Herbst, 2004; Militello, Schimmel, & Eberwein, 2009; Painter, 2001; Powell, 2010; Wagner & Katsiyannis, 2010; Yell, 2019). Despite nearly a half century of increased legal protections at both the federal and state levels assisting students with disabilities, many of the individuals who work closely with today's students with disabilities remain either uninformed or unaware of the legal rights and policies designed to protect students with disabilities (Umpstead, Decker, Brady, Schimmel, & Militello, 2015). Unfortunately, this lack of legal literacy is not without negative implications, including the unequal treatment, discrimination, and even abuse of students with disabilities in schools (Umpstead, Decker, Brady, Schimmel, & Militello, 2015). This introductory chapter begins with the premise that actively addressing and maintaining one's special education legal literacy can more effectively serve the interests and needs of children and youth with disabilities enrolled in schools. While the significance and overall impact of the law in contemporary schools is increasing nationwide, the research evidence suggests that today's educators and the variety of other school employees who work closely with students are often either ill-informed or completely unaware of critical legal knowledge directly related to their jobs (McCarthy, 2016; Decker, 2014; Gullat & Tollet, 1997). The direct and applicable benefits to educators and school employees of a having a better knowledge and understanding of the law as it impacts schools are significant, including the ability to "recognize the extent and limits of their discretion, to exercise leadership, to use the law to advance policy objectives, to avoid unnecessary litigation, and to make optimal use of limited resources" (Heubert, 1997, p. 566).

A lack of legal knowledge among contemporary school leaders, educators, parents, and other school employees is particularly evident as it relates to legal issues, policies, and practices involving students with disabilities (Umpstead, Decker, Brady, Schimmel, & Militello, 2015). Legal scholars maintain that special education legal compliance is one of the leading and "most contentious" topics involving the myriad of legal issues impacting schools (Eckes, 2008, pp. 8–9). Based on recent statistics, it is evident that the number of students receiving special education and related services is steadily rising. During the 2015–16 school year, for example, the number of eligible students ages three through twenty-one receiving special education services was calculated at approximately 6.7 million, or 13 percent of all enrolled public-school students in the U.S. (McFarland et al., 2018). It is a misconception to conclude that legal concerns of students with disabilities are restricted to special education teachers with classes comprised exclusively of students with disabilities. Instead, it is estimated that more than half of students identified with disabilities are enrolled in today's general education classrooms across the country (Institute of Education Sciences, 2010). While today's students with disabilities in the U.S. are afforded numerous legal entitlements and protections, a combination of confusion, misinformation, and general lack of legal knowledge has negatively impacted the delivery of legally mandated special education and related services to eligible students with disabilities. As a result, special education-related lawsuits are increasingly becoming a more common area of legal action initiated by parents against schools (Karanxha & Zirkel, 2014; Katsiyannis & Herbst, 2004).

While many of today's educational organizations recognize legal information and knowledge as an essential professional competency for today's educators, few states actually mandate training specifically targeting legal issues that impact schools as part of their pre-service or ongoing professional development for either educators or school administrators (Militello, Schimmel, & Eberwein, 2009). For over a half century, researchers have recommended that teachers and administrators receive additional and specialized legal training (McCarthy, 2008; Reglin, 1992). An increasing number of studies reveal a significant correlation between legal training and increased legal knowledge (Bull & McCarthy, 1995; Eberwein, 2008). Relatedly, other national surveys indicate that a majority of educators report not feeling legally prepared to properly handle legal issues arising in their own schools (Militello, Schimmel, & Eberwein, 2009). Despite real perceptions of feeling unprepared to handle legal concerns in schools, the research shows that surveyed school leaders and educators indicate a genuine desire to want more specialized training in legal issues, specifically the myriad of legal issues involving special education (Davidson & Algozzine, 2002).

Additionally, existing research reveals the need for substantially greater legal training for today's pre-service and in-service educators (Fischer, Schimmel, & Stellman, 2007; Gullatt & Tollett, 1997). For example, Gajda (2008) found that only one state currently requires its pre-service teachers to complete a single course in school law or a related course. In order to make better and more informed legal decisions involving students with disabilities, today's school administrators and educators must do more than simply learn the fundamentals of special education law (Decker & Pazey, 2017). Instead, the expectation should be that all school employees who work directly with students with disabilities and their families are taught the relevant skills of applying the law to the specific situations they encounter. In other words, school officials must not only be legally knowledgeable, but they must also be legally literate. Decker and Brady (2016) have defined legal literacy as:

> the legal knowledge, understanding, and skills that enable educators to apply relevant legal rules to their everyday practice. Those who are legally literate are able to spot legal issues, identify applicable laws or legal standards, and apply the relevant legal rules to solve legal dilemmas.
>
> (p. 231)

The research literature has identified the need to significantly increase the special education legal literacy of today's school communities (Decker & Brady, 2016; Katsiyannis & Herbst, 2004; Pazey & Cole, 2013; Wagner & Katsiyannis, 2010). More specifically, research evidence supports that an overwhelming majority of today's educators and school administrators receive little to no specialized training in legal issues involving special education (Eberwein, 2009; Militello & Schimmel, 2008). For instance, the overwhelming majority of college and university-level school administrator preparation programs in the U.S. currently do not require aspiring school principals to complete any formal coursework in legal aspects of special education (Bineham, 2014; Pazey & Cole, 2013; Powell, 2010). Decker and Brady (2016) argue that special education legal literacy must be prioritized in today's schools based on four primary justifications, including

1. Students with disabilities are already guaranteed a unique set of both federal and state-level legal protections and entitlements;
2. Existing research provides compelling evidence that a majority of today's educators as well as school-level administrators educators are significantly underprepared to competently handle special education-related legal situations;

3. Most schools are experiencing increases in legal challenges involving students with disabilities; and
4. Many of these special education-related legal challenges could be properly addressed with more effective and specialized training in special education legal concepts and principles.

Inadequate Professional Development and Specialized Legal Training

Administrators, educators, and pre-service teachers are not adequately trained in special education law despite the unique legal protections given to student with disabilities. According to Schimmel and Militello (2008), school principals rarely realize that they are "the chief teachers of law in their schools" (p. 54). In fact, the advice principals provide is "a mixture of accurate, inaccurate, and ambiguous" information that may confuse and misinform educators (Militello, Schimmel, & Eberwein, 2009, p. 39). It is especially problematic that today's school-level leadership lack requisite legal knowledge considering that one of their professional and ethical responsibilities is to ensure that all school employees comply with existing special education laws and practices serving eligible students with disabilities enrolled in their schools.

To date, for example, only two large-scale, multistate studies measuring educators' legal knowledge exist. In the first study, Schimmel and Militello (2007) surveyed 1,317 elementary though secondary public-school teachers across 17 states and concluded that approximately half of those educators who were surveyed were either uninformed or misinformed about the law. The authors of the study determined that "teachers' primary source of information and misinformation about school law was from other teachers who were often similarly uninformed" (p. 257). Eighty-five percent of the surveyed teachers indicated that they had not taken a school law-related course during their teacher preparation program while only 9 percent had previously taken a school law course since they started teaching. Schimmel and Militello's study reiterated previous concerns that teachers lacked legal literacy and offered new, additional research-based findings concerning the primary sources of teachers' legal information as well as direct implications involving the relationship between a teacher's legal literacy level(s) and how it impacts their professional practice as educators.

In addition to the legal literacy studies measuring principals' and teachers' legal knowledge, a few studies have examined whether pre-service teachers have received adequate legal training and professional development (Bruner & Bartlett, 2008). In a second study of pre-service teachers, Gullatt and Tollett (1997) discovered that only two states required pre-service teachers to complete an education law-related course. Specifically, this study also identified that over two-thirds of the 480 Louisiana teachers surveyed did not complete a postsecondary-level course in education law, and consequently, many reported feeling "underprepared in all legal areas of education" (Gullatt & Tollett, p. 133).

Furthermore, traditional public schools are not the only schools facing legal illiteracy. Evidence also suggests today's charter schools are experiencing significant challenges in addressing special education-related legal issues within their school environments (Garda, 2011; Drame, 2011; Estes, 2009). For instance, students with disabilities have been sometimes illegally counseled away from enrolling in charter schools and school officials have admitted to feeling unprepared to serve students with disabilities in charter school environments (Drame, 2011).

The Use of Case-Based Learning (CBL) to Address the Special Education Legal Literacy Gap

A review of existing research suggests that the adoption of a case-based learning, commonly referred to as CBL, can be an effective method for teaching the law to various members of today's educational community, especially instruction pertaining to relevant legal principles and strategies drawn from actual legal cases involving students (Decker & Pazey, 2017). In a review of the literature, Williams (2005) describes how CBL adopts collaborative learning, facilitates the integration of learning, develops students' intrinsic and extrinsic motivation to learn, encourages learner self-reflection and critical reflection, allows for scientific inquiry, integrates knowledge and practice, and supports the development of a variety of learning skills. If used appropriately, the case method instructional model can be effectively used to facilitate training and professional development initiatives for educators and school employees (Leko, Brownell, Sindelar, &

Murphy, 2012; McNergney, Ducharme, & Ducharme, 1999a). For example, a case-based instructional model affords educators the opportunity to examine specific details associated with an individual legal case as well as analyze a legally viable course of action grounded on legal principles and precedent discussed in the legal case (McNergney, Ducharme, & Ducharme, 1999b). Additionally, reading school-level legal cases actually exposes educators to alternative perspectives and potentially conflicting ethical and legal considerations, as well as the unique subtleties of a particular legal situation in a specific school environment. Moreover, all of these discussions allow the "learner" the unique opportunity to contemplate their own personal reactions and decision-making process in a "simulated and safe environment" but that also reflects situations and dilemmas that closely replicate what they can expect to encounter in their own school environments (Rodriguez, Gentilucci, & Sims, 2006).

Established legal case-based method of instruction as used extensively in legal education for over a century can be successfully transferred from a traditional legal education context to develop effective, contextualized learning environments for educators (Decker & Pazey, 2017; Lasky & Karge, 2006; Williams, 1992). Since the late nineteenth century, the dominant teaching method adopted by U.S. law schools across the country is the legal case method, which is often characterized by teacher-led, group-based discussions (Williams, 1992). The creation of the case method has been credited to Christopher Langdell, who became the dean of Harvard Law School in 1870. Presently, legal case-based instruction is used extensively at almost every accredited law school nationwide and provides law students with a useful structure for organizing legal knowledge that can be applied in professional practice. A major assumption of the legal case method instructional process is that it will assist individuals to learn and recognize important legal concepts and principles though the reading of actual situations that have already taken place. The authors of this book maintain that the legal case-based learning model holds significant potential for improving the special education legal literacy levels of those persons who work closely with children and youth with disabilities in educational settings.

The use of case-based learning requires learners to not only to acquire legal knowledge but simultaneously develop the necessary analytical thinking required for improving and maintaining their legal literacy, which for the purposes of this book is defined as "the legal knowledge, understanding, and skills enabling educators to apply relevant legal rules to their everyday practice" (Decker & Brady, 2016, p. 231). As illustrated in Figure 1.1, case-based learning (CBL) can be used as a conceptual learning model for improving a

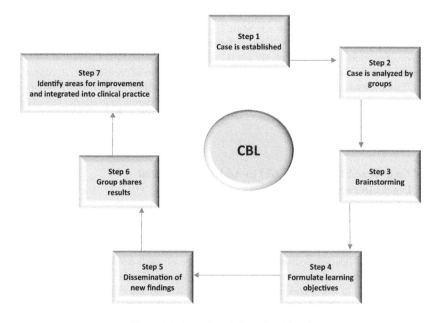

Figure 1.1 Case-Based Learning Model

person's special education legal literacy, especially for those in the education profession. The following seven steps can be applied to someone using the legal cases in this book as a means to learn more about important special education legal concepts and principles. These seven steps in a CBL–based model approach to improving special education legal literacy include:

1. Legal case is established
2. Legal case is analyzed in groups
3. Brainstorming occurs among group members
4. Formulate learning objectives surrounding the legal case
5. Dissemination of new findings
6. Group share results
7. Identify areas for improvement and integrate into clinical, or professional practice

Case-Based Learning (CBL) in Practice: Special Education Law in Practice

As a review of the existing research literature supports, today's schools are faced with the problem of a sizable gap in educators' and other school employees' lack of appropriate training and professional development addressing the unique legal protections and entitlements for eligible students with disabilities (Miles, 2011; MacNaughton, Hall, & Maccini, 2001; Merseth, 1990). The authors of this book believe that including specific, school-level legal cases combined with appropriate discussion of relevant legal concepts and principles as they impact eligible students with disabilities is an effective method to inform professional practitioners in education about the law and thus improve their overall special education legal literacy.

As seen with other landmark legal decisions involving education, including the seminal *Brown v. Board of Education* (1954) as well as numerous other cases, a single legal case and its impact has the potential to change the course of American schools. With this in mind, many of the chapters in this book include carefully selected and edited excerpts from specific legal cases involving students with disabilities, which contain important legal concepts and principles that are useful and directly applicable to educators as well as other practitioners who work closely with students with disabilities in school settings. At the end of certain chapters, one or more special education legal cases is profiled in a section the authors call "Special Education Law in Practice," which helps illustrate to the reader specific legal concepts or principles discussed in a particular chapter. Table 1.2 details the sixteen "Special Education Law in Practice" legal cases profiled in this book and the legal concepts and principles that derive from these cases. Sudzina (1999) recommends the following five steps in analyzing a legal case, including:

1. Identifying the issues and facts in a particular legal case
2. Considering the perspectives or values of the actors in a case
3. Identifying professional knowledge from practice, theory, and/or research that might be relevant in developing a particular course of action
4. Projecting actions that might be taken in a legal case
5. Forecasting likely consequences, both positive and negative, of particular actions

(p. 19)

By actively reading, analyzing, and discussing the actual legal language used by judges from various legal jurisdictions, including the U.S. Supreme Court, federal and state-level courts, as well as lower court opinions, readers develop an improved and more detailed understanding of the impact of judicial opinions on their own professional practice of working and serving the best interests of students with disabilities within their own school environments. The authors are keenly aware of the complexity associated with special education law, including the myriad of federal and state statutes, regulations, and multitude of legal cases spanning different legal jurisdictions that special education-related legal disputes between parents and/or legal guardians and schools have generated. Please note that it is a common practice not to reference the full names of students in the legal case names. This explains why the names of minor students are often abbreviated in the legal cases.

Table 1.2 Profiled "Special Education Law in Practice" Legal Cases

Case #	Case Name/Citation	Chapter	Legal Concept/Principle
No. 1	*Fry v. Napoleon Community Schools* 137 S. Ct. 743 (2017)	1	IDEA's "Exhaustion of Administrative Remedies" Rule
No. 2	*Watson v. City of Cambridge* 157 Mass. 561 (1893)	2	Sanctioned Exclusion of Students with Disabilities From Public Schools
No. 3	*Pennsylvania Association for Retarded Children (PARC) v. Commonwealth of Pennsylvania* 343 F. Supp. 279 (1972)	2	Rights of Students With Disabilities to a Public Education
No. 4	*Mills v. Board of Education of the District of Columbia* 348 F. Supp. 866 (1972)	2	Establishment of Due Process Rights for Students With Disabilities
No. 5	*Timothy W. v. Rochester, New Hampshire School District* 875 F. 2d 954 (1989)	5	IDEA's Zero Reject/Child Find Principle
No. 6	*J.D. v. Pawlet School District* 224 F. 3d 60 (2000)	5	IDEA Eligibility Requires That the Student's Disability(ies) "Adversely Impacts" the Student's Educational Performance
No. 7	*D.D. Ex. Rel. V.D. v. New York City Department of Education* 465 F. 3d 503 (2006)	6	Right to a Free Appropriate Public Education Requires That Individualized Education Programs Be Implemented as Soon as Possible
No. 8	*Board of Education of the Hendrick Hudson Central School District v. Rowley* 458 U.S. 176 (1982)	7	Definition of Free Appropriate Public Education (FAPE)
No. 9	*Endrew F. v. Douglas County School District RE-1* 137 S. Ct. 988 (2017)	7	Clarified Existing FAPE Standard. A Student's IEP Must Be "Reasonably Calculated to Enable a Child to Make Progress in Light of the Child's Circumstance."
No. 10	*Gibson v. Forest Hills School District* 655 Fed. Appx. 423 (6th Cir. 2016)	8	Postsecondary Transition Needs of a Student With Multiple Disabilities
No. 11	*Honig v. Doe* 484 U.S. 305 (1988)	9	IDEA's Stay-Put Provisions Involving Disciplinary Proceedings
No. 12	*Schaffer ex. Rel. Schaffer v. Weast* 546 U.S. 49 (2005)	10	Burden of Proof at Due Process Hearings
No. 13	*Florence County School District Four v. Carter* 510 U.S. 7 (1993)	11	Unilateral Placements in Private Schools If Free Appropriate Public Education Is Not Provided in Public Schools
No. 14	*Winkelman ex rel. Winkelman v. Parma City School District* 127 S. Ct. 1994 (2007)	12	Right of Non-Attorney Parents to Proceed *Pro Se* in IDEA Lawsuits
No. 15	*Doug C. v. Hawaii Department of Education* 720 F. 3d 1038 (2013)	12	Importance of Parental Participation in the IEP Process in the Change of Current Educational Placement
No. 16	*School Board of Nassau Country, Florida v. Arline* 480 U.S. 273 (1987)	13	Legal Defenses Under Section 504

IDEA's Exhaustion of Administrative Remedies

As reflected in a legal case from New Mexico, "[t]he IDEA favors prompt resolution of disputes" (*Sanders v. Santa Fe Public Schools*, 2004, p. 1311) involving the education of students with disabilities because Congress acknowledged the need to help children with disabilities who may be at formative stages in their development. As such, the IDEA requires parties (parents or school officials) to exhaust administrative remedies before filing suits unless it clearly is futile to do so. The first legal case involving a student with disabilities to be profiled in the "Special Education Law in Practice" section of this book is *Fry v. Napoleon Community Schools* (2017), a fairly recent case decided by the nation's highest court, the U.S. Supreme Court, meaning that this legal case ruling has implications on schools nationwide regardless of which state you currently reside. Under the Individuals with Disabilities Education Act, or IDEA, Congress created a detailed system of procedures and rules whereby schools are strongly encouraged to collaboratively work with families to resolve special education-related legal disputes in a non-adversarial manner, and if parents and school officials cannot successfully resolve their dispute, at some point the parents can file a lawsuit in either a state or federal-level court. The leading federal law impacting students with disabilities, the Individuals with Disabilities Education Act (hereafter referred to as IDEA 2004) has a specific rule governing legal enforcement under the IDEA 2004, Section 504 of the Rehabilitation Act (hereafter Section 504), and the Americans with Disabilities Act (hereafter the ADA) called the "IDEA exhaustion rule," meaning that any person filing a legal action under the IDEA 2004 must "exhaust" all those administrative remedies before pursuing legal relief under either Section 504 or the ADA (Colker, 2018). If a parent or legal guardian believes that their child is not receiving a free and appropriate public education, or FAPE, which is legally required under the IDEA 2004, they must seek legal relief from a state-level hearing officer prior to filing a formal legal complaint in either a state or federal-level court (Colker, 2018). The parents must "exhaust" their administrative remedies by formally requesting a special education due process hearing officer before going directly to the court system and filing legal action. One of the important practical considerations of the *Fry* ruling is that if a case does not expressly involve the discrimination of a student with disabilities, then the parent(s) or legal guardian is not legally required to exhaust IDEA procedures. The relevant part on the statute detailing the IDEA exhaustion rule states:

> Nothing in this chapter shall be construed to restrict or limit the rights, procedures, and remedies available under the Constitution, [the ADA, Section 504], or other federal laws protecting the rights of children with disabilities, except that before the filing of a civil action under such laws seeking relief that it is also available under this subchapter, the procedures under subsections (f) and (g) shall be exhausted to the same extent as would be required had the action been brought under this subchapter.
>
> (20 U.S.C. § 1415(l))

The U.S. Supreme Court's ruling in *Fry v. Napoleon Community Schools* (2017) provides useful and practical legal guidance on the issue of when a parent or legal guardian can actually seek legal relief under Section 504 instead of exhausting legal remedies under the IDEA. In this case, the student, Ehlena Fry, has cerebral palsy and her local public school district provided her with an Individualized Education Plan (IEP) when she entered kindergarten at the school. The main dispute between Ehlena's parents and the school was whether she could bring a trained service dog, a goldendoodle called Wonder, to school with her. The student's service dog was trained to do tasks that included retrieving dropped items, opening and closing doors, turning lights on and off, assisting the student in taking off her coat, and helping the student go to and from the toilet (*Fry*, 2017, p. 751). Initially, the school allowed the student's service dog to accompany the student to school on a 30-day trial basis. At the end of the trial of the 30-day trial basis, however, school officials informed Ehlena's parents that the service dog was no longer allowed in the school. Ehlena's parents filed a legal complaint with the U.S. Department of Education's Office for Civil Rights (OCR) for allegedly violating two federal civil rights laws, including Section 504 and the ADA. While the Office for Civil Rights (OCR) rendered a decision in the favor of Ehlena's parents, the parents decided to place Ehlena in a new school because they believed that school officials would "make her return to school difficult" (*Fry*, 2017, p. 751). Shortly after, Ehlena's parents sued the school district in federal court alleging that school officials had violated the student's legal rights under Section 504 and the ADA based on her emotional distress and pain, embarrassment, and mental anguish (*Fry*, 2017, p. 752). After reversing a legal decision by the federal

U.S. Court of Appeals for the Sixth Circuit in a unanimous 8–0 decision, the Supreme Court reversed the Court of Appeals decision and ruled in favor of the parents. The Court stated, "we hold that exhaustion is not necessary when the gravamen of the plaintiff's suit is something other than the denial of the IDEA's core guarantee—what the Act calls a 'free appropriate public education.'" One possible implication of the *Fry* decision is that it allows both parents and school officials to think more broadly about education, including the use of a service dog as an integral part of a student with disability's educational process (Colker, 2018). Under the IDEA 2004, a person seeking legal relief must "exhaust administrative remedies" prior to pursuing legal action under Section 504, the Americans with Disabilities Act (ADA), or other federal antidiscrimination laws. As a result, the *Fry* ruling can potentially serve as legal justification in situations where parents can now pursue legal remedies under the Americans with Disabilities Act (ADA) or Section 504 of the Rehabilitation Act of 1973 (Section 504) without exhausting their IDEA-based remedies.

IDEA's Exhaustion of Administrative Remedies Not Required

For the most part, courts agree that parents are not required to exhaust administrative remedies under the IDEA in a variety of circumstances. Parties may not have to exhaust administrative remedies when complaints allege systemic failures.

Challenges to school board policies that could violate the IDEA may not be subject to the administrative process. As such, the Ninth Circuit was convinced that a claim that the school day for specified special education students was shorter than for children in regular education was not subject to the exhaustion requirement because it had nothing to do with individual IEPs (*Christopher S. ex rel. Rita S. v. Stanislaus County Office of Education*, 2004).

Courts have considered exhaustion to be futile when hearing officers lacked authority to grant the requested relief. The Second Circuit decided that a father's complaint about the method by which hearing officers were selected was not subject to exhaustion since a sole hearing officer lacked the authority to alter the procedure (*Heldman v. Sobol*, 1992). Federal trial courts in New York also found that exhaustion was not required when the requested relief was that a child be placed in a school that was not on the state's list of approved placements because the hearing officer could not order a student to attend classes in an unapproved facility (*Straube v. Florida Union Free School District*, 1992), or in challenging an adjudication of officials of the state education department who rejected a parental request but declined to make an exception to general procedures (*Vander Malle v. Ambach*, 1987).

Yet, since not all courts agree, exhaustion may not be necessary in class action suits where the claims of plaintiffs are systemic in nature and hearing officers would not have the authority to the requested relief. For example, the Second Circuit affirmed that exhaustion was not required when a hearing officer could not order a systemwide change to correct the alleged wrongs (*J.G. v. Board of Education of the Rochester City School District*, 1987). Exhaustion may be unnecessary in emergency situations if it would cause severe or irreparable harm to students. However, the Third Circuit held that since mere allegations of irreparable harm are insufficient to excuse exhaustion, a plaintiff must present actual evidence to support such a claim (*Komninos v. Upper Saddle River Board of Education*, 1994).

When litigation involves issues that are purely legal rather than factual, the Third Circuit was of the opinion that exhaustion may not be required (*Lester H. v. Gilhool*, 1990). Similarly, the Second Circuit determined that exhaustion may not be necessary if a state persistently fails to render expeditious decisions regarding a student's educational placement (*Frutiger v. Hamilton Central School District*, 1991).

Finally, courts have refused to apply the exhaustion requirement when students are determined to not need special education. To this end, courts agree that parents do not have to exhaust administrative remedies in cases under Section 504 if their children are not receiving services under the IDEA, even if they are disabled (*Doe v. Belleville Public School District No. 118*, 1987; *Robertson v. Granite City Community Unit School District No. 9*, 1988).

⚖️

SPECIAL EDUCATION LAW IN PRACTICE
Legal Case No. 1—IDEA's "Exhaustion of Administrative Remedies" Rule

FRY V. NAPOLEON COMMUNITY SCHOOLS
137 S. CT. 743 (2017)

Justice KAGAN delivered the opinion of the Court.

The Individuals with Disabilities Education Act (IDEA or Act), 84 Stat. 175, as amended, 20 U.S.C. § 1400 *et seq.*, ensures that children with disabilities receive needed special education services. One of its provisions, § 1415(*l*), addresses the Act's relationship with other laws protecting those children. Section 1415(*l*) makes clear that nothing in the IDEA "restrict[s] or limit[s] the rights [or] remedies" that other federal laws, including antidiscrimination statutes, confer on children with disabilities. At the same time, the section states that if a suit brought under such a law "seek[s] relief that is also available under" the IDEA, the plaintiff must first exhaust the IDEA's administrative procedures. In this case, we consider the scope of that exhaustion requirement. We hold that exhaustion is not necessary when the gravamen of the plaintiff's suit is something other than the denial of the IDEA's core guarantee—what the Act calls a "free appropriate public education." § 1412(a)(1)(A).

I

A

Important as the IDEA is for children with disabilities, it is not the only federal statute protecting their interests. Of particular relevance to this case are two antidiscrimination laws—Title II of the Americans with Disabilities Act (ADA), 42 U.S.C. § 12131 *et seq.*, and § 504 of the Rehabilitation Act, 29 U.S.C. § 794—which cover both adults and children with disabilities, in both public schools and other settings. Title II forbids any "public entity" from discriminating based on disability; Section 504 applies the same prohibition to any federally funded "program or activity." 42 U.S.C. §§ 12131–12132; 29 U.S.C. § 794(a). A regulation implementing Title II requires a public entity to make "reasonable modifications" to its "policies, practices, or procedures" when necessary to avoid such discrimination. 28 C.F.R. § 35.130(b)(7) (2016); In similar vein, courts have interpreted § 504 as demanding certain "reasonable" modifications to existing practices in order to "accommodate" persons with disabilities. And both statutes authorize individuals to seek redress for violations of their substantive guarantees by bringing suits for injunctive relief or money damages. See 29 U.S.C. § 794a(a)(2); 42 U.S.C. § 12133.

This Court first considered the interaction between such laws and the IDEA in *Smith v. Robinson*, 468 U.S. 922. . . . The plaintiffs there sought "to secure a 'free appropriate public education' for [their] handicapped child." But instead of bringing suit under the IDEA alone, they appended "virtually identical" claims (again alleging the denial of a "free appropriate public education") under § 504 of the Rehabilitation Act and the Fourteenth Amendment's Equal Protection Clause.

Congress was quick to respond. In the Handicapped Children's Protection Act of 1986, it overturned *Smith*'s preclusion of non-IDEA claims while also adding a carefully defined exhaustion requirement. Now codified at 20 U.S.C. § 1415(*l*), the relevant provision of that statute reads:

"Nothing in [the IDEA] shall be construed to restrict or limit the rights, procedures, and remedies available under the Constitution, the [ADA], title V of the Rehabilitation Act [including § 504], or other Federal laws protecting the rights of children with disabilities, except that before the filing of a civil action under such laws seeking relief that is also available under [the IDEA], the [IDEA's administrative procedures] shall be exhausted to the same extent as would be required had the action been brought under [the IDEA]."

The first half of § 1415(*l*) (up until "except that") "reaffirm[s] the viability" of federal statutes like the ADA or Rehabilitation Act "as separate vehicles," no less integral than the IDEA, "for ensuring the rights of handicapped children." H.R.Rep. No. 99–296, p. 4 (1985). According to that opening phrase, the IDEA does not prevent a plaintiff from asserting claims under such laws even if, as in *Smith* itself, those claims allege the denial of an appropriate public education (much as an IDEA claim would). But the second half of § 1415(*l*) (from "except that" onward) imposes a limit on that "anything goes" regime, in the form of an exhaustion provision. According to that closing phrase, a plaintiff bringing suit under the ADA, the Rehabilitation Act, or similar laws must in certain circumstances—that is, when "seeking relief that is also available under" the IDEA—first exhaust the IDEA's administrative procedures. The reach of that requirement is the issue in this case.

B

Petitioner E.F. is a child with a severe form of cerebral palsy, which "significantly limits her motor skills and mobility." When E.F. was five years old, her parents—petitioners Stacy and Brent Fry—obtained a trained service dog for her, as recommended by her pediatrician. The dog, a goldendoodle named Wonder, "help[s E.F.] to live as independently as possible" by assisting her with various life activities. In particular, Wonder aids E.F. by "retrieving dropped items, helping her balance when she uses her walker, opening and closing doors, turning on and off lights, helping her take off her coat, [and] helping her transfer to and from the toilet."

But when the Frys sought permission for Wonder to join E.F. in kindergarten, officials at Ezra Eby Elementary School refused the request. Under E.F.'s existing IEP, a human aide provided E.F. with one-on-one support throughout the day; that two-legged assistance, the school officials thought, rendered Wonder superfluous. In the words of one administrator, Wonder should be barred from Ezra Eby because all of E.F.'s "physical and academic needs [were] being met through the services programs/accommodations" that the school had already agreed to. Later that year, the school officials briefly allowed Wonder to accompany E.F. to school on a trial basis; but even then, "the dog was required to remain in the back of the room during classes, and was forbidden from assisting [E.F.] with many tasks he had been specifically trained to do." And when the trial period concluded, the administrators again informed the Frys that Wonder was not welcome. As a result, the Frys removed E.F. from Ezra Eby and began homeschooling her.

C

The Frys then filed this suit in federal court against the local and regional school districts in which Ezra Eby is located, along with the school's principal (collectively, the school districts). The complaint alleged that the school districts violated Title II of the ADA and § 504 of the Rehabilitation Act by "denying [E.F.] equal access" to Ezra Eby and its programs, "refus[ing] to reasonably accommodate" E.F.'s use of a service animal, and otherwise "discriminat[ing] against [E.F.] as a person with disabilities." According

to the complaint, E.F. suffered harm as a result of that discrimination, including "emotional distress and pain, embarrassment, [and] mental anguish." In their prayer for relief, the Frys sought a declaration that the school districts had violated Title II and § 504, along with money damages to compensate for E.F.'s injuries.

The District Court granted the school districts' motion to dismiss the suit, holding that § 1415(*l*) required the Frys to first exhaust the IDEA's administrative procedures. A divided panel of the Court of Appeals for the Sixth Circuit affirmed on the same ground. In that court's view, § 1415(*l*) applies if "the injuries [alleged in a suit] relate to the specific substantive protections of the IDEA." And that means, the court continued, that exhaustion is necessary whenever "the genesis and the manifestations" of the complained-of harms were "educational" in nature. On that understanding of § 1415(*l*), the Sixth Circuit held, the Frys' suit could not proceed: Because the harms to E.F. were generally "educational"—most notably, the court reasoned, because "Wonder's absence hurt her sense of independence and social confidence at school"—the Frys had to exhaust the IDEA's procedures. 788 F.3d, at 627. Judge Daughtrey dissented, emphasizing that in bringing their Title II and § 504 claims, the Frys "did not allege the denial of a FAPE" or "seek to modify [E.F.'s] IEP in any way."

We granted certiorari to address confusion in the courts of appeals as to the scope of § 1415(*l*)'s exhaustion requirement. We now vacate the Sixth Circuit's decision.

II

Section 1415(*l*) requires that a plaintiff exhaust the IDEA's procedures before filing an action under the ADA, the Rehabilitation Act, or similar laws when (but only when) her suit "seek[s] relief that is also available" under the IDEA. We first hold that to meet that statutory standard, a suit must seek relief for the denial of a FAPE, because that is the only "relief" the IDEA makes "available."

A

In this Court, the parties have reached substantial agreement about what "relief" the IDEA makes "available" for children with disabilities—and about how the Sixth Circuit went wrong in addressing that question. The Frys maintain that such a child can obtain remedies under the IDEA for decisions that deprive her of a FAPE, but none for those that do not. So in the Frys' view, § 1415(*l*)'s exhaustion requirement can come into play only when a suit concerns the denial of a FAPE—and not, as the Sixth Circuit held, when it merely has some articulable connection to the education of a child with a disability. The school districts, for their part, also believe that the Sixth Circuit's exhaustion standard "goes too far" because it could mandate exhaustion when a plaintiff is "seeking relief that is *not* in substance available" under the IDEA. Brief for Respondents 30. And in particular, the school districts acknowledge that the IDEA makes remedies available only in suits that "directly implicate[ ]" a FAPE—so that only in those suits can § 1415(*l*) apply. Tr. of Oral Arg. 46. For the reasons that follow, we agree with the parties' shared view: The only relief that an IDEA officer can give—hence the thing a plaintiff must seek in order to trigger § 1415(*l*)'s exhaustion rule—is relief for the denial of a FAPE.

We begin, as always, with the statutory language at issue, which (at risk of repetition) compels exhaustion when a plaintiff seeks "relief" that is "available" under the IDEA. The ordinary meaning of "relief" in the context of a lawsuit is the "redress[ ] or benefit" that attends a favorable judgment. Black's Law Dictionary 1161 (5th ed. 1979). And such relief is "available," as we recently explained, when it is "accessible or may be obtained." (quoting Webster's Third New International Dictionary 150 (1993)). So to establish the scope of § 1415(*l*), we must identify the circumstances in which the IDEA enables a person to obtain redress (or, similarly, to access a benefit).

The IDEA's administrative procedures test whether a school has met that obligation—and so center on the Act's FAPE requirement. As noted earlier, any decision by a hearing officer on a request for substantive relief "shall" be "based on a determination of whether the child received a free appropriate public education." § 1415(f)(3)(E)(i); Suppose that a parent's complaint protests a school's failure to provide some accommodation for a child with a disability. If that accommodation is needed to fulfill the IDEA's FAPE requirement, the hearing officer must order relief. But if it is not, he cannot—even though the dispute is between a child with a disability and the school she attends. . . . For that reason, § 1415(*l*)'s exhaustion rule hinges on whether a lawsuit seeks relief for the denial of a free appropriate public education. Rather, that plaintiff must first submit her case to an IDEA hearing officer, experienced in addressing exactly the issues she raises. But if, in a suit brought under a different statute, the remedy sought is not for the denial of a FAPE, then exhaustion of the IDEA's procedures is not required. After all, the plaintiff could not get any relief from those procedures: A hearing officer, as just explained,

would have to send her away empty-handed. And that is true even when the suit arises directly from a school's treatment of a child with a disability—and so could be said to relate in some way to her education. A school's conduct toward such a child—say, some refusal to make an accommodation—might injure her in ways unrelated to a FAPE, which are addressed in statutes other than the IDEA. A complaint seeking redress for those other harms, independent of any FAPE denial, is not subject to § 1415(*l*)'s exhaustion rule because, once again, the only "relief" the IDEA makes "available" is relief for the denial of a FAPE.

B

Still, an important question remains: How is a court to tell when a plaintiff "seeks" relief for the denial of a FAPE and when she does not? Here, too, the parties have found some common ground: By looking, they both say, to the "substance" of, rather than the labels used in, the plaintiff's complaint. And here, too, we agree with that view: What matters is the crux—or, in legal-speak, the gravamen—of the plaintiff's complaint, setting aside any attempts at artful pleading.

That inquiry makes central the plaintiff's own claims, as § 1415(*l*) explicitly requires. The statutory language asks whether a lawsuit in fact "seeks" relief available under the IDEA—not, as a stricter exhaustion statute might, whether the suit "could have sought" relief available under the IDEA (or, what is much the same, whether any remedies "are" available under that law).

But that examination should consider substance, not surface. The use (or nonuse) of particular labels and terms is not what matters. The inquiry, for example, does not ride on whether a complaint includes (or, alternatively, omits) the precise words(?) "FAPE" or "IEP." After all, § 1415(*l*)'s premise is that the plaintiff is suing under a statute *other than* the IDEA, like the Rehabilitation Act; in such a suit, the plaintiff might see no need to use the IDEA's distinctive language—even if she is in essence contesting the adequacy of a special education program. And still more critically, a "magic words" approach would make § 1415(*l*)'s exhaustion rule too easy to bypass. It requires exhaustion when the gravamen of a complaint seeks redress for a school's failure to provide a FAPE, even if not phrased or framed in precisely that way.

In addressing whether a complaint fits that description, a court should attend to the diverse means and ends of the statutes covering persons with disabilities—the IDEA on the one hand, the ADA and Rehabilitation Act (most notably) on the other. The IDEA, of course, protects only "children" (well, really, adolescents too) and concerns only their schooling. § 1412(a)(1) (A). And as earlier noted, the statute's goal is to provide each child with meaningful access to education by offering individualized instruction and related services appropriate to her "unique needs." § 1401(29); by contrast, Title II of the ADA and § 504 of the Rehabilitation Act cover people with disabilities of all ages, and do so both inside and outside schools. And those statutes aim to root out disability-based discrimination, enabling each covered person (sometimes by means of reasonable accommodations) to participate equally to all others in public facilities and federally funded programs. In short, the IDEA guarantees individually tailored educational services, while Title II and § 504 promise non-discriminatory access to public institutions. That is not to deny some overlap in coverage: The same conduct might violate all three statutes—which is why, as in *Smith*, a plaintiff might seek relief for the denial of a FAPE under Title II and § 504 as well as the IDEA. But still, the statutory differences just discussed mean that a complaint brought under Title II and § 504 might instead seek relief for simple discrimination, irrespective of the IDEA's FAPE obligation.

One clue to whether the gravamen of a complaint against a school concerns the denial of a FAPE, or instead addresses disability-based discrimination, can come from asking a pair of hypothetical questions. First, could the plaintiff have brought essentially the same claim if the alleged conduct had occurred at a public facility that was *not* a school—say, a public theater or library? And second, could an *adult* at the school—say, an employee or visitor—have pressed essentially the same grievance? When the answer to those questions is yes, a complaint that does not expressly allege the denial of a FAPE is also unlikely to be truly about that subject; after all, in those other situations there is no FAPE obligation and yet the same basic suit could go forward. But when the answer is no, then the complaint probably does concern a FAPE, even if it does not explicitly say so; for the FAPE requirement is all that explains why only a child in the school setting (not an adult in that setting or a child in some other) has a viable claim.

Take two contrasting examples. Suppose first that a wheelchair-bound child sues his school for discrimination under Title II (again, without mentioning the denial of a FAPE) because the building lacks access ramps. In some sense, that architectural feature has educational consequences, and a different lawsuit might have alleged that it violates

the IDEA: After all, if the child cannot get inside the school, he cannot receive instruction there; and if he must be carried inside, he may not achieve the sense of independence conducive to academic (or later to real-world) success. But is the denial of a FAPE really the gravamen of the plaintiff's Title II complaint? Consider that the child could file the same basic complaint if a municipal library or theater had no ramps. And similarly, an employee or visitor could bring a mostly identical complaint against the school. That the claim can stay the same in those alternative scenarios suggests that its essence is equality of access to public facilities, not adequacy of special education.

But suppose next that a student with a learning disability sues his school under Title II for failing to provide remedial tutoring in mathematics. That suit, too, might be cast as one for disability-based discrimination, grounded on the school's refusal to make a reasonable accommodation; the complaint might make no reference at all to a FAPE or an IEP. But can anyone imagine the student making the same claim against a public theater or library? Or, similarly, imagine an adult visitor or employee suing the school to obtain a math tutorial? The difficulty of transplanting the complaint to those other contexts suggests that its essence—even though not its wording—is the provision of a FAPE, thus bringing § 1415(*l*) into play.

A further sign that the gravamen of a suit is the denial of a FAPE can emerge from the history of the proceedings. In particular, a court may consider that a plaintiff has previously invoked the IDEA's formal procedures to handle the dispute—thus starting to exhaust the Act's remedies before switching midstream. Recall that a parent dissatisfied with her child's education initiates those administrative procedures by filing a complaint, which triggers a preliminary meeting (or possibly mediation) and then a due process hearing. A plaintiff's initial choice to pursue that process may suggest that she is indeed seeking relief for the denial of a FAPE—with the shift to judicial proceedings prior to full exhaustion reflecting only strategic calculations about how to maximize the prospects of such a remedy. Whether that is so depends on the facts; a court may conclude, for example, that the move to a courtroom came from a late-acquired awareness that the school had fulfilled its FAPE obligation and that the grievance involves something else entirely But prior pursuit of the IDEA's administrative remedies will often provide strong evidence that the substance of a plaintiff's claim concerns the denial of a FAPE, even if the complaint never explicitly uses that term.

III

The Court of Appeals did not undertake the analysis we have just set forward. As noted above, it asked whether E.F.'s injuries were, broadly speaking, "educational" in nature That is not the same as asking whether the gravamen of E.F.'s complaint charges, and seeks relief for, the denial of a FAPE. And that difference in standard may have led to a difference in result in this case. Understood correctly, § 1415(*l*) might not require exhaustion of the Frys' claim. We lack some important information on that score, however, and so we remand the issue to the court below.

The Frys' complaint alleges only disability-based discrimination, without making any reference to the adequacy of the special education services E.F.'s school provided. The school districts' "refusal to allow Wonder to act as a service dog," the complaint states, "discriminated against [E.F.] as a person with disabilities . . . by denying her equal access" to public facilities. The complaint contains no allegation about the denial of a FAPE or about any deficiency in E.F.'s IEP. More, it does not accuse the school even in general terms of refusing to provide the educational instruction and services. As the Frys explained in this Court: The school district "have said all along that because they gave [E.F.] a one-on-one [human] aide, that all of her . . . educational needs were satisfied." The Frys instead maintained, just as OCR had earlier found, that the school districts infringed E.F.'s right to equal access—even if their actions complied in full with the IDEA's requirements.

And nothing in the nature of the Frys' suit suggests any implicit focus on the adequacy of E.F.'s education. Consider, as suggested above, that the Frys could have filed essentially the same complaint if a public library or theater had refused admittance to Wonder. Or similarly, consider that an adult visitor to the school could have leveled much the same charges if prevented from entering with his service dog. In each case, the plaintiff would challenge a public facility's policy of precluding service dogs (just as a blind person might challenge a policy of barring guide dogs, see *supra*, at 751) as violating Title II's and § 504's equal access requirements. The suit would have nothing to do with the provision of educational services. From all that we know now, that is exactly the kind of action the Frys have brought.

But we do not foreclose the possibility that the history of these proceedings might suggest something different. As earlier discussed, a plaintiff's initial pursuit of the IDEA's administrative remedies can serve as evidence that the gravamen of her later suit is the denial of a FAPE, even though that does not appear on the face of her complaint. The Frys may or may not have sought those remedies before filing this case: None of the parties here have addressed that issue, and the record is cloudy as to the relevant facts. Accordingly, on remand, the court below should establish whether (or to what extent) the Frys invoked the IDEA's dispute resolution process before bringing this suit. And if the Frys started down that road, the court should decide whether their actions reveal that the gravamen of their complaint is indeed the denial of a FAPE, thus necessitating further exhaustion.

With these instructions and for the reasons stated, we vacate the judgment of the Court of Appeals and remand the case for further proceedings consistent with this opinion.

It is so ordered.

Justice Alito, with whom Justice Thomas joins, concurring in part and concurring in the judgment.

The Court first instructs the lower courts to inquire whether the plaintiff could have brought "essentially the same claim if the alleged conduct had occurred at a public facility that was *not* a school—say, a public theater or library." Next, the Court says, a court should ask whether "an *adult* at the school—say, an employee or visitor—[could] have pressed essentially the same grievance." These clues make sense only if there is no overlap between the relief available under the following two sets of claims: (1) the relief provided by the Individuals with Disabilities Education Act (IDEA), and (2) the relief provided by other federal laws (including the Constitution, the Americans with Disabilities Act of 1990 (ADA), and the Rehabilitation Act of 1973). The Court does not show or even claim that there is no such overlap—to the contrary, it observes that "[t]he same conduct might violate" the ADA, the Rehabilitation Act and the IDEA. *Ibid*. And since these clues work only in the absence of overlap, I would not suggest them.

The Court provides another false clue by suggesting that lower courts take into account whether parents, before filing suit under the ADA or the Rehabilitation Act, began to pursue but then abandoned the IDEA's formal procedures. This clue also seems to me to be ill-advised. It is easy to imagine circumstances under which parents might start down the IDEA road and then change course and file an action under the ADA or the Rehabilitation Act that seeks relief that the IDEA cannot provide. The parents might be advised by their attorney that the relief they were seeking under the IDEA is not available under that law but is available under another. Or the parents might change their minds about the relief that they want, give up on the relief that the IDEA can provide, and turn to another statute.

Although the Court provides these clues for the purpose of assisting the lower courts, I am afraid that they may have the opposite effect. They are likely to confuse and lead courts astray.

Questions for Discussion

1. Do you think the 2017 Supreme Court's *Fry* ruling will encourage increased litigation of parents seeking monetary damages against school districts refusing to accommodate the requests of students with disabilities?
2. One of the goals of the Individuals with Disabilities Education Act (IDEA) is to encourage students with disabilities to "lead productive and independent adult lives" (See 20 U.S.C. § 1400(c)(5)(A)(ii)). Do you think certain student accommodations, such as a service dog, can be successful at improving the educational progression of students with disabilities?
3. As mandated under the IDEA's "exhaustion of administrative remedies rule", public school districts sued by parents under the Americans with Disabilities Act (ADA), Section 504 of the Rehabilitation Act, as well as other federal antidiscrimination statutes should evaluate the substance and validity of their legal claim(s) to determine whether the legal relief sought really is for a failure to provide a free appropriate public education (FAPE). If so, the parents of students with disabilities are required to exhaust IDEA's administrative remedies, and a failure to do so would likely result in dismissal of the case. Do you agree or disagree with the *Fry* case's interpretation of the IDEA's "exhaustion of administrative remedies" rule? Why or why not?

Summary of Important Legal Policies, Principles, and Practices

This chapter starts with the premise that "ignorantia juris non excusat" or "ignorance of the law is no excuse," a long-standing U.S. legal tradition that if individuals claim they are unaware of a particular law(s) or principle(s), they may not escape legal liability by simply responding they are either unaware or not knowledgeable of the law's content. The main concepts and principles of this chapter include:

1. Despite nationwide increases in the number of eligible students with disabilities enrolled in schools, a review of the research literature demonstrates that many educators and others who work closely with students with disabilities are either poorly informed or uninformed concerning their knowledge in special education law. As a result, today's school administrators, educators, and pre-service teachers are not adequately trained in special education law despite the unique federal and state-level legal protections afforded student with disabilities.
2. For the purposes of this book, special education legal literacy is defined as " the legal knowledge, understanding, and skills that enable educators to apply relevant legal rules to their everyday practice" (Decker & Brady, 2016, p. 231). Those individuals, who are legally literate in special education are better able to spot legal issues, identify applicable laws or legal standards, and apply the relevant legal rules to solve legal dilemmas.
3. The use of case-based learning, or CBL has been shown to be an effective method for teaching the law and legal principles to members of the educational community, especially instruction involving relevant legal principles and strategies drawn from actual legal cases involving students with disabilities. The legal case-based learning model has significant potential for improving the special education legal literacy levels of those persons who work closely with children and youth with disabilities in educational settings.
4. This chapter's *Special Education Law in Practice* legal case, *Fry v. Napoleon Community Schools* (2017) was decided by the U.S. Supreme Court and explains the IDEA's "exhaustion of administrative remedies" rule preferring alternative dispute resolution measures, including mediation and due process hearings over litigation proceedings in our nation's courts. In *Fry*, the Supreme Court developed a test for determining when students with disabilities are legally obligated to exhaust claims under the IDEA. The

IDEA's exhaustion requirement actively encourages alternative dispute resolution alternatives to formal litigation actions in federal or state-level courts. If the nature of the alleged legal complaint by a parent or legal guardian pertains to or arises based on a student with disability's education, then administrative relief as opposed to litigation in the court system remains the preferred remedy to settle IDEA-based legal disputes.

Useful Online Resources

Poorvu Center for Teaching and Learning at Yale University: Case-Based Learning (CBL)
Case-based learning (CBL) is an established approach used across disciplines where individuals apply their knowledge to real-world scenarios, promoting higher levels of cognition. CBL has a long history of successful implementation in medical, law, and business schools, and is increasingly used within undergraduate education, particularly within pre-professional majors and the sciences, including education. https://poorvucenter.yale.edu/faculty-resources/strategies-teaching/case-based-learning

Recommended Reading

Bateman, D., & Cline, J. (2019). *Special education law case studies: A review from practitioners*. Lanham, MD: Rowman & Littlefield.
Bateman, D., & Yell, M. L. (2019). *Current trends and legal issues in special education*. Thousand Oaks, CA: Corwin.
Weishaar, M. K. (2007). *Case studies in special education law: No Child Left Behind and Individuals with Disabilities Education Improvement Act*. Upper Saddle River, NJ: Pearson.

References

Ballentine, J. A. (1916). *Ballentine's Law Dictionary*. Indianapolis, IN: Bobbs-Merrill Company.
Bineham, S. C. (2014). *Knowledge and skills essential for secondary campus-base administrators to appropriately serve students with special needs* (unpublished doctoral dissertation), University of Texas at Austin, Austin.
Brady, K. P., & Bathon, J. (2012). Education law in a digital age: The growing impact of the open access legal movement. *Education Law Reporter, 227*, 589.
Brown v. Board of Education, 347 U.S. 483 (1954).
Bruner, D. Y., & Bartlett, M. J. (2008). Effective methods and materials for teaching law to preservice teachers. *Action in Teacher Education, 30*(2), 36–45.
Bull, B., & McCarthy, M. (1995). Reflections on the knowledge base in law and ethics for educational leaders. *Education Administration Quarterly, 31*(4), 613–631.
Christopher S. ex rel. Rita S. v. Stanislaus County Office of Education, 384 F.3d 1205 (9th Cir. 2004).
Christopher W. v. Portsmouth School Committee, 877 F.2d 1089 (1st Cir. 1989).
Colker, R. (2018). *Special education law in a nutshell*. St. Paul, MN: West Academic.
Davidson, D. N., & Algozzine, B. (2002). Administrators' perceptions of special education law. *Journal of Special Education Leadership, 15*(2), 43–48.
Davies, S. (1998). The jurisprudence of willfulness: An evolving theory of excusable ignorance, *Duke Law Journal, 48*(3), 341–427.
Decker, J. R. (2014). Legal literacy in education: An ideal time to increase research, advocacy, and action. *Education Law Reporter, 304*(1), 679–696.
Decker, J. R., & Brady, K. (2016). Increasing school employees' special education legal literacy. *Journal of School Public Relations, 36*(3), 231–259.
Decker, J. R., & Pazey, B. L. (2017). Case-based instruction to teach educators about the legal parameters surrounding the discipline of students with disabilities. *Action in Teacher Education, 39*(3), 255–273.
DiPaola, M., & Walther-Thomas, C. (2003). *Principals and special education: The critical role of school leaders* (COPSSE Document No. IB-7E). Gainesville, FL: University of Florida.
Doe v. Belleville Public School District No. 118, 672 F. Supp. 342 (S.D. Ill. 1987).
Drame, E. (2011, January/February). An analysis of the capacity of charter schools to address the needs of SWDs in Wisconsin. *Remedial and Special Education, 32*(1), 55–63.
Eberwein, H. J. (2008). *Raising legal literacy in public schools, a call for principal leadership: A national study of secondary principals' knowledge of public school law* (Unpublished doctoral dissertation), University of Massachusetts, Amherst.
Eckes, E. (2008, Summer). Significant issues for inclusion in pre-service teacher preparation. *Action in Teacher Education, 30*(2), 25–35.

Estes, M. (2009). Charter schools and students with disabilities: How far have we come? *Remedial and Special Education*, *30*(4), 216–224.

Fischer, L., Schimmel, D., & Stellman, L. (2007). *Teachers and the law* (7th ed.). Boston: Allyn & Bacon.

Fry v. Napoleon Community Schools, 137 S. Ct. 743 (2017).

Gajda, R. (2008). States' expectations for teachers' knowledge about school law. *Action in Teacher Education*, *30*(2), 15–24.

Garda, R. (2011). Culture clash: Special education in charter schools. *North Carolina Law Review*, *90*(3), 655–718.

Gullatt, D., & Tollett, J. (1997). Educational law: A requisite course for preservice and inservice teacher education programs. *Journal of Teacher Education*, *48*(2), 129–135.

Heldman v. Sobol, 962 F.2d 148 (2d Cir. 1992).

Heubert, J. (1997). The more we get together: Improving collaboration between educators and their lawyers. *Harvard Educational Review*, *67*(3), 531–583.

Imber, M. (2008). Pervasive myths in teacher beliefs about education law. *Action in Teacher Education*, *30*(2), 88–97.

Institute for Educational Sciences (IES). (2010, July). Do states have certification requirements for preparing general education teachers to teach students with disabilities (SWDs)? *Institute for Educational Sciences*, *90*. Retrieved from http://eric.ed.gov/?id=ED511104

J.G. v. Board of Education of the Rochester City School District, 830 F.2d 444 (2d Cir. 1987).

Karanxha, Z., & Zirkel, P. (2014). Longitudinal trends in special education case law: Frequencies and outcomes of published court decisions. *Journal of Special Education Leadership*, *27*, 55.

Katsiyannis, A., & Herbst, M. (2004). 20 Ways to minimize litigation in special education. *Intervention in School & Clinic*, *40*, 106–110.

Komninos v. Upper Saddle River Board of Education, 13 F.3d 775 (1994).

Lasky, B., & Karge, B. (2006). Meeting the needs of students with disabilities: Experience and confidence of principals. *NASSP Bulletin*, *90*, 19–36.

Leko, M. M., Brownell, M. T., Sindelar, P. T., & Murphy, K. (2012). Promoting special education preservice teacher expertise. *Focus on Exceptional Children*, *44*(7), 1–16.

Lester H. v. Gilhool, 916 F.2d 865 (3d Cir. 1990).

Littleton, M. (2008). Teachers' knowledge of education law. *Action in Teacher Education*, *30*(2), 71–78.

MacNaughton, D., Hall, T. E., & Maccini, P. (2001). Case-based instruction in special education teacher preparation. *Teacher Education and Special Education*, *24*(2), 84–94.

McCarthy, M. (2008, Summer). One model to infuse the law in teacher education. *Action in Teacher Education*, *30*(2), 59–70.

McCarthy, M. (2016). The marginalization of school law knowledge and research: Missed opportunities for educators. *Education Law Reporter*, *331*, 565–584.

McFarland, J., Hussar, B., Wang, X., Zhang, J., Wang, K., Rathbun, A., et al. (2018). *The condition of education 2018 (NCES 2018-144)*. U.S. Department of Education. Washington, DC: National Center for Education Statistics. Retrieved from https://nces.ed.gov/pubsearch/pubsinfo. asp?pubid=2018144.

McNergney, R. F., Ducharme, E. R., & Ducharme, M. K. (Eds.). (1999a). *Educating for democracy: Case method teaching and learning*. Mahwah, NJ: Lawrence Erlbaum.

McNergney, R. F., Ducharme, E. R., & Ducharme, M. K. (1999b). Teaching democracy through cases. In R. F. McNergney, E. R. Ducharme, & M. K. Ducharme (Eds.), *Educating for democracy: Case method teaching and learning* (pp. 3–13). Mahwah, NJ: Lawrence Erlbaum.

Merseth, K. K. (1990). Case methodology in the study and practice of teacher education. *Teacher Education Quarterly*, *17*(1), 53–62.

Miles, A. D. (2011). Bridging the gap between theory and application: Using the Harvard case study method to develop higher order thinking skills with college students. *Teaching and Learning Journal*, *1*(1), 1–22.

Militello, M., & Schimmel, D. (2008). Toward universal legal literacy in American schools. *Action in Teacher Education*, *30*(2), 98–106.

Militello, M., Schimmel, D., & Eberwein, H. J. (2009). If they knew, they would change: How legal knowledge impacts principals' practice. *NASSP Bulletin*, *93*(1), 27–52.

Osterman, K. F., & Hafner, M. (2009). Curriculum in leadership preparation programs. In M. Young, G. M. Crow, J. Murphy, & R. T. Ogawa (Eds.), *Handbook of research on the education of school leaders* (pp. 269–318). New York, NY: Routledge.

Painter, S. (2001). Improving the teaching of school law: A call for dialogue. *Brigham Young University Education and Law Journal*, *2001*(2), 213–230.

Pazey, B. L., & Cole, H. (2013). The role of special education training in the development of socially just leaders: Building an equity consciousness in educational leadership programs. *Educational Administration Quarterly*, *49*(2), 243–271.

Powell, P. R. (2010). *An exploratory study of the presentation of special education law in administrative preparation programs for aspiring administrators* (doctoral dissertation). Retrieved from Dissertation Abstracts International (Order No. AAI3390580).

Reglin, G. (1992). Public school educators' knowledge of selected Supreme Court decisions affecting daily public school operations. *Journal of Education Administration, 30*(2), 26–32.

Robertson v. Granite City Community Unit School District No. 9, 684 F. Supp. 1002 (S.D. Ill. 1988).

Rodriguez, M. A., Gentilucci, J., & Sims, P. G. (2006, November). *Preparing school leaders to effectively support special education programs: Using modules in educational leadership.* Paper presented at the University Council for Educational Administration, San Antonio, TX.

Sanders v. Santa Fe Public Schools, 383 F. Supp.2d 1305 (D.N.M. 2004).

Schimmel, D., & Militello, M. (2007). Legal literacy for teachers: A neglected responsibility. *Harvard Educational Review, 77*(3), 257–284.

Schimmel, D., & Militello, M. (2008, December). Legal literacy for teachers. *Principal Leadership, 9*(4), 54–58.

Straube v. Florida Union Free School District, 801 F. Supp. 1164 (S.D.N.Y. 1992).

Sudzina, M. R. (1999). Organizing instruction for case-based teaching. In R. F. McNergney, E. R. Ducharme, & M. K. Ducharme (Eds.), *Educating for democracy: Case method teaching and learning* (pp. 15–28). Mahwah, NJ: Lawrence Erlbaum.

Umpstead, R., Decker, J., Brady, K., Schimmel, D., & Militello, M. (2015). *How to prevent special education litigation: Eight legal lesson plans.* New York, NY: Teachers College Press.

Vander Malle v. Ambach, 667 F. Supp. 1015 (S.D.N.Y. 1987).

Wagner, J. Y., & Katsiyannis, A. (2010). Special education litigation update: Implications for school administrators. *NASSP Bulletin, 94*(1), 40–52.

Williams, B. (2005). Case-based learning: A review of the literature: Is there scope for this educational paradigm in pre-hospital education? *Emerging Medicine, 22*, 577–581.

Williams, S. M. (1992). Putting case-based instruction into context: Examples from legal and medical education. *The Journal of the Learning Sciences, 2*(4), 367–427.

Yell, M. L. (2019). *Law and special education* (5th ed.). Upper Saddle River, NJ: Pearson.

Zirkel, P. A. (2006). The effect of law on education: The common ungoodness of paralyzing fear? *Journal of Law and Education, 35*(4), 461–495.

Zirkel, P. A., & Lupini, W. H. (2003). An outcomes analysis of education litigation. *Educational Policy, 17*(2), 257–279.

2

Historical Development of Laws Impacting Students With Disabilities

---

Key Concepts and Terms in This Chapter

- Historical development of special educational laws
- Introduction to Individuals with Disabilities Education Act (IDEA 2004)
- Introduction to Section 504 of the Rehabilitation Act of 1973 (Section 504)
- Introduction to the Americans with Disabilities Act (ADA)

The primary purpose of this chapter is to provide readers with an overview of the historical development of laws relating to the inclusion of students with disabilities in the nation's public elementary through secondary schools. Next, the chapter reviews significant historical events and efforts to obtain equal educational opportunities for school-aged children and youth with disabilities. Specifically, this chapter highlights several landmark legal decisions that have led to federal legislation mandating a free appropriate public education, often referred to as FAPE in the least restrictive environment, commonly called LRE for students with disabilities. Readers who might be unfamiliar with certain legal terminology should consult the glossary found towards the back of this book for definitions of various legal terms used in this chapter as well as throughout the book.

When non-tuition, public schools in the U.S. emerged beginning in the 1820s, classrooms were largely unavailable to students with disabilities. In fact, the exclusion of students with disabilities was often legally sanctioned by the courts. In one of the earliest reported legal cases involving a child or youth with disabilities attempting to gain access to a public school, the Supreme Judicial Court of Massachusetts in 1893 upheld a public school committee's exclusion of a student who was considered "too weak-minded to derive profit from instruction," made "uncouth noises," and was "unable to take ordinary decent physical care of himself" (*Watson v. City of Cambridge*, 1893, p. 32) (for more details of this case, *see* Special Education Law in Practice: *Case 2*). In the court's legal decision, they indicated that by law the school committee (as school boards in Massachusetts are known) had general charge of the public schools and refused to interfere with its judgment. Furthermore, the court explained that if acts of disorder by a student interfered with the operation of the schools, whether committed voluntarily or based on the student's intellectual ability, the school committee should have been able to exclude a student with disabilities without being overruled by a jury that lacked expertise in educational matters.

Compulsory Education and the Exclusion of Students With Disabilities

The historical development of the laws and legislation allowing children and youth with disabilities to attend U.S. public schools was achieved through the combined efforts of many individuals, groups, and governmental entities, including the parents of students with disabilities, advocacy groups for individuals with disabilities, Congress, and individual state legislatures (Yell, 2019). As will be discussed in Chapter 3, it is important to realize that public education is not directly mentioned in the U.S. Constitution. According to the U.S. Constitution, the Tenth Amendment specifies that any authority or powers not expressly granted to the federal government are reserved to the states (Turnbull, Stowe, & Huerta, 2007). While the majority of states had passed compulsory education laws by 1918 requiring that students attend schools until a certain age, children and youth with disabilities were a group of students initially excluded from state compulsory education laws. Prior to 1975, no federal statute legally obligated states to provide comprehensive special education programming or individualized services for students with disabilities. Initially, some states enacted legislation offering limited special education services to students with disabilities, but these state jurisdictions were in the distinct minority (Yell, 2019). For example, in 1911, New Jersey became the first state to legally allow the education of students with disabilities in its public schools followed closely by New York in 1917 and Massachusetts in 1920 (Colker, 2018). Unfortunately, however, the actual enforcement of these state laws was largely ineffective. Prior to the enactment of state compulsory education laws, as discussed at the outset of this chapter, local public schools routinely excluded students with disabilities.

In a second legal case involving whether to permit a student with disabilities access to a public school, the Supreme Court of Wisconsin, in 1919, upheld the exclusion of a student with a form of paralysis (*State ex rel. Beattie v. Board of Education of Antigo*, 1919). The student was determined to have normal intelligence, but his medical condition caused him to drool and make facial contortions. The student attended public schools through the fifth grade but was excluded from advancing to the next grade level since school officials claimed his physical appearance nauseated teachers and other students, his disability required an undue amount of his teacher's time, and the student had a negative impact on the discipline and progress of the school. School officials suggested that the student attend a day school for students with hearing impairments and defective speech, but the student refused and was supported by his parents. When the local school board refused to reinstate the student, the court affirmed its decision, maintaining that the student's right to attend the public schools was not absolute when his presence at the school was harmful to the best interests of others. The court went so far as to suggest that as the student's presence was not in the best interest of the school, the local school board had a legal obligation to exclude the student. Despite the fact that the state of Wisconsin at the time had a compulsory education law requiring a free public education "to all children between the ages of four and twenty years," the court ruled "the right of a child of school age to attend the public schools of this state cannot be insisted upon when its presence therein is harmful to the best interest of the school" (*State ex rel. Beattie v. Board of Education of Antigo*, 1919, p. 154).

The Legal Significance of the Civil Rights Movement

The greatest historical legal advancements in special education have occurred since World War II. The impetus for ensuring equal educational opportunities for all American children can be traced back to the United States Supreme Court's landmark 1954 *Brown v. Board of Education* decision, a school desegregation case ruling that public schools that were segregated based on race are "inherently unequal." Although equal access to public education was addressed in the context of racial school desegregation as a result of the *Brown* ruling, a unanimous Supreme Court set the tone for later legal developments, including those leading to increased constitutional protections as well as access to public education for students with disabilities, in asserting that "education is perhaps the most important function of state and local governments." Unfortunately, immediately following the Supreme Court's 1954 *Brown* ruling, the legal rights of individuals with disabilities continued to be overlooked. Throughout the 1950s, for example, more than half of the states still had laws calling for the sterilization of individuals with disabilities, while other state jurisdictions limited the basic rights of persons with disabilities, including voting, marrying, and obtaining drivers' licenses (Russo, 2018). By the 1960s, the percentage of children with disabilities who were served in public schools began to rise. While 12 percent of the students in public schools in 1948 had disabilities, the number of students with disabilities increased to 21 percent by 1963 and to 38 percent by 1968 (Zerrel & Ballard, 1982). While advancements in the legal rights of students with disabilities attempting to gain access to the country's public schools did not come easily, these legal rights advanced gradually with improved professional research and knowledge about individuals with disabilities, social advancements, and legal mandates initiated by concerned parents, educators, politicians, and advocates.

More specifically, the legal movement to advance the equal educational opportunities for students with disabilities gained sizable momentum during the late 1960s and early 1970s when parent activists filed legal suits on behalf of their children attempting to advance educational equality for the poor, language minorities, and racial minorities. Much of the legal language emerging from some of these judicial opinions had direct implications influencing the legal cause of students with disabilities. In a 1967 groundbreaking federal lawsuit in Washington D.C., Judge Skelly Wright declared that the tracking system used by the District of Columbia School District to assign students to various classes purportedly based on academic ability and achievement was discriminatory (*Hobson v. Hansen*, 1967). As part of this student tracking system, students were placed in tracks, or curriculum levels, as early as elementary school based on an academic ability assessment that relied heavily on nationally normed standardized aptitude tests. Once placed, it was difficult for students to ever move out of their assigned tracks. The court ordered school board officials to abolish the tracking system after hearing testimony suggesting that the tests produced inaccurate and misleading results when used with populations other than white middle-class students. The court found that using these tests with poor minority students, especially African-American students often resulted in the students being placed according to environmental and psychological factors rather than academic ability.

The court saw that since the school board lacked the ability to render scores that accurately reflected the innate learning abilities of a majority of its students, the students' placements in lower tracks was not justified. The federal court concluded that the local school district unconstitutionally used the tracking system to place racial minorities, especially African-American students in segregated and academically inferior classrooms (Colker, 2018). Moreover, school officials denied students placed in the lower academic tracks equal educational opportunities by failing to provide these students with compensatory educational services that would have helped to bring them back into the mainstream of public education.

At least two courts disallowed school systems from placing students in segregated educational programs on the basis of culturally biased assessments. In the first case, a student who was Spanish-speaking was placed in a class with students with intellectual and developmental disabilities on the basis of an intelligence quotient, or IQ test administered in English (*Diana v. State Board of Education*, 1970, 1973). The legal issue was similar in the second legal case, except that the student was African-American (*Larry P. v. Riles*, 1972, 1974, 1979, 1984). In the latter case, the court ruled that standardized student IQ tests were inappropriate because they were not validated for the class of students on whom they were used. This resulted in the students being placed disproportionately in special education classes. In both instances, the courts ordered the respective local school boards to develop nondiscriminatory procedures for placing students in special education classes. However, in a separate case, another federal trial court commented that standardized IQ tests commonly used in schools were not culturally or racially biased (*Parents in Action on Special Education v. Hannon*, 1980).

In 1974, the U.S. Supreme Court ruled that the failure to provide remedial English language instruction to non-English-speaking students violated Section 601 of the Civil Rights Act of 1974 (*Lau v. Nichols*, 1974). Plaintiffs filed a class action suit on behalf of Chinese students in the San Francisco school system who did not speak English and who had not been provided with English language instruction. The Court found that the board's denying the students the chance to receive remedial instruction denied them of meaningful opportunities to participate in public education. The Court contended that, as a recipient of federal funds, the school board was bound by Title VI of the Civil Rights Act of 1964 and a Department of Health, Education, and Welfare regulation that required it to take affirmative steps to rectify language deficiencies.

The growing legal success that advocates for students with disabilities enjoyed in mostly lower court cases initially are considered landmark opinions despite their limited precedential legal value since they provided the impetus for Congress to pass sweeping federal legislation mandating a free appropriate public education for students with disabilities, regardless of the severity or nature of their disabilities. These legal cases, which are listed by their conceptually related holdings, rather than chronologically, occurred in less than a decade of each other and are important because they helped establish many of the legal principles that shaped the far-reaching federal legislation that is now known as the Individuals with Disabilities Education Act (IDEA).

Legal Entitlement to an Appropriate Education for Students With Disabilities

One of the first legal cases that shifted the tide in favor of students with disabilities, *Wolf v. State of Utah* (1969), was filed in a state court on behalf of two children with mental retardation (now referred to as intellectual disability) who were denied admission to public schools. As a result, the parents of these children enrolled them in a private daycare center at their own expense. As background to the dispute, the parents, through their lawyer, pointed out that according to Utah's state constitution, the public school system should have been open to all children, a provision that the state supreme court interpreted broadly; other state statutes stipulated that all children between the ages of six and twenty-one who had not completed high school were entitled to public education at taxpayers' expense. In light of these provisions, the *Wolf* court, in language that was remarkably similar to portions of *Brown*, declared that children who had an intellectual disability were entitled to a free appropriate public education under the state constitution.

Two Landmark Federal Court Cases: The Legal Significance of PARC and Mills

Two federal class action suits combined to have a profound impact on the education of students with disabilities. The first case, *Pennsylvania Association for Retarded Children v. Commonwealth of Pennsylvania* (*PARC*) (1972), was initiated on behalf of a class of individuals between the ages of six and twenty-one with intellectual disabilities who were excluded from public schools. School officials justified the exclusions on the basis of four statutes that relieved them of any obligation to educate children who were certified, in the terminology used at that time, as uneducable and untrainable by school psychologists, allowed officials to postpone the admission to any children who had not attained the mental age of five years, excused children who were found unable to profit from education from compulsory attendance, and defined compulsory school age as eight to seventeen while excluding children who were mentally not between those ages.

PARC was resolved by means of a consent agreement between the parties that was endorsed by a federal trial court. In language that preceded the IDEA, the stipulations maintained that no "mentally retarded" child, or child thought to be "mentally retarded," could be assigned to a special education program or be excluded from the public schools without due process. The consent agreement added that school systems in Pennsylvania had the obligation to provide all children with intellectual disabilities a free appropriate public education and training programs appropriate to their capacities. Even though *PARC* was a consent decree, thereby arguably limiting its legal value to the parties, there can be no doubt that it helped to usher in significant positive change with regard to protecting the educational rights of students. *PARC* helped to establish that students who were "mentally retarded" (now referred to as an "intellectual disability") were entitled to receive a free appropriate public education, or FAPE.

The second legal case, *Mills v. Board of Education of the District of Columbia* (*Mills*) (1972), extended the same legal right to other classes of students with disabilities, establishing the principle that a lack of funds was an insufficient basis for denying children with disabilities services. Moreover, *Mills* provided much of the due process language that was later incorporated into the IDEA and other federal legislation. The *Mills* case similar to *PARC*, was a class action lawsuit brought on behalf of children who were excluded from the public schools in the District of Columbia after they were classified as being behavior problems, mentally retarded, emotionally disturbed, and hyperactive. In fact, in an egregious oversight, the plaintiffs estimated that approximately 18,000 out of 22,000 students with disabilities in the school district were not receiving special education services. The plaintiff class sought a declaration of rights and an order directing the school board to provide a publicly supported education to all students with disabilities either within its system of public schools or at alternative programs at public expense. School officials responded that while the board had the responsibility to provide a publicly supported education to meet the needs of all children within its boundaries and that it had failed to do so, it was impossible to afford the plaintiff class the relief it sought due to a lack of funds. Additionally, school personnel admitted that they had not provided the plaintiffs with due process procedures prior to their exclusion.

Entering a judgment on the merits in favor of the plaintiffs, meaning that it went beyond the consent decree in *PARC*, the federal trial court pointed out that the United States Constitution, the District of Columbia Code, and its own regulations required the board to provide a publicly supported education to all children, including those with disabilities. The court explained that the board had to expend its available funds equitably so that all students would receive a publicly funded education consistent with their needs and abilities. If sufficient funds were not available, the court asserted that existing funds would have to be distributed in such a manner that no child was entirely excluded and the inadequacies could not be allowed to bear more heavily on one class of students. In so ruling, the court directed the board to provide due process safeguards before any children were excluded from the public schools, reassigned, or had their special education services terminated. At the same time, as part of its opinion, the court outlined elaborate due process procedures that it expected the school board to follow. These procedures later formed the foundation for the due process safeguards that were mandated in the federal special education statute.

Major Legislative Initiatives

With the prospect of additional litigation, Congress, along with select state legislatures, passed new laws expanding the rights of students with disabilities to receive an appropriate education. In so doing, the legislatures incorporated many of the legal principles that emerged from the legal cases discussed previously. Table 2.1 chronologically depicts the foundational legal cases and federal legislation that helped secure the access of students with disabilities in the nation's public schools.

Table 2.1 Case Law and Legislation That Influenced the Education of Students With Disabilities

Date	Case Law or Legislation	Description
1954	*Brown v. Board of Education*	• Legally prohibited segregation in public schools on the basis of race
1965	Elementary and Secondary Education Act (ESEA)(P.L. 89–10)	• Provided federal funding to assist states in educating students as part of the war on poverty
1966	Amendments to the ESEA, Title VI (P.L. 89–750)	• Provided federal funding to assist states to expand programs for children with disabilities
1970	Education of the Handicapped Act (P.L. 91–230)	• Expanded state grant programs for children with disabilities • Provided grants to institutions of higher education to train special education teachers • Created regional resource centers
1972	*PARC v. Commonwealth of Pennsylvania*	• Required the state of Pennsylvania to provide students with "mental retardation" with a free appropriate education
1972	*Mills v. Board of Education of the District of Columbia*	• Ruled that since segregation in public schools by race is illegal, it would be unconstitutional for the District of Columbia Board of Education to deprive students with disabilities from receiving an education
1973	Section 504 of the Rehabilitation Act (P.L. 93–112)	• Prohibits discrimination against otherwise qualified individuals with disabilities in programs that receive federal funding
1974	Education Amendments (P.L. 93–380)	• Incorporated the rights from the legal cases from *PARC* and *Mills* into federal law
1975	Education for All Handicapped Children (P.L. 94–142)	• Provided federal funding to states that agree to educate eligible students with disabilities as required in the EAHCA • Established the rights of eligible students with disabilities to a free appropriate public education in the least restrictive environment • Required public school to develop an Individualized Education Plan (IEP) for each eligible student with disabilities • Established procedural safeguards
1986	The Handicapped Children's Protection Act (P.L. 99–372)	• Allowed parents to recover attorney's fees if they prevail in a due process hearing or court case
1986	Education of the Handicapped Amendments (P.L. 99–457)	• Created federal financial incentives to educate infants (birth through age two) using early intervention strategies • Extended the EAHCA's Part B programs to 3-to-5-year olds in participating states

Date	Case Law or Legislation	Description
1990	Individuals with Disabilities Education Act (P.L. 101–476)	• Renamed the EAHCA to IDEA • Added traumatic brain injury and autism as new disability categories under the IDEA • Added a transition requirement to the IEP for students age sixteen or older • Added language that states that were not immune from lawsuits under the 11th Amendment for violations of the IDEA • Changed to "people first" language
1997	Individuals with Disabilities Education Act Amendments (P.L. 105–17)	• Added new IEP content and changed the IEP team composition • Added new disciplinary provisions • Required states to offer mediation to parents prior to due process hearings • Reorganized the structure of the IDEA
2004	Individuals with Disabilities Education Improvement Act (P.L. 108–446)	• Defined "highly qualified" special education teacher • Removed the short-term objectives requirement from IEPs, except for students with severe disabilities • Prohibited states from requiring school districts to use a discrepancy formula for determining eligibility of students with learning disabilities

Source: Yell, M.L. (2019). *The law and special education (5th Ed.).* New York, NY: Pearson.

The Standards-Based Reform Movement and Students With Disabilities

Beginning in the 1980s, the U.S. educational system experienced a standards-based reform movement. In 1983, the National Commission on Excellence in Education published an influential report, *A Nation at Risk*, highlighting the fact that U.S. students were lagging behind academically when compared with other students in other countries. In order to address this educational deficit, state and local school systems began to develop and implement educational reforms supporting the use of national academic standards promoting improvements in academic performance. As a way to incentivize the implementation of these education reforms, levels of federal funding were contingent on individual states demonstrating improvement in the academic performance of students.

Approximately a decade after the beginning of the standards-based education reform movement, the 1997 reauthorization of the Individuals with Disabilities Education Act (IDEA) included an expectation for encouraging high academic expectations for students with disabilities. Despite continued low overall student academic performance in U.S. schools throughout the 1990s, Congress passed the No Child Left Behind Act of 2001, often referred to as NCLB. President George W. Bush signed this bill into law on January 8, 2002. NCLB expanded the existing standards-based reforms of the 1990s and developed a comprehensive system of enforcement measures requiring the regular testing of students. Individual student test results were compared to specific state-defined standards of academic achievement. The regular testing of students mandated under NCLB included the reporting of traditionally underperforming subgroups of students, including students with disabilities. Prior to the passage of NCLB, many students with disabilities either did not participate or their test scores were withdrawn from state academic testing assessments. Under NCLB, schools were required to demonstrate through specific data assessment measures, a steady and measured increase in student achievement levels in order to satisfy NCLB's designated adequate yearly progress, or AYP goals. If schools were repeatedly unable to satisfy these designated AYP targets, there would be penalties imposed by the federal government, including the withholding of federal funds. Students with disabilities were one of the identified student subgroups under NCLB. As such, the academic performance of students with disabilities became an integral part of the NCLB student accountability system, which became a central theme of the 2004 IDEA reauthorization process. A primary focus of the most recent 2004 IDEA reauthorization was linking NCLB's objective of holding all schools accountable for the academic progress of its students, including students with disabilities as well as maintaining the IDEA's existing goal of providing eligible students with disabilities a free and appropriate public education (FAPE) in the least restrictive environment (LRE). Congress struggled to find a balance between NCLB demands for increased school accountability with the need to legally safeguard existing IDEA entitlements and protections for students with disabilities.

Today, special education in the U.S. is governed primarily by three federal laws as well as individual state laws. The three federal laws are the Individuals with Disabilities Education Act (IDEA), Section 504 of the Rehabilitation Act (Section 504), and the Americans with Disabilities Act (ADA). While the IDEA receives considerably more attention in this book, both Section 504 and the ADA are federal antidiscrimination statutes assisting students with disabilities achieve improved access in schools nationwide. These two federal statutes are discussed in more detail in Chapter 12.

Individuals With Disabilities Education Act (IDEA)

In 1975, Congress passed Public Law (P.L.) 94–142, which at that time was known as the Education for All Handicapped Children Act. In a 1990 amendment, this landmark statute was given its current title, the Individuals with Disabilities Education Act (IDEA). P.L. 94–142, signifying that it was the 142nd piece of legislation introduced during the Ninety-Fourth Congress, was not an independent act. Instead, the IDEA was an amendment to previous legislation that provided funds to the states for educating students with disabilities. The important aspect of the IDEA is that it is permanent legislation, while previous laws expired unless they were reauthorized.

The IDEA mandates a free appropriate public education (FAPE) in the least restrictive environment (LRE) for all students with disabilities between the ages of three and twenty-one based on the contents of their Individualized Education Programs (IEPs). Educators must develop IEPs in conferences with students' parents for any children who require special education and related services. The IDEA specifies how IEPs are to be developed and what they must contain. Additionally, the IDEA includes elaborate due process safeguards to protect the rights of students and ensure that its provisions are enforced. As part of the IDEA's funding formula that allows all school districts to qualify for funds, boards receiving funds are subject to fairly rigid auditing and management requirements.

The IDEA has been periodically amended, or reauthorized, since its original enactment in 1975. The Handicapped Children's Protection Act (1986), an important modification, added a clause that allows parents who prevail in litigation against their school boards to recover legal expenses. Another amendment, the Education of the Handicapped Amendments of 1986, provided grants to states that wish to provide services to children with disabilities from birth to age two. The 1990 amendments, mentioned previously, changed the statute's name and abrogated the states' Eleventh Amendment immunity to litigation.

Another important reauthorization, the Individuals with Disabilities Education Act Amendments of 1997, which was passed after a great deal of debate, incorporated disciplinary provisions into the IDEA. The most recent amendments, the Individuals with Disabilities Education Improvement Act of 2004, now codified as the IDEA, modified the 1997 disciplinary provisions and brought the IDEA in alignment with other federal legislation. More specifically, the most recent IDEA 2004 represents Congress' efforts to incorporate increased school and student accountability requirements of NCLB with the existing statutory structure of providing special education and related services to eligible students with disabilities. The most recent IDEA 2004 has altered and adjusted many provisions in the federal law compared to its predecessors, including requiring state educational agencies (SEAs) and local educational agencies (LEAs) to do the following:

1. Increase accountability and improve the educational performance for students with disabilities
2. Reduce the administrative burden on today's special education teachers and administrators
3. Reduce the over-identification or misidentification of nondisabled children and youth, including minority children and youth
4. Increase the flexibility of educational programs offered to students with disabilities
5. Improve the overall safety of school environments as they impact students with disabilities
6. Reduce the litigation of special education-related legal disputes
7. Support both general education and special education teachers
8. Improve early intervention strategies for students with disabilities

Section 504, the Rehabilitation Act of 1973

According to Section 504 of the Rehabilitation Act of 1973:

> No otherwise qualified individual with a disability in the United States . . . shall, solely by reason of her or his disability, be excluded from the participation in, be denied the benefits of, or be subjected to discrimination under any program or activity receiving Federal financial assistance or under any program or activity conducted by any Executive agency or by the United States Postal Service.

Section 504 was the first federal civil rights legislation that specifically guaranteed the rights of disabled persons, even though it relies on the broader term "impairment" in offering its protections to qualified individuals. Section 504's provisions that prohibit discrimination against individuals with disabilities in programs receiving federal funds are similar to those found in Titles VI (2005) and VII of the Civil Rights Act of 1964 (2005), which forbids employment discrimination in programs that receive federal financial assistance on the basis of race, color, religion, sex, or national origin. Section 504 effectively prohibits discrimination by any recipient of federal funds in the provision of services or employment. Individuals are covered by Section 504 if they have physical or mental impairments that substantially limit one or more of life's major life activities, have a record of such impairments, or are regarded as having impairments (29 U.S.C. § 706(7)(B)). Major life activities are "functions such as caring for oneself, performing manual tasks, walking, seeing, hearing, speaking, breathing, learning, and working" (28 C.F.R. § 41.31).

Americans With Disabilities Act (ADA)

The Americans with Disabilities Act (ADA), passed in 1990, prohibits discrimination against individuals with disabilities in the private sector. The ADA's preamble explains its purpose as acting "to provide a clear and comprehensive national mandate for the elimination of discrimination against individuals with disabilities" (42 U.S.C. § 12101). Basically, the intent of the ADA is to extend the protections afforded by Section 504 to programs and activities that are not covered by Section 504 because they do not receive federal funds. While the ADA is aimed primarily at the private sector, public agencies are not immune to its provisions. Compliance with Section 504 does not automatically translate to compliance with the ADA. The legislative history of the ADA indicates that it also addresses what the judiciary had perceived as shortcomings or loopholes in Section 504 (Marczely, 1993).

State Statutes

Since public education is a function of the states, rather than the federal government, special education is governed by state laws in addition to the federal statutes discussed earlier. While state special education laws must be consistent with federal laws, to the extent that they cannot do less than the federal statutes require, states can provide greater legal protection(s) for children with disabilities if they wish to do so. To this end, while most states have laws that are similar in scope and language to the federal IDEA statute, several jurisdictions include provisions in their legislation that exceed the federal IDEA's requirements. For example, some states have higher standards of what constitutes a free appropriate education for a student with disabilities. Other states have stricter procedural requirements designed to protect students with disabilities as well as their parents. Most states have established procedures for special education program implementation that are either not covered by federal law or have been left to the discretion of individual states to determine. If a conflict develops between provisions of the IDEA or other federal statutes and state laws, federal law is almost always considered to be supreme under Article VI of the United States Constitution.

A comprehensive discussion of the laws of each of the fifty states, the District of Columbia, and various American possessions and territories is beyond the scope of this book. Each of these governmental entities has its own terminology, laws, regulations, funding schemes, and legal systems. Indeed, entire books could be written on the special education laws of each state. The primary purpose of this book is to improve the special education legal literacy of persons who work closely with students with disabilities by providing comprehensive information on the federal mandate, the laws encompassing the entire nation. As such, readers are cautioned that they cannot acquire a complete understanding of special education law if they are not familiar with their existing state's law relating to students with disabilities. Thus, readers are advised to seek out sources of information involving the pertinent laws of their states to supplement this book.

⚖

SPECIAL EDUCATION LAW IN PRACTICE

Legal Case No. 2—Sanctioned Exclusion of Students With Disabilities From Public Schools

WATSON V. CITY OF CAMBRIDGE

157 Mass. 561 (1893)

OPINION

KNOWLTON, J.

The records of the school committee of the defendant city set forth that the plaintiff in 1885 was excluded from the schools "because he was too weak-minded to derive profit from instruction." He was afterwards taken again on trial for two weeks, and at the end of that time again excluded. The records further recite that "it appears from the statements of teachers who observed him, and from certificates of physicians, that he is so weak in mind as not to derive any marked benefit from instruction, and, further, that he is troublesome to other children, making unusual noises, pinching others, etc. He is also found unable to take ordinary, decent, physical care of himself." The evidence at the trial tended strongly to show that the matters set out in the records were true.

The defendant requested the court to rule that if the facts are true which are set forth in the records of the committee, as to the cause of the exclusion of the plaintiff from the public schools, the determination of the school committee thereon, acting in good faith, was final, and not subject to revision in the courts. The court refused so to rule, and submitted to the jury the question whether the facts stated, if proved, showed that the plaintiff's presence in school "was a serious disturbance to the good order and discipline of the school."

The exceptions present the question whether the decision of the school committee of a city or town, acting in good faith in the management of the schools, upon matters of fact directly affecting the good order and discipline of the schools, is final, so far as it relates to the rights of pupils to enjoy the privileges of the school, or is subject to revision by a court. In *Hodgkins v. Rockport*, it appeared that the school committee, acting in good faith, excluded the plaintiff from school on account "of his general persistence in disobeying the rules of the school, to the injury of the school." Of the plaintiff's acts of misconduct, it is said, in the opinion in that case, that "whether they had such an effect upon the welfare of the school as to require his expulsion was a question within the discretion of the committee, and upon which their action is conclusive." The principles there laid down are decisive of the present case. It was found by the presiding justice that the alleged misconduct of the plaintiff in that case was not mutinous or gross, and did not consist of a refusal to obey the commands of the teachers, or of any outrageous proceeding, but of acts of neglect, carelessness of posture in his seat, and recitation, tricks of playfulness, inattention to study and the regulations of the school in minor matters. The only difference between the acts of disorder in that case and in this is that in this they resulted from the incapacity and mental weakness of the plaintiff, and in the other they were willful or careless,-the result in part of youthful exuberance of spirits and impatience of restraint or control. In their general effect upon the school, they were alike; and the reasons for giving the school committee, acting in good faith, the power to decide finally a question affecting so vitally the rights and interests of all the other scholars of the school, are the same in both cases.

Under the law the school committee "have the general charge and superintendence of all the public schools in the town" or city. Pub. St. c. 44, § 21. The management of the schools involves many details; and it is important that a board of public officers, dealing with these details, and having jurisdiction to regulate the internal affairs of the schools, should not be interfered with or have their conduct called in question before another tribunal, so long as they act in good faith within their jurisdiction. Whether certain acts of disorder so seriously interfere with the school that one who persists in them, either voluntarily or by reason of imbecility, should not be permitted to continue in the school, is a question which the statute makes it their duty to answer; and if they answer honestly, in an effort to do their duty, a jury composed of men of no special fitness to decide educational questions should not be permitted to say that their answer is wrong. Spear v. Cummings, 23 Pick. 224, 226.

We are of opinion that the ruling requested should have been given.

Exceptions sustained.

Questions for Discussion

1. In this case, the courts indicate that ultimately local school boards have the discretion to make judgements concerning the admission of students to a school. What are your thoughts about the local school board having full legal authority to make admissions decisions on all students, especially students with disabilities?

2. The current IDEA provides parents significant procedural due process protections, including the ability to formally request a hearing to challenge a local school district's decision regarding the identification, evaluation, or educational program or placement of their child. Can you think of any modern-day practices of schools limiting the access of students with disabilities to educational programs and services?

⚖️

SPECIAL EDUCATION LAW IN PRACTICE
Legal Case No. 3—Rights of Students With Disabilities to a Public Education

PENNSYLVANIA ASSOCIATION FOR RETARDED CHILDREN (PARC) V. COMMONWEALTH OF PENNSYLVANIA
343 F. Supp. 279 (1972)

OPINION, ORDER AND INJUNCTION

MASTERSON, District Judge.

This civil rights case, a class action, was brought by the Pennsylvania Association for Retarded Children and the parents of thirteen individual retarded children on behalf of all mentally retarded persons between the ages 6 and 21 whom the Commonwealth of Pennsylvania, through its local school districts and intermediate units, is presently excluding from a program of education and training in the public schools. Named as defendants are the Commonwealth of Pennsylvania, Secretary of Welfare, State Board of Education and thirteen individual school districts scattered throughout the Commonwealth. In addition, plaintiffs have joined all other school districts in the Commonwealth as class defendants of which the named districts are said to be representative.

The exclusions of retarded children complained of are based upon four State statutes: (1) . . . which relieves the State Board of Education from any obligation to educate a child whom a public school psychologist certifies as uneducable and untrainable. The burden of caring for such a child then shifts to the Department of Welfare which has no obligation to provide any educational services for the child; (2) . . . which allows an indefinite postponement of admission to public school of any child who has not attained a mental age of five years; (3) . . . which appears to *excuse* any child from compulsory school attendance whom a psychologist finds unable to profit therefrom and (4) . . . which defines compulsory school age as 8 to 17 years but has been used in practice to postpone admissions of retarded children until 8 or to eliminate them from public schools at age 17.

[T]he parties agreed upon a Stipulation which basically provides that no child who is mentally retarded or thought to be mentally retarded can be assigned initially (or re-assigned) to either a regular or special educational status, or excluded from a public education without a prior recorded hearing before a special hearing officer. At that hearing, parents have the right to representation by counsel, to examine their child's records, to compel the attendance of school officials who may have relevant evidence to offer, to cross-examine witnesses testifying on behalf of school officials and to introduce evidence of their own . . . .

[T]he parties submitted a Consent Agreement to this Court which, along with the . . . Stipulation, would settle the entire case. Essentially, this Agreement deals with the four state statutes in an effort to eliminate the alleged equal protection problems. As a proposed cure, the defendants agreed, that since "the Commonwealth of Pennsylvania has undertaken to provide a free public education for all of its children between the ages of six and twenty-one years" . . . therefore, "it is the Commonwealth's obligation to place each mentally retarded child in a *free, public program of education and training appropriate to the child's capacity.*"

The lengthy Consent Agreement concludes by stating that "[e]very retarded person between the ages of six and twenty-one shall be provided access to a free public program of education and training appropriate to his capacities as soon as possible but in no event later than *September 1, 1972. . . .*" Finally, and perhaps most importantly, the Agreement states that:

"The defendants shall formulate and submit . . . *a plan to be effectuated by September 1, 1972*, to commence or recommence a free public program of education and training for all mentally retarded persons . . . aged between four and twenty-one years as of the date of this Order, and for all mentally retarded persons of such ages hereafter. The plan shall specify the range of programs of education and training, there [sic] kind and number, necessary to provide an appropriate program of education and training to all mentally retarded children, where they shall be conducted, arrangements for their financing, and, if additional teachers are found to be necessary, the plan shall specify recruitment, hiring, and training arrangements. "

Thus, if all goes according to plan, Pennsylvania should be providing a meaningful program of education and training to every retarded child in the Commonwealth by September, 1972 .

Questions for Discussion

1. Although the *PARC* legal case dealt only with the right to an education for students who suffered from intellectual difficulties (at the time, referred to as mental retardation) it is considered a landmark case involving the access of students with disabilities to an education. Why is this particular legal decision also important for students with other types of disabilities?

2. The fact that this legal dispute was settled by a stipulation and consent agreement indicates that the state of Pennsylvania accepted its legal obligation to provide appropriate *educational opportunities for its students with disabilities.* Compare this case to the *Mills v. Board of Education of the District of Columbia* case where the District of Columbia School District claimed that it did not have the proper financial resources to appropriately educate its students with disabilities. Do you think this is a valid argument? Why or why not? Many public school districts nationwide claim they do not have the necessary financial resources to appropriately educate their population of students with disabilities. Do you think this is a valid argument for today's public school districts to make?

⚖️

SPECIAL EDUCATION LAW IN PRACTICE
Legal Case No. 4—Establishment of Due Process Rights for Students With Disabilities

MILLS V. BOARD OF EDUCATION OF THE DISTRICT OF COLUMBIA
348 F. Supp. 866 (1972)

MEMORANDUM OPINION, JUDGMENT AND DECREE

WADDY, District Judge.

This is a civil action brought on behalf of seven children of school age by their next friends in which they seek a declaration of rights and to enjoin the defendants from excluding them from the District of Columbia Public Schools and/or denying them publicly supported education and to compel the defendants to provide them with immediate and adequate education and educational facilities in the public schools or alternative placement at public expense. They also seek additional and ancillary relief to effectuate the primary relief. They allege that although they can profit from an education either in regular classrooms with supportive services or in special classes adopted to their needs, they have been labeled as behavioral problems, mentally retarded, emotionally disturbed or hyperactive, and denied admission to the public schools or excluded therefrom after admission, with no provision for alternative educational placement or periodic review. . . .

The Problem

The genesis of this case is found (1) in the failure of the District of Columbia to provide publicly supported education and training to plaintiffs and other "exceptional" children, members of their class, and (2) the excluding, suspending, expelling, reassigning, and transferring of "exceptional" children from regular public school classes without affording them due process of law.

The problem of providing special education for "exceptional" children (mentally retarded, emotionally disturbed, physically handicapped, hyperactive and other children with behavioral problems) is one of major proportions in the District of Columbia. The precise number of such children cannot be stated because the District has continuously failed to comply with Section 31–208 of the District of Columbia Code which requires a census of all children aged 3 to 18 in the District to be taken. Plaintiffs estimate that there are " . . . 22,000 retarded,

emotionally disturbed, blind, deaf, and speech or learning disabled children, and perhaps as many as 18,000 of these children are not being furnished with programs of specialized education." According to data prepared by the Board of Education, . . . the District of Columbia provides publicly supported special education programs of various descriptions to at least 3880 school age children. However, in a 1971 report to the Department of Health, Education and Welfare, the District of Columbia Public Schools admitted that an estimated 12,340 handicapped children were not to be served in the 1971–72 school year. . . . Each of the minor plaintiffs in this case qualifies as an "exceptional" child. Plaintiffs allege in their complaint and defendants admit as follows:

"PETER MILLS is twelve years old, black, and a committed dependent ward of the District of Columbia resident at Junior Village. He was excluded from the Brent Elementary School on March 23, 1971, at which time he was in the fourth grade. Peter allegedly was a 'behavior problem' and was recommended and approved for exclusion by the principal. Defendants have not provided him with a full hearing or with a timely and adequate review of his status. Furthermore, Defendants have failed to provide for his reenrollment in the District of Columbia Public Schools or enrollment in private school. On information and belief, numerous other dependent children of school attendance age at Junior Village are denied a publicly-supported education. Peter remains excluded from any publicly-supported education.

• "DUANE BLACKSHEARE is thirteen years old, black, resident at Saint Elizabeth's Hospital, Washington, D. C., and a dependent committed child. He was excluded from the Giddings Elementary School in October, 1967, at which time he was in the third grade. Duane allegedly was a "behavior problem." Defendants have not provided him with a full hearing or with a timely and adequate review of his status. Despite repeated efforts by his mother, Duane remained largely excluded from all publicly-supported education until February, 1971. Education experts at the Child Study Center examined Duane and found him to be capable of returning to regular class if supportive services were provided. Following several articles in the Washington Post and Washington Star, Duane was placed in a regular seventh grade classroom on a two-hour a day basis without any catch-up assistance and without an evaluation or diagnostic interview of any kind. Duane has remained on a waiting list for a tuition grant and is now excluded from all publicly-supported education.

• "GEORGE LIDDELL, JR., is eight years old, black, resident with his mother, Daisy Liddell, at 601 Morton Street, N. W., Washington, D. C., and an AFDC recipient. George has never attended public school because of the denial of his application to the Maury Elementary School on the ground that he required a special class. George allegedly was retarded. Defendants have not provided him with a full hearing or with a timely and adequate review of his status. George remains excluded from all publicly-supported education, despite a medical opinion that he is capable of profiting from schooling, and despite his mother's efforts to secure a tuition grant from Defendants.

• "STEVEN GASTON is eight years old, black, resident with his mother, Ina Gaston, at 714 9th Street, N. E., Washington, D. C. and unable to afford private instruction. He has been excluded from the Taylor Elementary School since September, 1969, at which time he was in the first grade. Steven allegedly was slightly brain-damaged and hyperactive, and was excluded because he wandered around the classroom. Defendants have not provided him with a full hearing or with a timely and adequate review of his status. Steven was accepted in the Contemporary School, a private school, provided that tuition was paid in full in advance. Despite the efforts of his parents, Steven has remained on a waiting list for the requisite tuition grant from Defendant school system and excluded from all publicly-supported education.

• "MICHAEL WILLIAMS is sixteen years old, black, resident at Saint Elizabeth's Hospital, Washington, D. C., and unable to afford private instruction. Michael is epileptic and allegedly slightly retarded. He has been excluded from the Sharpe Health School since October, 1969, at which time he was temporarily hospitalized. Thereafter Michael was excluded from school because of health problems and school absences. Defendants have not provided him with a full

hearing or with a timely and adequate review of his status. Despite his mother's efforts, and his attending physician's medical opinion that he could attend school, Michael has remained on a waiting list for a tuition grant and excluded from all publicly-supported education.

• "JANICE KING is thirteen years old, black, resident with her father, Andrew King, at 233 Anacostia Avenue, N. E., Washington, D. C., and unable to afford private instruction. She has been denied access to public schools since reaching compulsory school attendance age, as a result of the rejection of her application, based on the lack of an appropriate educational program. Janice is brain-damaged and retarded, with right hemiplegia, resulting from a childhood illness. Defendants have not provided her with a full hearing or with a timely and adequate review of her status. Despite repeated efforts by her parents, Janice has been excluded from all publicly-supported education.

• "JEROME JAMES is twelve years old, black, resident with his mother, Mary James, at 2512 Ontario Avenue, N. W., Washington, D. C., and an AFDC recipient. Jerome is a retarded child and has been totally excluded from public school. Defendants have not given him a full hearing or a timely and adequate review of his status. Despite his mother's efforts to secure either public school placement or a tuition grant, Jerome has remained on a waiting list for a tuition grant and excluded from all publicly supported education."

• Although all of the named minor plaintiffs are identified as Negroes the class they represent is not limited by their race. They sue on behalf of and represent all other District of Columbia residents of school age who are eligible for a free public education and who have been, or may be, excluded from such education or otherwise deprived by defendants of access to publicly supported education.

Minor plaintiffs are poor and without financial means to obtain private instruction. There has been no determination that they may not benefit from specialized instruction adapted to their needs. Prior to the beginning of the 1971–72 school year minor plaintiffs, through their representatives, sought to obtain publicly supported education and certain of them were assured by the school authorities that they would be placed in programs of publicly supported education and certain others would be recommended for special tuition grants at private schools. However, none of the plaintiff children were placed for the 1971 Fall term and they continued to be entirely excluded from all publicly supported education. After thus trying unsuccessfully to obtain relief from the Board of Education the plaintiffs filed this action on September 24, 1971.

Judgment and Decree

Plaintiffs having filed their verified complaint seeking an injunction and declaration of rights as set forth more fully in the verified complaint and the prayer for relief contained therein; and having moved this Court for summary judgment pursuant to [the rules of civil procedure], and this Court having reviewed the record of this cause . . . it is hereby ordered, adjudged and decreed that summary judgment in favor of plaintiffs and against defendants be, and hereby is, granted, and judgment is entered in this action as follows:

1. That no child eligible for a publicly supported education in the District of Columbia public schools shall be excluded from a regular public school assignment by a Rule, policy, or practice of the Board of Education of the District of Columbia or its agents unless such child is provided (a) adequate alternative educational services suited to the child's needs, which may include special education or tuition grants, and (b) a constitutionally adequate prior hearing and periodic review of the child's status, progress, and the adequacy of any educational alternative.

2. The defendants, their officers, agents, servants, employees, and attorneys and all those in active concert or participation with them are hereby enjoined from maintaining, enforcing or otherwise continuing in effect any and all rules, policies and practices which exclude plaintiffs and the members of the class they represent from a regular public school assignment without providing them at public expense (a) adequate and immediate alternative education or tuition grants, consistent with their needs, and (b) a constitutionally adequate prior hearing and periodic review of their status, progress and the adequacy of any educational alternatives; and it is further ORDERED that:

3. The District of Columbia shall provide to each child of school age a free and suitable publicly-supported education regardless of the degree of the child's mental, physical or emotional disability or impairment. Furthermore, defendants shall not exclude any child resident in the District of Columbia from such publicly-supported

education on the basis of a claim of insufficient resources. . . . .

13. Hearing Procedures.

a. Each member of the plaintiff class is to be provided with a publicly-supported educational program suited to his needs, within the context of a presumption that among the alternative programs of education, placement in a regular public school class with appropriate ancillary services is preferable to placement in a special school class.

b. Before placing a member of the class in such a program, defendants shall notify his parent or guardian of the proposed educational placement, the reasons therefor, and the right to a hearing before a Hearing Officer if there is an objection to the placement proposed. Any such hearing shall be held in accordance with the provisions of Paragraph 13.e., below.

c. Hereinafter, children who are residents of the District of Columbia and are thought by any of the defendants, or by officials, parents or guardians, to be in need of a program of special education, shall neither be placed in, transferred from or to, nor denied placement in such a program unless defendants shall have first notified their parents or guardians of such proposed placement, transfer or denial, the reasons therefor, and of the right to a hearing before a Hearing Officer if there is an objection to the placement, transfer or denial of placement. Any such hearings shall be held in accordance with the provisions of Paragraph 13.e., below.

d. Defendants shall not, on grounds of discipline, cause the exclusion, suspension, expulsion, postponement, interschool transfer, or any other denial of access to regular instruction in the public schools to any child for more than two days without first notifying the child's parent or guardian of such proposed action, the reasons therefor, and of the hearing before a Hearing Officer in accordance with the provisions of Paragraph 13.f., below.

e. Whenever defendants take action regarding a child's placement, denial of placement, or transfer, as described in Paragraphs 13.b. or 13.c., above, the following procedures shall be followed.

 . . . .

(15) Pending a determination by the Hearing Officer, defendants shall take no action described in Paragraphs 13.b or 13.c, above, if the child's parent or guardian objects to such action. Such objection must be in writing and postmarked within five

(5) days of the date of receipt of notification herein above described.

Questions for Discussion

1. The plaintiffs in *Mills* estimated that as many as 18,000 of the District of Columbia's 22,000 students with disabilities were not receiving specialized educational services. In today's world that would be unconscionable, but sadly, in 1972 it was not that unusual.

2. The **local** board of education in *Mills* basically claimed that it could not afford to provide the required services to give the plaintiffs the relief they sought. The court responded that the available funds needed to be expended equitably so that students with disabilities would not be disproportionately deprived of an equal educational opportunity. How does this decision compare with other equal educational opportunity opinions?

3. Many legal commentators have expressed the view that *Mills* laid the groundwork for the elaborate due process provisions that are included in the IDEA. Compare the due process procedures outlined in this decision with those currently included in § 1415 of the IDEA. What are the similarities and differences?

Summary of Important Legal Policies, Principles, and Practices

This chapter provides a brief overview of major historical developments impacting the axis of students with disabilities to public schools. Prior to the mid-1970s, there was considerable exclusion of children and youth with disabilities from the nation's schools. The legal rights afforded children and youth with disabilities were gained through the efforts of many individuals. Some historical highlights in the development of influential case law and legislation impacting children and youth with disabilities and their access to schooling include

1. Despite compulsory education laws in many states by the 1900s, children and youth with disabilities were largely excluded from public schools and this exclusion was sanctioned by both the federal and state courts across the country.

2. The Civil Rights Movement, especially the U.S. Supreme Court's *Brown v. Board of Education* (1954) decision was a catalyst for subsequent litigation and legislation related to providing students with disabilities the right to a free appropriate public education (FAPE).

3. Two seminal legal cases, *PARC v. Pennsylvania* (1972) and *Mills v. Board of Education* (1972) became precursors to federal legislative efforts to improve the education of students with disabilities. These early major pieces of legislation were Section 504 of the Rehabilitation Act of 1973 (Section 504) and the Education for All Handicapped Children Act of 1975 (EAHCA).

4. More recent federal efforts to improve the educational rights of students with disabilities include the Individuals with Disabilities Education Act and the Americans with Disabilities Act (ADA).

5. Beginning with the passage of the No Child Left Behind Act of 2001(NCLB), increased nationwide school accountability efforts led to increased monitoring efforts of the academic progress of students with disabilities in conjunction with maintaining legal entitlements and protections already provided under the IDEA.

Useful Online Resources

Celebrating the 40th Anniversary of IDEA

This YouTube video provides an excellent 10-minute overview on the history and impact of the Individuals with Disabilities Education Act (IDEA). www.youtube.com/watch?v=Oj4b9d4XAdY

Recommended Reading

Ballard, J., Ramirez, B., & Weintraub, F. (Eds.). (1982). *Special education in America: Its legal and governmental foundations.* Reston, VA: Council for Exceptional Children.

Katsiyannis, A., Yell, M. L., & Bradley, R. (2001). Reflections on the 25th anniversary of the Individuals with Disabilities Act. *Remedial and Special Education, 22*, 324–334.

Martin, E. W. (2013). *Breakthrough: Special education legislation 1965–1981.* Sarasota, FL: Bardolf & Company.

Winzer, M. A. (1993). *History of special education from isolation to integration.* Washington, DC: Gallaudet Press.

Yell, M. L., Rogers, D., & Rogers, E. L. (1998, July/August). The legal history of special education: What a long, strange trip it's been! *Remedial and Special Education, 19*(4), 219–228.

References

Americans with Disabilities Act, 42 U.S.C. §§ 12101–12213 (1990).

Brown v. Board of Education, 347 U.S. 483 (1954).

Civil Rights Act of 1964, Title VI, 42 U.S.C. §§ 2000 *et seq.* (2005).

Colker, R. (2018). *Special education law in a nutshell.* St. Paul, MN: West Academic Publishing.

Diana v. State Board of Education, Civ. No. C-70-37 RFP (N.D. Cal. 1970 & 1973).

Education for All Handicapped Children Act, 20 U.S.C. § 1400 *et seq.* (1975).

Education of the Handicapped Amendments of 1986, P.L. 99–457, 100 Stat. 1145 (1986).

Hobson v. Hansen, 269 F. Supp. 401 (D.D.C. 1967).

Individuals with Disabilities Education Act Amendments of 1997, P.L. 105–17, 11 Stat. 37 (1997).

Individuals with Disabilities Education Improvement Act of 2004, P.L. 108–446, 118 Stat. 2647 (2004).

Larry P. v. Riles, 343 F. Supp. 1306 (N.D. Cal. 1972), *aff'd,* 502 F.2d 963 (9th Cir. 1974), *further action,* 495 F. Supp. 926 (N.D. Cal. 1979), *aff'd,* 793 F.2d 969 (9th Cir. 1984).

Lau v. Nichols, 414 U.S. 563 (1974).

Marczely, B. (1993). The Americans with Disabilities Act: Confronting the shortcomings of Section 504 in public education. *Education Law Reporter, 78,* 199–207.

Mills v. Board of Education of the District of Columbia, 348 F. Supp. 866 (D.D.C. 1972).

Parents in Action on Special Education v. Hannon, 506 F. Supp. 831 (N.D. Ill. 1980).

Pennsylvania Association for Retarded Children v. Commonwealth of Pennsylvania, 334 F. Supp. 1257 (E.D. Pa. 1971), 343 F. Supp. 279 (E.D. Pa. 1972).

Russo, C. J. (2018). *Russo's law of public education* (9th ed.). New York: Foundation Press.

State ex rel. Beattie v. Board of Education of Antigo, 169 Wis. 231 (Wis. 1919).

Turnbull, H. R., Stowe, M. J., & Huerta, N. E. (2007). *Free appropriate public education: The law and children with disabilities.* Denver, CO: Love.

Watson v. City of Cambridge, 157 Mass. 561 (Mass. 1893).

Wolf v. State of Utah, Civ. No. 182646 (Utah Dist. Ct. 1969).

Yell, M. L. (2019). *The law and special education* (5th ed.). New York: Pearson.

Zerrel, J. J., & Ballard, J. (1982). The Education for All Handicapped Children Act of 1975 (P.L. 94–142). Its history, origins, and concepts. In J. Ballard, B. Ramirez, & F. Weintraub (Eds.), *Special education in America: Its legal and governmental foundations* (pp. 11–22). Reston, VA. Council for Exceptional Children.

3
Finding Special Education Legal Information in a Digital Age

Key Concepts and Terms in This Chapter

- Primary sources of law
- Secondary sources of law
- Open-access online resources of special education legal information

Prior to the 1970s, the area of special education law was nonexistent. Many educators and parents have not had the opportunity to understand the origins and major legal sources involving the rights of children with disabilities. One definite way to improve someone's special education legal literacy is to familiarize yourself with the major legal sources of special education information and where to find these resources, many of which are now fully accessible online. Acquiring a working knowledge of the U.S. legal system is invaluable to recognizing the significant impact special education law, policies, and practices have on children with disabilities enrolled in our nation's elementary through secondary schools. When today's school employees are more legally literate about special education laws, policies, and procedures they are better able to identify legal issues, identify applicable laws or legal standards, and apply relevant legal rules to solve legal dilemmas (Decker & Brady, 2016). More importantly, acquiring special education legal literacy allows those that work closely with students with disabilities in school settings to more effectively and efficiently serve the best and individualized interests of children and youth with disabilities. In light of the various constitutional provisions, statutes, regulations, administrative rulings, and court cases protecting the rights of students with disabilities, this chapter begins with a brief overview of the American legal system, the legal process, and the structure of the courts in order to assist readers who might be less familiar with these general legal principles. Next, this chapter assists readers with effectively identifying and using special education legal resources, which now can be found almost entirely online at no cost. The final section of this chapter provides the reader with a concise overview of leading online primary and secondary legal resources addressing children and youth with disabilities in school environments. This part of the chapter also acknowledges that many states throughout the country have adopted similar laws protecting the educational rights of children and youth with disabilities and their parents/legal guardians. Readers who are less or not familiar with legal terminology should refer to the glossary found in the appendix section at the back of the book for definitions of various terms used in this specific chapter as well as throughout the book.

The United States legal system is inherently complex and is based largely on the concept of federalism (Turnbull, Stowe, & Huerta, 2007; Underwood & Mead, 1995). Federalism refers to the allocation of duties and responsibilities between the federal and individual state governments. Federalism also reflects the occasional imbalance of power between the federal and state governments involving important functions, including the provision of education to school age children and youth. Under the U.S. Constitution, the federal government has been given limited legal authority in certain areas that impact the general public.

Interestingly, the U.S. Constitution does not specifically address the issue and provision of education to its citizens. Based on this omission, the Tenth Amendment of the U.S. Constitution states, "The powers not delegated to the United States by the Constitution, nor prohibited by it to the states, are reserved to the states respectively, or to the people" (U.S. Constitution, Amendment X). Based on the legal doctrine called the "federal supremacy of the laws," however, both the U.S. Constitution and federal laws prevail over individual state constitutions and state laws (Turnbull, Stowe, & Huerta, 2007). Based on the federal supremacy of the laws doctrine, there have been instances when the federal government has intervened in education-related issues, including situations involving the access and provision of public education to students with disabilities. While the federal government does have limited legal authority over education-related issues, it can enact and enforce laws related to the U.S. Constitution as well as enforce those laws on individual states. For example, the U.S. Constitution's Fourteenth Amendment legally guarantees every citizen is afforded equal protection under the law and both the federal and state governments are mandated to provide all citizens due process, or fundamental fairness under the law. The U.S. Constitution's Fourteenth Amendment states:

> no state shall make or enforce any law which shall abridge the privileges or immunities of citizens of the United States; nor shall any State deprive any person of life, liberty, or property, without due process of law; nor deny to any person within its jurisdiction the equal protection of the laws.
>
> (U.S. Constitution, XIV)

Primary Sources of Special Education Legal Information

Laws applicable to special education come from a variety of sources. Yet, however, not all legal sources are inherently equal nor comparable. The source of law, or where a particular law(s) originates significantly informs the reader of a particular law's importance relative to other legal sources. Table 3.1 outlines the major sources of special education law found at the three different governmental levels: federal, state, and local. The four primary sources of legal authority in the U.S. include: (a) constitutions; (b) statutes; (c) regulations; and (d) judicial opinions, or court cases. A constitution is defined as the fundamental law of a nation or state (Garner, 2004). A statute is defined as a legal act of the legislative body; basically, a law that either Congress or an individual state legislature has passed (Garner, 2004). Statutes, whether they originate at the federal or state-level, must be consistent with their controlling federal or state constitutions. Most statutes are supplemented by regulations or guidelines written by federal or state-level governmental officials employed with administrative agencies charged with their implementation and enforcement. Regulations are often considerably more specific compared to statutes since they are designed to implement or carry out how the laws articulated in the statute should work in practice. Finally, the many legal cases, or case law

Table 3.1 Primary Governmental Sources of Special Education Law in the United States

Branches of Government	Levels of Government		
	Federal	*State*	*Local*
Legislative	**U.S. Congress** (statutes)	**State Legislature** (statutes)	**School Board** (school-level policies)
Executive	**Department of Education** (regulations)	**State Office of Education** (regulations)	**Superintendent** (school district rules)
Judicial	**Federal Courts** (court cases)	**State Courts** (court cases)	**Hearing Officers** (quasi-judicial administrative rulings)

decided by the nation's numerous courts interpreting the constitutions, statutes, and regulations comprise a body of law known as the common law, relying heavily on the concept of binding precedent, meaning that a legal ruling of the highest court within a particular legal jurisdiction is legally binding, or enforceable on all lower courts in that specific jurisdiction.

The ongoing judicial, or legal opinions involving school age children and youth with disabilities have the potential to significantly alter and impact the professional practices of today's educators, school leaders, and parents. Given the importance of school-based legal cases involving students with disabilities, a majority of the chapters contained in this book include a section(s) called, "Special Education Law in Practice," which includes carefully selected, and edited, excerpts drawn from actual and relevant legal cases across the country involving students with disabilities attending elementary through secondary school. The authors include excerpts from specific legal cases at the end of a chapter because these cases help illustrate essential legal concepts and principles that have or continue to influence special education law in the U.S. Furthermore, by reviewing the actual language of the justices of the United States Supreme Court or judges from a variety of other lower federal or state courts, readers develop a better appreciation and understanding of judicial opinions, even in instances when individuals may disagree with the actual legal outcome.

Federal and State Constitutions

The most influential source of legal authority in the U.S. rests with constitutions, which are found at both the federal and state levels. Constitutions provide the legal foundations upon which the entire U.S. legal system operates (Osborne & Russo, 2014). For example, the U.S. Constitution develops the legal rules under which the entire federal government functions and allocates legal authority and responsibilities to the three different branches of the federal government: executive, legislative, and judicial. Both federal and state constitutions contain broad legal rights and protections for children with disabilities (Weber, Mawdsley, & Redfield, 2013).

Despite the comprehensive and varied coverage of the U.S. Constitution on many important topics impacting the general public, the Constitution is notably silent on the topic of public education. In many instances, legal issues involving education are the legal responsibility of individual states. Under the U.S. Constitution's Tenth Amendment, "powers not delegated to the United States by the Constitution, nor prohibited by it to the states, are reserved to the states." Based on the U.S. Constitution's Tenth Amendment, individual states are legally bound under the Fourteenth Amendment of the U.S. Constitution to provide education on an equal basis as well as provide due process before denying equal educational programming to different students. (U.S. Constitution, X).

Analogous to their federal counterpart, state constitutions provide the primary source of law for a particular state. State constitutions can legally grant their citizens more, but not fewer, rights compared to the federal Constitution. As such, state constitutions are often considered the dominant laws within their own state boundaries, with which all state statutes, regulations, laws, and ordinances must follow. Typically, state constitutions encounter many of the same issues and concerns as their federal constitutional counterpart, but usually provide more detail when addressing educational issues.

Federal and State Statutes

The U.S. Constitution affords Congress the legal authority to make laws. The legislative branch of both the federal and state governments have been granted the authority to develop statutory law. Statutory law is comprised of those laws passed or enacted by the federal legislative body, which is represented by the U.S. Congress and at the state level by individual state legislatures. Once enacted by Congress or a state legislature, statutes take legal precedence over court cases, or judicial opinions. It is crucial for readers to know that statutory law, one of the four primary sources of law, comprises a majority of the laws impacting today's students with disabilities. The three leading federal statutes addressed in this book impacting students with disabilities at the elementary to secondary school level are the Individuals with Disabilities Education Act (2004), (hereafter IDEA 2004), Section 504 of the Rehabilitation Act of 1973 (hereafter Section 504), and the Americans with Disabilities Act (1990), (hereafter ADA). For example, Figure 3.1 provides a citation to a specific section in the current IDEA 2004 statute.

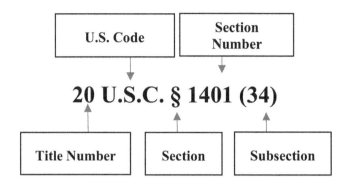

Figure 3.1 Legal Citation of Section in the Federal IDEA 2004 Statute

Federal and State Regulations

Essentially, the primary task of regulations is to help clarify the *United States Code* (U.S.C). A regulation has the same force of law as a statute. When federal or state statutes are passed, they often provide only a general and limited framework of the policies involving a particular issue, including policies regulating the education of students with disabilities in schools. In order to provide additional details and clarifications regarding statutory laws, Congress and state legislatures often delegate to administrative agencies the task of developing regulations pursuant to federal and state statutes. Additionally, today's administrative agencies have the quasi-judicial authority, or the ability to develop and enforce judicial rulings involving the compliance of regulations as well as develop guidelines suggesting how the laws should be interpreted (Yell, 2019). While the guidelines of administrative agencies do not have judicial authority, these guidelines are often seen as influential by national and state-level policymakers as well as the nation's courts. In special education, for example, many of the procedural legal safeguards contained in the regulations implementing the federal statute, the Individuals with Disabilities Education Act (IDEA 2004), are codified, or legally arranged in what is referred to as the Code of Federal Regulations, or C.F.R. The C.F.R. regulations covering the IDEA 2004 are published in Volume 34, Part 300 of the Code of Federal Regulations (C.F.R.). The legal citation for the Individuals with Disabilities Education Act (IDEA) regulations is 34 CFR § 300. Figure 3.2 shows a legal citation to the IDEA 2004 regulations. The first number in the legal citation, 34, refers to the title number, which is "education." *Code of Federal Regulations* is abbreviated as C.F.R. The next number, 300.39 refers to the section number and (a) (1) refer to the subsection letter and number. A violation of either federal or state regulations is comparable to a constitutional or statutory violation of law.

The U.S. Department of Education is the leading administrative agency, which authorizes programs and services related to education. For instance, the U.S. Department of Education develops and publishes a majority of the federal special education regulations. Regulations clarify and explain the United States Code. A regulation must be consistent with the United States Code and has the same force of law. Before the Department publishes the regulations, the agency must publish the proposed regulations in the *Federal Register* (F. R.) and solicit comments from citizens about the proposed regulations. The special education regulations are published in Volume 34, Part 300 of the Code of Federal Regulations. The legal citation for the regulations is 34 CFR § 300.

Federal and State Court System

Generally, the U.S. courts serve three primary functions including (a) settling controversies, (b) interpreting legislation, and (c) determining the constitutionality of governmental actions. The United States has a total of fifty-one different systems of courts. Figure 3.3 illustrates the federal court system, which contains three hierarchal levels including: (a) the United States Supreme Court at the top, (b) the United States Courts of Appeals (with thirteen circuits), and (c) 94 district, or trial courts. Most court cases begin at the bottom of their respective federal or state court level.

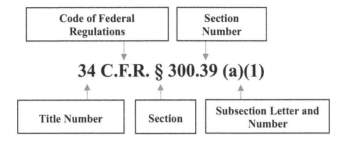

Figure 3.2 Legal Citation for a Section of the IDEA 2004 Regulations

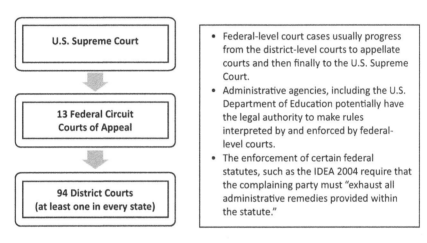

Figure 3.3 Federal Court System

At the lowest level, trial courts are known as federal district courts. Each state has at least one federal district court, while some states, such as California and New York, have as many as four. Trial courts are the basic triers of fact in legal disputes. As triers of fact in a special education suit, federal trial courts review the record of administrative hearings, additional evidence, and hear the testimony of witnesses. Trial courts render judgments based on the evidence presented by the parties to the dispute. Parties not satisfied with the decisions of federal-level trial courts may appeal to federal circuit courts of appeals based on where they are located. Figure 3.4 displays the geographical boundaries of the 13 Federal Circuit Courts of Appeal. For example, the First Circuit Court of Appeals consists of Maine, New Hampshire, Massachusetts, Rhode Island, and Puerto Rico. Table 3.2 shows the distribution of states and geographical territories associated with the thirteen Federal Circuit Courts of Appeal. Parties not satisfied with the judgments of the federal circuit courts may appeal to the U.S. Supreme Court, which also does not hear all legal cases brought before it on appeal. In fact, the U.S. Supreme Court actually accepts only a very small percentage of requests to hear legal cases. In a given year, for example, the U.S. Supreme Court receives in excess of 7,000 legal case requests annually but accepts about only 100–150 appeals (Imber, Van Geel, Blokhuis, & Feldman, 2014). Legal cases typically reach the U.S. Supreme Court in requests for a writ of *certiorari*, literally "to be informed of" (Russo, 2018). The U.S. Supreme Court may decide, for whatever reason, that a case is not worthy of its review. Generally, if the Supreme Court agrees to hear an appeal, the justices grant a writ of *certiorari*. At least four of the nine justices must vote to grant *certiorari* in order for a case to be heard (Russo, 2018). Denying a writ of certiorari has the effect of leaving a lower court's decision unchanged (Garner, 2004). In Figure 3.4 each Federal Circuit Court of Appeal is designated by the number inside the blackened circle. Each Federal Circuit Court of Appeal represents the same color-coded states associated with the number.

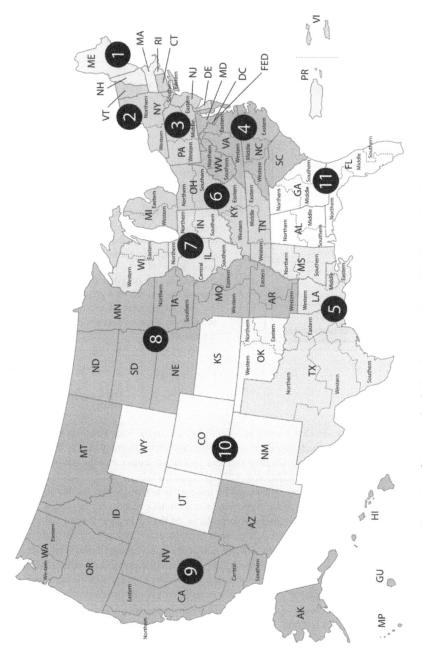

Figure 3.4 Thirteen Federal Circuit Courts of Appeal By Geographical Boundaries

Table 3.2 Geographical Jurisdiction of Federal Circuit Courts of Appeal

Circuit	Jurisdiction
1st	Maine, Massachusetts, New Hampshire, Puerto Rico, Rhode Island
2nd	Connecticut, New York, Vermont
3rd	Delaware, New Jersey, Pennsylvania, Virgin Islands
4th	Maryland, North Carolina, South Carolina, Virginia, West Virginia
5th	Louisiana, Mississippi, Texas
6th	Kentucky, Ohio, Michigan, Tennessee
7th	Illinois, Indiana, Wisconsin
8th	Arkansas, Iowa, Minnesota, Missouri, Nebraska, North Dakota, South Dakota
9th	Alaska, Arizona, California, Guam, Hawaii, Idaho, Montana, Nevada, Northern Mariana Islands, Oregon, Washington
10th	Colorado, Kansas, New Mexico, Oklahoma, Utah, Wyoming
11th	Alabama, Florida, Georgia
12th (D.C.)	Washington, D.C.
13th (Federal)	Washington, D.C. (specialized courts)

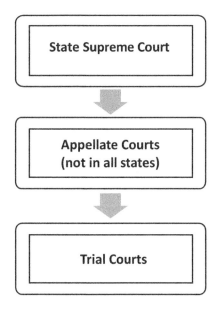

- State-level courts have the ability to resolve both state and federal claims.
- State supreme court decisions can be appealed directly to the U.S. Supreme Court on issues of federal law.

Figure 3.5 Typical State Court System

Each of the fifty states and various territories has a similar arrangement for its state court system, except that the names of the courts vary. Generally speaking, there are three levels of state courts: trial courts, intermediate appellate courts, and courts of last resort. One has to be careful with the names of state courts. For example, most people probably think of "supreme court" being the name of a state's highest court; however, in New York, the trial court is known as the Supreme Court, while the highest court in the state is called the Court of Appeals. Figure 3.5 illustrates the typical state court system.

When a court delivers a legal ruling, its judgment is binding only within its jurisdiction. Keeping in mind that the concept of jurisdiction can refer to either the types of cases that courts can hear or the geographic area over which they have authority, this instance refers to the latter situation. By way of illustration, a judgment of the federal district court for New Hampshire is binding only in New Hampshire. The federal district court in Massachusetts might find a decision of the New Hampshire court persuasive, but it is not bound by its order. However, a decision of the First Circuit Court of Appeals is binding on all states within its jurisdiction, and lower courts in those states must rule consistently. A decision by the Supreme Court of the United States is enforceable in all fifty states as well as the American territories.

The written opinions of most legal cases are readily available in a variety of published formats. The official versions of Supreme Court opinions are in the *United States Reports*, abbreviated U.S. The same opinions, with additional research aids, are published in the *Supreme Court Reporter* (S. Ct.) and the *Lawyer's Edition*, now in its second series (L. Ed.2d). Decisions of the federal circuit courts are found in the *Federal Reporter*, now in its third series (F.3d), while federal trial court opinions are in the *Federal Supplement*, now in its second series (F. Supp.2d). State cases are published in a variety of publications, most notably West's National Reporter System, which divides the country up into seven regions: Atlantic, North Eastern, North Western, Pacific, South Eastern, South Western, and Southern. Prior to being published in bound volumes, most court cases are available in what are known as slip opinions, a variety of loose-leaf services, and electronic sources. Special education cases, as well as due process hearing decisions, are reproduced in a loose-leaf format called the *Individuals with Disabilities Education Law Reporter* (IDELR) published by LRP Publications.

Special Education Administrative Rules and Regulations

Administrative decisions are made at the federal, state, and local levels. For example, the U.S. Department of Education frequently issues interpretative statements and letters of opinion on a variety of legal issues involving education. Specifically, several administrative agencies within the U.S. Department of Education, including the Office for Civil Rights (OCR), Office of Special Education Programs (OSEP), and the Office of Special Education and Rehabilitative Services (OSERS) comment on legal issues and concerns involving special education. While these administrative decisions and opinions serve as important guides related to how a particular agency is going to interpret a matter, these decisions and opinions do not carry the same legal weight compared to statutes, regulations, or legal cases. Nevertheless, it is quite useful for individuals interested in special education law and policy issues to obtain access to these materials. Fortunately, many of these administrative decisions, especially at the federal level are now accessible online. For example, the U.S. Department of Education's Office of Special Education Programs (OSEP) issues guidance to support the implementation of the Individuals with Disabilities Education Act (IDEA). Anyone can search policy guidance documents related to the IDEA by going to the website, https://sites.ed.gov/idea/policy-guidance/. Additionally, state administrative hearing decisions involving both federal statutes, the IDEA 2004 and Section 504, are cited in the Individuals with Disabilities Education Law Report' (IDELR, formerly the *Education of the Handicapped Law Report*, or EHLR). IDELR is a fee-based, comprehensive service published by LRP Publications that reports administrative hearing decisions at the state level and policy guidance at the federal level. It publishes these administrative hearing decision materials in loose-leaf binders, which are generally available in state offices of education as well as college and university libraries, including law school libraries. An IDELR citation follows the general rule for legal citations: the name of the ruling, the volume number, the abbreviated name of the reporting service, the page number, and the document source and date in parentheses. Table 3.3 provides illustrative examples of different types of special education-related legal citations, including court cases, statutes, regulations, and administrative regulations and hearing decisions.

Secondary Sources of Special Education Legal Information

Unlike primary legal sources, secondary legal sources refer to materials that describe and explain the law. Since secondary legal materials are not actual statements of the law, they do not have legal authority but may serve as persuasive authority (Yell, 2019). When starting your search for special education legal information, secondary legal sources can be extremely useful because they explain a particular area of special education

Table 3.3 Examples of Various Special Education Legal Citations

Federal Court Cases

U.S. Supreme Court	*Endrew F. v. Douglas County School District RE-1*, 137 S.Ct. 988 (2017)
U.S. Court of Appeals	*Doug C. v. State of Hawaii Dept. of Educ.*, 720 F.3d 1038 (9th Cir., 2013)
Federal District Court	*Evans v. Bd. of Educ. of Rhinebeck Central Sch. Dist.*, 930 F. Supp. 83 (S.D.N.Y. 1996)

Federal Statutes and Regulations

Individuals with Disabilities Education Act (IDEA 2004)	20 U.S.C. §§ 1400–1482 (2006)
IDEA 2004 Regulations for Parts A and B	34 C.F.R. Part 300 (2006)
Section 504 of the Rehabilitation Act of 1973 (Section 504)	29 U.S.C. § 794(a) (2006)
Section 504 Regulations	34 C.F.R. Part 104 (2009)

OSEP/OSERS/OCR Documents

Letter to Rangel-Diaz, 58 IDELR 78 (OSEP 2011)
Letter to Davilia, 18 IDELR 1036 (OSERS 1992)
OCR Senior Staff Memorandum, 19 IDELR 894 (OCR 1992)

IDEA Administrative Hearing Decisions

Greater Lowell Tech. High Sch., 45 IDELR 28 (Mass. SEA 2006)
In re Student with a Disability, 40 IDELR 139 (Vt. SEA 2003)

Note: OSEP=Office of Special Education Programs, U.S. Department of Education; OSERS=Office of Special Education and Rehabilitative Services, U.S. Department of Education; OCR=Office of Civil Rights, U.S. Department of Education

Table 3.4 Online Blogs of Special Education Legal Information

Name	*URL*
Disability Scoop: Politics and Law Blog	www.disabilityscoop.com/politics/
Education Law Prof Blog	https://lawprofessors.typepad.com/education_law/
SpedLawBlog	https://spedlawblog.com/author/mitchellyell/
The Wrightslaw Law to Special Education Law and Advocacy	www.wrightslaw.com/blog/

law and detail the specific issues involved. Similar to primary sources of special education information, many secondary sources are available online. Examples of secondary sources that contain special education legal information include: (a) legal citation guides; (b) legal dictionaries and encyclopedias; (c) law review and journal articles; and (d) loose-leaf or topical services; and newspapers, newsletters, and blogs. In response to the limited availability of traditional legal scholarship in an open access format, there has been a definite growth in legally oriented blogs, including those specifically covering special education law and policy issues. Special education legal blog online conversations are expanding legal scholarship and increasing online communications among many different groups interested in special education legal issues, including but not limited to legal scholars, school practitioners, as well as laypersons interested in certain areas of legal research and scholarship (Brady & Bathon, 2012). Table 3.4 displays secondary sources of special education drawn from online blogs, or regularly updated websites or web pages that focus on particularized topics or subject areas.

Finding Primary Sources of Special Education Legal Information Online

Since many of the legal sources involving children with disabilities originated in federal statutory laws, it is a good place to begin your search of special education-related legal information. Federal and state statutes are readily available in both print and online versions. Federal statutes are located in the *United States Code*

(U.S.C.), the official version. Federal statutes are organized by topic, or subject and are published in the United States Code as a series of volumes. All three of the leading federal statutes impacting students with disabilities can be found in specific titles of the *United States Code*, including the Individuals with Disabilities Education Act (IDEA)), Section 504 of the Rehabilitation Act of 1973 (Section 504), and the Americans with Disabilities Act (ADA). For example, the Individuals with Disabilities Education Act (IDEA) can be found in Title 20 (Education) of the *United States Code*; Section 504 of the Rehabilitation Act of 1973 can be found in Title 29 (Labor Statutes); and the Americans with Disabilities Act (ADA) can be found under Title 42 (Public Health and Welfare). Due to significant advances in the accessibility of online legal information, there are many online resources providing free access to the *United States Code*, allowing users to browse or search by a specific title, chapter or section. The official website of the *United States Code* can be found on the Govinfo website: www.govinfo.gov/app/collection/USCODE

Additionally, the *United States Code* can be accessed online through a variety of nongovernmental websites, including Cornell's Legal Information Institute (LII) (www.law.cornell.edu/uscode/text) or FindLaw's (https://codes.findlaw.com/us/) *United States Code* online sites.

Regulations are published in the *Code of Federal Regulations (C.F.R.)*. State laws and regulations are generally available online from the websites of their states. Legal citations are fairly easy to read. The first number indicates the volume number where the case, statute, or regulation is located; the abbreviation refers to the book or series in which the material may be found; the second number indicates the page on which a case begins or the section number of a statute or regulation; the last part of a citation includes the name of the court, for lower court cases, and the year in which the dispute was resolved. For instance, the citation for *Barnett v. Memphis City School System*, 294 F. Supp.2d 924 (W.D. Tenn. 2003) can be located in volume 294 of the *Federal Supplement, Second Series* beginning on page 924. The case was resolved at the federal trial court in the Western Division of Tennessee.

Similar to federal statutes, the federal regulations—the Code of Federal Regulations (C.F.R.)—are all available online. Two useful online resources for accessing the federal regulations relating to special education include: (a) Electronic Code of Federal Regulations (e-CFR), (www.ecfr.gov) a currently updated version of the Code of Federal Regulations (CFR); and (b) the U.S. Department of Education's IDEA website detailing both the statute and regulations (https://sites.ed.gov/idea/statuteregulations/#regulations).

Individual state statutes and regulations often organize their statutes based on subject (e.g., education). In many states, you can find specific websites that provide access to specific state statutes and regulations. For example, Cornell's Legal Information Institute (LII) allows you to search education statutes by individual state (www.law.cornell.edu/wex/table_education) or jurisdiction type (www.law.cornell.edu/states/listing).

The Internet has made finding legal cases at the federal, state, and local levels much more accessible. Today, for example, legal opinions are accessible on a daily basis from official federal and state court websites as well as secondary websites, including Google Scholar, FindLaw, and Justica. The United States courts website provides access to U.S. Supreme Court, U.S. Courts of Appeals and U.S. District Court websites. Table 3.5 lists

Table 3.5 Useful Online Resources for Searching Special Education Federal and State Case Law

Website	*URL*
Cornell's Legal Information Institute (LII)	www.law.cornell.edu/
Findlaw's Legal Cases	https://caselaw.findlaw.com/
Google Scholar	https://scholar.google.com/scholar_courts?hl=en&as_sdt=1006
Justia	https://law.justia.com/
Oyez	www.oyez.org
PACER (Public Access to Court Electronic Records) (there is a nominal fee associated with accessing legal case information)	www.pacer.gov/
U.S. Supreme Court	http://supremecourt.gov
U.S. Courts	http://uscourts.gov

Table 3.6 Online Resources of Special Education Statutes, Regulations, and Administrative Agency Policy and Guidance Documents

Website Name	URL
American with Disability Act's (ADA) Homepage	www.ada.gov/pubs/adastatute08.htm
Cornell Legal Information Institute (CII): State Law Resources By Jurisdiction	www.law.cornell.edu/states/listing
e-CFR (Electronic Code of Federal Regulations)	www.ecfr.gov
U.S. Department of Education, Office of Special Education Programs (OSEP) policy letters and guidance to support the implementation of the Individuals with Disabilities Education Act (IDEA)	https://sites.ed.gov/idea/policy-guidance/
U.S. Department of Education, IDEA Stature and Regulations	https://sites.ed.gov/idea/statuteregulations/
U.S. Department of Labor-Section 504 of the Rehabilitation Act of 1973	www.dol.gov/oasam/regs/statutes/sec504.htm
U.S. House of Representatives, Office of the Law Revision Counsel	http://uscode.house.gov

online resources for searching federal and state-level court decisions or rulings. Additionally, open access websites, including Cornell's Legal Information Institute (LII) and Google Scholar allow users to search federal and state legal cases individually or together (Yell, 2019). Beginning in 2001, the Public Access to Court Electronic Records (PACER) website (www.pacer.gov/findcase.html) became available allowing users to retrieve individual legal cases online from both federal appellate and district-level jurisdictions. Currently, there is a maximum charge of $3.00 for online access to any single court case document other than name searches, reports that are not case-specific, and transcripts of federal court proceedings. Table 3.6 provides leading online resources of special education statutes, regulations, and administrative agency policy and guidance documents.

Summary of Important Legal Policies, Principles, and Practices

This chapter provides the reader with an overview of the U.S. legal system and the many sources of law, including those relating to special education. As individuals begin their legal research involving special education issues, they need to be aware as well as distinguish primary legal sources, or actual statements of the law compared to secondary legal sources, with analysis and explanations of the law.

1. There are four primary sources of law that may potentially include special education legal information, including (a) constitutions; (b) statutes; (c) regulations; and (d) judicial opinions, or court cases. Given increased accessibility online, anyone with access to the Internet can find a majority of primary sources of law online.
2. Secondary legal sources, including online blogs, law review articles, peer-reviewed journal articles, and loose-leaf or online topical services do not have legal authority, but can provide useful explanations of special education law and policy issues for those persons that work closely with children and youth with disabilities in school settings, especially those with little or no prior experience with the law.
3. The Internet is increasingly becoming a more effective and efficient method to retrieve legal information, including the myriad of legal information, federal and state-level statutes, regulations, administrative decisions and court cases impacting students with disabilities. Moreover, many of the necessary, online resources regarding special education are available at little or no cost to the general public.

Useful Online Resources

FreshEd Podcast with Will Brehm, FreshEd Audio Podcast #153, May 6, 2019
Special Education Law in the United States and Beyond (with Charles J. Russo) at www.freshedpodcast. com/charlesrusso/
One of the book's coauthors, Charlie Russo, the Joseph Panzer Chair in Education in the School of Education and Health Sciences and Research Professor of Law in the School of Law at the University of Dayton, details the legal power of the Individuals with Disabilities Education Act (IDEA) and places this federal law in an international context.

Wrightslaw: Special Education Law and Advocacy
The Wrightslaw website provides parents, educators, advocates, and attorneys with comprehensive online resources of accurate and reliable information concerning special education law for children with disabilities. For those beginning their special education legal research, it is suggested that you begin viewing the Wrightlaw's online "law library," which contains a plethora of links to articles, case law, IDEA 2004, and Section 504 information.

Recommended Reading

Colker, R. (2018). *Special education law in a nutshell*. St. Paul, MN: West Academic Publishing.

Sloan, A. E. (2017). *Researching the law: Finding what you need when you need it* (2nd ed.). New York, NY: Wolters Kluwer Law & Business.

References

Brady, K. P., & Bathon, J. (2012). Education law in a digital age: The growing impact of the open access legal movement. *Education Law Reporter, 227,* 589–612.

Decker, J. R., & Brady, K. (2016). Increasing school employees' special education legal literacy. *Journal of School Public Relations, 36*(3), 231–259.

Garner, B. A. (2004). *Black's Law Dictionary* (8th ed.). St. Paul, MN: West.

Imber, M., Van Geel, T., Blokhuis, J. C., & Feldman, J. (2014). *Education law* (5th ed.). New York, NY: Routledge.

Osborne, A. G., & Russo, C. J. (2014). *Special education and the law: A guide for practitioners* (3rd ed.). Thousand Oaks, CA: Corwin.

Russo, C. J. (2018). *Russo's the law and public education* (10th ed.). St. Paul, MN: West Academic.

Turnbull, H. R., Stowe, M. J., & Huerta, N. E. (2007). *Free appropriate public education: The law and children with disabilities*. Denver, CO: Love Publishing.

Underwood, J. K., & Mead, J. E. (1995). *Legal aspects of special education and pupil services*. Boston, MA: Allyn and Bacon.

Weber, M. C., Mawdsley, R., & Redfield, S. (2013). *Special education law: Cases and materials* (4th ed.). Durham, NC: Carolina Academic Press.

Yell, M. L. (2019). *The law and special education* (5th ed.). New York, NY: Pearson.

II
IDEA 2004
A Legal Primer

4

IDEA 2004

Basic Structure and Major Principles

Key Concepts and Terms in This Chapter

- IDEA 2004 Part A: General Provisions
- IDEA 2004 Part B: Assistance for Education of All Children With Disabilities
- IDEA 2004 Part C: Infants and Toddlers With Disabilities
- IDEA 2004 Part D: National Activities to Improve Education of Children With Disabilities
- Six major principles of the IDEA 2004

In 1975, Congress enacted Public Law 94–142, a federal statute known as the Education for All Handicapped Children Act (EAHCA), created to improve the educational opportunities for children and youth with disabilities. More specifically, EAHCA provided federal monies to states based on the provision of special education programs and services to school-aged children and youth with disabilities. As a funding statute, the federal government provides limited, supportive funding to individual states that provide special education and related services to eligible children and youth within a framework of federally developed guidelines (Rothstein & Johnson, 2014). However, the IDEA was never developed to cover the full costs of providing special education and related services to eligible students. Rather, the assumption is that federal monies assist individual states but the majority of these costs are shared between the states and local school systems. While the EAHCA statute has been amended and renamed numerous times since its original enactment in 1975, the four original purposes of this statute remain an integral part of the current IDEA 2004 statute, including

1. To assure the rights of all students with disabilities to a free appropriate public education
2. To protect the rights of the students and their parents in securing such an education
3. To assist state and local agencies to provide for the education of those students, and
4. To assess and assure the effectiveness of state and local efforts to educate those students

(P.L. 94–142, 20 U.S.C. §1400(d))

On November 29, 1975, President Gerald Ford signed EAHCA officially into law to address some of the critical and previously underserved or unserved educational needs of students with disabilities. EAHCA, also referred to as P.L. (Public Law) 94–142 provided federal funding to individual states in exchange for the provision of educational services to specified categories of students with disabilities (Yell, 2019). Amendments to the EAHCA were enacted in 1990, which changed the name of the federal statute to the Individuals with Disabilities Education Act (IDEA). In 1997, further amendments to the IDEA were made.

The most recent reauthorization, or revision to the IDEA federal statute was enacted by Congress on November 19, 2004 and is currently known as the Individuals with Disabilities Education Improvement Act of 2004 (hereafter referred throughout this book as the IDEA 2004). Former President George Bush signed the IDEA 2004 into law on December 3, 2004 and the federal statute went officially into effect on July 1, 2005. It is important to point out that almost two years later on August 14, 2006, the U.S. Department of Education officially published the "Final Regulations" based on the IDEA 2004 statute, which is published in the *Federal Register* (pages 46540 to page 46845) and is also available online at (http://sites.ed.gov/idea/regs). As you may recall from Chapter 3, the U.S. Department of Education issues regulations for the purpose of assisting with the implementation of the legal requirements detailed in the statute. At the time, Congress informed the U.S. Department of Education to specifically limit its regulations to discuss only those provisions within the scope and necessary to be in accordance with the statutory language of the IDEA 2004 (Snow-Huefner & Herr, 2012). Mainly, the 2006 IDEA federal regulations repeat the language of the IDEA 2004 statute. Yet, there are some instances where the federal regulations assist in clarifying certain provisions of the statute. Therefore, as you familiarize yourself with the structure of the IDEA 2004 statute, you should also access the 2006 IDEA 2004 Regulations, especially the section named, "An Analysis of Comments and Changes," which provides clarifications, definitions, and more detailed discussions of legal terminology and principles found in the IDEA 2004 statute as well as providing "plain meanings" of those terms (Wright & Wright, 2011, p. 5). The "An Analysis of Comments and Changes" section of the IDEA 2004 regulations can be found either in hardcopy in the *Federal Register* (pages 46547 through 46743) or online from Wrightslaw at (www.wright-slaw.com/idea/commentary.htm).

The IDEA 2004 is known as a "conditional grant in-aid statute," which means that if a particular state or local education agency (LEA), including a local public school district accepts IDEA 2004 funds, it must comply with the many provisions of the IDEA 2004 (Turnbull, Stowe, & Huerta, 2007). A major focus of the IDEA 2004 is holding schools accountable for the academic and functional (skills or activities not related to academic achievement) performance of students with disabilities by attempting to better align the IDEA 2004 with another federal statute, The No Child Left Behind Act of 2001. As a result, the reauthorized IDEA 2004 attempts to improve the academic achievement of students with disabilities as well as develop stricter accountability measures to motivate both local schools and individual states to improve the overall academic achievement of students with disabilities.

While the most recent reauthorization of the IDEA occurred in 2004, this federal law has been due for a reauthorization since 2009 (Winters-Kesslar, Fridman, & Munin 2018). While the current IDEA 2004 is overdue for a reauthorization, it continues to operate under its current provisions until Congress officially changes it.

Navigating the Statutory Structure of the IDEA 2004

Similar to its federal statutory predecessor, the Education for All Handicapped Children Act, the IDEA 2004 is divided into four major sections: Parts A through D. As reflected in Figure 4.1, the IDEA 2004 federal statute is comprised of four major parts, or components.

The four parts, or components of the IDEA 2004 include:

Part A—General Provisions (20 U.S.C. §§ 1400–1410)

Part A of the IDEA 2004 is a mandatory component of the federal statute and includes Sections 1400 through 1409 of Title 20 of the *United States Code* (U.S.C.). (*Note:* when a legal citation is referenced, the symbol for Section is §). The three primary purposes of Part A of the IDEA 2004 include:

1. Containing the major terms and definitions used throughout the IDEA 2004 federal statute.
2. Discussing Congress' primary findings and purposes of the IDEA 2004 law.
3. Establishing that the U.S. Department of Education's Office of Special Education Programs (OSEP) has the direct legal authority to implement as well as oversee the statute.

(20 U.S.C. § 1400(d))

A review of Part A's General Provisions section guides the reader through the varied terminology and definitions used throughout the lengthy statute. Part A is a recommended starting point for advocates,

Part A	Part B	Part C	Part D
General Provisions • States congressional findings and purposes of the law. • Contains all relevant definitions used in the statute.	*Assistance to States for All Children With Disabilities* • Covers ages three through twenty-one. • Authorizes federal funds to be distributed to individual states which submit plans that detail how a state will ensure a free appropriate public education (FAPE) to qualified children and youth. • Details legal rights for parents and children with disabilities and establishes the procedural due process system.	*Infants and Toddlers With Disabilities* • Provides categorical grants to states providing appropriate special education services to infants and toddlers with disabilities.	*National Activities to Improve Education of Children With Disabilities* • Provides federal grant monies that support the implementation of the IDEA, including the support of personnel preparation and research projects that support effective early intervention strategies.

Figure 4.1 Basic Structure of IDEA 2004 Statute

attorneys, educators, and parents to begin their reading of the IDEA 2004, especially those who might be less familiar with legal or specialized special education terminology. Part A of the IDEA 2004 also details Congress's justifications, or "findings" for the reauthorization of the federal statute and how special education programs and services for children and youth with disabilities can be improved and made more effective. For example, Congress discussed eight specific methods on how following the IDEA 2004 provisions can improve the education of students with disabilities. Congress' eight recommendations stated in Part A: Findings and Purposes (Section 1400–1410) of the statute include:

1. "Having high expectations for such children and ensuring their access to the general education curriculum in the regular classroom, to the extent possible, in order to

    a. meet developmental goals and, to the maximum extent possible, the challenging expectations that have been established for all children; and
    b. be prepared to lead productive an independent adult lives, to the maximum extent possible"
    (20 U.S.C. 1400(c)(5)(A))

2. "Strengthening the role and responsibility of parents and ensuring that families of such children have meaningful opportunities to participate in the education of their children at school and at home"
    (20 U.S.C. 1400(c)(5)(B))

3. "Coordinating this title with other local, educational service agency, state, and federal school improvement efforts, including improvement efforts under the elementary and secondary education act of 1965, in order to ensure that such children benefit from such efforts in that special education can become a service for such children rather than a place where such children are sent"
    (20 U.S.C. 1400(c)(5)(C)

4. "Providing appropriate special education and related services, and aids and supports in the regular classroom, to such children, whenever appropriate"

(20 U.S.C. §1400(c)(5)(D))

5. "Supporting high-quality, intensive preservice preparation and professional development for all personnel who work with children with disabilities in order to assure that such personnel have the skills and knowledge necessary to improve the academic achievement and functional performance of children with disabilities, including the use of scientifically-based instructional practices, to the maximum extent possible"

(20 U.S.C. 1400(c)(5)(E))

6. "Providing incentives for whole school approaches, scientifically-based early reading programs, positive behavioral interventions and supports, and early intervening services to reduce the need to label children as disabled in order to advance the learning and behavioral needs of such children"

(20 U.S.C. 1400(c)(5)(F))

7. "Focusing resources on teaching and learning while reducing paperwork and requirements that do not assist in improving educational results"

(20 U.S.C. 1400(c)(5)(G))

8. "Supporting the development and use of technology, including assistive technology devices and assistive technology services, to maximize accessibility for children with disabilities"

(20 U.S.C. 1400(c)(5)(H))

Relatedly, Congress in Part A details the six primary purposes of the IDEA 2004. These six purposes include:

1. "To ensure that all children with disabilities have available to them a free appropriate public education that emphasizes special education and related services designed to meet their unique needs and prepare them for further education, employment, and independent living"

(20 U.S.C. 1400(d)(1)(A))

2. "To ensure that the rights of children with disabilities and parents of such children are protected"

(20 U.S.C. 1400(d)(1)(B))

3. "To assist states, localities, educational service agencies, and federal agencies to provide for the education of all children with disabilities"

(20 U.S.C. 1400(d)(1)(C))

4. "To assist states in the implementation of a statewide, comprehensive, coordinated, multidisciplinary, interagency system of early intervention services for infants and toddlers with disabilities and their families"

(20 U.S.C. 1400(d)(2))

5. "To ensure that educators and parents have the necessary tools to improve educational results for children with disabilities by supporting system improvement activities; coordinated research and personnel preparation; coordinated technical assistance; dissemination in support; and technology development and media services"

(20 U.S.C. 1400(d)(3))

6. "To assess, and ensure the effectiveness of efforts to educate children with disabilities"

(20 U.S.C. 1400(d)(4))

Overall, the two most relevant sections of Part A of the IDEA 2004 include the following two sections: (1.) Section (§) 1400: Findings and Purposes; and (2.) Section (§) 1401: Definitions.

Part B—Assistance for Education of All Children With Disabilities (20 U.S.C. §§ 1411–1419)

Comparable to Part A, Part B of the IDEA 2004 is a mandatory, or necessary component of the federal statute. Part B of the IDEA 2004 primarily governs special education and related services for children with disabilities between the ages of three and twenty-one. For the majority of people interested in familiarizing themselves with the IDEA statute, the most important sections of Part B are Sections 1412, 1414, and 1415 (Wright & Wright, 2011). These three sections of the IDEA 2004 encompass the following topics:

1. *Section 1412: State Eligibility*, which is often called the "Catch-All" statute because it covers so many diverse topics under the IDEA, including provisions related to child find, free appropriate public education, children with disabilities who attend private or religiously affiliated schools, least restrictive environment, mandatory medication prohibition provision, over-identification of minority children and youth with disabilities, qualifications of special education teachers, unilateral placements, tuition reimbursements, and state and district assessments;
2. *Section 1414: Evaluations, Eligibility, Individualized Education Programs, and Educational Placements.* Part B, Section 1414 is an important component of the IDEA 2004 statute because it describes both the process and requirements covering initial student evaluations, parental consent, reevaluations, student eligibility, individualized education programs, or IEPs, and educational placements;
3. *Section 1415: Procedural Safeguards.* Section 1415 details the various procedural safeguards designed to protect both the rights of children and youth with disabilities and their parents (Wright & Wright, 2011). Under the IDEA 2004, the number of parental responsibilities has been expanded. More specifically, procedural safeguards include the right to examine a student with disabilities' educational records, obtain an independent educational evaluation (IEE), as well as the numerous legal requirements associated with acquiring prior written notice, due process hearings, mediation, attorneys' fees, and disciplinary provisions (Wright & Wright, 2011).

Part C—Infants and Toddlers With Disabilities (20 U.S.C. Sections 1431–1444)

While the IDEA statute focuses primarily on children and youth with disabilities aged three years and older, Part C of the IDEA was developed in 1986 in response to the need for special education services for children with developmental disabilities beginning at birth to three years of age (Lipkin & Okamoto, 2015). More specifically, Part C governs early intervention special education programs and services for infants and toddlers under the age of three. In many respects, the statutory structure of Part C aligns closely with the structure found in Part B. Unlike Part B, however, Part C recognizes the unique needs of infants and toddlers with disabilities and places increased emphasis on providing special education services within home and community settings instead of schools and requires family involvement in the process. Since compliance with Part C is non-mandatory, the U.S. Department of Education authorizes grants to individual states to incentivize the improvement of special education programs and services serving infants and toddlers with identified disabilities. Therefore, the decision of whether to comply with the Part C provisions of the IDEA is at the discretion of individual states.

Part D—National Activities to Improve Education of Children With Disabilities (20 U.S.C. §§ 1450–1482)

Congress has made noteworthy changes to Part D of the IDEA 2004 statute. Specifically, Section 1450: Findings, which expressly detail a major theme of this book, namely the critical need for appropriately trained school personnel, including school administrators, general education and special education teachers, and other school personnel as well as "high quality, comprehensive professional development programs . . . to ensure that the persons responsible for the education or transition of children with disabilities possess the skills and knowledge necessary to address the needs of those children" (20 U.S.C. §1450(6)). In addition to a focus on improving professional development for today's educators to improve special education programs and services for children and youth with disabilities, Congress emphasizes the invaluable role parents play in the education of their children with disabilities. As such, Congress created Parent Training and Information Centers (PTI) and Parent Resource Centers (CPRC); the goal of both centers is to assist parents in learning more about their child's disabilities and unique educational needs, both the parents' and their child's legal rights and responsibilities in the special education process, how to more effectively communicate with school personnel, and how to more actively participate in the educational decision-making process involving their child (20 U.S.C. §1471). Each year, the U.S. Department of Education awards grants to at least one parent organization in every state for either a CRPC or PTI (Wright & Wright, 2011).

While the IDEA has been revised numerous times, the original and primary goal of this federal law assisting students with disabilities remains unchanged, namely that states and local school districts must offer IDEA-eligible students a free and appropriate public education (FAPE). As evidence of the importance of FAPE, Congress states that the primary purpose of the IDEA is "to ensure that all children with disabilities have available to them a free appropriate public education that emphasizes special education and related services designed to meet their unique needs and prepare them for further education, employment, and independent living" (20 U.S.C. 1401(d)(d)(1)(A)) and to "ensure that the rights of children with disabilities in parents of such children are protected" (20 U.S.C. 1401(d)(d)(1)(B)). Additionally, the IDEA federal statute and regulations contain certain important principles and provisions that help maximize that all eligible students with disabilities receive FAPE. There are six key principles associated with the IDEA 2004. These six principles include:

1. Free Appropriate Public Education (FAPE)
2. Appropriate Student Eligibility and Evaluation Practices
3. Individualized Education Program (IEP)
4. Least Restrictive Environment (LRE)
5. Parental and Student Participation in the Decision-Making Process
6. Procedural Due Process and Safeguards

Collectively, these IDEA 2004 principles and provisions will be discussed throughout this book. Additionally, these particular principles and provisions will be profiled and discussed in select legal cases involving students with disabilities, especially in the "Special Education Law in Practice" sections found in the majority of the chapters in this book. As illustrated in Figure 4.2, the provision of a free appropriate public education (FAPE) in the least restrictive environment (LRE) to eligible students with disabilities remains the primary goal and the foundation upon which all other IDEA principles and provisions are based. Each of the major IDEA principles and provisions will be briefly discussed here and in more detail in the relevant sections of the book.

Free Appropriate Public Education (FAPE)

A free appropriate public education (hereafter FAPE) is the primary legal entitlement that the IDEA provides to eligible children or youth with disabilities. More specifically, the IDEA 2004 requires that states and local school systems provide FAPE to all eligible children and youth with disabilities residing in a particular state or local educational agency (LEA), such as a local school district between the ages of three and twenty-one years old. Individual states have the discretion of whether or not to provide FAPE to children under the age of three. Based on the IDEA 2004 statute, FAPE has four requirements. Specifically, FAPE is defined as special education and related services that:

1. Are provided at public expense, under public supervision and direction, and without charge;
2. Meet the standards of the State educational agency;
3. Include an appropriate preschool, elementary, or secondary school education in the State involved; and
4. Are provided in conformity with the individualized educational program (IEP).

(20 U.S.C. §1401[a][18])

While the four aforementioned requirements necessary to satisfy the IDEA 2004 FAPE provision appear fairly straightforward, what FAPE actually means in professional practice continues to be a contentiously litigated issue at the highest level of the U.S. judicial system, the U.S. Supreme Court. For the past several decades, for example, the courts have struggled to legally define the specific nature of FAPE for students

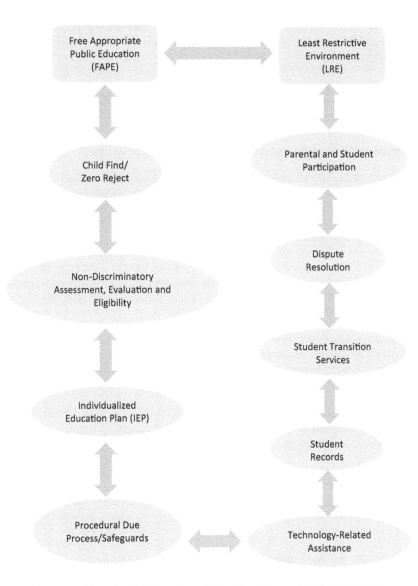

Figure 4.2 Major Legal Principles and Provisions Covered in the IDEA 2004

identified with disabilities under the IDEA. The lack of a clear and detailed definition of FAPE has led to numerous disagreements between parents and schools as to what properly constitutes an appropriate education for an IDEA–eligible student with disabilities (Yell, 2019). Throughout the 1980s and 1990s, the legal standard for FAPE was in a constant state of confusion based on numerous and conflicting judicial interpretations among the nation's federal and lower-level courts. Two leading legal cases that reached the U.S. Supreme Court have attempted to clarify the varying legal interpretations of the IDEA's FAPE provision. One of these landmark decisions, *Board of Education of Hendrick Hudson Central School District v. Rowley* (458 U.S. 176 (1982) held that the IDEA does not legally require that local school districts provide educational programs and services to IDEA-eligible students with disabilities that maximize their educational potential. More recently, in 2017, the 1982 Supreme Court's *Rowley* legal ruling was actively challenged and clarified but ultimately not overruled. In the 2017 case, *Endrew F. v. Douglas County Schools District RE-1* (137 S. Ct. 988 (2017)), the U.S. Supreme Court, in a 8–0 unanimous decision, clarified the existing FAPE provision under the 1982 *Rowley* Supreme Court decision and developed a new legal standard. Based on the more recent *Endrew* (2017) Supreme Court ruling, in order "to meet its substantive obligation under the IDEA, a school must offer an IEP reasonably calculated to enable the child to make progress appropriate in light of the child's circumstances" (*Endrew*, 2017, p. 15). A critical distinction in the *Endrew* ruling is that it clarifies but does not overrule the *Rowley* FAPE legal standard. Writing the majority opinion of the U.S. Supreme Court, Chief Justice John Roberts stated that the "IDEA cannot and does not promise any particular outcome" and "a substantive standard not focused on student progress would do little to remedy the pervasive and tragic academic stagnation that prompted Congress to act back in 1975" (*Endrew*, 2017, p. 11).

Nondiscriminatory Evaluation and Appropriate Eligibility Practices

Under the IDEA 2004, fair and accurate evaluation practices are necessary for the proper and most beneficial placement of students with disabilities. As such, the IDEA 2004 includes what are called protection evaluation procedures, or PEPs. These PEPs were formally written into the IDEA provisions to address a variety of abuses in the student assessment process, including the use of inappropriate assessments, placing children in special education based on only a single assessment, or the use of invalid or discriminatory assessment tests to illegally and falsely identify some students as eligible for special education and related services. The IDEA requires the establishment of policies, practices, and procedures ensuring that all children with disabilities who reside within a particular state or local educational agency (LEA) are "identified, located, and evaluated" (20 U.S.C. § 1412(a)(3)). It is the legal responsibility of LEAs, including local public school districts, to determine whether or not a particular student is eligible for special education services under the IDEA by conducting an initial evaluation, which should determine if the student has a qualifying disability under the IDEA (more detailed information related to student eligibility under the IDEA 2004 will be discussed in Chapter 5) as well as both the type and level of services the student needs. In fact, no provision of special education programs or services may take place unless the student receives a full, individualized evaluation of their unique, individualized educational needs (20 U.S.C. § 1412(a)(3)(2006)).

School officials should not initiate an evaluation for possible special education eligibility under the IDEA without receiving the informed, written consent of the parent or designated legal guardian of the student (20 U.S.C. § 1414(a)(1)(D)). In some circumstances, school officials may explain, in writing, reasons they believe a student does not have an eligible disability and does require an initial evaluation, satisfying the requirement of notifying parents when they refuse to perform a requested evaluation (34 C.F.R. §300.503). If parents are not satisfied with an evaluation performed on their children by the local school system, the IDEA provides them the legal right to an independent educational evaluation, commonly referred to as an IEE. Moreover, if the parents disagree with a school's refusal to have a student evaluated for potential IDEA eligibility, the parent can request a due process hearing to dispute the school's decision (Snow-Huefner & Herr, 2012).

Currently, the IDEA 2004 has established a 60-day time period in which a student evaluation for student eligibility under the IDEA must be completed after initial parental consent (or legal guardian(s) has been received (20 U.S.C. §1414(a)(1)(C)(i)). The 2006 IDEA regulations provide further details and establish that an individualized education plan (IEP) meeting must be held within a 30-day period of a student eligibility determination and strongly suggest that the student's actual IEP be implemented as soon as possible after its initial development (34 § C.F.R. 300.323(c)).

Under the IDEA 2004, two necessary criteria are required to establish eligibility under the IDEA. First, a student over the age of nine must be determined to have one or more of the existing thirteen eligibility categories under the IDEA; and second, the student's disability(ies) must be shown through academic and functional performance data to adversely affect the student's educational performance (20 U.S.C. § 1401(3)(A)(2)). Currently, the thirteen disability categories under the IDEA include: intellectual disability; hearing impairment (including deafness); speech or language impairment; visual impairment (including blindness); serious emotional disturbance; orthopedic impairment; autism; traumatic brain injury; another health impairment; specific learning disability; deaf-blindness; multiple disabilities; and developmental delay (the IDEA gives discretion to individual states and LEAs to potentially include children ages three through nine who do not meet the other eligibility requirements if a child experiences a "developmental delay" in either their physical, cognitive, communication, social/emotional, or adaptive development that results in a possible need for special education and related services (34 C.F.R. § 300.8)).

Individualized Education Plan (IEP)

After a formal evaluation or reevaluation has identified a particular student as in need of special education and related services, a team of individuals use the information gathered from the student's evaluation process to develop an individualized education program (IEP) for the student. An IEP is a mandatory written statement developed for every IDEA–eligible student with a disability. The IEP document contains information related to an individualized program of special education instruction, supports, and relevant services that a student will receive. Relatedly, the IEP also serves the role of a mandatory document utilized to legally monitor the delivery of special education and related services as well as evaluate its overall effectiveness. Under the current IDEA 2004, the composition of an IEP team must consist of at least one special educator (or special education provider); at least one general education teacher; the parent(s); a representative of the local school district (LEA); someone who can interpret the implications of the student's evaluation results; the student, when appropriate; and, at the discretion of the parent(s) or school, others who may have specialized knowledge or expertise about the student (20 U.S.C. §1414(d)(1)(B)). The IDEA regulations require that all of the student's teachers or service providers have direct access to the IEP if they have any duties or responsibilities for its implementation (34 C.F.R. § 300.323(d)). The current IDEA 2004 statute, regulations, and emerging case law are in agreement that a student's IEP must be developed collaboratively with the child's parent(s) and school officials. While the IEP does not legally guarantee that the student will make progress, the IEP must be developed in order that the child "make progress appropriate in light of the child's circumstances" (*Endrew*, 2017, p. 988). The Individualized Education Plan, or IEP will be discussed in much greater detail in Chapter 6.

Least Restrictive Environment (LRE)

Legal issues pertaining to the educational placement of students with disabilities has and continues to be a controversial provision in the IDEA 2004. Some of the earlier, significant court cases involving students with disabilities' access to public schools prior to the passage of the IDEA, including *PARC v. Pennsylvania* (1972) and *Mills v. Board of Education* (1972), established the legal principle that the exclusion of children with disabilities from public schools was a denial of equal protection under the law based on the Fourteenth Amendment of the U.S. Constitution. Moreover, the *PARC* and *Mills* cases established the initial legal precedent advocating the education of students with disabilities alongside children without disabilities to the maximum extent possible (Snow-Huefner & Herr, 2012). This legal preference is now called least restrictive environment, or LRE, which was a term borrowed from a series of court cases involving the deinstitutionalization of persons with mental illness (Snow-Huefner & Herr, 2012). A common misconception among educational practitioners and laypersons alike is that the term LRE can be used interchangeably with the terms "mainstreaming" and "inclusion" (Snow-Huefner & Herr, 2012). Neither the IDEA statute nor regulations make any reference to the terms "mainstreaming" or "inclusion" in relation to LRE. In terms of the IDEA, the meaning of LRE refers to the educational setting that most closely resembles the general educational setting as well as an educational placement in which FAPE can be appropriately delivered to a student with disabilities. More specifically, the IDEA mandates that eligible students with disabilities are educated with their student peers without disabilities in general education classrooms to the maximum extent appropriate (34 C.F.R. § 300.550(b)(2)). Eligible students with disabilities can only be removed to separate or self-contained special education classrooms when the nature or severity of their disabilities is such that they are unable to receive an appropriate education within a general education classroom environment with supplementary aids and services (34 C.F.R. § 300.550(b)(2)). When students with disabilities are placed in segregated classroom settings, such as physical education, school officials are required to provide students with disabilities in these restrictive educational settings with appropriate opportunities to interact alongside their student peers without disabilities (Yell, 2019). A more detailed discussion of LRE will be provided in Chapter 7.

Parental and Student Participation in the Decision-Making Process

Since the inception of the Education for All Handicapped Children Act (EAHCA) in 1975 up to the present IDEA 2004 statute, Congress has consistently stressed the important role of parents in the education of children and youth with disabilities. Ideally, the goal of this IDEA principle is to ensure that parents participate in a meaningful way in the process of providing special education and related services education to their child. Relatedly, the IDEA statute strongly encourages positive, non-adversarial partnerships between school officials and families as both groups strive to serve the best interests of children with disabilities in school settings. As a result, parental involvement is mandated at every stage of the special education process, including the critical stages of initial evaluation, IEP meetings, and student placement decisions. More recently, emerging research is highlighting the importance and positive effects associated with active student participation, when feasible, in the decision-making process, including a more student-centered and collaborative process between families and schools (Danneker & Bottge, 2009). A lingering issue involving the monitoring and enforcement of the parental participation principle is defining "who" the student's parent is. For example, school officials cannot automatically assume the "biological parent" as the sole option. Instead, the 2006 IDEA regulations clarify who constitutes a parent under the IDEA among the following five options, including:

1. A student's biological or adoptive parent(s)

    (34 C.F.R. § 300.30)

2. A foster parent(s), unless state law prohibits a foster parent(s) from acting in the role as parent(s)
    (34 C.F.R. § 300.30)

3. A designated guardian authorized to act as the legal minor's parent(s) or legally authorized to make educational decisions for the legal minor (not the state if the legal minor is a beneficial ward of the state)
    (34 C.F.R. § 300.30)

4. A designated individual acting in the place of either a biological or adoptive parent(s), including a grandparent, stepparent, or other relative with whom the legal minor lives, or any designated individual who is legally responsible for the legal minor's welfare

    (34 C.F.R. § 300.30)

5. A surrogate parent(s), who has been appointed in accordance with the 2006 regulations
    (34 C.F.R. § 300.519)

Recent legal cases, most notably, *Doug C. v. Hawaii Department of Education* (2013), a case decided by the federal U.S. Court of Appeals for the Ninth Circuit, illustrates the central and vital role of parents in the IEP process of IDEA–eligible students. A more detailed discussion of the importance of parental participation in the IDEA special education process will be discussed in Chapter 12.

Procedural Due Process and Safeguards

Among the many unique elements of the IDEA is its complex system of procedural due process and safeguards developed to ensure IDEA-eligible students with disabilities are properly identified, evaluated, and placed according to the detailed procedures found in the provisions (20 U.S.C. § 1415). Basically, the IDEA mandate of procedural due process ensures that both an eligible student and their parents' rights are appropriately protected or safeguarded. Currently, the IDEA 2004 provides a detailed and extensive system of procedural safeguards for eligible students with disabilities and their parents to ensure equitable participation in the special education process (34 C.F.R. § 300.500 *et seq.*). These procedural safeguards consist of four specific component areas, including: (a) general safeguards; (b) the independent educational evaluation (IEE); (c) the appointment of a dispute resolution session; and a due process hearing (if necessary) (34 C.F.R. § 300.500 *et seq.*). The primary legal safeguards afforded eligible students with disabilities and their parents are the requirements of notice and consent. First, the requirement of notice must be provided to parents within a reasonable amount of time prior to a school's starting, changing, or refusing to initiate a student's identification, evaluation, or educational placement (34 C.F.R. § 300.504(a)). Second, in terms of the parental consent requirement, school officials must obtain "informed consent" from an eligible student's parents before conducting a pre-placement student evaluation as well as an initial student placement to a special education program (34 C.F.R. § 300.504(b)).

Additional IDEA 2004 Legal Principles and Provisions Addressed in the Book

In addition to these six major principles, there are other important IDEA 2004 provisions and legally related topics necessary for individuals working closely with IDEA–eligible students with disabilities to recognize, understand, and improve their special education legal literacy. These additional topics are discussed throughout various sections of both the IDEA 2004 statute as well as the 2006 regulations. For a variety of reasons, including lack of awareness, noncompliance, and disagreements over the interpretation of these IDEA principles and provisions, certain IDEA principles and provisions have continually been the center of legal discussions and debate as well as litigated at all levels of our judicial system, ranging from the nation's highest court, the U.S. Supreme Court to the numerous federal and lower-level courts throughout the country. Therefore, in addition to the six major IDEA principles, the following topics will also be discussed in the book, including:

- Bullying/harassment of students with disabilities
- Child Find/ Zero Reject
- Discipling students with disabilities
- Student eligibility/evaluation/assessment requirements
- Placement of students in private facilities
- Related, supplementary, and nonacademic services under the IDEA 2004
- Available legal remedies under the IDEA 2004
- Student records and privacy issues
- Technology-related assistance
- Transition services

A better working knowledge of the general structure of the IDEA 2004 and a brief overview of the federal law's major legal principles and provisions will assist persons who work closely with today's students with disabilities in varied, diverse school settings, including school board members, superintendents, principals, general education teachers, special education teachers, parents, and other advocates by providing improved legal knowledge and literacy of the major provisions and legal requirements expected of the current IDEA 2004. Also, this legal primer of the IDEA 2004's general statutory structure and major principles can significantly benefit future educational practitioners, including those enrolled in teacher preparation programs or specialized practitioner training programs, including school counseling, educational leadership, law, school psychology, social work, and special education.

Summary of Important Legal Policies, Principles, and Practices

The focus of this chapter addresses the major statutory structure of the federal Individuals with Disabilities Education Improvement Act, or IDEA 2004. The IDEA 2004 is divided into four major components, or sections.

1. IDEA 2004: Part A: General Provisions. This mandatory section of the IDEA 2004 details the primary findings and purposes of the law developed by Congress. Additionally, Part A contains definitions of the major terms used in the statute.
2. IDEA 2004: Part B: Assistance for Education. The IDEA 2004's Part B section is also mandatory and establishes the requirements both individual states and local school districts must meet to receive federal funding serving children and youth with disabilities. Part B also stipulates that states must ensure a free appropriate public education (FAPE) to all qualified children and youth with disabilities who live in a particular state.
3. IDEA 2004: Part C: Infants and Toddlers with Disabilities. While not a required section of the federal law, the IDEA 2004's Part C provides federal, categorical grants to states that establish systems to provide appropriate early intervention special education services to eligible infants and toddlers with disabilities.
4. IDEA 2004: Part D: National Activities to Improve Education of Children with Disabilities. The IDEA 2004's Part D provides federal grants that support a variety of activities, including support for the development of instructional methods, professional development, and research projects that address effective early intervention strategies for infants and toddlers with disabilities.

5. Despite numerous reauthorizations, the original purpose of the IDEA remains intact and unchanged, namely to provide eligible students with disabilities a free appropriate public education (FAPE). Achieving this goal is based upon six principles: (a) zero reject/child find; (b) nondiscriminatory student evaluation and appropriate eligibility practices; (c) an individualized education program (IEP); (d) procedural due process and safeguards for parents and students with disabilities; (e) student placements in the least restrictive environment (LRE); and (f) parental and student participation in the decision-making process.

Useful Online Resources

U.S. House of Representatives-Office of the Law Revision Council (OLRC): U.S. Code
> **IDEA 2004: Part A. General Provisions** outlines the federal statute's general provisions, including the purpose of the IDEA and definitions used throughout the statute. http://uscode.house.gov/view.xhtml?path=/prelim@title20/chapter33/subchapter1&edition=prelim
> **IDEA 2004: Part B: Assistance for All Children with Disabilities** includes provisions related to IDEA formula grants that assist states in providing a free appropriate public education (FAPE) in the least restrictive environment (LRE) for children with disabilities ages three through twenty-one. http://uscode.house.gov/view.xhtml?path=/prelim@title20/chapter33/subchapter2&edition=prelim
> **Part C. Infants and Toddlers with Disabilities** includes provisions related to formula grants that assist states in providing early intervention services for infants and toddlers birth through age two and their families. http://uscode.house.gov/view.xhtml?path=/prelim@title20/chapter33/subchapter3&edition=prelim
> **Part D. National Activities to Improve Education of Children with Disabilities** includes provisions related to discretionary grants to support state personnel development, technical assistance and dissemination, technology, and parent training and information centers. http://uscode.house.gov/view.xhtml?path=/prelim@title20/chapter33/subchapter4&edition=prelim

Full IDEA 2004 Statute http://uscode.house.gov/view.xhtml?path=/prelim@title20/chapter33&edition=prelim

U.S. Department of Education-Office of Special Education and Rehabilitative Services
> **IDEA 2006 Regulation: Part 300 (Part B)** Assistance to States for the Education of Children with Disabilities (Sections 300.1 to 300.818) https://sites.ed.gov/idea/regs/b
> **IDEA 2006 Regulations: Part 303 (Part C)** Early Intervention Program for Infants and Toddlers with Disabilities (Sections 303.1 to 303.734) https://sites.ed.gov/idea/regs/c

Recommended Reading

Ballard, J., Ramirez, B., & Weintraub, F. (Eds.). (1982). *Special education in America: Its legal and governmental foundations.* Reston, VA: Council for Exceptional Children.

Huefner, D. S. (1997). The legalization and federalization of special education. In J. W. Lloyd, E. J. Kameenui, & D. Chard (Eds.), *Issues in educating students with disabilities* (pp. 343–362). Mahwah. NJ: Erlbaum.

References

Board of Education of the Hendrick Hudson School District v. Rowley, 458 U.S. 176 (1982).

Danneker, J. E., & Bottge, B. A. (2009). Benefits of and barriers to elementary student-led individualized education programs. *Remedial and Special Education, 30*, 225–233.

Doug C. v. Hawaii Department of Education, 720 F.2d 1038 (9th Cir. 2013).

Education for All Handicapped Children Act of 1975, 20 U.S.C. §1401 *et seq. Endrew F. v. Douglas County School District RE-1*, 137 S.Ct. 988 (2017).

Lipkin, P. H., & Okamoto, J. (2015). The Individuals with Disabilities Education Act (IDEA) for children with special educational needs. *Pediatrics, 136*(6), 1650–1662.

Mills v. Board of Education, 348 F. Supp. 866 (D.D.C. 1972).

Pennsylvania Association of Retarded Citizens (PARC) v. Commonwealth of Pennsylvania, 343 F. Supp. 279 (E.D. Pa. 1972).

Rothstein, L., & Johnson, S. F. (2014). *Special education law* (5th ed.). Thousand Oaks, CA: Sage Publications.

Snow-Huefner, D., & Herr, C. H. (2012). *Navigating special education law and policy.* Verona, WI: Attainment Company, Inc.

Turnbull, H. R., Stowe, M. J., & Huerta, N. E. (2007). *Free appropriate public education: The law and children with disabilities.* Denver, CO: Love Publishing.

Winters-Kesslar, T., Fridman, E., & Munin, M. (2018). *IDEA: New expectations for schools and students.* Palm Beach Gardens, FL: LRP Publications.

Wright, P. W. D., & Wright, P. D. (2011). *Wrightslaw special education law* (2nd ed.). Hartfield, VA: Harbor House Law Press, Inc.

Yell, M. L. (2019). *The law and special education* (5th ed.). New York, NY: Pearson.

5
Student Identification, Evaluation, and Eligibility

Key Concepts and Terms in This Chapter

- Child find provision/Zero reject principle
- Nondiscriminatory evaluation procedures and practices under the IDEA 2004
- Student eligibility criteria under the IDEA 2004
- Eligibility criteria under the IDEA 2004 for students enrolled in private schools

Zero Reject and the Child Find Provision

The IDEA 2004 provides today's students with disabilities unprecedented access to U.S. public schools, especially when compared to a long history of exclusion from the nation's public schools until the mid-1970s. One of the IDEA's core six principles, "zero reject" reflects the process of student enrollment and expressly stipulates that every eligible child with a disability under the IDEA is entitled to a free appropriate public education, or FAPE (Turnbull, Stowe, & Huerta, 2007). The essence of the IDEA's zero reject principle is "providing full educational opportunities to all children with disabilities" (20 U.S.C. §1412(a)(2)). Thus, students with disabilities cannot be either physically or functionally excluded from today's public schools (Turnbull, Stowe, & Huerta, 2007). With respect to the meaning of functional performance, the U.S. Department of Education defines functional performance as "skills or activities that are not considered academic or related to a child's academic achievement" and "the range of functional skills is as varied as the individual needs of children with disabilities" (71 Fed. Reg. at 46661).

However, before students with disabilities can actually benefit from the legal protections and services afforded by the IDEA, children and youth must be located and identified. School environments are the logical place to initiate searches for children and youth suspected of having disabilities that would quality them to receive special education and related services under the IDEA. The "child find" legal obligation requires each state receiving federal funds based on the IDEA responsible for having policies and procedures in place ensuring that all students with disabilities are "identified, located and evaluated" and "a practical method is developed and implemented to determine which children are currently receiving needed special education and related services" (34 C.F.R. § 300.111(a)). State educational agencies (hereafter SEAs) including state education departments bear the primary responsibility of complying with the IDEA's child find provision (20 U.S.C. §1412(a)(3)). Relatedly, local education agencies (hereafter LEAs) are responsible for complying with individual state policies and procedures as a precondition of receiving federal funds based on compliance with the enumerated provisions of the IDEA (20 U.S.C. §1412(a)(1)). The IDEA 2004 child find provision has three primary purposes, including: (a) ensuring no student with a disability is denied a free appropriate education based on not being identified, or located; (b) facilitating cooperation between state and local educational agencies with other agencies that work with students with disabilities on a regular basis, including health, social services, correction facilities, and private schools; and (c) requiring that state and local educational agencies are held accountable in identifying all potential students with disabilities (Turnbull, Stowe, & Huerta, 2007).

While the U.S. Supreme Court has not yet addressed the IDEA principle of zero reject requiring individual states and local school systems to provide education to all students with disabilities, regardless of the severity of the student's disability, a seminal, federal-level case involving a child from New Hampshire with severe disabilities has established the legal precedent. In *Timothy W. v. Rochester, N.H. School District* (1989), the First Circuit ruled that the IDEA's language is unequivocal and does not include exceptions for those students with exceptionally severe disabilities nor does the IDEA require students with disabilities to demonstrate the ability to benefit from special education services in order to be considered eligible. This particular case, profiled at the end of this chapter in the "Special Education Law in Practice" section is an important and illustrative case of the essential IDEA concept and legal principle of "zero reject," mandating that once children or youth are identified as being in need of IDEA special education and related services, it does not need to be proven that the student will benefit from the provision of individualized special education and related services. The court in the *Timothy W.* case also defined education in a broad sense, encompassing nonacademic, functional skills, including training a student in basic life skills.

In the case, Timothy W. was born two months premature and weighed only four pounds at the time of birth. He had numerous, severe developmental disabilities, including brain damage, cerebral palsy, cortical blindness, quadriplegia, severe respiratory problems, and hearing defects. While Timothy W. received some assistive services from a local child development center, he did not receive any such services from his local school district when he reached school age. Based on the school's initial evaluation of Timothy W's eligibility for special education under the IDEA, it was determined he was not educationally handicapped since he was "not capable of benefiting" from an education. The primary legal issue involving eligibility in the *Timothy W.* case involved whether it must be proven that a child or youth will benefit from special education before they are considered eligible to receive special education services under the IDEA. Timothy W., a child who was severely disabled, was denied special education services by the school district, who claimed that he was allegedly unable to actually benefit from these special education services. A previous district court ruled in favor of the local school district indicating that the school district was not legally obligated to provide special education services to the child since the state legislature could not have mandated it to do a futile act (Underwood & Mead, 1995). Since the *Timothy W.* legal decision, the zero reject principle has been generally universally accepted across the country and no court to date has disagreed with the decision (Rothstein & Johnson, 2014).

As previously discussed in Chapter 2, students with disabilities were until the mid-1970s largely excluded and denied access to public school programs and these exclusionary practices were often legally sanctioned by the courts at both the federal and individual state levels. Children and youth with disabilities who were not excluded from schools generally were relegated to second-class citizenship status insofar as they did not receive adequate nor appropriate educational programs or services. This chapter contains important information related to the identification, evaluation, and eligibility requirements stipulated under the present IDEA 2004.

Generally, the special education process under the IDEA 2004 contains five mandatory steps, including:

1. Identification and/or referral of a potential student(s) with disabilities
2. Initial evaluation and reevaluation procedures
3. Eligibility requirements
4. Individualized Education Plan (IEP)
5. Student placement

Under the IDEA 2004, the first step in the special education process is the identification and referral process, which mandates that students suspected of having a disability(ies), without regard to whether or not they are progressing from grade to grade, must initially be located prior to being evaluated and determined eligible for special education and related services (34 C.F.R. § 300.111(c)). A referral is defined as someone requesting an LEA to determine whether a particular student satisfies the definition of a child with a disability under the IDEA (Rothstein & Johnson, 2014).

The child find principle operates at two levels: the state (usually through a state educational agency (SEA), such as a state education department, and locally through an LEA, such as a local school district). The goal of the IDEA's child find provision is comparable at both the state and local levels, namely identify, locate,

Table 5.1 Examples of Child Find Responsibilities

State educational agency (SEA)	Local educational agency (LEA)
• Coordinate services and delivery of free and appropriate education (FAPE) • Develop statewide plan of compliance • Monitor the effectiveness of statewide system • Report total number of students eligible statewide	• Develop effective student screening methods • Parental-community outreach efforts • Pre-referral system for at-risk students, including optional, early intervention services

and evaluate students so that their need(s) for special education and related services are appropriately and fairly assessed. Table 5.1 details some examples of specific child find responsibilities at both the state and local educational agency levels.

Under the IDEA 2004, the child find provision is fairly comprehensive in scope encompassing "all children residing in the State" including those children and youth with disabilities, regardless of the severity of their disability, who are determined to be wards of the state, homeless children, highly mobile students with disabilities, including migrant children, students with disabilities residing in juvenile correctional facilities, and students with disabilities attending private schools (34 C.F.R. § 300.111(a)(1)(i)). Interestingly, the IDEA's child find provision does not cover children and youth residing in federal prisons or other federal residential facilities, including the Department of Homeland Security Immigration and Customs Enforcement Facilities (*see: Letter to Anderson*, OSEP, 2008). The IDEA 2004 statute and regulations does not specify the specific extent to which SEAs or LEAs must ensure that the child find obligations have been successfully met. Therefore, SEAs and LEAs are given wide latitude to develop and implement child find plans to ensure that children and youth are located, identified, and evaluated in accordance with the federal IDEA provisions (Colker & Waterstone, 2011). The 2006 IDEA regulations provide suggested activities local educational agencies could possibly implement to satisfy the child find provision, which

> [I]nclude, but is not limited to, such activities as widely distributed informational brochures, providing regular public service announcements, staffing exhibits at health fairs and other community activities, and creating direct liaisons with private schools.
>
> (71 Fed. Reg. 46593 (2006))

Basically, any activity designed to inform parents or public awareness of the nature of special education and related services that an LEA provides to students with disabilities satisfies the IDEA 2004's child find provision. Analysis of litigation involving alleged violations of the child find provision have identified several areas of concern for today's school officials, including compliance with regulatory timelines, monitoring student progress, and student mental health issues (Ennis, Blanton, & Katsiyannis, 2017). Table 5.2 summarizes the most common child find legal compliance mistakes made by local school officials.

Child Find Requirement for Children With Disabilities in Private School Settings

The IDEA 2004 requires LEAs to locate, or identify all children and youth with disabilities residing within their local boundaries, including students attending private elementary through secondary schools as well as religious schools (34 C.F.R § 300.131(a)). More specifically, the IDEA 2004 requires individual states to develop policies and procedures assuring that

> to the extent consistent with the number and location of children with disabilities in the state were enrolled in private elementary and secondary schools, provision is made for the participation of such children in the program assisted or carried out under this subchapter by providing for such children special education and related services.
>
> (20 U.S.C. 1412(a)(10)(A)(i))

Table 5.2 Child Find Activities Under IDEA

Area of Concern	Child Find Mistake	How to Address
Timelines	• Waiting to initiate a school-based evaluation because assessments from outside agencies are pending • Failing to conduct student evaluations within 60 calendar days • Delaying referral for special education because of other concerns	• Always initiate a school-based evaluation if there is a suspected need of special education services. Assessments from outside agencies can supplement, but should never supersede, school evaluations. • Create a checklist to promote adherence to evaluation timelines. • Consult with the IEP team to determined efficient timelines for determining eligibility. • Although IDEA provides that cultural factors, environmental or economic disadvantage, and limited English proficiency must be ruled out before a child can be classified as having a specific learning disability, document these other concerns with a plan to monitor progress to help prevent concerns being wrongly attributed to other factors.
Student Progress	• Incorrectly attributing high cognition to a lack of disability • Incorrectly attributing student grades or promotion to a lack of disability when other triggers are present	• Encourage teachers and other school personnel to be mindful of students' behavioral, social, physical, and mental health needs in addition to academics. • Use the response to intervention (RTI) process to support student needs in a timely and systematic way rather than as a substitute for special education services. • Note that students who require several informal supports over a long period of time may necessitate formal special education services for continued success.
Student Mental Health Concerns	• Failing to refer a child or youth with mental health needs • Failing to respond to social and behavioral concerns	• Encourage an open dialogue between school personnel and students and their families to increase awareness of mental health needs. • Encourage an open dialogue between school personnel and students and their families to increase awareness of mental health needs. • Be aware that an emotional disturbance may be present even if the student has not received a formal diagnosis or treatment from mental health professionals. • Be mindful that if behavior or interpersonal relationships are impacting a student's educational performance, a referral is warranted.

Source: Ennis, R.P., Blanton, K, & Katsiyannis, A. (2017). Child find activities under the Individuals with Disabilities Education Act: Recent case law. *TEACHING Exceptional Children*, 49(5), p. 305.

LEAs are mandated to develop plans to permit students enrolled in private schools to participate in special education programs delivered pursuant to the IDEA 2004 so that they can gather an accurate count of parentally placed private school children with disabilities (34 C.F.R. § 300.132). This accurate count is used to calculate federal part B monies available to provide students enrolled in private schools with what are referred to as "equitable participation services" (34 C.F.R. § 300.137). The IDEA 2004 regulations define students in private schools as those whose parents voluntarily enroll them in such schools or facilities (34 C.F.R. § 300.130). Thus, this definition does not include students whose local school districts placed them in private facilities at public expense to provide each of them with a free appropriate public education (FAPE). Therefore, children with disabilities who are voluntarily enrolled in private schools by their parents do not have a legal right to a free appropriate public education (FAPE) compared to students with disabilities enrolled in public schools. Instead, both individual states and LEAs are required to provide students enrolled in private schools only what a "genuine opportunity for equitable participation" in programs delivered only under Part B of the IDEA (34 C.F.R. § 300.137 and 300.138). Importantly, local public school districts are not legally required to pay for the education of a child or youth with disabilities at a private school when the school district has offered an appropriate placement.

In summary, the IDEA's zero reject principle actively supports the identification and education of students with disabilities regardless of the educational setting, including those students enrolled in private elementary and secondary schools as well as students enrolled in religiously affiliated schools (34 C.F.R § 300.131(a)). As such, child find activities used for public school students must be similar to those adopted in private school settings. For example, an LEA must locate, or identify all private elementary and secondary schools located within its boundaries to determine if there are any parentally placed children with disabilities enrolled in those schools. A 2017 U.S. Government Accountability Office (GAO) report found that many parents are not aware of the specific legal protections available to students with disabilities enrolled in private school settings. One of the primary recommendations derived from this GAO report was that Congress require states to notify parents about changes in existing federal special education legal rights and entitlements when a parent decides to change the enrollment of their child from a public to a private school environment. There are specific IDEA requirements that apply to children with disabilities enrolled in private schools (34 C.F.R. § 300.130 to 300.144). For example, LEAs where a particular private school is located are responsible for conducting a "thorough and complete child find process to determine the number of parentally placed children with disabilities attending private schools located in the local educational agency" (20 U.S.C. §1412(a)(10)(A)(i)(II)). The child find process must be developed to ensure "equitable participation" of parentally placed children in private schools as well as obtain an accurate count of these children (34 C.F.R. § 300.131(b)). The LEA where the private school is located must also conduct "activities similar to activities undertaken" for public school students that ensure timelines are consistent with those of public school children (34 C.F.R. § 300.131(c)).

The IDEA 2004 statute (20 U.S.C.A. § 1412(a)(10)) and its regulatory guidelines (34 C.F.R. § 300.132) make it clear that children whose parents voluntarily enroll them in private schools are entitled to at least some level of special education services. Furthermore, the IDEA 2004 permits the on-site delivery of special education and related services for students with disabilities whose parents have placed them in "private," including religious, elementary, and secondary schools (20 U.S.C.A. § 1412(a)(10)(A)(i)(III)), as long as certain procedural safeguards are in place to avoid "excessive entanglement" between public school systems and religious institutions (Osborne & Russo, 2014). Such an approach is consistent with settled law that public school personnel can conduct diagnostic tests on-site in religiously affiliated nonpublic schools to evaluate whether children are eligible for services in programs that are supported by public funds (*Meek v. Pittenger*, 1975; *Wolman v. Walter*, 1977).

The IDEA 2004 regulations point out that students whose parents voluntarily place them in private schools do not have the individual right to receive some or all of the special education and related services that they might have been entitled to had they attended public schools (34 C.F.R. § 300.137(a); *Fowler v. Unified School District*, 1997). Even so, this does not mean that children in private schools are denied all services under the IDEA. Instead, the current IDEA 2004 regulations afford public school officials the authority to develop service plans and to decide which students from private schools are to be served (34 C.F.R. § 300.137(b)(2)). The regulations also require public school officials to ensure that representatives of private or religious schools have the opportunity to attend these meetings or participate by other means, including individual or group-based conference calls (34 C.F.R. § 300.137(c)).

Evaluation Requirements Under the IDEA 2004

Initiating Student Evaluations and Notifying Parents

The IDEA 2004 has extensive and detailed rules involving evaluation procedures to determine student eligibility. Evaluation of a child or youth suspected of having a disability is a critical part of the special education process since it is the mechanism not only for establishing student eligibility for special education and related services but also for determining the specific nature of necessary educational and related services (20 U.S.C. § 1414(a)(1)(C)). When conducting an evaluation to determine IDEA eligibility, a local school district must ensure that they do the following:

1. use a variety of assessment tools and strategies to gather relevant functional, developmental, and academic information, including information provided by the parent, that may assist in determining whether the child is a child with a disability; and the content of the child's individualized education program, including information related to enabling the child to be involved in and progress in the general curriculum, or, for preschool children, to participate in appropriate activities;
2. not use any single measure or assessment as the sole criterion for determining whether a child is a child with a disability or determining an appropriate educational program for the child; and
3. use technically sound instruments that may assess the relative contribution of cognitive and behavioral factors, in addition to physical or developmental factors.

(20 U.S.C. § 1414(b)(2))

When a student is suspected of being eligible to receive special education and related services under the IDEA 2004, a local school district has the legal duty to ensure that the student is fully "assessed in all areas of suspected disability" (20 U.S.C. § 1414(b)(3)(B)) and all student assessments must be "administered by trained and knowledgeable personnel" (20 U.S.C. § 1414(b)(3)(A)(iv)). A failure by the local school district to locate and evaluate a potential child or youth with disabilities constitutes a direct violation of the IDEA and can result in school district liability (20 U.S.C. § 1412 (a)(3)). For example, a recent legal case brought by the parents of a elementary school-aged child with disabilities, *Greenwich Board of Education v. G.M. and J.M.* (2016) provides an instructive example of a local school district's violation of the child find obligation related to the IDEA evaluation process, namely that a local school district cannot rely exclusively upon a single assessment criterion for determining student eligibility under the IDEA. In this case, the student, K.M. was in kindergarten and first grade at the time of the child find violation. K.M.'s parents notified her teacher that their family had an extensive history of learning disabilities. Shortly after providing this information, K.M. was assigned a response to intervention team, where she began to receive specialized instruction. The term, response to intervention, or RTI, refers to a policy that is encouraged but not required under the IDEA whereby students identified as needing assistance are provided additional educational programming and formally evaluated before they are identified as qualifying for special education and related services. K.M.'s parents supplemented the school district's RTI assistance with both a private reading tutor as well as hiring a private psychologist, who assessed that K.M. had a specific reading disorder, ADHD, and generalized anxiety. Based on the psychologist's evaluation, K.M.'s parents notified the elementary school's principal and requested a referral to have K.M. evaluated to determine possible eligibility for special education and related services under the IDEA. Instead of conducting an evaluation, however, the school district gathered a team of school officials, who concluded that K.M. was "ineligible for special education and related services because she responded to the current level of interaction" provided during the RTI process (*Greenwich Board of Education v. G.M. and J.M.*, 2016, p. 4). K.M.'s parents challenged the school district's denial of their request to have their child, K.M., evaluated. A district court judge ruled in favor of K.M.'s parents, finding that the school district "prematurely and improperly cut off the disability review process" (p. 14).

Procedural Safeguards Notice for Parents in the Evaluation Process

The IDEA 2004 requires a "full and individual initial evaluation" before a local school district can deliver special education and related services to a student with a disability (34 C.F.R. § 300.301(a)). Either the parent of the child or a public agency may initiate a formal request for an initial evaluation (34 C.F.R. § 300.301(b)).

A public agency could be an individual from a state educational agency, another state agency or an LEA. "Upon initial referral or parent request for an evaluation," a parent must be given a document referred to as the "procedural safeguards notice" (34 C.F.R. § 300.504(a)(1)). The procedural safeguards notice includes a detailed explanation of the parents' many procedural rights under the IDEA, including the right to an independent educational evaluation, prior written notice, parental consent, access to education records, disclosure of evaluation results, and the opportunity to present and resolve complaints (34 C.F.R. § 300.504(a)(1)(c)).

Prior Written Notice Requirement

The legal obligation of providing prior written notice to parents occurs after the request for an initial evaluation has been made is a important part of the evaluation process under the IDEA. A local school district must notify a parent in writing that it either intends to, or refuses to, evaluate a student to determine if they are eligible or not for IDEA special education and related services. More specifically, the written notice must describe the rationale(s) behind the local school district's decision as well as describe each evaluation procedure, assessment, student record, or report that the school district used as a basis for its decision (34 C.F.R. § 300.503). The local school district must also describe any future evaluation procedures that they propose to initiate on the student (34 C.F.R. § 300.503). A copy of the student's evaluation report as well as the supplemental documentation of eligibility must be given to the parent at no cost (20 U.S.C. § 1414(b)(4)(B)). Who actually writes the report is left completely to the discretion of the local school district.

The IDEA 2004 statute establishes a 60-day timeframe under which evaluation for student eligibility must be completed after parental consent for the initial evaluation has been obtained (20 U.S.C. § 1414(a)(1)(C)(i)). The timeframe applies solely to student eligibility determinations, not to the actual completion of the local school district's determination of all required special education and related services. Some individual states have opted to develop their own timelines, and these state-initiated timelines are allowed to override those stipulated in the IDEA federal statute (20 U.S.C. § 1414(a)(1)(C)(i)).

The IDEA 2004 contains two exceptions to the stated 60-day or state-initiated timeframes for initial student evaluations. First, if a parent repeatedly refuses to have their child available for an initial evaluation, a local school district is not legally bound by either the 60-day or state-initiated timeframe limit. Second, if a student transfers to a school within a new LEA after the previous LEA has begun but not completed an initial evaluation, the new LEA is not bound by either the 60-day or state-initiated timeframe so long as the new LEA is determined to be making "significant progress" to ensure prompt completion of an initial student evaluation and the parents and new LEA agree to a date when the evaluation will be completed (34 C.F.R. § 300.301(d)).

Informed Written Consent Requirement

The IDEA 2004 requires that local school districts make "reasonable efforts" to acquire a parents' informed written consent based on the initial evaluation of their child for potential IDEA eligibility (34 C.F.R. § 300.300(a)). If parental consent is not obtained, a local school district can use the IDEA mediation or due process hearing procedures to override lack of parental consent, unless the procedures conflict with existing state law governing parental consent (20 U.S.C. § 1414(a)(1)(D)). In deciding whether or not to consent, parents are legally entitled to descriptions of each evaluation procedure to be used (20 U.S.C. § 1415(c)(1)(B)). School district failure to provide explanations can be a serious enough legal error to produce liability. Based on the 2006 IDEA regulatory language, informed parental written consent is defined as follows:

1. The parent has been fully informed, in their native language or other primary mode of communication, of all information relevant to the activity for which the consent is sought;
2. The parent understands and agrees in writing to the activity(ies) for which their consent is sought, and the consent describes that activity and list the records (if any) that will be released and to whom;
3. The parent understands that providing consent is voluntary and may be revoked at any time. If the parent revokes consent, that revocation is not retroactive (i.e., it does not negate an action that occurred after the consent was given and before the consent was revoked.

(34 C.F.R. § 300.9)

While a local school district is held legally accountable to make "reasonable efforts" to obtain parental consent for a student's initial evaluation, there are specific circumstances discussed under the IDEA statute whereby the informed parental consent requirement is waived if: (a) the whereabouts of the parent are unknown after "reasonable efforts" to contact them; (b) the parents' rights have been legally terminated; or (c) the parents' rights to make educational decisions "have been subrogated by a judge" and "consent for an initial evaluation has been given by an individual appointed by the judge to represent the child" (20 U.S.C. §1414(a)(1)(D)(iii)(II)).

According to present IDEA regulations, local school districts must document their "reasonable efforts" to obtain the informed written consent of parents. As such, the IDEA requires local school districts to keep up-to-date and ongoing records of their ten attempts to gain informed parental consent including:

1. Detailed records of telephone calls made or attempted and the results of those calls;
2. Copies of all correspondence sent to parents in any responses received, including email;
3. Detailed records of visits made to a parent's home or place of employment and the results of those visits (34 C.F.R. § 300.322(d)).

Independent Educational Evaluations (IEE)

A local school district has the legal responsibility to conduct an appropriate student evaluation in all areas of a student's suspected disability(ies) (Colker, 2018). If a local school district fails in this responsibility, the IDEA provides parents the right to an independent educational evaluation (IEE). An IEE is defined as a student evaluation conducted by a qualified examiner who is not employed by the local school district responsible for educating the particular child (34 C.F.R. § 300.502(a)(3)(i)). An appropriate evaluation is considered one that uses professionals to evaluate the child within all areas of suspected disability. If parents disagree with a school district's evaluation of their child, they are legally entitled to request that a school district pay for an independent educational evaluation, or IEE. It is important to point out that parents should not confuse an IEE with merely a "second opinion" to have their child evaluated by another qualified evaluator (Colker, 2018). The IEE is supposed to be "independent" and a school district cannot restrict a list of qualified, potential evaluators. It is strongly suggested that parents put their disagreement in writing and provide an opportunity for the local school district to respond by agreeing to pay for an independent evaluation or filing for due process (Colker, 2018). The IDEA 2004 federal statute or regulations does not mention a specific amount of time in which the school district must respond. Instead, some states have developed a timeframe while others have not. The following five IDEA 2004 regulatory provisions apply to IEE's, including:

1. A parent has the right to an independent educational evaluation at public expense if the parent disagrees with an evaluation obtained by the public agency, subject to the conditions in paragraphs (b)(2) through (4) of this section.
2. If a parent requests an independent educational evaluation at public expense, the public agency must, without unnecessary delay, either—
   a. File a due process complaint to request a hearing to show that its evaluation is appropriate; or
   b. Ensure that an independent educational evaluation is provided at public expense, unless the agency demonstrates in a hearing pursuant to §§ 300.507 through 300.513 that the evaluation obtained by the parent did not meet agency criteria.
3. If the public agency files a due process complaint notice to request a hearing and the final decision is that the agency's evaluation is appropriate, the parent still has the right to an independent educational evaluation, but not at public expense.
4. If a parent requests an independent educational evaluation, the public agency may ask for the parent's reason why he or she objects to the public evaluation. However, the public agency may not require the parent to provide an explanation and may not unreasonably delay either providing the independent educational evaluation at public expense or filing a due process complaint to request a due process hearing to defend the public evaluation.
5. A parent is entitled to only one independent educational evaluation at public expense each time the public agency conducts an evaluation with which the parent disagrees.

(34 C.F.R. § 300.502(b))

Reevaluations

A local school district is legally required to periodically reevaluate students determined to be eligible for special education and related services under the IDEA. More specifically, a local school district must complete a reevaluation of the student with a disability if two situations arise, including

1. The local educational agency (LEA) determines that the educational or related service needs, including improved academic achievement and functional performance, of the child warrant reevaluation, or;
2. The child's parents or teachers request a reevaluation.

(34 C.F.R. § 300.303)

Comparable to the IDEA statutory and regulatory standard for initial student evaluations, local school districts must make reasonable efforts to acquire the parent's informed written consent for all reevaluations. If a parent(s) refuses consent, a local school district is allowed, but not required, to use mediation or due process procedures to acquire parental consent. Additionally, if parents do not respond to a local school district's reasonable efforts to obtain written informed consent, the local school district is permitted to conduct reevaluations without obtaining written informed consent.

The IDEA 2004 specifies that a reevaluation for student eligibility will take place no more than once a year, and no less than once every three years, unless in either situation the parent and the local school district agree otherwise (20 U.S.C. § 1414(a)(2)). During this time interval, a reevaluation will be performed at the request of the student's parent or teacher, or at the initiative of the local school system. The possibility of evaluation errors or a significant change in the student's needs or performance may dictate a reevaluation more often than every three years. Similar to an initial evaluation, a local school district must seek parental consent before conducting a reevaluation. If the parent fails to respond after multiple attempts by the local school district, the school can proceed with the reevaluation if it can demonstrate that it took "reasonable measures" to seek consent (20 U.S.C. § 1414(c)(3)). In the 2006 regulations, reasonable measures mean measures that are consistent with those used to obtain parental attendance at IEP meetings—for instance, a record of telephone calls, correspondence, and home visits (34 C.F.R § 300.300(d)(5)).

When a reevaluation is initiated, IEP team members and other qualified professionals review existing student evaluation data and determine if additional data are needed. If no more data is needed, no further reevaluation is required unless the parent requests it. Reevaluation is required prior to determining that a student no longer needs special education, unless the student is graduating with a regular diploma or has aged out of eligibility.

Student Eligibility

After an initial evaluation or reevaluation of a student has been completed, a local school system must compile and review all of the student's evaluation data to determine whether the child or youth is a "child with a disability" and eligible for special education and related services under the IDEA. Under the IDEA 2004, the definition of eligibility for special education and related services has three primary parameters, which are necessary prerequisites, including

1. The age of the student at the time of seeking eligibility;
2. The student's specified disability; and
3. The determined "need" for special education and related services.

(34 C.F.R § 300.7(a)(2))

Eligibility Criteria Under the IDEA's Part B: School Age Children

As straightforward as the IDEA statute and its regulations appear, controversies continue regarding who is actually eligible for special education and related services (Osborne & Russo, 2014). Much of the ensuing litigation evolved over the specified disability categories defined in the IDEA statute and its regulations and whether students were eligible for services under those definitions. Students who are classified under any of the categories of disabilities specifically defined in the IDEA's regulations (34 C.F.R. § 300.8) are eligible for services as long as they are necessary. Students are generally considered to require services if their educational performances are adversely affected by their disabilities. Individual states may specify disability categories in addition to those listed in the IDEA or may provide special education services on a noncategorical basis.

Part B of the IDEA provides federal funding to individual states who provide a free appropriate public education, or FAPE to all eligible students with disabilities defined under the law, including those children and youth ranging in age from three to twenty-one (inclusive), including those students who have been suspended or expelled from school (20 U.S.C.§1412(a)(1)(A) & (B)). However, an individual state is not legally required to satisfy the IDEA's FAPE provision for children with disabilities ages three to five or young adults ages eighteen to twenty-one "if inconsistent with state law or practice or the order of any court" in relation to public education for nondisabled children in those age groups (34 C.F.R. § 300.102(a)(1)).

For a student to be legally entitled to receive special education and related services, the student must meet the IDEA's two-part definition of a child with a disability. According to the IDEA 2004 statute, a "child with a disability" is defined as a child—

(i)   with intellectual disabilities, hearing impairments (including deafness), speech or language impairments, visual impairments (including blindness), serious emotional disturbance (referred to in this chapter as "emotional disturbance"), orthopedic impairments, autism, traumatic brain injury, other health impairments, or specific learning disabilities; and

(ii) who, by reason thereof, needs special education and related services.

$$(20 \text{ U.S.C. } \S 1401(3))$$

In terms of student eligibility under the IDEA 2004, it is critical for educational practitioners to understand that establishing student eligibility is not satisfied exclusively when a student meets one or more of the current thirteen IDEA disability categories found in the regulations. In other words, satisfying one or more of the current thirteen disability categories alone does not establish IDEA eligibility. Rather, once a child or youth is determined to have one or more of the thirteen present disability conditions, there needs to be evidence that the disabling condition adversely impact(s) the child or youth's educational performance (20 U.S.C. § 1401(3)(A)). The courts have struggled with how broadly to interpret "educational performance" and determine based on the student's disability(ies) how significant the adverse impact is on the educational performance of the child or youth to meet current IDEA eligibility requirements (Archer & Marsico, 2017). Since the IDEA has not clearly defined "educational performance," there is confusion as to whether a student's educational performance under the IDEA is limited exclusively to traditional measures of educational performance, including grades and standardized test scores or a broader definition that encompasses nonacademic performance indicators, such as behavior, emotional development, and interpersonal relationships (Garda, 2006). One such legal case, *J.D. v. Pawlet School District* (224 F.3d 60 2d. Cir. 2000), which is profiled in the "Special Education Law in Practice" section at the end of this chapter addresses this legal dilemma. On the one hand, school officials who utilize a narrow definition of educational performance to solely academic factors deny IDEA eligibility to children and youth whose disability impacts areas of performance other than academic performance. In contrast, school officials employing a broader definition of educational performance find students qualify as eligible under the IDEA when their disability(ies) adversely impact nonacademic areas of their performance in schools, including their attendance, socialization or behavior. The *J.D. v. Pawlet School District* (2000) case reflects this judicial split among the U.S. courts. In this case, the court ruled that while the student experienced "difficulty with interpersonal relationships and negative feelings," the student's parents did not demonstrate that the student's disability had an "adverse impact on his educational performance," which is necessary to establish IDEA eligibility (p. 68). The case *J.D. v. Pawlet School District* (2000) can be distinguished from another case, *Mr. I. v. Maine School Administrative District* (416 F. Supp. 2d 147 (D. Maine 2006), where the court held that a child with an autism spectrum disorder performed at an average level academically but his disability was determined to have an adverse impact on the student's social functioning at school.

Thus, these two legal cases represent differing legal interpretations of the IDEA's "educational performance" eligibility clause. As stated earlier, there is presently no clear federal IDEA definition of "educational performance." In the absence of a clear definition under the IDEA, the federal Second Circuit court in

J.D. v. Pawlet School District (2000) concluded that the IDEA gives discretion to each state to define "educational performance" (Garda, 2006). In the case of student J.D., the Second Circuit of the U.S. Circuit Court of Appeals denied eligibility to a child experiencing difficulty with his interpersonal relationships and negative feelings in school because these were not included in Vermont's regulations defining "educational performance" for disabled students. In the case *Mr. and Mrs. I. v. Maine School Administrative District No. 55* (2005), the school denied eligibility to a student with Asperger's syndrome because she performed well academically and was not disruptive in class. In this case, however, the court disagreed, finding that the state of Maine's definition of "educational performance" encompassed communications skills, interpersonal relationships, career preparation, and health education, all of which were directly impacted by the child's disability (Garda, 2006).

As Figure 5.1 illustrates, the most commonly used IDEA disability classifications are specific learning disability, speech or language impairment, and other heath impairment (OHI) (Colker, 2018). In recent years, the IDEA disability classification of autism spectrum disorder has experienced the most significant increase. Table 5.3 provides definitions for each of the current disability categories detailed in the IDEA regulations. On October 5, 2010, former President Barack Obama signed federal legislation, "Rosa's Law" (Pub. L. No. 111–256), requiring the use of the term "intellectual disability" in lieu of "mental retardation" (Huefner & Herr, 2012). Rosa's law changes references in several federal statutes, including the IDEA 2004. The 2006 IDEA Regulations provide more detail about the disability categories compared to the statute as well as provide additional definitions for deaf-blindness and multiple disabilities since they represent special combinations of disabilities (34 C.F.R. § 300.8(a)(1)(2006)).

For children ages three through nine (or any subgroup of those ages, including preschoolers ages three through five), these IDEA eligibility categories need not be used. Instead, the IDEA allows individual states and LEAs (local educational agencies) to include children ages three through nine who do

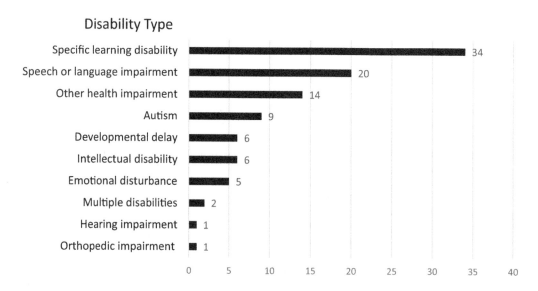

Figure 5.1 Percentage Distribution of Students Ages 3–21 Served Under the Individuals With Disabilities Education Act (IDEA), Part B, by Disability Type: School Year 2015–16

Note: Deaf-blindness, traumatic brain injury, and visual impairment are not shown because they each account for less than 0.5 percent of students served under IDEA. Due to categories not shown, detail does not sum to 100 percent. Although rounded numbers are displayed, the figures are based on unrounded estimates.

Source: U.S. Department of Education, Office of Special Education Programs, Individuals with Disabilities Education Act (IDEA) database, retrieved May10, 2019, from www2.ed.gov/programs/osepidea/618-data/state-level-data-files/index. html#bcc. *See Digest of Education Statistics 2017*, table 204.30.

Table 5.3 IDEA Disability Classification Definitions

IDEA Disability Category	IDEA Regulatory Definition	Key Elements
Autism	(1) (i) *Autism* means a developmental disability significantly affecting verbal and nonverbal communication and social interaction, generally evident before age three, that adversely affects a child's educational performance. Other characteristics often associated with autism are engagement in repetitive activities and stereotyped movements, resistance to environmental change or change in daily routines, and unusual responses to sensory experiences. (ii) Autism does not apply if a child's educational performance is adversely affected primarily because the child has an emotional disturbance, as defined in . . . this section. (iii) A child who manifests the characteristics of "autism" after age three could be diagnosed as having "autism" if the criteria in paragraph (c)(1)(i) . . . are satisfied (34 CFR § 300.8 (c)).	• Acknowledged in the 1999 IDEA regulations, autism is the most recent disability classification category • The number of children ages six to twenty-one diagnosed as having autism has grown dramatically • According to the American Psychiatric Association Diagnostic and Statistical Manual of Mental Disorders (Fifth Edition, 2015), or DSM-5, the two essential features of autism spectrum disorder include: • Persistent deficits in social communication and social interaction among multiple contexts; • Restricted, repetitive patterns of behavior, interest, interest, or activities (See DSM-5 at 50–51) • Based on a medical diagnosis, the term "Asperger's" is no longer used to describe persons who have autism spectrum disorder and are high functioning (Colker, 2018)
Deaf-blindness	The IDEA regulations define this disability as concomitant hearing and visual impairments, the combination of which causes such severe communication and other developmental and educational needs that they cannot be accommodated in special education programs solely for children with deafness or children with blindness (34 CFR § 300.8 (c)(2)).	• No new recent developments
Deafness	The IDEA regulations define this disability as a hearing impairment that is so severe that the child is impaired in processing linguistic information through hearing, with or without amplification, that adversely affects a child's educational performance (34 CFR § 300.8).	• No new recent developments

(Continued)

Table 5.3 (Continued)

IDEA Disability Category	IDEA Regulatory Definition	Key Elements
*Developmental delay	The IDEA statute defines this disability category as including a child age three through nine that is experiencing developmental delays, as defined by the State and as measured by appropriate diagnostic instruments and procedures, in one or more of the following areas: physical development; cognitive development; communication development; social or emotional development; or adaptive development and who, by reason thereof, needs special education and related services (20 U.S.C. § 1401(3)(B).	• The developmental delay" category is usually used only for preschool aged children • Individual states have discretion to classify students ages three to nine by meeting the broader definition of developmental delay found in the IDEA statute • By the time the student reaches age nine, the local school district and parent need to develop a more defined disability classification in order for the student to continue to receive special education and related services under the IDEA
Emotional Disturbance (ED)	The IDEA regulations define this disability as: (i) a condition exhibiting one or more of the following characteristics over a long period of time and to a marked degree that adversely affects a child's educational performance: (a) An inability to learn that cannot be explained by intellectual, sensory, or health factors, (b) An inability to build or maintain satisfactory interpersonal relationships with peers and teachers, (c) Inappropriate types of behavior or feelings under normal circumstances, (d) A general pervasive mood of unhappiness or depression, (e) A tendency to develop physical symptoms or fears associated with personal or school problems (34 § CFR 300.8 (c)(4)(i), (ii) Emotional disturbance includes schizophrenia. The term does not apply to children who are socially maladjusted, unless it is determined that they have an emotional disturbance under [subsection (i) above] (34 § CFR 300.8 (c)(4)(ii)).	• Formerly labeled as "serious emotional disturbance" • Serves as a disability category for various disorders, including anxiety, bipolar, and depressive disorders; obsessive-compulsive disorders; trauma and stress-related disorders; somatic symptoms; feeding and eating disorders; and sleep-wake disorders • Courts have continued to struggle to distinguish between emotional disturbance and social maladjustment. Currently, a child or youth who is classified as "socially maladjusted" is not classified under emotional disturbance
Hearing impairment	The IDEA regulations define this disability as: "an impairment in hearing, whether permanent or fluctuating, that adversely affects a child's educational performance but that is not included under the definition of deafness in this section" (34 §CFR 300.8 (c)(5)).	• In some instances, it may be difficult to determine whether a student's hearing impairment is adversely affecting a child or youth's classroom performance

Category	Definition	Recent Developments
Intellectual Disability	The IDEA regulations define this disability as: "significantly subaverage general intellectual functioning, existing concurrently with deficits in adaptive behavior and manifested during the developmental period that adversely affects a child's educational performance" (34 CFR 300.8 (c)(6))	• Previously referred to as "mental retardation" • Intelligence quotient (IQ) scores are not the sole determinant as to whether a child or youth has an intellectual disability • In order for a student to be IDEA eligible under the category of intellectual disability, there must be evaluated evidence in adaptive behavior including issues in social judgment or understanding
Multiple Disabilities	The IDEA regulations define this disability as: "concomitant impairments (such as mental retardation[intellectual disability]-blindness or mental retardation[intellectual disability]-orthopedic impairment), the combination of which causes such severe educational needs that they cannot be accommodated in special education programs solely for one of the impairments. Multiple disabilities does not include deaf-blindness" (34 CFR 300.8 (c)(7)). *Note: The term "mental retardation" has been replaced in brackets with the term now used in the IDEA regulations, "intellectual disability."	
Orthopedic Impairment	The IDEA regulations define this disability as: "to mean a severe orthopedic impairment that adversely affects a child's educational performance caused by a congenital anomaly, impairments caused by disease (e.g., poliomyelitis, bone tuberculosis), and impairments from other causes (e.g., cerebral palsy, amputations, and fractures or burns that cause contractures" (34 C.F.R. § 300.8 (c)(8).	• No new recent developments
Other Heath Impairment (OHI)	The IDEA regulations define this disability as: "a student with OHI having limited strength, vitality, or alertness, including a heightened alertness to environmental stimuli, that results in limited alertness with respect to the educational environment, that is due to chronic or acute health problems such as asthma, attention deficit disorder or attention deficit hyperactivity disorder, diabetes, epilepsy, a heart condition, hemophilia, lead poisoning, leukemia, nephritis, rheumatic fever, sickle cell anemia, and Tourette syndrome." (34 C.F.R. § 300.8 (c)(9))	• The broadest of all the current IDEA disability classification categories and can potentially include a student with the following: attention deficit/hyperactivity disorder (ADHD), epilepsy, sickle cell anemia, and Tourette syndrome • ADHD is the most common impairment classified under the other health impairment, or OHI disability classification category comprising nearly 10 percent of the special education population (ages six to twenty-one) classified as IDEA eligible (Huefner & Herr, 2012)

(Continued)

Table 5.3 (Continued)

IDEA Disability Category	IDEA Regulatory Definition	Key Elements
Specific Learning Disability (SLD)	The IDEA regulations define this disability as: "a disorder in one or more of the basic psychological processes involved in understanding or in using language, spoken or written, that may manifest itself in the imperfect ability to listen, think, speak, read, write, spell, or to do mathematical calculations, including conditions such as perceptual disabilities, brain injury, minimal brain dysfunction, dyslexia, and developmental aphasia." The term does not include learning problems that are primarily the result of visual, hearing, or motor disabilities, of intellectual disability, of emotional disturbance, or of environmental, cultural, or economic disadvantage (34 C.F.R. §300.8 (c)(10).	• According to the DSM-5, this disability is referred to as a "Specific Learning Disorder" • Controversy has generated because the medical diagnosis definition under the DSM-5 for Specific Learning Disorder (SLD) does not include dyslexia, dyscalculia, or dysgraphia • A 2015 Dear Colleague (*Dear Colleague Guidance on Dyslexia*) issued by the U.S. Department of Education indicated that dyslexia, dyscalculia, or dysgraphia could all be included in IDEA-related eligibility documents
Speech or Language Impairment	The IDEA regulations define this disability as: "means a communication disorder, such as stuttering, impaired articulation, a language impairment, or a voice impairment, that adversely affects a child's educational performance" 34 C.F.R. § 300.8 (c)(11).	• No new recent developments
Traumatic Brain Injury	The IDEA regulations define this disability as: "an acquired injury to the brain caused by an external physical force, resulting in total or partial functional disability or psychosocial impairment or both, that adversely affects a child's educational performance. The term applies to open or closed head injuries resulting in impairments in one or more areas, such as cognition; language; memory; attention; reasoning; abstract thinking; judgment; problem solving; sensory, perceptual, and motor abilities; psychosocial behavior; physical functions; information processing; and speech. The term does not apply to brain injuries that are congenial or degenerative, or to brain injuries induced by birth trauma." (34 C.F.R. § 300.8 (c)(12).	• The primary controversy surrounding the traumatic brain injury disability classification is its limitation to injuries to the brain caused by "external force" • The traumatic brain injury disability classification does not include those injuries that are congenial or degenerative, including brain injuries resulting from strokes or birth trauma
Visual impairment (including blindness)	The IDEA regulations define this disability as: "an impairment in vision that, even with correction, adversely affects a child's educational performance. The term includes both partial sight and blindness." (34 C.F.R. § 300.8 (c)(12).	• No new recent developments

Note: When Congress reauthorized the IDEA in 1997, it provided states flexibility in using the "developmental delay" disability category to children aged three through nine under Part B of the IDEA.

not meet the present thirteen disability categories but experience a "developmental delay" resulting in a potential need for special education and related services. A student's developmental delay may be in one or more of the following areas: (a) physical development; (b) cognitive development; (c) communication development; (d) social or emotional development. An individual state may define the various kinds of developmental delays at its discretion, so long as they are measured by "appropriate diagnostic instruments and procedures" (20 U.S.C. § 1401 (3)(B)(i)). The relatively relaxed criteria for the disability category of "developmental delay" compared to other IDEA disability categories reflect the reality that it is often more difficult to pinpoint an exact disability during a child's early developmental years. Therefore, educational practitioners should exercise caution about prematurely making a disability classification for children three years of age or younger.

Eligibility Criteria Under the IDEA's Part C: Early Intervention for Infants and Toddlers

Beginning in 1986, early intervention services were added to the IDEA. Part C of the IDEA (20 U.S.C. § 1431 through 1444) provides federal funding to individual states serving children with disabilities beginning at birth through age two. Figure 5.2, illustrates a summary of age-related coverage under the IDEA 2004. With the reauthorization of the IDEA 2004, Congress identified an urgent need to provide early, research-based intervention services to infants and toddlers with disabilities nationwide (Chapman, 2015). The five major goals of the IDEA eligibility criteria detailed in Part C are:

1. to enhance the development of infants and toddlers with disabilities, to minimize their attentional for developmental delay, and to recognize the significant brain development that occurs during the child's first three years of life;
2. to reduce the educational cost to our society, including our nation's schools, by minimizing the need for special education and related services after infants and toddlers reach school age;
3. to maximize the potential for individuals with disabilities to live independently in our society;
4. to enhance the capacity of families to meet the special needs of their infants and toddlers with disabilities; and
5. to enhance the capacity of state and local agencies and service providers to identify, evaluate, and meet the needs of all children, particularly minority, low income, inner-city, and rural children, and infants and toddlers in foster care.

(20 U.S.C. § 1431(a))

Under Part C of the IDEA 2004, a child qualifies as an infant or toddler with a disability when the child is under three years of age and requires early intervention services based on the following two conditions:

1. Is experiencing developmental delays, as measured by appropriate diagnostic instruments and procedures in one or more of the areas of cognitive development, physical development, communication development, social or emotional development, and adaptive development
2. Has a diagnosed physical or mental condition that has a high probability of resulting in developmental delay

(20 U.S.C. § 1432(5)(A)); and (34 C.F.R. § 303.21(a)(1))

It is critical to highlight that eligibility criteria requirements for early intervention services for infants and toddlers are separate from Part B because the services need not be primarily educational in nature and are frequently coordinated by health or social services agencies (Huefner & Herr, 2012). IDEA 2004 eligibility is provided to infants and toddlers who need early intervention services because they are experiencing "developmental delays" or have a diagnosed condition likely to result in developmental delay. At an individual state's discretion, an infant or toddler's eligibility can also be expanded to include those infants and toddlers considered "at risk" of experiencing a substantial developmental delay if early intervention services are not provided. For example, a current provision under the IDEA 2004 allows

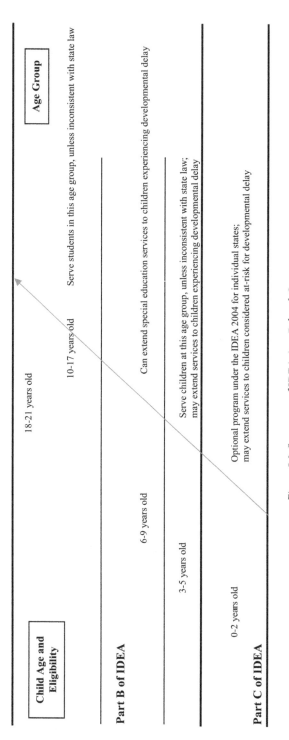

Figure 5.2 Summary of IDEA Age-Related Coverage

Source: Turnbull, H.R, Stowe, M.J., & Huerta, N.E., *Free appropriate public education: The law and children with disabilities* (2007). Denver, CO: Love Publishing, p. 63.

states to expand Part C services beyond a child's third birthday, if an education component is present that addresses school readiness and pre-literacy, language, and numeracy skills (20 U.S.C. § 1432(5)(B)). Additionally, Part C special education services may continue until these children are eligible to enter kindergarten. If a state chooses to adopt such a policy, parents must be given the choice of either continuing Part C services or have their child served under Part B of the IDEA (20 U.S.C. § 1435(c)). If the preschooler remains eligible under Part C, the state is not obligated to provide FAPE under Part B (20 U.S.C. § 1412(a)(1)(C)). Some possible examples of early intervention services offered to infants and toddlers can include the following:

1. Assistive technology devices and services
2. Audiology services
3. Early identification, screening, and assessment services
4. Family training, counseling, and home visits
5. Health services necessary to enable the infant or toddler to benefit from other early intervention services
6. Medical services for diagnostic and evaluation purposes
7. Physical therapy
8. Psychological services
9. Occupational therapy
10. Special instruction
11. Speech language pathology

Another important consideration of Part C eligibility is that early intervention services to infants and toddlers with disabilities are designed and delivered based on a document referred to as an Individualized Family Service Plan (IFSP). The IFSP document is similar to an Individualized Education Plan, or IEP in many ways but is family-centered rather than child-centered, which is the focus of the IEP. An IFSP must be written and contain, at a minimum, the following eight statements of information about the particular infant or toddler as well as their family, including:

1. a statement about the infant or toddler's present levels of physical development, cognitive development, communication development, social or emotional development, and adaptive development, based on objective criteria;
2. statement about the family's present resources, priorities, and concerns relating to enhancing the development of the family's infant or toddler with a disability;
3. a statement detailing the measurable results or outcomes expected to be achieved for the infant or toddler and the family, including pre-literacy and language skills, as developmentally appropriate for the child, and the criteria, procedures, and timeline used to determine the degree to which progress towards achieving the results or outcomes is being made and whether modifications or revisions of the results or services are necessary;
4. a statement of the "natural environments" in which early intervention services will appropriately be provided, including a justification of the extent, if any, to which the services will not be provided in a natural environment;
5. a statement of specific early intervention services based on peer-reviewed research, to the extent practicable, necessary to meet the unique needs of the infant or toddler in the family, including frequency, intensity, and method of delivering services;
6. the projected dates for initiation of services and the anticipated length, duration, and frequency of the services;
7. identification of the service coordinator from the profession most immediately relevant to the infant's or toddler's or family's needs (or which is otherwise qualified to carry out all applicable responsibilities under this part who will be responsible for the implementation of the plan and the coordination with other agencies and persons, including transition services; and
8. the steps to be taken to support the transition of the infant or toddler with a disability to preschool or other appropriate services.

(20 U.S.C. §1436(d))

Thus, the IFSP not only details specific special education services tailored to the individualized needs of the infant or toddler, but also provides services to assist the child's family members. The IFSP includes various statements detailing the family's resources, priorities, and concerns and requires written parental consent prior to being implemented. Additionally, a service coordinator must be identified, and transition plans must be included in the IFSP. Part C also requires that special education services be delivered to the maximum extent appropriate in "natural environments," which primarily consist of the home and community settings in which children without disabilities participate (20 U.S.C. § 1432(4)(G)). While state participation in Part C of the IDEA's early intervention program is optional, a fiscal incentive for states to actively participate in the early intervention of infants and toddlers with disabilities is to significantly minimize the need(s) for and financial cost(s) associated with special education and related services after infants and toddlers reach school age.

Eligibility and Homeschooled Students

Whether students who are homeschooled by their parents, a practice that should not be confused with the delivery of homebound instruction under the IDEA, are entitled to special education and related services depends largely on state law. The Ninth Circuit ruled that the IDEA grants states discretion to decide whether home education that is exempted from a state's compulsory attendance requirements constitutes an IDEA–qualifying private school (*Hooks v. Clark County School District*, 2000). Accordingly, individual states may consider whether students with disabilities who are homeschooled are to be counted as part of a district's private school population. If state law treats children who are being homeschooled as private school students, then all of the IDEA's provisions regarding private school students with disabilities apply to eligible children.

Termination of Student Eligibility

Under the IDEA 2004, a student's eligibility terminates based on the earlier of the following dates: (a) the date the student reaches the maximum age for eligibility under the IDEA (21 years old); or (b) the student graduates from high school with a regular high school diploma (34 C.F.R. § 300.101(a); 34 C.F.R. § 300.102(a)(1); 34 C.F.R. § 300.102(a)(3)(i)). Moreover, the IDEA 2004 affords individual state discretion to terminate student eligibility prior to either reaching the maximum age of twenty-one or earning a regular high school diploma under the following conditions, including:

1. the student is between the ages of 18 and 21;
2. the student is incarcerated in an adult correctional facility;
3. the student was not identified as a child with a disability during their last educational placement prior to incarceration; and
4. the student did not have an individualized education plan (IEP) during their last educational placement prior to incarceration.

(34 C.F.R. § 300.102(a)(2))

⚖️

SPECIAL EDUCATION LAW IN PRACTICE
Legal Case No. 5—IDEA's Zero Reject/Child Find Principle

TIMOTHY W. V. ROCHESTER, NEW HAMPSHIRE SCHOOL DISTRICT
United States Court of Appeals, First Circuit

875 F.2d 954 (1989)

BOWNES, Circuit Judge.

I. Background

Timothy W. was born two months prematurely on December 8, 1975 with severe respiratory problems, and shortly thereafter experienced an intracranial hemorrhage, subdural effusions, seizures, hydrocephalus, and meningitis. As a result, Timothy is multiply handicapped and profoundly mentally retarded. He suffers from complex developmental disabilities, spastic quadriplegia, cerebral palsy, seizure disorder and cortical blindness. His mother attempted to obtain appropriate services for him, and while he did receive some services from the Rochester Child Development Center, he did not receive any educational program from the Rochester School District when he became of school age.

On February 19, 1980, the Rochester School District convened a meeting to decide if Timothy was considered educationally handicapped under the state and federal statutes, thereby entitling him to special education and related services. . . . The school district adjourned without making a finding. In a meeting on March 7, 1980, the school district decided that Timothy was not educationally handicapped—that since his handicap was so severe he was not "capable of benefitting" from an education, and therefore was not entitled to one. During 1981 and 1982, the school district did not provide Timothy with any educational program.

In May, 1982, the New Hampshire Department of Education reviewed the Rochester School District's special education programs and made a finding of noncompliance, stating that the school district was not allowed to use "capable of benefitting" as a criterion for eligibility. No action was taken in response to this finding until one year later, on June 20, 1983, when the school district met to discuss Timothy's case. . . . The school district, however, continued its refusal to provide Timothy with any educational program or services.

In response to a letter from Timothy's attorney, on January 17, 1984, the school district's placement team met. . . . The placement team recommended that Timothy be placed at the Child Development Center so that he could be provided with a special education program. The Rochester School Board, however, refused to authorize the placement team's recommendation to provide educational services for Timothy, contending that it still needed more information. The school district's request to have Timothy be given a neurological evaluation, including a CAT Scan, was refused by his mother.

On April 24, 1984, Timothy filed a complaint with the New Hampshire Department of Education requesting that he be placed in an educational program immediately. On October 9, 1984, the Department of Education issued an order requiring the school district to place him, within five days, in an educational program, until the appeals process on the issue of whether Timothy was educationally handicapped was completed. The school district, however, refused to make any such educational placement. On October 31, 1984, the school district filed an appeal of the order. There was also a meeting on November 8, 1984, in which the Rochester School Board reviewed Timothy's case and concluded he was not eligible for special education.

On November 17, 1984, Timothy filed a complaint in the United States District Court, . . . alleging that his rights under the Education for All Handicapped Children Act [now IDEA] . . ., the corresponding New Hampshire state law (RSA 186-C), § 504 of the Rehabilitation Act of 1973 . . ., and the equal protection and due process clauses of the United States and New Hampshire Constitutions, had been violated by the Rochester School District. The complaint sought preliminary and permanent injunctions directing the school district to provide him with special education, and $175,000 in damages.

A hearing was held in the district court on December 21, 1984. . . . On January 3, 1985, the district court denied Timothy's motion for a preliminary injunction, and on January 8, stated it would abstain on the damage claim pending exhaustion of the state administrative procedures.

In September, 1986, Timothy again requested a special education program. In October, 1986, the school district continued to refuse to provide him with such a program, claiming it still needed more information. Various evaluations were done at the behest of the school district. . . .

On May 20, 1987, the district court found that Timothy had not exhausted his state administrative remedies before the New Hampshire Department of Education, and precluded pretrial discovery until this had been done. On September 15, 1987, the hearing officer in the administrative hearings ruled that Timothy's capacity to benefit was not a legally permissible standard for determining his eligibility to receive a public education, and that the Rochester School District must provide him with an education. The Rochester School District, on November 12, 1987, appealed this decision to the United States District Court by filing a counterclaim, and on March 29, 1988, moved for summary judgment. Timothy filed a cross motion for summary judgment. . . .

On July 15, 1988, the district court rendered its opinion. . . . It first ruled that "under EAHCA [the Education for All Handicapped Children Act], an initial determination as to the child's ability to benefit from special education, must be made in order for a handicapped child to qualify for education under the Act." After noting that the New Hampshire statute (RSA 186-C) was intended to implement the EAHCA, the court held: "Under New Hampshire law, an initial decision must be made concerning the ability of a handicapped child to benefit from special education before an entitlement to the education can exist." The court then . . . found that "Timothy W. is not capable of benefitting from special education. . . . As a result, the defendant [school district] is not obligated to provide special education under either EAHCA [the federal statute] or RSA 186-C [the New Hampshire statute]." Timothy W. has appealed this order. . . .

The primary issue is whether the district court erred in its rulings of law. Since we find that it did, we do not review its findings of fact.

II. The Language of the Act

A. The Plain Meaning of the Act Mandates a Public Education for All Handicapped Children

The Education for All Handicapped Children Act, enacted in 1975 to ensure that handicapped children receive an education which is appropriate to their unique needs. In assessing the plain meaning of the Act, we first look to its title: The Education for *All* Handicapped Children Act. (Emphasis added). . . . Congress concluded that "State and local educational agencies have a responsibility to provide education for *all* handicapped children . . . ." (emphasis added). . . . The Act's stated purpose was "to assure that *all* handicapped children have available to them . . . a free appropriate public education which emphasizes special education and related services designed to meet their unique needs, . . . [and] to assist states and localities to provide for the education of *all* handicapped children . . ."

The Act's mandatory provisions require that for a state to qualify for financial assistance, it must have "in effect a policy that assures *all* handicapped children the right to a free appropriate education." . . . The state must "set forth in detail the policies and procedures which the State will undertake . . . to assure that—there is established a goal of providing full educational opportunity to *all* handicapped children . . ., [and that] a free appropriate public education will be available for *all* handicapped children between the ages of three and eighteen . . . not later than September 1, 1978, and for *all* handicapped children between the ages of three and twenty-one . . . not later than September 1, 1980. . . . " (emphasis added). The state must also assure that "*all* children residing in the State who are handicapped, *regardless of the severity of their handicap*, and who are in need of special education and related services are identified, located, and evaluated . . ." (emphasis added). . . . The Act further requires a state to:

Establish priorities for providing a free appropriate public education to *all* handicapped children, . . . first with respect to handicapped children who are not receiving an education, and second *with respect to handicapped children, within each disability, with the most severe handicaps* who are receiving an inadequate education

(emphasis added) . . . .

Thus, not only are severely handicapped children not excluded from the Act, but the most severely handicapped are actually given *priority* under the Act. . . .

The language of the Act could not be more unequivocal. The statute is permeated with the words "*all* handicapped children" whenever it refers to the target population. It never speaks of any exceptions for severely handicapped children. Indeed, as indicated *supra*, the Act gives priority to the most severely handicapped. Nor is there any language whatsoever which requires as a prerequisite to being covered by the Act, that a handicapped child must demonstrate that he or she will "benefit" from the educational program. Rather, the Act speaks of the *state's* responsibility to design a special education and related services program that will meet the unique "needs" of all handicapped children. The language of the Act in its entirety makes clear that a "zero-reject" policy is at the core of the Act, and that no child, regardless of the severity of his or her handicap, is to ever again be subjected to the deplorable state of affairs which existed at the time of the Act's passage, in which millions of handicapped children received inadequate education or none at all. In summary, the Act mandates an appropriate public education for all handicapped children, regardless of the level of achievement that such children might attain.

B. Timothy W.: A Handicapped Child Entitled to an Appropriate Education

Given that the Act's language mandates that all handicapped children are entitled to a free appropriate education, we must next inquire if Timothy W. is a handicapped child, and if he is, what constitutes an appropriate education to meet his unique needs.

(1) handicapped children:

The implementing regulations define handicapped children as "being mentally retarded, hard of hearing, deaf, speech impaired, visually handicapped, seriously emotionally disturbed, orthopedically impaired, other health impaired, deaf-blind, multi-handicapped, or as having specific learning disabilities, who because of those impairments need special education and related services." . . . "Mentally retarded" is described as "significantly subaverage general intellectual functioning existing concurrently with deficits in adaptive behavior and manifested during the developmental period, which adversely affects a child's educational performance." . . . "Multi-handicapped" is defined as "concomitant impairments (such as mentally retarded—blind, mentally retarded—orthopedically impaired, etc.), the combination of which causes such severe educational problems that they cannot be accommodated in special education programs solely for one of the impairments." . . .

There is no question that Timothy W. fits within the Act's definition of a handicapped child: he is multiply handicapped and profoundly mentally retarded. He has been described as suffering from severe spasticity, cerebral palsy, brain damage, joint contractures, cortical blindness, is not ambulatory, and is quadriplegic.

(2) appropriate public education:

The Act and the implementing regulations define a "free appropriate public education" to mean "special education and related services which are provided at public expense . . . [and] are provided in conformity with an individualized education program." . . .

The record shows that Timothy W. is a severely handicapped and profoundly retarded child in need of special education and related services. Much of the expert testimony was to the effect that he is aware of his surrounding environment, makes or attempts to make purposeful movements, responds to tactile stimulation, responds to his mother's voice and touch, recognizes familiar voices, responds to noises, and parts his lips when spoon fed. The record contains testimony that Timothy W.'s needs include sensory stimulation, physical therapy, improved head control, socialization, consistency in responding to sound sources, and partial participation in eating. The educational consultants who drafted Timothy's individualized education program recommended that Timothy's special education program should include goals and objectives in the areas of motor control, communication, socialization, daily living skills, and recreation. The special education and related services that have been recommended to meet Timothy W.'s needs fit well within the statutory and regulatory definitions of the Act.

We conclude that the Act's language dictates the holding that Timothy W. is a handicapped child who is in need of special education and related services because of his handicaps. He must, therefore, according to the Act, be provided with such an educational program. There is nothing in the Act's language which even remotely supports the district court's conclusion that "under [the Act], an initial determination as to a child's ability to benefit from special education, must be made in order for a handicapped child to qualify for education under the Act." The language of the Act is directly to the contrary: a school district has a duty to provide an educational program for every handicapped child in the district, regardless of the severity of the handicap.

III. Legislative History

An examination of the legislative history reveals that Congress intended the Act to provide a public education for all handicapped children, without exception; that the most severely handicapped were in fact to be given priority attention; and that an educational benefit was neither guaranteed nor required as a prerequisite for a child to receive such education. These factors were central, and were repeated over and over again, in the more than three years of congressional hearings and debates, which culminated in passage of the 1975 Act. . . .

Moreover, the legislative history is unambiguous that the primary purpose of the Act was to remedy the then current state of affairs, and provide a public education for *all* handicapped children. . . .

B. Priority for the Most Severely Handicapped

Not only did Congress intend that all handicapped children be educated, it expressly indicated its intent that the most severely handicapped be given priority. This resolve was reiterated over and over again in the floor debates and congressional reports, as well as in the final legislation. . . .

This priority reflected congressional acceptance of the thesis that early educational intervention was very important for severely handicapped children. . . .

If the order of the district court denying Timothy W. the benefits of the Act were to be implemented, he would be classified by the Act as in even greater need for receiving educational services than a severely multi-handicapped child receiving inadequate education. He would be in the *highest priority*—as a child who was not receiving any education at all.

C. Guarantees of Educational Benefit Are Not a Requirement for Child Eligibility

In mandating a public education for all handicapped children, Congress explicitly faced the issue of the possibility of the non-educability of the most severely handicapped. . . .

Thus, the district court's major holding, that proof of an educational benefit is a prerequisite before a handicapped child is entitled to a public education, is specifically belied, not only by the statutory language, but by the legislative history as well. We have not found in the Act's voluminous legislative history, nor has the school district directed our attention to, a single affirmative averment to support a benefit/eligibility requirement. But there is explicit evidence of a contrary congressional intent, that *no* guarantee of any particular educational outcome is required for a child to be eligible for public education.

We sum up. In the more than three years of legislative history leading to passage of the 1975 Act, covering House and Senate floor debates, hearings, and Congressional reports, the Congressional intention is unequivocal: Public education is to be provided to all handicapped children, unconditionally and without exception. It encompasses a universal right, and is not predicated upon any type of guarantees that the child will benefit from the special education and services before he or she is considered eligible to receive such education. Congress explicitly recognized the particular plight and special needs of the severely handicapped, and rather than excluding them from the Act's coverage, gave them priority status. The district court's holding is directly contradicted by the Act's legislative history, as well as the statutory language.

IV. Case Law

A. Cases Relied on in the Act

In its deliberations over the Act, Congress relied heavily on two landmark cases, *Pennsylvania Association for Retarded Children v. Commonwealth of Pennsylvania (PARC)* and *Mills v. Board of Education of the District of Columbia* which established the principle that exclusion from public education of any handicapped child is unconstitutional. . . .

B. All Handicapped Children Are Entitled to a Public Education

Subsequent to the enactment of the Act, the courts have continued to embrace the principle that all handicapped children are entitled to a public education, and have consistently interpreted the Act as embodying this principle. . . .

C. Education Is Broadly Defined

The courts have also made it clear that education for the severely handicapped under the Act is to be broadly defined. . . .

In the instant case, the district court's conclusion that education must be measured by the acquirement of traditional "cognitive skills" has no basis whatsoever in the 14 years of case law since the passage of the Act. All other courts have consistently held that education under the Act encompasses a wide spectrum of training, and that for the severely handicapped it may include the most elemental of life skills.

D. Proof of Benefit Is Not Required

The district court relied heavily on *Rowley* in concluding that as a matter of law a child is not entitled to a public education unless he or she can benefit from it. The district court, however, has misconstrued *Rowley*. In that case, the Supreme Court held that a deaf child, who was an above average student and was advancing from grade to grade in a regular public school classroom, and who was already receiving substantial specialized instruction and related services, was not entitled, in addition, to a full-time sign-language interpreter, because she was already benefitting from the special education and services she was receiving. The Court held that the school district was not required to *maximize* her educational achievement. It stated, "if personalized instruction is being provided with sufficient supportive services to permit the child to benefit from the instruction, . . . the child is receiving a 'free appropriate public education' as defined by the Act," . . ., and that "certainly the language of the statute contains no requirement . . . that States maximize the potential of handicapped children." . . .

Rowley focused on the *level* of services and the quality of programs that a *state* must provide, not the criteria for *access* to those programs. . . . The Court's use of "benefit" in *Rowley* was a substantive limitation placed on the state's choice of an educational program; it was not a license for the state to exclude certain handicapped children. In ruling that a state was not required to provide the maximum benefit possible, the Court was *not* saying that there must be proof that a child will benefit before the state is obligated to provide any education at all. Indeed, the Court in *Rowley* explicitly acknowledged Congress' intent to ensure public education to all handicapped children without regard to the level of achievement that they might attain. . . .

Rowley simply does not lend support to the district court's finding of a benefit/eligibility standard in the Act. As the Court explained, while the Act does not require a school to maximize a child's potential for learning, it does provide a "basic floor of opportunity" for the handicapped, consisting of "*access* to specialized instruction and related services" . . . (emphasis added). Nowhere does the Court imply that such a "floor" contains a trap door for the severely handicapped. Indeed, *Rowley* explicitly states: "[t]he Act requires special educational services for children 'regardless of the severity of their handicap,'" . . ., and "[t]he Act requires participating States to educate a wide spectrum of handicapped children, from the marginally hearing-impaired to the profoundly retarded and palsied." . . .

And most recently, the Supreme Court, in *Honig v. Doe* has made it quite clear that it will not rewrite the language of the Act to include exceptions which are not there. The Court, relying on the plain language and legislative history of the Act, ruled that dangerous and disruptive disabled children were not excluded from the requirement of [the IDEA], that a child "shall remain in the then current educational placement" pending any proceedings, unless the parents consent to a change. The Court rejected the argument that Congress could not possibly have meant to allow dangerous children to remain in the classroom. The analogous holding by the district court in the instant case—that Congress could not possibly have meant to "legislate futility," i.e. to educate children who could not benefit from it—falls for the reasons stated in *Honig*. The Court concluded that the language and legislative history of the Act was unequivocal in its mandate to educate all handicapped children, with no exceptions. The statute "means what it says," and the Court was "not at liberty to engraft onto the statute an exception Congress chose not to create." . . . As Justice Brennan stated: "We think it clear . . . that Congress very much meant to strip schools of the *unilateral* authority they had traditionally employed to exclude disabled students . . . from school" . . . (emphasis in original). Such a stricture applies with equal force to the case of Timothy W., where the school is attempting to employ its unilateral authority to exclude a disabled student that it deems "uneducable."

The district court in the instant case, is, as far as we know, the only court in the 14 years subsequent to passage of the Act, to hold that a handicapped child was not entitled to a public education under the Act because he could not benefit from the education. This holding is contrary to the language of the Act, its legislative history, and the case law.

V. Conclusion

The statutory language of the Act, its legislative history, and the case law construing it, mandate that all handicapped children, regardless of the severity of their handicap, are entitled to a public education. The district court erred in requiring a benefit/eligibility test as a prerequisite to implicating the Act. School districts cannot avoid the provisions of the Act by returning to the practices that were widespread prior to the Act's passage, and which indeed were the impetus for the Act's passage, of unilaterally excluding certain handicapped children from a public education on the ground that they are uneducable.

The law explicitly recognizes that education for the severely handicapped is to be broadly defined, to include not only traditional academic skills, but also basic functional life skills, and that educational methodologies in these areas are not static, but are constantly evolving and improving. It is the school district's responsibility to avail itself of these new approaches in providing an education program geared to each child's individual needs. The only question for the school district to determine, in conjunction with the child's parents, is what constitutes an appropriate individualized education program (IEP) for the handicapped child. We emphasize that the phrase "appropriate individualized education program" cannot be interpreted, as the school district has done, to mean "no educational program." . . .

The judgment of the district court is reversed, judgment shall issue for Timothy W. The case is remanded to the district court which shall retain jurisdiction until a suitable individualized education program (IEP) for Timothy W. is effectuated by the school district. Timothy W. is entitled to an interim special educational placement until a final IEP is developed and agreed upon by the parties. The district court shall also determine the question of damages. . . .

Questions for Discussion

1. At the time of this 1989 legal decision, Timothy W. was already 14 years old. The legal dispute involving whether Timothy was or was not capable of benefitting from special education based on his severe disabilities took many years of lengthy disputes between Timothy's parents and school officials as well as litigation at several different court levels. What do you think made the stakes in this special education legal dispute so high?

2. In this case, there was expert witness testimony presented by individuals who knew Timothy. How credible was this testimony related to Timothy's educational potential and whether or not he could benefit from special education and related services?

3. Many students with severe disabilities require expensive special education and related services. Should the cost of services be a significant factor in a local school district's decision of what specific special education services it will provide to these students? Why or why not? Should local school districts be able to use a data-driven, cost-benefit analysis in evaluating whether or not to provide expensive special education services to students with disabilities? Why or why not?

SPECIAL EDUCATION LAW IN PRACTICE

Legal Case No. 6—IDEA Eligibility Requires That the Student's Disability(ies)
"Adversely Impact" the Student's Educational Performance

J. D. V. PAWLET SCHOOL DISTRICT

United States Court of Appeals, Second Circuit

224 F.3d 60 (2000)

KATZMANN, Circuit Judge:

I. Background

A. Factual Background

The following facts are undisputed except where noted. J.D., a minor of high school age at all times relevant to this action, is an academically gifted child who also has emotional and behavioral problems.

J.D. attended Pawlet Elementary School through the third grade when he transferred to Poultney Elementary School outside the Pawlet School District for the fourth and fifth grades. Partly because of his academic progress, he skipped the sixth grade and was placed in Poultney High School ("PHS") for the seventh grade, where he was allowed to take ninth grade English. While in the seventh grade, J.D. took an IQ test on which he scored in the top two percent of his age group. In the eighth grade, J.D. took the Comprehensive Test of Basic Skills, a norm-based examination on which he received grade equivalency scores for reading, language, and mathematics that were predominantly in the tenth, eleventh, and twelfth grade levels. Even his lowest score, in spelling, placed him at the mid-eighth grade level. In the ninth grade, he took classes at or above his grade level in a variety of subjects and achieved grades ranging from B to A+.

1. The IDEA Evaluation

During the summer of 1996, between J.D.'s ninth and tenth grade years, J.D.'s parents requested that he be evaluated for special education because they were concerned that PHS was not meeting their son's intellectual or emotional needs. In response, the School District convened an Evaluation and Planning Team (the "EPT") to determine J.D.'s eligibility for special education. The EPT considered J.D.'s results on standardized academic achievement tests, his cumulative school file consisting of grades, progress reports, and teacher comments, and a psychological evaluation conducted by Dr. Roger Meisenhelder, a psychologist selected by J.D.'s parents.

According to Dr. Meisenhelder, J.D. had "superior" verbal and language skills, together with good concentration and "highly developed" conceptual and abstract thinking skills. These conclusions were largely consistent with J.D.'s academic record from kindergarten through the ninth grade.

However, Dr. Meisenhelder also observed that J.D. experienced "frustration, boredom, alienation, apathy, and hopelessness" because of an absence of intellectual peers at PHS, and that these feelings persisted despite a "somewhat differentiated curriculum at school," leading to passive resistance as well as aggressive behavior at school. Dr. Meisenhelder recommended that J.D. be: (1) classified as a student with an "emotional and behavioral" disability; (2) placed in a school environment in which he has academically challenging courses and intellectual peers; and (3) given individual and family counseling.

Based on Dr. Meisenhelder's report, the EPT concluded that J.D. had an emotional-behavioral disability within the meaning of Rule 2362.1(h) of the VSER, as further explained below. When the EPT members were unable to reach consensus on whether J.D.'s disability adversely affected his educational performance, the School District, pursuant to Rule 2364.1, offered its decision that J.D. did not meet this criterion and notified J.D.'s parents of their right to challenge this decision.

3. The Proceedings Below

Not satisfied with the offered program, J.D.'s parents requested an administrative due process hearing on or about March 6, 1997, seeking reimbursement for J.D.'s tuition and costs at Simon's Rock. On April 21, 1997, J.D.'s attorney informed the State hearing officer that J.D. intended to proceed pro se and had authorized him to waive up to that date the regulatory requirement that a decision be issued within 45 days of the receipt of a request for a hearing. The parties dispute as to whether J.D., by his father or other representative, consented to any further delay after April 21. The State Defendants allege, and J.D. does not dispute, that J.D. asserted a 45-day violation for the first time in a reply brief submitted to the hearing officer on June 16.

On June 18, the hearing officer rendered an oral decision granting partial summary judgment for the School District on the substantive IDEA claim. The oral decision was confirmed by a thorough written opinion dated July 8, 1997, which held that:

(1) J.D. was ineligible for special education under the IDEA because he was performing at or above age and grade norms in each of eight basic skill areas;

(2) the School District had provided J.D. with a free appropriate public education under § 504 of the Rehabilitation Act and was not further obligated to place him among his intellectual peers outside his residential community; and

(3) summary disposition of the complaint was proper and the failure to decide the complaint within 45 days was harmless error.

II. Discussion

B. The Substantive IDEA Claim

We begin with the substantive IDEA claim because its resolution will facilitate our decision as to the procedural IDEA claim. The substantive claim presents a matter of first impression: whether an academically gifted child with an emotional-behavioral disability is eligible for special education under the IDEA and the corresponding Vermont regulations. We agree with the district court that he is not.

1. The IDEA

The IDEA was enacted, in part, "to assure that all children with disabilities have available to them . . . a free appropriate public education which emphasizes special education and related services designed to meet their unique needs." Accordingly, implementation responsibilities are delegated to the State educational service agencies—in this case, the Vermont Department of Education—by means of financial incentives. A local educational agency, such as the School District, also qualifies to receive federal funds if it provides a free appropriate public education consistent with the IDEA.

. . . . .

2. The Vermont Special Education Regulations

The VSER, promulgated by the Vermont Department of Education, have been approved by the U.S. Department of Education. Rule 2362(1) establishes three eligibility criteria for special education that are consistent with the IDEA:

To be determined eligible for special education, an elementary or secondary student must receive a comprehensive evaluation . . . under the auspices of a Basic Staffing Team[3] . . .; and based on the results of the comprehensive evaluation, the Basic Staffing Team must determine that the student:

(a) meets one or more disability categories (Rule 2362.1);

(b) *exhibits the adverse effect of the disability on educational performance;* and

(c) is in need of special education.
> VSER 2362(1) (emphasis added).

Rule 2362(2)(b) defines "adverse effect of the disability on educational performance" as follows:

To establish that a disability has an adverse effect on the student's educational performance, the Basic Staffing Team shall determine and document that the student is functioning significantly below expected age or grade norms, *in one or more of the basic skills.* This determination of adverse effect, usually defined as 1.0 standard deviation or its equivalent, shall be documented and supported by two or more measures of school performance. These measures may include but are not limited to:

• parent or teacher observation
• grades
• curriculum-based measures
• work or language samples
• other test results.
> VSER 2362(2)(b) (emphasis added).

Rule 2362(3) further provides:

[U]nless otherwise stated in an individual category of disability (Rule 2362.1), basic skill areas are defined as:

(a) oral expression;
(b) listening comprehension;
(c) written expression;
(d) basic reading skills;
(e) reading comprehension;
(f) mathematics calculation;
(g) mathematics reasoning; and
(h) motor skills.
> VSER 2362(3).

3. J.D.'s Eligibility

a. "Adverse Effect" Measured by Effect on Basic Skills

An emotional-behavioral disability shall be identified by the occurrence of one or more of the following conditions exhibited over a long period of time and to a marked degree:. . . . .

2. An inability to build or maintain satisfactory interpersonal relationships with peers and teachers;
3. Inappropriate types of behavior or feelings under normal circumstances;
4. A general pervasive mood of unhappiness or depression[.]

VSER 2362.1(1)(h). J.D. argues that the 2362.1(1)(h) list, not the 2362(3) list, must be used to discern whether his emotional-behavioral disability has caused an adverse effect.

Based on the language and structure of the VSER, we have no choice but to reject J.D.'s interpretation. First, Rule 2362.1(1)(h) provides that the criteria set forth therein shall be used to establish "the existence of" a covered disability (*i.e.*, the *first* eligibility criterion under Rule 2362(1)), not the presence of an adverse effect on educational performance (*i.e.*, the *second* eligibility criterion under Rule 2362(1)). This is confirmed by Rule 2362(1)(a) (existence of a disability), which specifically cross-references Rule 2362.1. In contrast, Rule 2362(1)(b) (adverse effect) does not cross-reference Rule 2362.1. Second, Rule 2362.1(1)(c), which defines the disability of visual impairment, expressly states: "For the purposes of this disability, mobility and orientation skills shall also be considered to be basic skills." Such modification of the 2362(3) list of basic skills is what is meant by the phrase "unless otherwise stated in an individual category of disability" in Rule 2362(3). Thus, the district court correctly evaluated the effect of J.D.'s emotional-behavioral disability on his educational performance by reference to the basic skills in Rule 2362(3).

b. Measures of Educational Performance

J.D. also argues that his educational performance cannot be measured by his grades and achievement test results alone, which were indisputably at or above the norm for his age group. Rule 2362(2)(b) provides that the determination of adverse effect "shall be documented and supported by two or more measures of school performance," including, among others, grades and "other test results." Conversely, if a plaintiff is unable to identify at least two school performance measures that point to an adverse effect, the plaintiff would not qualify for special education under the IDEA. In this case, the district court highlighted J.D.'s grades and norm-referenced achievement test results as well as the psychologist's comments.

In sum, although we sympathize with the understandable desire of J.D.'s parents to provide the best possible education for their academically gifted child, we find no error in the district court's holding that the defendants did not discriminate against J.D. in violation of § 504 by declining to reimburse him for tuition and costs at an out-of-state residential school.

Conclusion

For the reasons explained above, the judgment of the district court is affirmed.

Questions for Discussion

1. In this case, the student, J.D. is described as "an academically gifted child who has emotional and behavioral problems." In your opinion, do you think it is a school's responsibility to ensure that a student is surrounded by their "intellectual peers"? Why or why not?
2. Under the current IDEA 2004, academically gifted students are not considered for eligibility. Is it possible for students with an emotional-behavior disability(ies), who are also satisfying educational performance requirements, to be in need of the types of special education services provided under the IDEA?
3. Should schools look more broadly or narrowly at an individual student's academic environment when determining eligibility under the IDEA? Develop a list comparing both perspectives of viewing potentially how a student's disability may have an adverse impact on their educational performance in the classroom.

⚖

Summary of Important Legal Policies, Principles, and Practices

1. Under Part B of the IDEA 2004, children and youth between the ages of three and twenty-one are potentially eligible to receive special education and related services. In order to become eligible to receive special education services under the IDEA 2004, a student must be (a) an appropriate age, (b) meet the IDEA's definition of a "child with a disability," and (c) based on the particular disability(ies) need special education and related services.

2. One of the foundational principles of the IDEA 2004 is the "child find" provision, which requires that states and local school districts develop comprehensive plans and procedures to locate, identify, and evaluate all children and youth potentially eligible for special education and related services under Part B of the IDEA 2004.

3. Related to the IDEA 2004's child find provision is the zero-reject principal, which means that students with disabilities cannot be excluded, either physically or functionally, from public schools. The IDEA 2004 requires both individual states and local school districts to follow the zero reject principle and fulfill the goal of "providing full educational opportunities to all children with disabilities" (20 U.S.C. § 1412 (a)(2)).

4. The IDEA 2004 mandates that local school districts conduct a "full and individual initial evaluation" before local educational agencies (LEA's) can provide special education and related services to a student with a disability (34 C.F.R. § 300.301(a)). Relatedly, local educational agencies (LEAs) are required to always make "reasonable efforts" to acquire the parents' informed written consent prior to performing an initial evaluation of their child for possible IDEA eligibility (34 C.F.R. § 300.300(a)).

5. After completing an initial evaluation or reevaluation, local educational agencies (LEAs) need to compile all student evaluation data for review and consideration to determine whether the student is a "child with a disability." The local school district is required to provide a copy of a student's evaluation report as well as all supporting documentation at no cost to the parent (34 C.F.R. § 300.306(a)).

6. Presently, there are thirteen IDEA 2004 disability classification categories, including: (1) autism; (2) deaf-blindness; (3) developmental delay; (4) hearing impairment (including deafness); (5) intellectual disability; (6) multiple disabilities; (7) other health impairment (OHI); (8) orthopedic impairment; (9) multiple disabilities; (10) serious emotional disturbance; (11) speech or language impairment; (12) traumatic brain injury; and (13) visual impairment (including blindness).

Useful Online Resources

Child Find
Early Childhood Technical Assistance Center (ECTA) overview of Child Find and Early Identification under the IDEA 2004: http://ectacenter.org/topics/earlyid/idoverview.asp
State Resources check your specific state to locate child find policies and procedures

Student Identification
Center for Parent Information and Resources includes ten basic steps in the student evaluation, identification, and IEP process: www.parentcenterhub.org/steps/
U.S. Department of Education, Model Forms-Prior Written Notice Requirement
A requirement of the 2004 IDEA reauthorization was that the U.S. Department of Education publish and widely disseminate "model forms" and that these forms be made available "no later than the date that the Secretary publishes final regulations" (20 U.S.C. § 1417(e)). Prior Written Notice Requirement: https://sites.ed.gov/idea/files/modelform2_Prior_Written_Notice.pdf

Recommended Reading

Boundy, K. B., & Cortiella, C. (2018, April). *Chronic absenteeism: Recognizing child find obligations.* Minneapolis, MN: University of Minnesota, National Center on Educational Outcomes.

Dinnesen, M. S., & Kroeger, S. D. (2018). Toward active partnership: Notice of procedural safeguards designed for parent use. *Journal of Disability Policy Studies, 29*(1), 54–64.

Smith, C. R., Katsiyannis, A., Losinski, M., & Ryan, J. B. (2015). Eligibility for students with emotional or behavioral disorders: The social maladjustment dilemma continues. *Journal of Disability Policy Studies, 25*(4), 252–259.

Weber, M. C. (2006). Reflections on the new Individuals with Disabilities Education Improvement Act. *Florida Law Review, 58,* 8–51.

Wright, P., & Wright, P. (2019). *The child find mandate: What does it mean to you?* Retrieved from www.wrightslaw.com/info/child.find.mandate.htm

References

Archer, D. N., & Marsico, R. D. (2017). *Special education law and practice: Cases and materials.* Durham, NC: Carolina Academic Press.

Chapman, R. (2015). *The everyday guide to special education law: A handbook for parents, teachers, and other professionals* (3rd ed.). Denver, CO: Mighty Rights Press.

Colker, R. (2018). *Special education law in a nutshell.* St. Paul: MN: West Academic Publishing.

Colker, R., & Waterstone, J. K. (2011). *Special education advocacy.* San Francisco, CA: LexisNexis.

Ennis, R. P., Blanton, K., & Katsiyannis, A. (2017). Child find activities under the Individuals with Disabilities Education Act: Recent case law. *Teaching Exceptional Children, 49*(5), 301–308.

Fowler v. Unified School District, 107 F.3d 797, 129 F.3d 1431 (10th Cir. 1997).

Garda, R. A. (2006). Who is eligible under the Individuals with Disabilities Education Improvement Act? *Journal of Law and Education, 35,* 291–334.

Greenwich Board of Education v. G.M. and J.M. (2016), 2016 WL 3512120 (D. Conn. June 22, 2016).

Hooks v. Clark County School District, 228 F.3d 1036 (9th Cir. 2000).

Huefner, D. S., & Herr, C. M. (2012). *Navigating special education law and policy.* Verona, WI: Attainment Company, Inc.

Individuals with Disabilities Education Act, 20 U.S.C. §§ 1400–1491 (2004).

J.D. v. Pawlet School District, 224 F.3d 600 (2nd Cir. 2000).

Letter to Anderson, 30 LRP 70096 (OSEP 2008).

Meek v. Pittenger, 421 U.S. 349 (1975).

Mr. and Mrs. I. v. Maine School Administrative District No. 55, 2005 WL 1389135 (2005).

Osborne, A. G., & Russo, C. J. (2014). *Special education and the law: A guide for practitioners.* Thousand Oaks, CA: Corwin.

Rothstein, L., & Johnson, S. F. (2014). *Special education law.* Thousand Oaks, CA: Sage Publications.

Timothy W. v. Rochester, N.H. School District, 875 F.2d 954 (1st Cir. 1989).

Turnbull, H. R., Stowe, M. J., & Huerta, N. E. (2007). *Free appropriate public education: The law and children with disabilities* (7th ed.). Denver, CO: Love Publishing.

Underwood, J. K., & Mead, J. F. (1995). *Legal aspects of special education and pupil services.* Needham Heights, MA: Allyn & Bacon.

U.S. Government Accountability Office (GAO). (2017, November 30). *Private school choice: Federal activities needed to ensure parents are notified about changes in rights for students with disabilities* (GAO 18–94). Washington, DC: U.S. Government Printing Office. Retrieved from www.gao.gov/assets/690/688444.pdf

Wolman v. Walter, 433 U.S. 229 (1977).

6

The Individualized Education Program (IEP)

Key Concepts and Terms in This Chapter

- Developing an IEP
- IEP and student placement
- Team members and meetings
- Parental participation
- Implementation
- Drafts, interim, and revisions

The Individuals with Disabilities Education Act of 2004 requires school personnel, in conjunction with parents, to develop individualized education programs (IEPs) for every child found to need special education and related services (20 U.S.C. § 1414(d)(5)). An important element of this process is that the parents of children with disabilities must be provided with opportunities to participate in the development of their IEPs (20 U.S.C. § 1414(d)(1)(B)(i)).

An IEP is a written document that includes statements of the student's present levels of academic achievement and functional performance; measurable annual goals, including academic and functional goals; how the child's progress will be measured and when progress reports will be provided; the special education, related services, and supplementary aids and services to be provided; the extent, if any, to which the child will not participate in regular classes; accommodations necessary for state and district-wide assessments; the projected date for the beginning of services, and the anticipated frequency, location, and duration of those services; and (for students 16 and over) transition goals and services (20 U.S.C. § 1414(d)(1)(A)). The IEP team is a group of individuals composed of the parents of a child with a disability; at least one regular education teacher of the child (if the child is, or may be, participating in the regular education environment); at least one special education teacher, or where appropriate, at least one of the child's special education providers; a representative of the local educational agency who is qualified to provide or supervise the provision of specially designed instruction to meet the unique needs of children with disabilities, is knowledgeable about the general education curriculum, and is knowledgeable about the availability of resources of the local educational agency; an individual who can interpret the instructional implications of evaluation results; at the discretion of the parent or the agency, other individuals who have knowledge or special expertise regarding the child, including related services personnel as appropriate; and whenever appropriate, the child with a disability (20 U.S.C. § 1414(d)(1)(B)).

Before the IDEA's initial implementation school officials could make placement decisions concerning children with disabilities without regard to the wishes of their parents. This approach led to exclusionary policies. The IDEA changed that by ensuring that school boards do not act without parental knowledge by requiring school personnel to obtain parental consent prior to evaluating students or making initial placements (20 U.S.C. § 1414(a)(D)) and by mandating proper notice before initiating changes in placements once students are in their original placements (20 U.S.C. § 1415(b)(3)). The framers of the IDEA anticipated that parents and school officials would work together. Even so, Congress understood that agreements regarding classification and placement would not always be reached easily. Thus, it included a dispute resolution mechanism in the IDEA where parents can bring grievances to impartial hearing officers and eventually to the courts, if necessary. The IDEA's dispute resolution process is discussed more fully in Chapter 10.

This chapter reviews the IDEA's process for developing IEPs. In this respect, the importance of procedural compliance cannot be ignored. As the Supreme Court stipulated, an IEP is not appropriate if it is not developed according to the IDEA's procedures (*Board of Education of the Hendrick Hudson Central School District v. Rowley*, 1982).

Development of Individualized Education Programs

School personnel, acting in conjunction with parents, must develop IEPs before providing students with disabilities with special education and related services. Further, IEPs must be in effect at the beginning of each school year (34 C.F.R. § 300.323). The specific content of IEPs may vary from state-to-state, but most contain some basic elements. For example, the IDEA does not require benchmarks and short-term objectives for children with disabilities, other than for those who take alternate assessments aligned to alternate achievement standards (20 U.S.C. § 1414(d)(1)(A)(I)). Even so, some state laws require IEPs to include benchmarks and short-term objectives. Thus, it is important for educators and parents to be familiar with their own states' laws and regulations regarding the content of IEPs.

One of the IDEA's overriding themes is that IEPs and educational programs for students with disabilities must be individualized. This means that IEPs must be customized according to the unique characteristics of each child, taking into consideration the child's individual circumstances (*Endrew F. ex rel. Joseph F. v. Douglas County School District RE-1*, 2017). To this end, courts have invalidated IEPs that are not individualized. In one such case, a federal trial court insisted that an IEP that did not contain academic objectives and methods of evaluation targeting the student's unique needs and abilities was not appropriate (*Chris D. v. Montgomery County Board of Education*, 1990). Another court criticized an IEP that was not specific to the student but, rather, was assembled using portions of IEPs that had been developed for other students (*Gerstmyer v. Howard County Public Schools*, 1994). Although boilerplate IEPs may not be illegal if they address a student's needs, they are frowned upon (*M.H. and E.K. ex rel. P.H. v. New York City Department of Education*, 2012).

IEPs do not have to be written perfectly to pass judicial review. Recognizing the IDEA's myriad of requirements, courts generally allow some flaws in IEPs if they do not compromise the appropriateness of student educational programming (Osborne, 2004). Courts are more forgiving if the missing information was available or provided in another form. For example, the Sixth Circuit noted that an IEP that did not include current levels of performance or the objective criteria for evaluating progress was still appropriate because the information was known to all concerned (*Doe v. Defendant I*, 1990). The court was unwilling to exalt form over substance, stating that the emphasis on procedural safeguards referred to the process by which an IEP was developed, not the numerous technical items that should be included in the written document. In contrast, a federal trial court in California nullified an IEP that did not address all areas of the student's disabilities and did not contain any statement of the specific services to be provided (*Russell v. Jefferson*, 1985). The court posited that an IEP with those defects compromised the integrity of the student's educational program. Therefore, it is in the best interest of the school district to include all components of the IEP as noted in Table 6.1.

Table 6.1 Mandatory Components of a Student's IEP

---

1. A statement of a student's present levels of academic achievement and functional performance;
2. A statement of a student's measurable annual goals, including academic and functional goals, short-term instructional objectives for students who take alternative assessments;
3. A statement of how the student's progress toward meeting the annual goals will be measured and when periodic reports on the student's progress toward the goals will be provided to the parents;
4. A statement of the special education, related services, and supplemental aids and services, based on peer-reviewed research, be provided to the student and a statement of the program modifications or support school personnel;

(Continued)

Table 6.1 (Continued)

5. An examination of the extent, if any, to which the student will not participate with students without disabilities in general education;
6. A statement of any accommodations necessary to measure the academic and functional performance of the students on states wide assessment of student achievement or a statement of why a student cannot participate in the regular assessment and how the alternate assessment was selected;
7. The projected date for beginning the services and modifications and the anticipated frequency, location, and duration of services; and
8. A statement of appropriate measurable postsecondary goals based on age-appropriate services in the transition services needed to assist student in reaching the goals (transitional services must be included in the IEP's of students who are 16 years old or older).

Another of the IDEA's tenets is that student placements must be based on IEPs, not the other way around. Placements should be developed to fit the unique, individual needs of children. Courts have struck down the practice of writing IEPs to fit placements. In such a situation, the Fourth Circuit agreed that school officials violated the IDEA when they placed a child in a county facility and developed an IEP to carry out their judgment (*Spielberg v. Henrico County Public Schools*, 1988). In another case, the federal trial court in Connecticut held that school officials violated the IDEA when they proposed a placement without first evaluating the child or writing an IEP (*P.J. v. State of Connecticut Board of Education*, 1992).

IEP Teams

As stated previously, IEPs are developed by teams that include parents, a regular education teacher (if the child is or will be participating in regular education), a special education teacher or provider, a school board representative, and an individual who can interpret evaluation results (20 U.S.C. § 1414(d)(1)(B)). The school board representative must be qualified to either provide or supervise special education, know the general education curriculum, and know the availability of school board resources. Failure to include a board representative can result in an IEP being invalidated, as it can be taken as an indication that the parents were denied a full opportunity to discuss all options (*Pitchford ex rel. M. v. Salem-Keizer School District No. 24J*, 2001). At the same time, the requirement that the IEP team include persons knowledgeable about placement options does not mandate the presence of an expert in the parents' preferred methodology (*Dong v. Board of Education of the Rochester Community Schools*, 1999).

Given the IDEA's emphasis on inclusion, the need for the participation of a regular education teacher on IEP teams cannot be overemphasized. Courts have struck down IEPs when regular education teachers were not included on teams and students either were or would be participating in the general education curricula (*Deal ex rel. Deal v. Hamilton County Department of Education*, 2004; *M.L. v. Federal Way School District*, 2005). In one case, a federal trial court in Pennsylvania held that the absence of a general education teacher who had actually taught the student meant that an IEP team was not properly constituted (*L.R. v. Manheim Township School District*, 2008). Even so, when participation in general education is not a consideration, it is unnecessary for regular education teachers to be part of IEP teams (*Cone ex rel. Cone v. Randolph County Schools*, 2004). Other persons may be present during IEP conferences at the request of either the parents or school boards, and students may attend if appropriate. Individual members of IEP teams may be excused from attending meetings with the consent of the parents, but they must file written reports (20 U.S.C. § 1414(d)(1)(C)).

The presence of a special education provider at the IEP team meeting is equally as important. This does not mean, however, that the child's current special educator must be in attendance. The Ninth Circuit explained that an IEP meeting is valid as long as it includes a special education teacher or provider who has actually taught the student, even if it is not the child's current teacher (*A.G. ex rel. Groves v. Placentia-Yorba Linda Unified School District*, 2009). That said, the availability and input of the child's current special education teacher can be extremely helpful to the IEP Team.

IEP Team Conferences

IEP meetings are designed to provide parents with the best opportunity to participate in the development of appropriate educational programs for their children. The purpose of IEP meetings is to share evaluation results, discuss progress, develop or revise IEPs, review specially designed instruction and supplementary aides and services, and to discuss placement options. While parents may have attended meetings where they provided school personnel with information about and discussed the educational status of their children, most decisions regarding the contents of the IEPs are made during a meeting of the full team. The IDEA's regulations specify that school officials must take steps to ensure that at least one of a student's parents is present at IEP meetings (34 C.F.R. § 300.322). Schools should also be mindful of parent custodial issues that could impact IEP meeting notifications and participation. IEP meetings must occur within thirty calendar days of a determination that children need special education and related services (34 C.F.R. § 300.323(c)(1)). Failure to meet this timeline may result in IEPs being invalidated (*Knable v. Bexley City School District*, 2001). For students who attend private schools, a representative of the private schools must be present at IEP meetings (34 C.F.R. § 300.325).

As stated earlier, one of the IDEA's unique features is that it provides for parental participation. This aspect of the IDEA cannot be minimized. Parents cannot simply be given token opportunities for participation. As such, parental input into the IEP process must be genuine. In one instance, the Ninth Circuit affirmed that an IEP that was developed without input from a student's parents and his teacher in a religiously affiliated school was invalid (*W.G. and B.G. v. Board of Trustees of Target Range School District No. 23*, 1992). The court emphasized that procedural violations that infringe on parents' opportunity to participate in the formulation of their child's IEP resulted in a denial of a free appropriate public education (FAPE). In this respect, informal contacts between parents and school officials do not fully meet the IDEA's parental participation requirements. For example, a state court in Pennsylvania proclaimed that impromptu meetings between a student's mother and school officials did not satisfy the IDEA's requirement of affording her the opportunity to participate in the development of an IEP (*Big Beaver Falls Area School District v. Jackson*, 1992). When parents are unable to attend scheduled IEP team meetings, school officials should either reschedule the meetings (*Doug C. ex rel. Spencer C. v. Hawaii Department of Education*, 2013) or arrange for the parents to participate via other means such as conference calls or video conferences (20 U.S.C. § 1414(f)).

The Third Circuit advised that the fact that parents may disagree with recommendations made by an IEP team does not mean that they were denied meaningful participation in the process (*W.R. and K.R. ex rel. H.R. v. Union Beach Board of Education*, 2011). In this case, the court viewed evidence that there was considerable communication between the parents and school personnel as an indication that they had been given a full opportunity to participate in the development of their child's IEP.

Parental participation is meaningless if parents do not understand what is going on at IEP (or other) meetings. Accordingly, IEP teams must take necessary steps to ensure that parents do understand the proceedings. This may require officials to provide interpreters if the parents' primary mode of communication is not standard English (*Rothschild v. Grottenthaler*, 1990). School officials should take whatever steps are necessary to ensure that parents fully understand the proceedings. In two separate cases, a federal trial court in Connecticut ruled that parents have the right to tape-record IEP meetings. In the first dispute, the student's mother had limited English proficiency and requested permission to tape-record the proceedings so that she could better understand and follow what was said at the meeting (*E.H. and H.H. v. Tirozzi*, 1990). In the second case, the mother could not take notes at the meeting due to a disabling hand injury (*V.W. and R.W. v. Favolise*, 1990). In each case, since the court interpreted the IDEA's intent of parental participation as meaning more than mere presence at the IEP conference, it decided that tape recordings would have allowed the parents to become active and meaningful participants in planning for the education of their children. Parents must also be provided with up-to-date and accurate information about their children's status for them to be able to make informed decisions (*M.M.; E.M. ex rel. C.M. v. Lafayette School District*, 2014; *Marc M. ex rel. Aidan M. v. Department of Education, State of Hawaii*, 2011).

As the preceding cases illustrate, procedural errors can be fatal to school boards in that they may cause courts to rule in favor of parents in disputes involving IEPs. However, as a ruling of the Sixth Circuit demonstrates, parents may give up some of their rights by not fully cooperating (*Cordrey v. Euckert*, 1990). Here, the parents unsuccessfully challenged the adequacy of an IEP because all the required participants were not present at the conference, but they rejected the school board's offer to convene a properly constituted IEP meeting. The court found that the parents relinquished their right to a procedurally correct IEP conference when they rejected the board's offer to reschedule the meeting. By the same token, the Ninth and Eleventh Circuits ruled that IEP team meetings may be held without parents when reasonable efforts have been made to include them, but the parents resist those efforts (*A.L. v. Jackson County School Board*, 2015; *K.D. ex rel. C.L. v. Department of Education, State of Hawaii*, 2011). The Fifth Circuit dismissed a parent's claim that she had been denied a full opportunity to participate in the development of her child's IEP because the meetings had been terminated early (*R.P. ex rel. R.P. and C.P. v. Alamo Heights Independent School District*, 2012). Evidence showed that the meetings had been terminated early because of the parent's behavior and follow-up meetings had been scheduled.

Implementation

The IDEA does not specify a timeframe for implementation of an IEP, except to say that it should be as soon as possible after it is developed. The Second Circuit interpreted *as soon as possible* as a flexible, rather than rigid, requirement, permitting some delay between development and implementation. In evaluating whether the *as soon as possible* criterion has been met, the court advised that the length of the delay, the reasons for the delay, including the availability of the mandated services, and the steps taken to overcome whatever obstacles have delayed implementation of the IEP should be considered (*D.D. ex rel. V.D. v. New York City Board of Education*, 2006).

Whenever possible, IEPs should be in place at the start of a school year, even if this means that IEP teams must meet over the summer school vacation (20 U.S.C. § 1414(d)(2)(A)). For example, two courts agreed that school boards must have permanent IEPs in place by the beginning of a school year, even if they had to conduct meetings over the summer (*Gerstmyer v. Howard County Public Schools*, 1994; *Myles S. v. Montgomery County Board of Education*, 1993). Even so, as a case from the Third Circuit demonstrates, school officials cannot be held liable for not having an IEP in place at the start of a school year if the reason for the delay is the fault of the child's parents (*C.H. v. Cape Henlopen School District*, 2010).

Once an IEP has been implemented, school personnel may find that adjustments may need to be made to the child's program. When this happens, it is imperative for school officials to contact parents, discuss the proposed changes with them, and amend the IEP if necessary. The Ninth Circuit made it clear that a school board is not allowed to make unilateral changes to an IEP document without parental notification and consent (*M.C. ex rel. M.N. v. Antelope Valley Union High School District*, 2017).

Draft IEPs and Interim IEPs

School personnel may present draft IEPs at meetings for purposes of discussion. Such a practice is acceptable if the drafts are true drafts subject to revision. In fact, nothing in the IDEA or its regulations prohibits school personnel from coming to IEP meetings with tentative recommendations for IEPs (*Blackmon v. Springfield R-XII School District*, 1999). Along the same lines, school personnel are not prohibited from meeting informally, reviewing evaluations, or discussing placement options prior to convening formal IEP meetings (*Tracy v. Beaufort County Board of Education*, 2004). In one case, a federal trial court in Rhode Island stressed that presenting parents with a completed IEP at the meeting did not mean that the parents were denied a meaningful opportunity to participate in the development of the IEP (*Scituate School Committee v. Robert B.*, 1986). In a related vein, the First Circuit declared that it is acceptable for one person to draft an IEP if the parents and other members of the team have an opportunity to provide input into its contents (*Hampton School District v. Dobrowolski*, 1992). In an analogous situation, the Third Circuit affirmed that a draft IEP did not violate the IDEA's parental participation requirement where there was evidence that the parents made suggestions for changes, some of which were incorporated into the final IEP (*Fuhrmann v. East Hanover Board of Education*, 1993).

In this regard, a federal trial court in Virginia ascertained that while school officials must come to IEP conferences with open minds, this does not mean they must come with blank minds (*Doyle v. Arlington County School Board*, 1992). The court emphasized that school board officials may not finalize placement decisions before IEP meetings but should have given prior thought to such issues. Of course, school board representatives must remain receptive to all parental concerns. The Second Circuit emphasized that the

IDEA allows school personnel to engage in preparatory activities to develop a proposal or response to parental requests to be discussed at the IEP meeting (*T.P. and S.P. ex rel. S.P. v. Mamaroneck Union Free School District*, 2009). Even school personnel holding a preparatory meeting prior to the actual IEP conference does not violate the IDEA according to the Ninth Circuit (*J.L., M.L., K.L. v. Mercer Island School District*, 2010).

The courts certainly frown on attempts by school officials to develop IEPs beforehand and then force them on parents without any meaningful discussion of the educational needs of their children. Thus, while coming to IEP meetings with draft IEPs is certainly an acceptable practice, school personnel must take care that they do not predetermine the outcome. After seeing evidence that school personnel had come to definitive conclusions on a child's placement without parental input, failed to incorporate any suggestions the parents made, or discuss possible prospective placements with the parents, the Third Circuit affirmed that they had predetermined the child's IEP (*D.B. and L.B. ex rel. H.B. v. Gloucester Township School District*, 2012). The Eleventh Circuit also ascertained that an IEP team had predetermined a child's placement because evidence indicated that school personnel came to the meeting with closed minds, were unwilling to consider other options, and anything the parents said or any information they provided would not have changed their minds (*R.L., S.L. ex rel. O.L. v. Miami-Dade County School Board*, 2014).

School board officials sometimes develop interim IEPs for students to cover short periods of time while preparing permanent IEPs. Some courts have frowned on this practice, while others have allowed it to be employed (Mehfoud & Osborne, 1998). Interim IEPs may be acceptable for short periods of time once special education students move into school districts. In these instances, school personnel can develop interim IEPs to cover short periods of time while they assess the needs of students and write long-range IEPs. The IDEA specifically outlines IEP requirements for students who move from one district to another but makes a distinction between those who transfer within the state and those who transfer from another state. When students transfer within states, receiving boards must provide services that are comparable to those in the student's previous IEP until such time as they either adopt the previous IEPs or develop new ones (20 U.S.C. § 1414(d)(2)(C)(i)(I)). On the other hand, when students transfer to districts in new states, receiving school boards must provide services comparable to those in their previous IEPs until such time as officials conduct evaluations, if necessary, and develop new IEPs (20 U.S.C. § 1414(d)(2)(C)(i)(II)). Although the difference is slight, this provision recognizes the fact that students who were eligible for services in one state may not necessarily qualify for them in another due to differing state standards.

IEP Revisions

From time to time school officials may need to modify IEPs. These alterations may be necessary due to changing circumstances in either educational environments or the needs of students. Minor adjustments that do not result in changes in student placements are of little consequence. Changes that alter IEPs substantially or result in their not being implemented as written trigger the IDEA's procedural protections (Osborne & Mawdsley, 2013). Parents must be notified of changes in the educational placements of their children and must be given the opportunity to object (20 U.S.C. § 1415(b)(3); 34 C.F.R. § 300.504).

IEPs for students with disabilities must be reviewed and revised, if necessary, at least annually (20 U.S.C. § 1414(d)(4)), but more frequently if needed. Procedures for reviewing and amending IEPs are generally similar to those for developing initial IEPs. All the IDEA's procedural and notification rights apply to meetings to review and possibly revise IEPs. Naturally, parents must be given input into the process just as they are with initial IEPs.

IEPs should be reviewed if parents express any dissatisfaction with the educational programs of their children. In one case, the federal trial court in the District of Columbia ruled that a parent's request for a due process hearing put the school board on notice that she was dissatisfied with her daughter's placement status and that school personnel were obligated to review and possibly revise her IEP (*Edwards-White v. District of Columbia*, 1992). Conversely, where parents unilaterally withdrew their son from a public school and placed him in a private school, the First Circuit affirmed that the board was not obligated to review and revise the child's IEP (*Amann v. Stow School System*, 1992).

⚖

SPECIAL EDUCATION LAW IN PRACTICE

Legal Case No. 7—Right to a Free Appropriate Public Education Requires
That Individualized Education Programs Be Implemented as Soon as Possible

D. D. EX REL. V.D. V. NEW YORK CITY BOARD OF EDUCATION

United States Court of Appeals, Second Circuit

465 F.3d 503 (2006)

HALL, Circuit Judge.

Three New York City preschool children with disabilities . . . filed a class action alleging, that Defendants failed to provide them immediately with the educational services mandated by their Individualized Education Programs ("IEPs") under the IDEA. Plaintiffs moved for a preliminary injunction ordering Defendants to implement all services required by the IEPs immediately. The United States District Court for the Eastern District of New York (Trager, *J.*) denied the motion. The District Court based its denial of the preliminary injunction in principal part on its determination that . . . the IDEA, "raise[d] some question as to whether defendants can be held to an absolute standard of timely providing services to 100% of preschool children with IEPs."

On appeal, Plaintiffs argue that in evaluating whether they were entitled to a preliminary injunction, the District Court incorrectly used a "substantial compliance" standard to assess the Defendants' obligation to meet Plaintiffs' rights. They contend the IDEA confers upon them and all disabled children the right to a "free appropriate public education," and the Act's requirement to "comply substantially" with its provisions applies only to the States' entitlement to continue receiving federal funds.

We agree that the IDEA provides Plaintiffs the right to a free appropriate public education. We also agree that the District Court erred in using the "substantial compliance" standard to determine whether Plaintiffs could prove that right was being denied. We disagree, however, with Plaintiffs' assertion that their right to a free appropriate public education entitles them to receive the required educational services immediately upon development of their IEPs or within a specific time thereafter. Instead, we hold that the right to a free appropriate public education entitles Plaintiffs to their IEP-mandated services "as soon as possible" after the IEPs have been developed. Because the District Court applied the wrong legal standard, we vacate that portion of the District Court's order denying Plaintiffs' motion for

a preliminary injunction and remand it for reconsideration under the proper legal standard.

Background

I. Factual History

The named plaintiffs are three disabled New York City preschool students whose IEPs have been determined. After named plaintiffs received their IEPs, the DOE placed them on a list referred to as the "PN" list. The PN list is a waiting list for students who have received IEPs, but for whom educational services cannot be found immediately. A brief description of named plaintiffs' circumstances is warranted.

D.D. was born on July 27, 1998, and was a New York City resident until July of 2003. D.D. received an IEP in November of 2002 and an amended IEP on March 31, 2003, but he received none of the services required by either IEP through May of 2003. A.C. is a New York City resident born on December 21, 1999. He received an IEP on February 26, 2003, with a projected start date of March 10, 2003. Although A.C. eventually received speech therapy on an interim basis, he did not receive the occupational therapy, counseling, or school placements required by his IEP for at least three months. B.T. was born on October 7, 1999, and is also a New York City resident. He received his IEP on January 3, 2003. Although the projected start date for B.T.'s IEP was "ASAP" meaning "as soon as possible," he received none of his required services through March of 2003 and only partial services through June of 2003. B.T. was not offered a placement at a school until June 25, 2003.

II. The Statutory and Regulatory Framework

The IDEA does not specify a time frame for implementing an IEP after it has been developed. Federal regulations require that once an IEP is adopted for a disabled child, "[e]ach public agency shall ensure that (1)[a]n IEP . . . [i]s implemented as soon as possible following the [IEP] meeting[ ]." . . .

New York uses a private provider system to provide disabled preschool children with the programs and services required by their IEPs. As of the fall of 2003, 96 providers approved by the SED operated 420 private preschool special education programs in New York City. For services, the DOE maintains a list of more than 900 independent related service providers with whom it contracts to provide related services to disabled preschool students.

In New York City, there are students for whom services cannot be found immediately. These students are placed on the PN list. In order to supply the educational services needed by students on the PN list, the DOE disseminates a monthly report to all approved preschool providers asking whether they can provide the identified services to the children on the PN list, provide partial services, or request a child-specific allowance to exceed temporarily an approved class size in order to provide the needed services . . . .

III. Procedural History

On June 16, 2003, plaintiffs filed an Amended Class Action Complaint on behalf of "all present and future New York City preschool children with IEPs who have not or will not receive all of the services recommended in their IEPs." The named plaintiffs alleged that by failing to provide immediately all services recommended in the IEPs, the Defendants "have deprived and will continue to deprive [them] of rights . . . including, but not limited to, rights guaranteed by the IDEA. On June 19, the named plaintiffs moved to certify the class . . . and sought a preliminary injunction requiring Defendants "to immediately implement all services required by [IEPs] to all members of the plaintiff class."

On March 30, 2004, the District Court issued a Memorandum and Order granting class certification, but denying the preliminary injunction. The District Court found that Plaintiffs satisfied the first prong of the preliminary injunction test by demonstrating that continued delays in the delivery of the educational services would result in irreparable harm. The District Court held, however, that Plaintiffs failed to demonstrate a clear or substantial likelihood of success on the merits, and thus failed to satisfy the second prong of the preliminary injunction test. Relying on the Act's substantial compliance provision, the District Court assumed that to prevail on their claim Plaintiffs must demonstrate

that Defendants are not in "substantial compliance" with the provisions of the IDEA. Because the record revealed that Defendants timely provide services to at least 97% of children with IEPs, the District Court concluded it was not clear that Plaintiffs could demonstrate that Defendants were not in "substantial compliance" with the IDEA, and therefore denied the preliminary injunction.

Discussion

A. Substantial Compliance

The IDEA contains a substantial compliance provision authorizing the Secretary of Education to, inter alia, withhold further payments pursuant to the Act if she determines the state has failed to comply substantially with the provisions of the Act. Relying on that provision, the District Court ruled Plaintiffs could not succeed on the merits of their claim without demonstrating that Defendants did not substantially comply with the provisions of the IDEA. This was error.

It is by now well-settled that the IDEA confers upon disabled students the right to a free appropriate public education. . . . The responsibility for providing the required education remains on the States. . . . [T]he Act establishes an enforceable substantive right to a free appropriate public education.").

It is also clear that the right to a free appropriate public education is afforded to each disabled child as an individual. . . .

B. As Soon as Possible

To conclude the District Court employed the wrong standard does not settle whether Plaintiffs have established a clear or substantial likelihood of success on the merits of their claim and are thus entitled to a preliminary injunction. Plaintiffs appear to claim that their right to a free appropriate public education entitles them to have their IEPs implemented immediately, or at least within 30 days, after their IEPs are developed. We disagree.

The term "free appropriate public education" is defined in part as "special education and related services that . . . are provided in conformity with the individualized education program required under [the Act]. [The IDEA] does not provide a time frame for implementing an IEP after its development, but federal regulations require that an IEP be implemented "as soon as possible" after the requisite IEP meetings. . . .

[The IDEA regulations], however, require only that IEPs be implemented "as soon as possible," not "immediately," or within 30 days, as Plaintiffs assert. In 1997, Congress amended various parts of the IDEA. The Secretary of Education subsequently published a notice of proposed rulemaking in the Federal Register to amend certain portions of the regulations governing the IDEA. The notice invited comments on the proposed regulatory changes. The Secretary declined [the suggested comments], stating it "would not be appropriate to add an outside time-line under [the regulations] for implementing IEPs, especially when there is not a specific statutory basis to do so." Nevertheless, the Secretary commented that "with very limited exceptions" IEPs "should be implemented without undue delay following the IEP meetings." The Secretary listed the following examples of "situations" that may warrant "a short delay":

(1) when the IEP meetings occur at the end of the school year or during the summer, and the IEP team determines that the child does not need special education and related services until the next school year begins[ ] or
(2) when there are circumstances that require a short delay in the provision of services (e.g., finding a qualified service provider, or making transportation arrangements for the child).

The Secretary cautioned that:
If it is determined, through the monitoring efforts of the Department, that there is a pattern o[r] practice within a given State of not making services available within a reasonable period of time (e.g., within a week or two following the meetings described in § 300.343(b)), this could raise a question as to whether the State is in compliance with that provision, unless one of the exceptions noted above applies.

Based on this commentary, we conclude that [the regulation] means what it says: States must implement a student's IEP "as soon as possible" after it has been developed. In other words, Plaintiffs' right to a free appropriate public education requires that their IEPs be implemented as soon as possible. "As soon as possible" is, by design, a flexible requirement. It permits some delay between when the IEP is developed and when the IEP is implemented. It does not impose a rigid, outside time frame for implementation. Moreover, the requirement necessitates a specific inquiry into the causes of the delay. Factors to be considered include, but are not limited to: (1) the length of the delay, (2) the reasons for the delay, including the availability of the mandated educational services, and (3) the steps taken to overcome whatever obstacles have delayed prompt implementation of the IEP. Nonetheless, just because the as-soon-as-possible-requirement is flexible does not mean it lacks a breaking point. "It is no doubt true that administrative delays, in certain circumstances, can violate the IDEA by depriving a student of his right to a 'free appropriate public education.'"

Because the District Court applied the wrong standard in evaluating Plaintiffs' motion for preliminary injunction, we vacate its denial of that motion and remand for reconsideration utilizing the proper standard. . . .

Conclusion

For the reasons set forth above, we vacate the District Court's order denying Plaintiffs' motion for a preliminary injunction and remand the case for further proceedings consistent with this opinion.

Questions for Discussion

1. Although the IDEA does not specify a timeframe for implementation of an IEP, state laws may do so. Does your state have such a requirement in either its special education statute or regulations?
2. As stated in this case, the Secretary of Education did not want to impose a timeline for implementing an IEP when the IDEA's regulations were revised, despite urging from several commenters. Why do you think the Secretary preferred to keep the implementation requirement flexible? Does this work to the advantage or disadvantage of students with disabilities?
3. Did the court in *D.D.* establish a realistic, workable test for when an IEP's implementation met the *as soon as possible* criteria set out in the IDEA's regulations? Why or why not?

Summary of Important Legal Policies, Principles, and Practices

An IEP is a legally binding road map that delineates the type of special education and related services for a student who meets eligibility requirements under the IDEA. A fundamental requirement of an IEP is that it is constructed to meet the "individual" needs of the student. This individual program is then implemented in an environment to ensure that students with disabilities are educated with children who do not have disabilities to the maximum extent appropriate. An IEP is implemented outside of the general educational environments only to the extent necessary for them to be provided with special education services. The following are considerations for designing and creating a legally sound IEP.

1. Avoid using boilerplate IEPs which can put the district at risk of violating the requirement to customize the IEP according to the unique characteristics of each child and take into consideration individual circumstances.
2. An IEP directs the placement decisions to fit the unique needs of the children and not based on the availability of classroom space or staffing.
3. Demonstrate that the school district convenes a fully staffed IEP team including parents, a regular education teacher (if the child is or will be participating in regular education), a special education teacher or provider, a school board representative, and an individual who can interpret evaluation results.
4. Actively engage parents in the IEP process with evidence that parental input is genuine.

Useful Online Resources

Individualized Education Program (IEP)—ECTA Center
A simulated IEP for a three-year old child with data included for all sections of the IEP.
https://ectacenter.org/eco/assets/pdfs/EEE-IEPSAMPLENovember15th2012.pdf

The IRIS Center (2018)
IEPs: Developing high-quality individualized education programs. Retrieved from https://iris.peabody.vanderbilt.edu/module/iep01/
Online module discusses IEP requirements under IDEA with particularly emphasis on the Supreme Court ruling in *Endrew F. v. Douglas County School District*.

Recommended Reading

Kurth, J. A., Ruppar, A. L., Toews, S. G., McCabe, K. M., McQueston, J. A., & Johnston, R. (2019). Considerations in placement decisions for students with extensive support needs: An analysis of LRE statements. *Research and Practice for Persons with Severe Disabilities*, 44(1), 3–19. doi:10.1177/1540796918825479

More, C. M., & Hart, J. E. (2013). Maximizing the use of electronic individualized education program software. *Teaching Exceptional Children*, 45(6), 24–29.

Mueller, T. G., & Vick, A. M. (2019). An investigation of facilitated individualized education program meeting practice: Promising procedures that foster family-professional collaboration. *Teacher Education and Special Education*, 42(1), 67–81. doi:10.1177/0888406417

Royer, D. J. (2017). My IEP: A student-directed individualized education program model. *Exceptionality*, 25(4), 235–252. doi:10.1080/09362835.2016.1216850

Seong, Y., Wehmeyer, M. L., Palmer, S. B., & Little, T. D. (2015). Effects of the self-directed individualized education program on self-determination and transition of adolescents with disabilities. *Career Development and Transition for Exceptional Individuals*, 38(3), 132–141. doi:10.1177/2165143414544359

Yell, M. L., Katsiyannis, A., Ennis, R. P., Losinski, M., & Christle, C. A. (2016). Avoiding substantive errors in individualized education program development. *Teaching Exceptional Children*, 49(1), 31–40. doi:10.1177/0040059916662204

References

A.G. ex rel. Groves v. Placentia-Yorba Linda Unified School District, 320 F. App'x 519 (9th Cir. 2009).

A.L. v. Jackson County School Board, 635 F. App'x 774 (11th Cir. 2015).

Amann v. Stow School System, 982 F.2d 644 (1st Cir. 1992).

Big Beaver Falls Area School District v. Jackson, 615 A.2d 910 (Pa. Commw. Ct. 1992).

Blackmon v. Springfield R-XII School District, 198 F.3d 648 (8th Cir. 1999).

Board of Education of the Hendrick Hudson Central School District v. Rowley, 458 U.S. 176 (1982).

Chris D. v. Montgomery County Board of Education, 753 F. Supp. 922 (M.D. Ala. 1990).

C.H. v. Cape Henlopen School District, 606 F.3d 59 (3d Cir. 2010).

Cone ex rel. Cone v. Randolph County Schools, 302 F. Supp.2d 500 (M.D.N.C. 2004).

Cordrey v. Euckert, 917 F.2d 1460 (6th Cir. 1990).

D.B. and L.B. ex rel. H.B. v. Gloucester Township School District, 489 F. App'x 564 (3d Cir. 2012).

D.D. ex rel. V.D. v. New York City Board of Education, 465 F.3d 503 (2d Cir. 2006).

Deal ex rel. Deal v. Hamilton County Department of Education, 392 F.3d 840 (6th Cir. 2004).

Doe v. Defendant I, 898 F.2d 1186 (6th Cir. 1990).

Dong v. Board of Education of the Rochester Community Schools, 197 F.3d 703 (6th Cir. 1999).

Doug C. ex rel. Spencer C. v. Hawaii Department of Education, 720 F.3d 1038 (9th Cir. 2013).

Doyle v. Arlington County School Board, 806 F. Supp. 1253 (E.D. Va. 1992).

Edwards-White v. District of Columbia, 785 F. Supp. 1022 (D.D.C. 1992).

E.H. and H.H. v. Tirozzi, 735 F. Supp. 53 (D. Conn. 1990).

Endrew F. ex rel. Joseph F. v. Douglas County School District RE-1, 137 S. Ct. 988 (2017).

Fuhrmann v. East Hanover Board of Education, 993 F.2d 1031 (3d Cir. 1993).

Gerstmyer v. Howard County Public Schools, 850 F. Supp. 361 (D. Md. 1994).

Hampton School District v. Dobrowolski, 976 F.2d 48 (1st Cir. 1992).

J.L., M.L., K.L. v. Mercer Island School District, 592 F.3d 938 (9th Cir. 2010).

K.D. ex rel. C.L. v. Department of Education, State of Hawaii, 665 F.3d 1110 (9th Cir. 2011).

Knable v. Bexley City School District, 238 F.3d 755 (6th Cir. 2001).

L.R. v. Manheim Township School District, 540 F. Supp.2d 603 (E.D. Pa. 2008).

Marc M. ex rel. Aidan M. v. Department of Education, State of Hawaii, 762 F. Supp.2d 1235 (D. Haw. 2011).

M.C. ex rel. M.N. v. Antelope Valley Union High School District, 858 F.3d 1189 (9th Cir. 2017).

Mehfoud, K. S., & Osborne, A. G. (1998). Making a successful "interim" placement under the IDEA. *Education Law Reporter, 124*, 7–12. Reprinted in ELA Notes, *33*(7), 3–6 (1998).

M.H. and E.K. ex rel. P.H. v. New York City Department of Education, 685 F.3d 217 (2d Cir. 2012).

M.L. v. Federal Way School District, 394 F.3d 634 (9th Cir. 2005).

M.M.; E.M. ex rel. C.M. v. Lafayette School District, 767 F.3d 842 (9th Cir. 2014).

Myles S. v. Montgomery County Board of Education, 824 F. Supp. 1549 (M.D. Ala. 1993).

Osborne, A. G. (2004). To what extent can procedural violations of the IDEA render an IEP invalid? *Education Law Reporter, 185*, 15–29.

Osborne, A. G., & Mawdsley, R. D. (2013). When does the failure to implement terms of an IEP result in the denial of a FAPE? *Education Law Reporter, 296*, 1–21 (2015).

Pitchford ex rel. M. v. Salem-Keizer School District No. 24J, 155 F. Supp.2d 1213 (D. Or. 2001).

P.J. v. State of Connecticut Board of Education, 788 F. Supp. 673 (D. Conn. 1992).

R.L., S.L. ex rel. O.L. v. Miami-Dade County School Board, 757 F.3d 1173 (11th Cir. 2014).

Rothschild v. Grottenthaler, 907 F.2d 286 (2d Cir. 1990).

R.P. ex rel. R.P. and C.P. v. Alamo Heights Independent School District, 703 F.3d 801 (5th Cir. 2012).

Russell v. Jefferson, 609 F. Supp. 605 (N.D. Cal. 1985).

Scituate School Committee v. Robert B, 795 F.2d 77 (1st Cir. 1986).

Spielberg v. Henrico County Public Schools, 853 F.2d 256 (4th Cir. 1988).

T.P. and S.P. ex rel. S.P. v. Mamaroneck Union Free School District, 554 F.3d 247 (2d Cir. 2009).

Tracy v. Beaufort County Board of Education, 335 F. Supp.2d 675 (D.S.C. 2004).

V.W. and R.W. v. Favolise, 131 F.R.D. 654 (D. Conn. 1990).

W.G. and B.G. v. Board of Trustees of Target Range School District No. 23, 960 F.2d 1479 (9th Cir. 1992).

W.R. and K.R. ex rel. H.R. v. Union Beach Board of Education, 414 F. App'x 499 (3d Cir. 2011).

7

Free Appropriate Public Education (FAPE) in the Least Restrictive Environment (LRE)

Key Concepts and Terms in This Chapter

- Appropriate Education
- Free Appropriate Public Education (FAPE)
- Least Restrictive Environment (LRE)
- Extended School Year Programs (ESY)

The Individuals with Disabilities Education Act (IDEA, 2004) entitles eligible children and youth with disabilities to specialized instruction and services specifically tailored to meet a student's unique special education needs at no cost to parents. Since its inception in 1975, a legal cornerstone of the federal law is that all eligible students are entitled to a free appropriate public education (FAPE). Based on the IDEA statute, FAPE requires that eligible students receive special education and related services that:

1. are provided at public expense, under public supervision and direction, and without charge;
2. meet the standards of the state educational agency;
3. include an appropriate education; and
4. are provided in conformity with the individualized education program (IEP).

(20 U.S.C. § 1402(9))

In addition to the mandatory FAPE requirement, the IDEA 2004 also stipulates that students with disabilities be educated alongside their peers without disabilities "to the maximum extent possible" (20 U.S.C. § 1412).

The creation of the IDEA's LRE provision was heavily influenced by the U.S. Civil Rights Movement, especially the landmark *Brown v. Board of Education* (1954) ruling and subsequent legal efforts to eradicate racial discrimination, segregated schools, and the "separate-but-equal" doctrine in educational settings. As the Supreme Court stated in *Brown*, "Separate educational facilities are inherently unequal" and deprive students of the "benefits they would receive in a(n) . . . integrated school system" (Brown, p. 484). In fact, some researchers and legal scholars view the IDEA's LRE provision akin to the disability community's version of the 1954 *Brown* ruling (Turnbull, Stowe, & Huerta, 2007). Analogous to the *Brown* ruling addressing the prior unequal, systematic segregation of African-American students attending public schools, the IDEA's LRE provision addresses the prior unequal and historical segregation of students with disabilities from public schools. Therefore, under the IDEA's LRE provision, Congress concluded that the research supports the general rule that educating children with disabilities alongside their student peers without disabilities provides an educationally enriching experience. In justifying the IDEA's least restrictive environment provision, Congress states:

almost 30 years of research and experience has demonstrated that the education of children with disabilities can be made more effective by . . . [h]aving high expectations for such children and ensuring their access to the general education curriculum in the regular classroom to the maximum extent possible.

(20 U.S.C. § 1400(c)(5))

More specifically, the least restrictive environment requirement is described in the IDEA statute as:

to the maximum extent appropriate, children with disabilities, including children in public or private institutions or other care facilities, are educated with children who are not disabled, and that special classes, separate schooling, or other removal of children with disabilities from the regular educational environment occurs only when the nature or severity of the disability is such that education in regular classes with the use of supplementary aids and services cannot be achieved satisfactorily.

(20 U.S.C. § 1412)

The IDEA's LRE requirement is one of the few substantive requirements found in the IDEA statute and assumes that any eligible student with a disability will be in a general education classroom "to the maximum extent appropriate" (Colker, 2018). In fact, if an IDEA-eligible student is removed from the regular classroom to a self-contained special education classroom, or similar placement outside the regular classroom, then that student's removal needs to be justified based on the student's individualized education plan, or IEP. The IDEA regulations provide some additional guidance regarding an instance when the removal of a student with disabilities from a regular classroom is legally permissible, stating:

If the nature or severity of the disability is such that education in regular classes with the use of supplementary aids and services cannot be achieved satisfactorily.

(34 C.F.R. § 300.114(a)(2)(ii))

Under the LRE requirement, local school districts also need to maintain a "continuum of alternative placements" to provide students with disabilities with a free appropriate public education (FAPE) mandated in its provisions (34 C.F.R. § 300.115). The LRE's continuum of alternative placements rule, for example, does not allow school districts to justify that a student's placement is not appropriate solely because the school has not made that kind of student placement previously available (Colker, 2018). As Figure 7.1 illustrates, the LRE continuum of alternative student placements range substantially from placements in general education classrooms to private residential facilities to homebound or hospital instruction to instruction in residential facilities. Furthermore, all student placements must be made in the least restrictive environment (LRE) and students with disabilities can be removed from general educational environments only to the extent necessary for them to be provided with special education services (20 U.S.C. § 1412(a)(5)). While individual states are required to adopt policies and procedures consistent with federal law, they may provide greater benefits than those required by the IDEA. If states establish higher standards, parents and children can enforce those higher standards in federal courts (*David D. v. Dartmouth School Committee*, 1985).

This chapter begins with an examination of how the courts have defined the term *appropriate* as used in the IDEA. Then the chapter traces the evolving case law regarding the IDEA's least restrictive environment (LRE) provision, particularly as it relates to the inclusion of students with disabilities in general educational

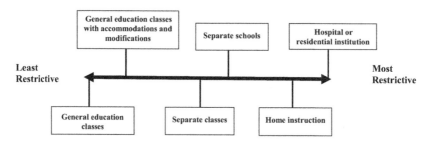

Figure 7.1 Continuum of Alternative Student Placements

settings. Next, the chapter outlines situations in which local school districts may be required to place students with disabilities in private day or residential school facilities. The chapter also looks at circumstances under which local school districts must provide educational programs for students with disabilities beyond the usual 180-day school year. Finally, the chapter examines the most common legal remedies associated with failure to provide a free appropriate public education (FAPE), including tuition reimbursement, compensatory educational services, and attorney fees and costs.

Definition of Appropriate Education

School administrators, special educators, and parents began to speculate about what constituted an appropriate education soon after the IDEA came into law. Yet, the IDEA's language and legislative history provided little guidance. The IDEA's implementing regulations, echoing the statute, stipulate that an appropriate education consists of special education and related services that are provided in conformance with an individualized education program (IEP) (34 C.F.R. § 300.17). Another regulation defines special education as "specially designed instruction, at no cost to the parents, to meet the unique needs of a child with a disability" (34 C.F.R. § 300.38). Insofar as all of these terms and definitions were open to interpretation, it is not surprising that a great deal of the early litigation concerned the meaning of the term *appropriate* as used in the IDEA (Osborne, 1992).

Early judicial opinions and interpretations of the IDEA defined an appropriate education as one that provided more than simple access to educational programs but fell somewhat short of the best that could possibly be provided (O'Hara, 1985). The courts emphasized that although appropriate did not mean best, the educational programs provided needed to be individually tailored to meet the specific needs of students (*Norris v. Massachusetts Department of Education*, 1981; *Rettig v. Kent City School District*, 1986; *Springdale School District v. Grace*, 1981). The courts did support the legal principle that when school personnel proposed IEPs for students with disabilities, they had to be developed to meet the needs of the children rather than those of the school systems (*Anderson v. Thompson*, 1981; *Gladys J. v. Pearland Independent School District*, 1981; *Campbell v. Talladega County Board of Education*, 1981; *Laura M. v. Special School District*, 1980).

Legal Significance of *Board of Education v. Rowley*

In 1982, in *Board of Education of the Hendrick Hudson Central School District v. Rowley*, the first case wherein the Supreme Court resolved a dispute under the IDEA, the Court defined the term appropriate as used in the act. The *Rowley* legal suit was filed based on a dispute over the special education and related services to be provided to a student, Amy Rowley, who was hearing impaired. The student, who had minimal residual hearing but was an excellent lip-reader, was placed in a regular kindergarten class on a trial basis when she entered the public schools. The school's staff took sign-language courses and installed a teletype machine to communicate with her parents, who were also deaf. While the student was given a sign-language interpreter, at the end of the trial period the interpreter reported that these special education services were not needed.

The dispute between the school district and the parents began when officials proposed an IEP for the student's first-grade placement. That IEP called for regular class placement, an FM hearing aid to amplify the spoken words of her teacher and classmates, one hour per day of instruction from a tutor for the deaf, and three hours per week of speech therapy. The parents agreed to the IEP but asked the board to continue the assistance of a sign-language interpreter. When the board refused to provide an interpreter, the parents asked for a due process hearing.

At issue before the U.S. Supreme Court in *Rowley* was the legal question concerning the level of special education services that school officials were required to provide in a student's IEP, and a student's educational placement, in order to be appropriate under the IDEA. In a divided, six-to-three decision, the Supreme Court reversed in favor of the local school district, reasoning that the lower courts erred in interpreting the IDEA as requiring the school district to provide a level of special education services that was such that the potential of students with disabilities must be maximized to be commensurate with opportunities provided to their peers who were not disabled. In *Rowley*, the Supreme Court held that local school districts are not required to provide educational programs that "maximize" the potential of students with disabilities. Instead, the court in *Rowley* offered minimum requirements to satisfy the FAPE provision. When determining whether a student's individualized education plan (IEP) is reasonably calculated to offer an appropriate education under the IDEA, three necessary conditions must be met, including:

1. "[I]f personalized instruction is being provided with sufficient supportive services to permit the child benefit from the instruction, and the other items on the definitional checklists are satisfied, the child is receiving a free appropriate public education is defined by the Act"

(Rowley, p. 189)

2. The "basic floor of opportunity" provided by the Act requires access to specialized instruction and related services which are individually designed to provide "educational benefit to the handicapped child"

(Rowley, p. 201)

3. Access to instruction should be "meaningful"

(Rowley, p. 192)

Trivial Educational Benefit Is Not Sufficient

The *Rowley* decision resulted in considerable ambiguity concerning the meaning of an "appropriate education" since it only addressed that question in the context of a student with disabilities who was receiving significant assistance and performing above grade level (Colker, 2018). Most courts responded to *Rowley* by deciding that IEPs and the educational programs that they called for were appropriate if they resulted in some educational benefit to students, even if the resulting benefits were minimal (Osborne, 1992). In the years immediately following *Rowley*, lower federal courts agreed that Congress only intended for the IDEA to provide students with disabilities with access to educational programs.

The Supreme Court's *Rowley* decision clearly stands for the legal proposition that students with disabilities must be placed in educational programs that confer at least some educational benefit. Approximately three years after *Rowley*, the lower courts began to expand their interpretation of the "*some educational benefit*" criteria. For example, the Fourth Circuit affirmed that *Rowley* allowed the courts to make case-by-case analyses of the substantive standards needed to meet the criteria that IEPs must reasonably have been calculated to enable students to receive educational benefits (*Hall v. Vance County Board of Education*, 1985). In this case, the court agreed that the minimal progress that the student made was insufficient in view of his intellectual potential. The court thought that Congress certainly did not intend for this, or any, school board to provide programs that produced only trivial academic advancements.

Best Available Educational Option Is Not Legally Required

Rowley made it clear that local school districts are not required to develop IEPs designed to maximize the potential of students with disabilities. In *Rowley*, the Court rejected the notion that the IDEA requires programs to provide students with disabilities with opportunities to achieve their full potential commensurate with the chances afforded peers who are not disabled.

In accord with *Rowley*, lower courts unanimously agreed that school boards are not required to maximize the potential of children with disabilities insofar as they are only obligated to meet the some educational benefit standard (*J.S.K. v. Hendry County School Board*, 1991).

In *Rowley* the Supreme Court cautioned judges not to substitute their views of proper educational methodology for that of competent school officials. Most jurists, recognizing that they are not experts in the field of education, typically defer to school officials on matters of methodology. It is thus well-settled that parents do not have the right to compel school boards to provide specific programs or employ specific methodologies (*Blackmon v. Springfield R-XII School District*, 1999; *Logue v. Shawnee Mission Public School Unified School District No. 512*, 1998; *Renner v. Board of Education of the Public Schools of the City of Ann Arbor*, 1999; *Tucker v. Calloway County Board of Education*, 1998). In this regard, a federal trial court in Kansas commented that the IDEA did not require a school board to use one proven method over another (*O'Toole v. Olathe District Schools Unified School District No. 233*, 1998). The Second Circuit explained that the fact that experts privately hired by parents may have recommended a different methodology did not undermine the deference that the judiciary owed to school officials (*Watson ex rel. Watson v. Kingston City School District*, 2005). As such, courts ordinarily support proposals from school board officials as long as the programs they select meet the IDEA's standards of appropriateness and are based on legitimate educational methodologies (*Dong v. Board of Education of the Rochester Community Schools*, 1999; *E.S. v. Independent School District, No 196*, 1998).

The Effect(s) of Individual State Standards

States may establish standards of appropriateness that are higher than the federal benchmark set in *Rowley*. In fact, the Court emphasized that programs also must meet state educational standards in order to be appropriate. The First Circuit noted that the IDEA incorporates state procedural and substantive standards that exceed the federal level by reference (*Burlington School Committee v. Department of Education of the Commonwealth of Massachusetts*, 1985). When state standards exceed their federal counterparts, the former are employed in evaluating whether proposed IEPs are appropriate. Even though the vast majority of jurisdictions have statutes and regulations that define an appropriate education in a manner not unlike the federal standard, at least five states have established higher standards.

Courts agree that North Carolina (*Burke County Board of Education v. Denton*, 1990), New Jersey (*Geis v. Board of Education of Parsippany-Troy Hills*, 1985), Michigan (*Barwacz v. Michigan Department of Education*, 1988), Missouri (*Lagares v. Camdenton R-III School District*, 2001), and California (*Pink v. Mt. Diablo Unified School District*, 1990) have higher standards of appropriateness. These courts treated the higher state standards as incorporated into federal law because one of the IDEA's requirements is that special education programs must meet "the standards of the state educational agency" (20 U.S.C. § 1401(9)(B)). To this end, state statutes may require school boards to provide programs to maximize the potential of students with disabilities commensurate with the educational opportunities provided to their peers who are not disabled (*Brimmer v. Traverse City Area Public Schools*, 1994). In these states, the *Rowley* standard simply does not apply because it has been superseded.

Clarifying the *Rowley* FAPE Standard: The Impact of *Endrew F.*

While the defining legal case addressing the term "appropriate" under FAPE continues to be *Board of Education v. Rowley* (1982), a recent decision by the U.S. Supreme Court, *Endrew F. v. Douglas County School District RE-1* (2017) has helped clarify the existing *Rowley* standard. On March 22, 2017, the U.S. Supreme Court issued a unanimous ruling in *Endrew F. v. Douglas Country School District RE-1* finding that the lower *de minimus*, or the "slightly more than trivial" educational benefit standard is inappropriate for successfully conferring a FAPE for eligible students receiving special education and related services. As stated by Chief Justice Roberts, who wrote the majority opinion in the *Endrew F.* decision, "a student offered an educational program providing merely more than de minimus progress from year to year can hardly be said to have been offered an education at all" (*Endrew F.*, 2017, p. 1001). Essentially, the Supreme Court rejected the *de minimus* test as being inconsistent with the *existing Rowley* decision's focus on a student's IEP to produce adequate educational benefits (Colker, 2018).

The *Endrew F.* case was brought by parents on behalf of their son Endrew, a student diagnosed with autism spectrum disorder (ASD) and attention deficit/hyperactivity disorder (ADHD), who attended the Douglas County School District from preschool to the fourth grade. Endrew's parents claimed their son was not provided appropriate special education programming as legally required under the IDEA. More specifically, Endrew's parents believed the strategies used by the school district to address his challenging behaviors did not improve his learning. Behaviors of concern were when Endrew would scream in class, climb over furniture and other students, and occasionally run away from school. Additionally, Endrew had phobias to things such as flies, spills, and public restrooms. According to his parents, "Endrew's [Individualized Education Programs (IEPs)] largely carried over the same basic goals and objectives from one year to the next, indicating that he was failing to make meaningful progress toward his aims" (*Endrew F.*, 2017, p. 996). At the end of fourth grade, when the school district failed to change Endrew's goals and objectives, his parents enrolled him in Firefly Autism, a private school setting. Within a month his parents noticed a major difference allowing him to make academic improvements that never occurred while enrolled in public school.

Interestingly, prior to the case coming before the Supreme Court, the school district legally prevailed at all levels, including the U.S. Court of Appeals for the Tenth Circuit. In each instance, the court ruled that Endrew's IEP met the existing IDEA's FAPE requirement as long as it was calculated to confer "educational benefit mandated by IDEA must merely be 'more than *de minimus*'" (*Endrew F.*, 2017, p. 1338). However, the Supreme Court mandated a far more robust, outcome-oriented FAPE standard. In *Endrew F.* (2017), the Supreme Court articulated a *new* FAPE standard, clarifying that FAPE is required to be "appropriately ambitious in light of his circumstances" (p. 992) [and must be] "markedly more demanding than the 'merely more than de minimus'" (p. 1000) with the expectation that a student with disability's educational program should be designed with parents and schools working collaboratively throughout the IEP process to ensure that parents and school leaders have opportunities to "fully air their respective opinions" (p. 993) to create an individualized program that (a) includes goals that are appropriately ambitious for each student, (b) recognizes goals differ between students, and (c) affords each student an opportunity "to meet challenging objectives" (*Endrew F.*, 2017, p. 992). This new standard established by the Supreme Court rejected the argument set by federal courts that "some educational benefit" is defined as any benefit above no benefit at all (Prince, Yell, & Katsiyannis, 2018). As stated by Chief Justice Roberts "a student offered an educational program providing merely more than *de minimus progress* from year to year can hardly be said to have been offered an education at all" (*Endrew F.*, 2017, p. 1001). While the Supreme Court's 2017 decision in *Endrew F.* did not expressly overrule the Supreme Court's 1982 *Rowley* ruling, it has clarified the existing FAPE standard.

For over three decades, the nation's courts have struggled to legally define what FAPE means for students with disabilities. As a result, this lack of legal clarity and guidance regarding the use of the appropriate FAPE legal standard has placed today's school personnel and parents of students with disabilities in challenging situations of trying to interpret the FAPE standard under the IDEA with limited guidance. The Supreme Court's *Endrew F.* decision has clarified, but not replaced, the prior *Rowley* legal standard for meeting the FAPE provision of IDEA. More specifically, the Supreme Court's *Endrew F.* decision did clarify that a student's progress on their IEP must be considerably more demanding than the "*merely de minimis*" standard previously applied by many courts. An important legal takeaway from the *Endrew F.* ruling is that any review of a student's IEP must address the issue of whether the IEP is reasonable and that determination must be made on an individual, case-by-case basis. In making these determinations, the Supreme Court in *Endrew F.* stressed that deference be given to local school officials, who use evidence-based practices (EBP), including timely data and assessments to accurately determine a student's appropriate level of progress.

Least Restrictive Environment (LRE)

One of the main tenets of the IDEA is that all placements for students with disabilities must be in the least restrictive environment (LRE). Under this provision, students with disabilities can be removed from general educational environments only to the extent necessary for them to be provided with special education services (20 U.S.C. § 1412(a)(5)). This does not, however, mean that students with disabilities can never be placed in restrictive settings. The basic principle is that each student should be placed in the setting that is least restrictive for that child. When developing Individualized Education Programs (IEPs) for students with disabilities, school personnel must balance their needs for specialized, special education services with the nonacademic benefits gained from the inclusion of students with disabilities alongside their nondisabled student peers in regular classrooms.

Consistent with the IDEA, school districts must establish procedures to ensure that students with disabilities are educated with children who do not have disabilities to the maximum extent appropriate. Thus, the IDEA allows school boards to place children with disabilities in special classes and/or separate facilities or remove them from the general education environment only when the nature or severity of their disabilities is such that instruction in general education classes cannot be achieved satisfactorily, even with supplementary aids and services. These provisions apply to students in private schools, institutions, and/or other care facilities as well as to students in public schools and facilities (20 U.S.C. § 1412(a)(5)(A)).

The terms *least restrictive environment*, *inclusion*, and *mainstreaming*, while often used interchangeably, are distinct. The difference between inclusion and mainstreaming is one of degree. Mainstreaming refers to the practice of placing special education class students in general education classes for a portion of the school day. Inclusion, on the other hand, refers to a philosophy where students with disabilities are enrolled in general education classes and are removed only when necessary to receive special education services. In many situations, special education services are provided within the general education environment so that students are not removed at all. *LRE* is the legal term used in the IDEA. The IDEA does not require inclusion in every situation but does mandate that all children be educated in environments that are the least restrictive possible and that removal from general education occur only when necessary.

The IDEA Does Not Prohibit Segregated Placements

When the IDEA was first implemented, courts weighed the benefits of student placements in less restrictive settings against the advantages of providing greater or more specialized services in segregated settings (*Bonadonna v. Cooperman*, 1985). Early courts typically agreed that the LRE mandate was secondary to the provision of an appropriate instructional program (*Johnston v. Ann Arbor Public Schools*, 1983).

Insofar as the IDEA is premised on the notion that students with disabilities may be removed from the general education environment only to the extent necessary to provide needed special education services, one task hearing officers and courts face is to determine whether required services warrant removal from the general education environment or if they can be provided in less restrictive settings. Even so, in the early days of the IDEA, courts agreed that the LRE requirement could not be used to preclude placements in segregated settings when such placements were necessary to provide students with a FAPE (*Board of Education of East Windsor Regional School District v. Diamond*, 1986; *St. Louis Developmental Disabilities Center v. Mallory*, 1984). The courts thus allowed placements in restrictive environments when school officials showed that they could not deliver satisfactory education for children with disabilities in less restrictive settings, even with supplementary aids and services (*Lachman v. Illinois State Board of Education*, 1988; *Wilson v. Marana Unified School District*, 1984). Even with the more recent emphasis on inclusion, these legal principles are still valid.

Federal Courts Still Split on What Is "Appropriate" LRE

Given the current absence of a Supreme Court decision providing guidance on interpreting what is an "appropriate" student placement in the least restrictive environment, there are a number of federal U.S. Circuit Court of Appeals decisions that can serve as useful guides to school officials for "best practices" in determining LRE for eligible student with disabilities (Rozalski, Steward, & Miller, 2010). Table 7.1 outlines the leading federal legal cases and the questions IEP team members should consider when making an LRE placement.

In the 1980s most courts deciding LRE issues agreed that mainstreaming was not required for every student with disabilities but had to be provided, where appropriate, to the maximum extent feasible. While recognizing the social benefits of inclusion, these courts nevertheless asserted that students should not be placed in general education solely for the sake of inclusion. In balancing the need for specialized services against the LRE provision of the IDEA, early courts tipped the scales in favor of specialized services. In one notable exception, the Sixth Circuit, acknowledging that the IDEA does not require mainstreaming or inclusion in every case, commented that it only had to be provided to the maximum extent appropriate (*Roncker v. Walter*, 1983). In what has become known as the portability standard, the court wrote that if the services that make particular placements better could be provided in less segregated settings, then the more restrictive placement would be inappropriate.

Towards the end of the 1980s and extending into the 1990s, the LRE provision of the IDEA played a more prominent role in litigation concerning the proper placement for students with disabilities. During this time, courts departed from previous case law and tipped the scales in favor of inclusive programming for students with severe disabilities. As a result of cases from the Third (*Oberti v. Board of Education of the Borough of Clementon School District*, 1993), Fifth (*Daniel R.R. v. State Board of Education*, 1989), Ninth (*Sacramento City Unified School District, Board of Education v. Rachel H.*, 1994), and Eleventh (*Greer v. Rome City School District*, 1991) Circuits, courts now view the LRE provision as a mandatory requirement rather than a general goal of the IDEA.

Table 7.1 Questions for Consideration When an IEP Team Is Making an LRE Decision

Court Case	Federal Circuit Court	Questions to Consider Based on Court Ruling
Clyde K. v. Puyallup School District (1994)	9th	• Is the student making adequate progress in benefiting academically from a general education placement?
Daniel R.R. v. Board of Education (1989)	5th	*Daniel Two-Part Test* • Can the education be achieved in the general education classroom with supplemental services? • If the student is placed in a restrictive setting, is the student integrated to the maximum extent possible?
Flour Bluff School District v. Katherine M. (1996)	5th	• Is the student placed in the school and district that is closest to home? • Does the school closest to home have the support/resources necessary for an appropriate education program for the student?
Greer v. Rome City School District (1991) Oberti v. Board of Education (1993)	11th 3d	• Is a placement in the least restrictive environment (general education classroom) appropriate for the student's needs? • If so, will the student receive an appropriate education with supplemental aids and services?
Hartmann v. Lououn County Board of Education (1997)	4th	• Is the student placed with nondisabled peers to the maximum extent appropriate under the IDEA?
Poolaw v. Bishop (1995)	9th	• Will mainstreaming the student be the most academically beneficial placement for them?
Roncker v. Walter (1983)	6th	*Roncker Portability Test* • If a segregated student setting appears to be the preferable placement, could the special education services provided in the segregated setting be feasibly provided in a setting that is not segregated?

Source: Rozalski, M., Stewart, A., & Miller, J. (2010). How to determine the least restrictive environment for students with disabilities. *Exceptionality, 18*, 151–163.

The Fifth Circuit provided considerable guidance on the LRE issue in *Daniel R.R. v. State Board of Education (Daniel R.R)* (1989). Although the court affirmed that a substantially separate class was appropriate for a child with Down syndrome, it offered a general test for evaluating when students could be removed from general education settings. The court stipulated that students with severe disabilities may be removed from the general education environment when they cannot be satisfactorily educated in such a setting. To assist lower courts with LRE decisions, the court developed a test for determining when school boards have met their obligations under the LRE provision.

Echoing language from the statute, the Fifth Circuit instructed lower courts to first examine whether education in general classrooms with supplementary aids and services could have been achieved satisfactorily. If an appropriate education could not be achieved in an inclusive setting, and school personnel needed to place children in special education classes, the court directed trial courts to consider whether schools included students in general education to the maximum extent appropriate. When answering this two-part inquiry, the Fifth Circuit advised lower courts to consider the ability of students to grasp the general education curriculum, the nature and severity of their disabilities, the effect that their presence would have on the functioning of the general education classroom, their overall experience in the general education setting, and the amount of exposure the special education students would have to children who are not disabled. The Fifth Circuit's two-part became the benchmark for LRE cases in the years that followed. Other courts expanded on the *Daniel R.R.* test to provide a comprehensive set of guidelines for reviewing whether school boards have met their LRE obligations.

Decisions Ordering Less Restrictive Placements

The Eleventh Circuit, citing *Daniel R.R.*, upheld an earlier order placing a student with Down syndrome in a general education classroom (*Greer v. Rome City School District*, 1991). According to the court, before school boards could place children outside the general education setting, IEP teams must evaluate whether their education can be achieved satisfactorily with one or more supplemental aids or services. When making such a determination, the court explained school boards should assess the educational benefits that children will receive in regular classes as opposed to the benefits they might acquire in special education environments. Observing that academic achievement is not the only benefit of inclusion, the court added that boards should also consider the nonacademic benefits that children will receive, the effect that students with disabilities will have on classrooms and the education of peers, and the cost of the supplemental aids and services. Still, the court noted that inclusion may not be appropriate if children would make significantly more progress in special education settings rather than in general education classrooms.

The Third Circuit enunciated guidelines on the extent to which school boards must go before recommending more restrictive placements. In another case involving the placement of a student with Down syndrome, the federal trial court in New Jersey insisted that school boards have an affirmative obligation to consider placing students with disabilities in general education classrooms with the use of supplementary aids and services before exploring other alternatives (*Oberti v. Board of Education of the Borough of Clementon School District*, 1993). Citing the Fifth Circuit's *Daniel R.R.* test, the court maintained that to meet the IDEA's goals, school officials must maximize opportunities for inclusion. The trial court contended that the preference for placements in the LRE can be rebutted only if officials can show that students' disabilities are so severe that they will receive little or no benefit from inclusion in regular classrooms, that they are so disruptive that the education of peers is impaired, or that the cost of providing supplementary services will have a negative effect on the provision of services to other children.

The trial court added that the IDEA requires school boards to supplement and realign their resources to move beyond the systems, structures, and practices that tend to unnecessarily segregate students with disabilities. The court recognized that including the student at the center of this case in a general education classroom clearly would have required a modification of the curriculum but declared that this alone was not a legitimate basis on which to justify his exclusion. Describing inclusion as a right, not a privilege for a select few, the court placed ultimate responsibility on the board to show that the student could not have been educated in a general education setting with supplementary aids and services. Inasmuch as school officials were unable to do as the court directed, it ordered them to develop an inclusive educational plan for the student.

On review, the Third Circuit affirmed the original order but applied a slightly different rationale. The court adopted the Fifth Circuit's *Daniel R.R.* two-part test but expanded it with the notation that the judiciary should also consider the benefits that students with disabilities would receive in regular classrooms as opposed to segregated settings, along with the possible negative effects that their inclusion could have on the education of other children. The court agreed that a fundamental value of the right of a student with disabilities to an education is to associate with peers who do not have disabilities. The court emphasized that a full range of supplementary aids and services must be available to modify regular classroom programs to accommodate students with disabilities and the fact that these children may learn differently from their being placed in general educational settings did not justify their exclusion from these kinds of placements.

In another major LRE dispute, the Ninth Circuit combined elements of the three previous decisions in providing a general summary of a school board's obligations (*Sacramento City Unified School District, Board of Education v. Rachel H.*, 1994). In affirming an earlier order, the Ninth Circuit decided school officials must consider four factors when devising LREs for students: the educational benefits of placements in regular classrooms, the nonacademic benefits of such placements, the effect that students would have on their teachers and other children in classes, and the costs of inclusion.

Hybrid Placements

While students with mild to moderate disabilities may benefit most from education in inclusive environments, those with more severe disabilities requiring specialized services may need to be removed from general education for a portion of each day to receive the needed services. Thus, many students' IEPs call for a mix of general and special education class placements. In one such situation the Second Circuit agreed with a lower court that a school board made reasonable efforts to facilitate a student's placement in general education for a significant portion of the school day, as he required some services in a more segregated setting to increase his focus and minimize distractions (*P. ex rel. Mr. P. v. Newington Board of Education*, 2008). The Ninth Circuit was satisfied that a blended program was better suited to the student's needs and abilities and was sufficient to overcome the preference for mainstreaming (*B.S. ex rel. R.S. and P.S. v. Placentia-Yorba Linda Unified School District*, 2009).

As students with disabilities advance through the educational system it can become more difficult to provide genuine inclusion in academic classes because the gap between their achievement levels and those of their peers widens. This was illustrated in a case from Michigan where the school board proposed an IEP that called for a student with Down syndrome to spend more time in special education when he entered high school. The federal trial court found that the student, whose achievement levels ranged from kindergarten to second grade, would not benefit from attending core academic classes in general education because he could not participate in those classes, take similar tests, or achieve at a level comparable to other ninth grade students (*Dick-Friedman ex rel. Friedman v. Board of Education of West Bloomfield Public Schools*, 2006).

More recently, the Sixth Circuit affirmed a lower court's ruling that a segregated special education class was too restrictive for a student with Down syndrome who had previously been educated in a general education setting (*L.H. v. Hamilton County Department of Education*, 2018). Even though the child's behavior had become more disruptive, the court saw that mainstreaming had provided him with some educational benefit. The court commented that a child does not need to master the general education curriculum for mainstreaming to be a viable option, but rather, the appropriate measure is whether the child, with supplemental aids and services can make progress toward the IEP goals in a general education setting.

Legal Decisions Approving More Restrictive Placements

The preceding opinions notwithstanding, school boards may place students in more restrictive settings when necessary. In fact, the Ninth Circuit applied its own test in affirming that officials had the authority to transfer a student with serious behavioral problems to an off-campus alternative program (*Clyde K. v. Puyallup School District*, 1994). After ascertaining that the student's disruptive behavior prevented him from learning in a general education setting and that he was receiving minimal nonacademic benefits from inclusion, the court approved the transfer. The court was persuaded by evidence that the student's presence had a negative effect on the staff and other children in the general education setting. In subsequent cases approving segregated placements, the same court was satisfied that inclusion that results in total failure is inappropriate (*Capistrano Unified School District v. Wartenberg*, 1995) and that some students may not derive any benefit from inclusion until they develop other skills (*Poolaw v. Bishop*, 1995).

Students may be moved from general educational environments to more restrictive settings if they are not making sufficient progress. The Fourth Circuit affirmed that a student with autism would not receive an appropriate education at a public high school and that the vocational school provided an appropriate education in the least restrictive environment (*DeVries v. Fairfax County School Board*, 1989). The court noted that the trial court found that the student had depressed cognitive and academic functioning, exhibited immature behavior, had difficulty with interpersonal communication and relationships, and required a predictable environment. That same court also allowed a school board to transfer a student with autism to a self-contained special education class after finding that the evidence clearly demonstrated that he failed to make academic progress in a regular classroom even with supplementary aids and services (*Hartman v. Loudoun County Board of Education*, 1997).

The Fifth Circuit upheld a school board's proposal to place a student in special education classes for science and social studies after concluding that he had not benefitted from general education classes in those subjects, even with accommodations (*J.H. ex rel. A.H. and S.H. v. Fort Bend Independent School District*, 2012). The court also observed that the student had not received any nonacademic benefit from placement in general education and that his misbehavior increased as classes became more difficult. Further, the Seventh Circuit permitted the transfer of a student with severe disabilities to a more restrictive setting after seeing that her academic progress in inclusionary settings was practically nonexistent (*Beth B. v. Van Clay*, 2002).

As in the other cases, the student received supplementary aids and services in the general education setting. Similarly, the Tenth Circuit also approved a more restrictive placement when a child could not be educated in a regular classroom even with supplementary aids and services (*T.W. ex rel. McCullough v. Unified School District No. 259*, 2005).

The Seventh Circuit, commenting that a student's history in a public school setting with special education and related services was disastrous, affirmed a homebound instruction program (*School District of Wisconsin Dells v. Z.S. ex rel. Littlegeorge*, 2002). Since the student had a long record of assaulting peers and staff members, the court was satisfied that school administrators were reasonable in thinking that he would not have functioned in a regular school environment (Hazelkorn, 2004).

Student Placements in Neighborhood Schools

The LRE mandate does not require school boards to place students in their neighborhood schools in all situations. For reasons of economy, many school systems centralize parts of their special education programs, a practice that the courts have consistently upheld. For example, the federal trial court in Virginia approved, and the Fourth Circuit affirmed, a centralized program for a high school student who was hearing impaired (*Barnett v. Fairfax County School Board*, 1991). The high school that the student was required to attend was located five miles farther from his home than the neighborhood school and his parents, objecting to this arrangement, requested that a similar program be developed in the neighborhood school. His parents argued that the student was earning satisfactory grades, was participating in extracurricular activities, and was successfully included in the general education program, so the court approved the centralized placement. Acknowledging the limited resources available to school boards, the court reasoned that centralized programs better served the interests of all students. The court concluded that centralizing programs for children with low-incidence disabilities allows school boards to better provide for all their students. Using a similar rationale, the Fifth Circuit approved the placement of a hearing-impaired student in a regional school program (*Flour Bluff Independent School District v. Katherine M.*, 1996).

The Eighth Circuit approved a centralized program for a student who requires a wheelchair, stating that the school board was not required to modify her neighborhood school to make it accessible (*Schuldt v. Mankato Independent School District No. 77*, 1991). Along the same vein, the First Circuit approved the placement of a student who had medical concerns in a program some distance from his home because it had a full-time nurse (*Kevin G. by Jo-Ann G. v. Cranston School Committee*, 1997). Collectively, these rulings show that if the services that students need are available only at centralized locations, the IDEA does not require school boards to duplicate them in neighborhood schools. In fact, school officials have significant authority to select school sites for providing special education and related services for students with disabilities (*White v. Ascension Parish School Board*, 2003).

Student Placements Should Be as Close to Home as Possible

When it is not feasible for students with disabilities to be educated in their neighborhood schools, The IDEA's regulations require their placements to be as close to their homes as possible (34 C.F.R. § 300.116(a)(3)). This is particularly important when placements must be made outside school district boundaries as is illustrated by an order from the federal trial court in New Jersey. The court approved a mother's request to have her daughter with autism transferred from the facility she attended to one closer to her home (*Remis v. New Jersey Department of Human Services*, 1993). The court was convinced that the requested placement would have provided the child with an education that was comparable to the one that she received but would have been located within her hometown. In another case, the Tenth Circuit, acknowledging that students with disabilities should attend the schools they would have gone to if they were not disabled unless their IEPs required other arrangements, noted that when students' IEPs call for other arrangements, placements should be as close to their homes as possible (*Murray v. Montrose County School District*, 1995). The court added that the preference for placing students in neighborhood schools did not amount to a mandate.

LRE and Extended School Year (ESY) Programs

Providing extended school year (ESY) programs in an inclusive setting can be challenging for school boards, particularly if they do not offer general education during school vacations. Courts have been mixed regarding the applicability of the LRE provision when providing services to students with disabilities beyond the traditional school calendar. The Second Circuit posited that a summer program was part of a child's overall placement and was subject to the same LRE requirement (*T.M. ex rel. A.M. v. Cornwall Central School District*, 2014). The court advised that an ESY program is defined by the child's disabilities and needs, not the placements the board chooses to offer. In contrast, the Eleventh Circuit insisted that the IDEA did not require a school board to create a mainstream summer program to serve the needs of one student (*A.L. v. Jackson County School Board*, 2015). The court reasoned that the board was required to offer the child the least restrictive appropriate option in its continuum of placements. Similarly, a federal trial court in Pennsylvania was convinced that because a school board was not required to provide summer school to general education students, it could not mainstream a student with disabilities during his ESY program (*Travis G. v. New Hope-Solebury School District*, 2008).

⚖️

SPECIAL EDUCATION LAW IN PRACTICE
Legal Case No. 8—Definition of Free Appropriate Public Education (FAPE)

BOARD OF EDUCATION OF THE HENDRICK HUDSON CENTRAL SCHOOL DISTRICT V. ROWLEY
Supreme Court of the United States, 1982

458 U.S. 176

Justice REHNQUIST delivered the opinion of the Court.

This case presents a question of statutory interpretation. Petitioners contend that the Court of Appeals and the District Court misconstrued the requirements imposed by Congress upon States which receive federal funds under the Education of the Handicapped Act. We agree and reverse the judgment of the Court of Appeals.

I

The Education of the Handicapped Act (Act) [now IDEA] ... provides federal money to assist state and local agencies in educating handicapped children, and conditions such funding upon a State's compliance with extensive goals and procedures. The Act represents an ambitious federal effort to promote the education of handicapped children, ... The Act's evolution and major provisions shed light on the question of statutory interpretation which is at the heart of this case ....

In order to qualify for federal financial assistance under the Act, a State must demonstrate that it "has in effect a policy that assures all handicapped children the right to a free appropriate public education." ...

The "free appropriate public education" required by the Act is tailored to the unique needs of the handicapped child by means of an "individualized educational program" (IEP) .... The IEP, which is prepared at a meeting between a qualified representative of the local educational agency, the child's teacher, the child's parents or guardian, and, where appropriate, the child, consists of a written document....

II

This case arose in connection with the education of Amy Rowley, a deaf student at the Furnace Woods School in the Hendrick Hudson Central School District, Peekskill, N.Y. Amy has minimal residual hearing and is an excellent lipreader. During the

year before she began attending Furnace Woods, a meeting between her parents and school administrators resulted in a decision to place her in a regular kindergarten class in order to determine what supplemental services would be necessary to her education. Several members of the school administration prepared for Amy's arrival by attending a course in sign-language interpretation, and a teletype machine was installed in the principal's office to facilitate communication with her parents who are also deaf. At the end of the trial period it was determined that Amy should remain in the kindergarten class, but that she should be provided with an FM hearing aid which would amplify words spoken into a wireless receiver by the teacher or fellow students during certain classroom activities. Amy successfully completed her kindergarten year.

As required by the Act, an IEP was prepared for Amy during the fall of her first-grade year. The IEP provided that Amy should be educated in a regular classroom at Furnace Woods, should continue to use the FM hearing aid, and should receive instruction from a tutor for the deaf for one hour each day and from a speech therapist for three hours each week. The Rowleys agreed with parts of the IEP, but insisted that Amy also be provided a qualified sign-language interpreter in all her academic classes in lieu of the assistance proposed in other parts of the IEP. Such an interpreter had been placed in Amy's kindergarten class for a 2-week experimental period, but the interpreter had reported that Amy did not need his services at that time. The school administrators likewise concluded that Amy did not need such an interpreter in her first-grade classroom. They reached this conclusion after consulting the school district's Committee on the Handicapped, which had received expert evidence from Amy's parents on the importance of a sign-language interpreter, received testimony from Amy's teacher and other persons familiar with her academic and social progress, and visited a class for the deaf.

When their request for an interpreter was denied, the Rowleys demanded and received a hearing before an independent examiner. After receiving evidence from both sides, the examiner agreed with the administrators' determination that an interpreter was not necessary because "Amy was achieving educationally, academically, and socially" without such assistance. . . . The examiner's decision was affirmed on appeal by the New York Commissioner of Education on the basis of substantial evidence in the record. . . . Pursuant to the Act's provision for judicial review, the Rowleys then brought an action in the United States District Court for the Southern District of New York, claiming that the administrators' denial of the sign-language interpreter constituted a denial of the "free appropriate public education" guaranteed by the Act.

The District Court found that Amy "is a remarkably well-adjusted child" who interacts and communicates well with her classmates and has "developed an extraordinary rapport" with her teachers. . . . It also found that "she performs better than the average child in her class and is advancing easily from grade to grade," but "that she understands considerably less of what goes on in class than she could if she were not deaf" and thus "is not learning as much, or performing as well academically, as she would without her handicap," This disparity between Amy's achievement and her potential led the court to decide that she was not receiving a "free appropriate public education," which the court defined as "an opportunity to achieve [her] full potential commensurate with the opportunity provided to other children." . . . According to the District Court, such a standard "requires that the potential of the handicapped child be measured and compared to his or her performance, and that the resulting differential or 'shortfall' be compared to the shortfall experienced by nonhandicapped children." The District Court's definition arose from its assumption that the responsibility for "giv[ing] content to the requirement of an 'appropriate education'" had "been left entirely to the [federal] courts and the hearing officers." . . .

A divided panel of the United States Court of Appeals for the Second Circuit affirmed. The Court of Appeals "agree[d] with the [D]istrict [C]ourt's conclusions of law," and held that its "findings of fact [were] not clearly erroneous." . . .

We granted certiorari to review the lower courts' interpretation of the Act. . . . Such review requires us to consider two questions: What is meant by the Act's requirement of a "free appropriate public education"? And what is the role of state and federal courts in exercising the review granted by [the Act]? We consider these questions separately.

III

A

This is the first case in which this Court has been called upon to interpret any provision of the Act. As noted previously, the District Court and the Court of Appeals concluded that "[t]he Act itself does not define 'appropriate education,'" . . . but leaves "to the courts and the hearing officers" the responsibility of "giv[ing] content to the requirement of an 'appropriate education. . . . '" Petitioners contend that the definition of the phrase "free appropriate public education" used by the courts below overlooks the definition of that phrase actually found in the Act. Respondents agree that the Act defines "free appropriate public education," but contend that the statutory definition is not "functional" and thus "offers judges no guidance in their consideration of controversies involving 'the identification, evaluation, or educational placement of the child or the provision of a free appropriate public education. . . . '" The United States, appearing as *amicus curiae* on behalf of respondents, states that "[a]lthough the Act includes definitions of a 'free appropriate public education' and other related terms, the statutory definitions do not adequately explain what is meant by 'appropriate.' . . ."

We are loath to conclude that Congress failed to offer any assistance in defining the meaning of the principal substantive phrase used in the Act. It is beyond dispute that, contrary to the conclusions of the courts below, the Act does expressly define "free appropriate public education":

"The term 'free appropriate public education' means *special education* and *related services* which (A) have been provided at public expense, under public supervision and direction, and without charge, (B) meet the standards of the State educational agency, (C) include an appropriate preschool, elementary, or secondary school education in the State involved, and (D) are provided in conformity with the individualized education program required under [this Act]."

"Special education," as referred to in this definition, means "specially designed instruction, at no cost to parents or guardians, to meet the unique needs of a handicapped child, including classroom instruction, instruction in physical education, home instruction, and instruction in hospitals and institutions." . . . "Related services" are defined as "transportation, and such developmental, corrective, and other supportive services . . . as may be required to assist a handicapped child to benefit from special education."

Like many statutory definitions, this one tends toward the cryptic rather than the comprehensive, but that is scarcely a reason for abandoning the quest for legislative intent

According to the definitions contained in the Act, a "free appropriate public education" consists of educational instruction specially designed to meet the unique needs of the handicapped child, supported by such services as are necessary to permit the child "to benefit" from the instruction. Almost as a checklist for adequacy under the Act, the definition also requires that such instruction and services be provided at public expense and under public supervision, meet the State's educational standards, approximate the grade levels used in the State's regular education, and comport with the child's IEP. Thus, if personalized instruction is being provided with sufficient supportive services to permit the child to benefit from the instruction, and the other items on the definitional checklist are satisfied, the child is receiving a "free appropriate public education" as defined by the Act.

Other portions of the statute also shed light upon congressional intent. Congress found that of the roughly eight million handicapped children in the United States at the time of enactment, one million were "excluded entirely from the public school system" and more than half were receiving an inappropriate education. . . . When these express statutory findings and priorities are read together with the Act's extensive procedural requirements and its definition of "free appropriate public education," the face of the statute evinces a congressional intent to bring previously excluded handicapped children into the public education systems of the States and to require the States to adopt *procedures* which would result in individualized consideration of and instruction for each child.

Noticeably absent from the language of the statute is any substantive standard prescribing the level of education to be accorded handicapped children. Certainly the language of the statute contains no requirement like the one imposed by the lower courts-that States maximize the potential of handicapped children "commensurate with the opportunity provided to other children." . . . That standard was expounded by the District Court without reference to the statutory definitions or even to the legislative history of the Act. Although we find the statutory definition of "free appropriate public education" to be helpful in our interpretation of the Act, there remains the question of whether the legislative history indicates a congressional intent that such education meet some

additional substantive standard. For an answer, we turn to that history.

B

(i)

. . . By passing the Act, Congress sought primarily to make public education available to handicapped children. But in seeking to provide such access to public education, Congress did not impose upon the States any greater substantive educational standard than would be necessary to make such access meaningful. Indeed, Congress expressly "recognize[d] that in many instances the process of providing special education and related services to handicapped children is not guaranteed to produce any particular outcome." . . . Thus, the intent of the Act was more to open the door of public education to handicapped children on appropriate terms than to guarantee any particular level of education once inside.

Both the House and the Senate Reports attribute the impetus for the Act and its predecessors to two federal court judgments rendered in 1971 and 1972. As the Senate Report states, passage of the Act "followed a series of landmark court cases establishing in law the right to education for all handicapped children." . . . The first case, *Pennsylvania Assn. for Retarded Children v. Commonwealth* (PARC), was a suit on behalf of retarded children challenging the constitutionality of a Pennsylvania statute which acted to exclude them from public education and training. The case ended in a consent decree which enjoined the State from "deny[ing] to any mentally retarded child *access* to a free public program of education and training." . . .

PARC was followed by *Mills v. Board of Education of District of Columbia*, . . . a case in which the plaintiff handicapped children had been excluded from the District of Columbia public schools. The court's judgment . . . provided that

"no [handicapped] child eligible for a publicly supported education in the District of Columbia public schools shall be *excluded* from a regular school assignment by a Rule, policy, or practice of the Board of Education of the District of Columbia or its agents unless such child is provided (a) *adequate* alternative educational services suited to the child's needs, which may include special education or tuition grants, and (b) a constitutionally adequate prior hearing and periodic review of the child's status, progress, and the *adequacy* of any educational alternative." . . .

Mills and *PARC* both held that handicapped children must be given *access* to an adequate, publicly supported education. Neither case purports to require any particular substantive level of education. Rather, like the language of the Act, the cases set forth extensive procedures to be followed in formulating personalized educational programs for handicapped children . . . . The fact that both *PARC* and *Mills* are discussed at length in the legislative Reports suggests that the principles which they established are the principles which, to a significant extent, guided the drafters of the Act. Indeed, immediately after discussing these cases the Senate Report describes the 1974 statute as having "incorporated the major principles of the right to education cases." . . . Those principles in turn became the basis of the Act, which itself was designed to effectuate the purposes of the 1974 statute. . . .

That the Act imposes no clear obligation upon recipient States beyond the requirement that handicapped children receive some form of specialized education is perhaps best demonstrated by the fact that Congress, in explaining the need for the Act, equated an "appropriate education" to the receipt of some specialized educational services. . . .

(ii)

Respondents contend that "the goal of the Act is to provide each handicapped child with an equal educational opportunity." . . . We think, however, that the requirement that a State provide specialized educational services to handicapped children generates no additional requirement that the services so provided be sufficient to maximize each child's potential "commensurate with the opportunity provided other children . . ." and the United States correctly note that Congress sought "to provide assistance to the States in carrying out their responsibilities under . . . the Constitution of the United States to provide equal protection of the laws." . . . But we do not think that such statements imply a congressional intent to achieve strict equality of opportunity or services.

The educational opportunities provided by our public school systems undoubtedly differ from student to student, depending upon a myriad of factors that might affect a particular student's ability to assimilate information presented in the classroom. The requirement that States provide "equal" educational opportunities would thus seem to present an entirely unworkable standard requiring impossible measurements and comparisons. Similarly, furnishing handicapped children with only such services as are available to nonhandicapped children would in all probability fall short of the statutory requirement of "free appropriate public education"; to require, on the other hand, the furnishing of every special service necessary to maximize each handicapped child's potential is, we think, further than Congress intended to go. Thus to speak in terms of "equal" services in one instance gives less than what is required by the Act and in another instance more. The theme of the Act is "free appropriate public education," a phrase which is too complex to be captured by the word "equal" whether one is speaking of opportunities or services.

The legislative conception of the requirements of equal protection was undoubtedly informed by the two District Court decisions referred to above. But cases such as *Mills* and *PARC* held simply that handicapped children may not be excluded entirely from public education. In *Mills*, the District Court said:

"If sufficient funds are not available to finance all of the services and programs that are needed and desirable in the system then the available funds must be expended equitably in such a manner that no child is entirely excluded from a publicly supported education consistent with his needs and ability to benefit therefrom." . . .

The *PARC* court used similar language, saying "[i]t is the commonwealth's obligation to place each mentally retarded child in a free, public program of education and training appropriate to the child's capacity." . . . The right of access to free public education enunciated by these cases is significantly different from any notion of absolute equality of opportunity regardless of capacity. To the extent that Congress might have looked further than these cases which are mentioned in the legislative history, at the time of enactment of the Act this Court had held at least twice that the Equal Protection Clause of the Fourteenth Amendment does not require States to expend equal financial resources on the education of each child. . . .

In explaining the need for federal legislation, the House Report noted that "no congressional legislation has required a precise guarantee for handicapped children, i.e. a basic floor of opportunity that would bring into compliance all school districts with the constitutional right of equal protection with respect to handicapped children." Assuming that the Act was designed to fill the need identified in the House Report-that is, to provide a "basic floor of opportunity" consistent with equal protection-neither the Act nor its history persuasively demonstrates that Congress thought that equal protection required anything more than equal access. Therefore, Congress' desire to provide specialized educational services, even in furtherance of "equality," cannot be read as imposing any particular substantive educational standard upon the States.

The District Court and the Court of Appeals thus erred when they held that the Act requires New York to maximize the potential of each handicapped child commensurate with the opportunity provided nonhandicapped children. Desirable though that goal might be, it is not the standard that Congress imposed upon States which receive funding under the Act. Rather, Congress sought primarily to identify and evaluate handicapped children, and to provide them with access to a free public education.

(iii)

Implicit in the congressional purpose of providing access to a "free appropriate public education" is the requirement that the education to which access is provided be sufficient to confer some educational benefit upon the handicapped child. It would do little good for Congress to spend millions of dollars in providing access to a public education only to have the handicapped child receive no benefit from that education. The statutory definition of "free appropriate public education," in addition to requiring that States provide each child with "specially designed instruction," expressly requires the provision of "such ... supportive services ... as may be required to assist a handicapped child *to benefit* from special education." ... We therefore conclude that the "basic floor of opportunity" provided by the Act consists of access to specialized instruction and related services which are individually designed to provide educational benefit to the handicapped child. ...

The determination of when handicapped children are receiving sufficient educational benefits to satisfy the requirements of the Act presents a more difficult problem. The Act requires participating States to educate a wide spectrum of handicapped children, from the marginally hearing impaired to the profoundly retarded and palsied. It is clear that the benefits obtainable by children at one end of the spectrum will differ dramatically from those obtainable by children at the other end, with infinite variations in between. One child may have little difficulty competing successfully in an academic setting with nonhandicapped children while another child may encounter great difficulty in acquiring even the most basic of self-maintenance skills. We do not attempt today to establish any one test for determining the adequacy of educational benefits conferred upon

all children covered by the Act. Because in this case we are presented with a handicapped child who is receiving substantial specialized instruction and related services, and who is performing above average in the regular classrooms of a public school system, we confine our analysis to that situation.

The Act requires participating States to educate handicapped children with nonhandicapped children whenever possible. When that "mainstreaming" preference of the Act has been met and a child is being educated in the regular classrooms of a public school system, the system itself monitors the educational progress of the child. Regular examinations are administered, grades are awarded, and yearly advancement to higher grade levels is permitted for those children who attain an adequate knowledge of the course material. The grading and advancement system thus constitutes an important factor in determining educational benefit. Children who graduate from our public school systems are considered by our society to have been "educated" at least to the grade level they have completed, and access to an "education" for handicapped children is precisely what Congress sought to provide in the Act.

C

When the language of the Act and its legislative history are considered together, the requirements imposed by Congress become tolerably clear. Insofar as a State is required to provide a handicapped child with a "free appropriate public education," we hold that it satisfies this requirement by providing personalized instruction with sufficient support services to permit the child to benefit educationally from that instruction. Such instruction and services must be provided at public expense, must meet the State's educational standards, must approximate the grade levels used in the State's regular education, and must comport with the child's IEP. In addition, the IEP, and therefore the personalized instruction, should be formulated in accordance with the requirements of the Act and, if the child is being educated in the regular classrooms of the public education system, should be reasonably calculated to enable the child to achieve passing marks and advance from grade to grade. ...

IV

A

As mentioned in Part I, the Act permits "[a]ny party aggrieved by the findings and decision" of the state administrative hearings "to bring a civil action" in "any State court of competent jurisdiction or in a district court of the United States without regard to the amount in controversy." The complaint, and therefore the civil action, may concern "any matter relating to the identification, evaluation, or educational placement of the child, or the provision of a free appropriate public education to such child." . . . In reviewing the complaint, the Act provides that a court "shall receive the record of the [state] administrative proceedings, shall hear additional evidence at the request of a party, and, basing its decision on the preponderance of the evidence, shall grant such relief as the court determines is appropriate." . . .

The parties disagree sharply over the meaning of these provisions, petitioners contending that courts are given only limited authority to review for state compliance with the Act's procedural requirements and no power to review the substance of the state program, and respondents contending that the Act requires courts to exercise *de novo* review over state educational decisions and policies. We find petitioners' contention unpersuasive, for Congress expressly rejected provisions that would have so severely restricted the role of reviewing courts. In substituting the current language of the statute for language that would have made state administrative findings conclusive if supported by substantial evidence, the Conference Committee explained that courts were to make "independent decision[s] based on a preponderance of the evidence." . . .

But although we find that this grant of authority is broader than claimed by petitioners, we think the fact that it is found in § 1415, which is entitled "Procedural safeguards," is not without significance. When the elaborate and highly specific procedural safeguards embodied in § 1415 are contrasted with the general and somewhat imprecise substantive admonitions contained in the Act, we think that the importance Congress attached to these procedural safeguards cannot be gainsaid. It seems to us no exaggeration to say that Congress placed every bit as much emphasis upon compliance with procedures giving parents and guardians a large measure of participation at every stage of the administrative process, . . . as it did upon the measurement of the resulting IEP against a substantive standard. We think that the congressional emphasis upon full participation of concerned parties throughout the development of the IEP, as well as the requirements that state and local plans be submitted to the Secretary for approval, demonstrates the legislative conviction that adequate compliance with the procedures prescribed would in most cases assure much if not all of what Congress wished in the way of substantive content in an IEP.

Thus the provision that a reviewing court base its decision on the "preponderance of the evidence" is by no means an invitation to the courts to substitute their own notions of sound educational policy for those of the school authorities which they review. The very importance which Congress has attached to compliance with certain procedures in the preparation of an IEP would be frustrated if a court were permitted simply to set state decisions at nought. The fact that § 1415(e) requires that the reviewing court "receive the records of the [state] administrative proceedings" carries with it the implied requirement that due weight shall be given to these proceedings. And we find nothing in the Act to suggest that merely because Congress was rather sketchy in establishing substantive requirements, as opposed to procedural requirements for the preparation of an IEP, it intended that reviewing courts should have a free hand to impose substantive standards of review which cannot be derived from the Act itself. In short, the statutory authorization to grant "such relief as the court determines is appropriate" cannot be read without reference to the obligations, largely procedural in nature, which are imposed upon recipient States by Congress.

Therefore, a court's inquiry in suits brought under [the Act] is twofold. First, has the State complied with the procedures set forth in the Act? And second, is the individualized educational program developed through the Act's procedures reasonably calculated to enable the child to receive educational benefits? If these requirements are met, the State has complied with the obligations imposed by Congress and the courts can require no more.

B

In assuring that the requirements of the Act have been met, courts must be careful to avoid imposing their view of preferable educational methods upon the States. The primary responsibility for formulating the education to be accorded a handicapped child, and for choosing the educational method most suitable to the child's needs, was left by the Act to state and local educational agencies in cooperation with the parents or guardian of the child. . . .

We previously have cautioned that courts lack the "specialized knowledge and experience" necessary to resolve "persistent and difficult questions of educational policy." . . . We think that Congress shared that view when it passed the Act. As already demonstrated, Congress' intention was not that the Act displace the primacy of States in the field of education, but that States receive funds to assist them in extending their educational systems to the handicapped. Therefore, once a court determines that the requirements of the Act have been met, questions of methodology are for resolution by the States.

V

Entrusting a child's education to state and local agencies does not leave the child without protection. Congress sought to protect individual children by providing for parental involvement in the development of state plans and policies . . . and in the formulation of the child's individual educational program. . . . As this very case demonstrates, parents and guardians will not lack ardor in seeking to ensure that handicapped children receive all of the benefits to which they are entitled by the Act.

VI

Applying these principles to the facts of this case, we conclude that the Court of Appeals erred in affirming the decision of the District Court. Neither the District Court nor the Court of Appeals found that petitioners had failed to comply with the procedures of the Act, and the findings of neither court would support a conclusion that Amy's educational program failed to comply with the substantive requirements of the Act. On the contrary, the District Court found that the "evidence firmly establishes that Amy is receiving an 'adequate' education, since she performs better than the average child in her class and is advancing easily from grade to grade." . . . In light of this finding, and of the fact that Amy was receiving personalized instruction and related services calculated by the Furnace Woods school administrators to meet her educational needs, the lower courts should not have concluded that the Act requires the provision of a sign-language interpreter. Accordingly, the decision of the Court of Appeals is reversed, and the case is remanded for further proceedings consistent with this opinion.

So ordered.

Questions for Discussion

1. In a dissenting opinion Justice White wrote:

   Providing a teacher with a loud voice would not meet Amy's needs and would not satisfy the Act. The basic floor of opportunity is instead, as the courts below recognized, intended to eliminate the effects of the handicap, at least to the extent that the child will be given an equal opportunity to learn if that is reasonably possible. Amy Rowley, without a sign-language interpreter, comprehends less than half of what is said in the classroom-less than half of what normal children comprehend. This is hardly an equal opportunity to learn, even if Amy makes passing grades (p. 215).

   In your opinion, did the Court do little more than provide Amy Rowley with a "teacher with a loud voice"?

2. In addition to providing a more concrete definition of what constitutes an appropriate education, *Rowley* provided instructions for lower courts on how to resolve cases involving an appropriate education. This is discussed in greater detail in Chapter 7.

3. As noted, states are free to establish higher standards of appropriateness. As such, states may adopt the "commensurate with the opportunities provided to other children" standard enunciated by the lower courts in *Rowley*. Check the standard in your state.

4. Despite a hearing disability, Amy Rowley was identified early as a gifted academic student in school. It is evident that she experienced academic success throughout her schooling experience. By way of update, Amy Rowley is currently an Associate Professor and the Coordinator of the American Sign Language Program in the Department of Modern Languages and Literatures at California State University, East Bay in Hayward, California. Dr. Rowley received her Ph.D. in Urban Education and Second Language at the University of Wisconsin-Milwaukee. Dr. Rowley's current scholarly research involves examining the relationships among students, interpreters, and the Deaf community.

⚖️

SPECIAL EDUCATION LAW IN PRACTICE

Legal Case No. 9—Clarified Existing FAPE Standard. A Student's IEP Must Be
"Reasonably Calculated to Enable a Child to Make Progress in Light of the Child's Circumstance."

ENDREW F. V. DOUGLAS COUNTY SCHOOL DISTRICT RE-1
Supreme Court of the United States, 2017

137 S. Ct. 988

Chief Justice ROBERTS delivered the opinion of the Court

Thirty-five years ago, this Court held that the Individuals with Disabilities Education Act establishes a substantive right to a "free appropriate public education" for certain children with disabilities. *Board of Ed. of Hendrick Hudson Central School Dist., Westchester Cty. v. Rowley*, 458 U.S. 176 (1982). We declined, however, to endorse any one standard for determining "when handicapped children are receiving sufficient educational benefits to satisfy the requirements of the Act." *Id.*, at 202, 102 S.Ct. 3034. That "more difficult problem" is before us today.

I

A

The Individuals with Disabilities Education Act (IDEA or Act) offers States federal funds to assist in educating children with disabilities. In exchange for the funds, a State pledges to comply with a number of statutory conditions. Among them, the State must provide a free appropriate public education—a FAPE, for short—to all eligible children.

A FAPE, as the Act defines it, includes both "special education" and "related services." "Special education" is "specially designed instruction . . . to meet the unique needs of a child with a disability"; "related services" are the support services "required to assist a child . . . to benefit from" that instruction. A State covered by the IDEA must provide a disabled child with such special education and related services "in conformity with the [child's] individualized education program," or IE. . . .

The IDEA requires that every IEP include "a statement of the child's present levels of academic achievement and functional performance," describe "how the child's disability affects the child's involvement and progress in the general education curriculum," and set out "measurable annual goals, including academic and functional goals," along with

a "description of how the child's progress toward meeting" those goals will be gauged. The IEP must also describe the "special education and related services . . . that will be provided" so that the child may "advance appropriately toward attaining the annual goals" and, when possible, "be involved in and make progress in the general education curriculum."

B

In view of Amy Rowley's excellent progress and the "substantial" suite of specialized instruction and services offered in her IEP, we concluded that her program satisfied the FAPE requirement. But we went no further. Instead, we expressly "confine[d] our analysis" to the facts of the case before us. Observing that the Act requires States to "educate a wide spectrum" of children with disabilities and that "the benefits obtainable by children at one end of the spectrum will differ dramatically from those obtainable by children at the other end," we declined "to establish any one test for determining the adequacy of educational benefits conferred upon all children covered by the Act."

C

Petitioner Endrew F. was diagnosed with autism at age two. Autism is a neurodevelopmental disorder generally marked by impaired social and communicative skills, "engagement in repetitive activities and stereotyped movements, resistance to environmental change or change in daily routines, and unusual responses to sensory experiences." A child with autism qualifies as a "[c]hild with a disability" under the IDEA, and Colorado (where Endrew resides) accepts IDEA funding. Endrew is therefore entitled to the benefits of the Act, including a FAPE provided by the State.

Endrew attended school in respondent Douglas County School District from preschool through fourth grade. Each year, his IEP Team drafted an IEP addressed to his educational and functional needs. By Endrew's fourth grade year, however, his parents had become dissatisfied with his progress. Although Endrew displayed a number of strengths—his teachers described him as a humorous child with a "sweet disposition" who "show[ed] concern[ ] for friends"—he still "exhibited multiple behaviors that inhibited his ability to access learning in the classroom." Endrew would scream in class, climb over furniture and other students, and occasionally run away from school. He was afflicted by severe fears of commonplace things like flies, spills, and public restrooms. As Endrew's parents saw it, his academic and functional progress had essentially stalled: Endrew's IEPs largely carried over the same basic goals and objectives from one year to the next, indicating that he was failing to make meaningful progress toward his aims. His parents believed that only a thorough overhaul of the school district's approach to Endrew's behavioral problems could reverse the trend. But in April 2010, the school district presented Endrew's parents with a proposed fifth grade IEP that was, in their view, pretty much the same as his past ones. So his parents removed Endrew from public school and enrolled him at Firefly Autism House, a private school that specializes in educating children with autism.

Endrew did much better at Firefly. The school developed a "behavioral intervention plan" that identified Endrew's most problematic behaviors and set out particular strategies for addressing them. Firefly also added heft to Endrew's academic goals. Within months, Endrew's behavior improved significantly, permitting him to make a degree of academic progress that had eluded him in public school.

In November 2010, some six months after Endrew started classes at Firefly, his parents again met with representatives of the Douglas County School District. The district presented a new IEP. Endrew's parents considered the IEP no more adequate than the one proposed in April, and rejected it. They were particularly concerned that the stated plan for addressing Endrew's behavior did not differ meaningfully from the plan in his fourth grade IEP, despite the fact that his experience at Firefly suggested that he would benefit from a different approach.

Endrew's parents sought review in Federal District Court. Giving "due weight" to the decision of the ALJ, the District Court affirmed. The court acknowledged that Endrew's performance under past IEPs "did not reveal immense educational growth." But it concluded that annual modifications to Endrew's IEP objectives were "sufficient to show a pattern of, at the least, minimal progress." Because Endrew's previous IEPs had enabled him to make this sort of progress, the court reasoned, his latest,

similar IEP was reasonably calculated to do the same thing. In the court's view, that was all *Rowley* demanded. The Tenth Circuit affirmed. The Court of Appeals recited language from *Rowley* stating that the instruction and services furnished to children with disabilities must be calculated to confer "*some* educational benefit." The court noted that it had long interpreted this language to mean that a child's IEP is adequate as long as it is calculated to confer an "educational benefit [that is] merely . . . more than *de minimis.*" Applying this standard, the Tenth Circuit held that Endrew's IEP had been "reasonably calculated to enable [him] to make *some* progress." Accordingly, he had not been denied a FAPE.

We granted certiorari.

II

A

The Court in *Rowley* declined "to establish any one test for determining the adequacy of educational benefits conferred upon all children covered by the Act." The school district, however, contends that *Rowley* nonetheless established that "an IEP need not promise any particular *level* of benefit," so long as it is 'reasonably calculated' to provide *some* benefit, as opposed to *none.*"

The district relies on several passages from *Rowley* to make its case. It points to our observation that "any substantive standard prescribing the level of education to be accorded" children with disabilities was "[n]oticeably absent from the language of the statute." The district also emphasizes the Court's statement that the Act requires States to provide access to instruction "sufficient to confer *some* educational benefit," reasoning that any benefit, however minimal, satisfies this mandate. Finally, the district urges that the Court conclusively adopted a "some educational benefit" standard when it wrote that "the intent of the Act was more to open the door of public education to handicapped children . . . than to guarantee any particular level of education."

These statements in isolation do support the school district's argument. But the district makes too much of them. Our statement that the face of the IDEA imposed no explicit substantive standard must be evaluated alongside our statement that a substantive standard was "implicit in the Act." Similarly, we find little significance in the Court's language concerning the requirement that States provide instruction calculated to "confer some educational benefit." The Court had no need to say anything more particular, since the case before it involved a child whose progress plainly demonstrated that her IEP was designed to deliver more than adequate educational benefits. The Court's principal concern was to correct what it viewed as the surprising rulings below: that the IDEA effectively empowers judges to elaborate a federal common law of public education, and that a child performing *better* than most in her class had been denied a FAPE. The Court was not concerned with precisely articulating a governing standard for closer cases. And the statement that the Act did not "guarantee any particular level of education" simply reflects the unobjectionable proposition that the IDEA cannot and does not promise "any particular [educational] outcome." No law could do that—for any child.

More important, the school district's reading of these isolated statements runs headlong into several points on which *Rowley* is crystal clear. For instance—just after saying that the Act requires instruction that is "sufficient to confer some educational benefit"—we noted that "[t]he determination of when handicapped children are receiving *sufficient* educational benefits . . . presents a . . . difficult problem." And then we expressly declined "to establish any one test for determining the *adequacy* of educational benefits" under the Act. It would not have been "difficult" for us to say when educational benefits are sufficient if we had just said that *any* educational benefit was enough. And it would have been strange to refuse to set out a test for the adequacy of educational benefits if we had just done exactly that. We cannot accept the school district's reading of *Rowley*.

B

While *Rowley* declined to articulate an overarching standard to evaluate the adequacy of the education provided under the Act, the decision and the statutory language point to a general approach: To meet its substantive obligation under the IDEA, a school must offer an IEP reasonably calculated to enable a child to make progress appropriate in light of the child's circumstances. The "reasonably calculated" qualification reflects a recognition that crafting an appropriate program of education requires a prospective judgment by school officials. The Act contemplates that this fact-intensive exercise will be informed not only by the expertise of school officials, but also by the input of the child's parents or guardians. Any review of an IEP must appreciate that the question is whether the IEP is *reasonable*, not whether the court regards it as ideal.

The IEP must aim to enable the child to make progress. After all, the essential function of an IEP is to set out a plan for pursuing academic and functional advancement. This reflects the broad purpose of the IDEA, an "ambitious" piece of legislation enacted "in response to Congress' perception that a majority of handicapped children in the United States 'were either totally excluded from schools or [were] sitting idly in regular classrooms awaiting the time when they were old enough to "drop out."'" A substantive standard not focused on student progress would do little to remedy the pervasive and tragic academic stagnation that prompted Congress to act. That the progress contemplated by the IEP must be appropriate in light of the child's circumstances should come as no surprise. A focus on the particular child is at the core of the IDEA. The instruction offered must be "*specially designed*" to meet a child's "*unique* needs" through an "[*i*]*ndividualized* education program." An IEP is not a form document. It is constructed only after careful consideration of the child's present levels of achievement, disability, and potential for growth. As we observed in *Rowley*, the IDEA "requires participating States to educate a wide spectrum of handicapped children," and "the benefits obtainable by children at one end of the spectrum will differ dramatically from those obtainable by children at the other end, with infinite variations in between." *Rowley* sheds light on what appropriate progress will look like in many cases. There, the Court recognized that the IDEA requires that children with disabilities receive education in the regular classroom "whenever possible." When this preference is met, "the system itself monitors the educational progress of the child." "Regular examinations are administered, grades are awarded, and yearly advancement to higher grade levels is permitted for those children who attain an adequate knowledge of the course material." Progress through this system is what our society generally means by an "education." And access to an "education" is what the IDEA promises. Accordingly, for a child fully integrated in the regular classroom, an IEP typically should, as *Rowley* put it, be "reasonably calculated to enable the child to achieve passing marks and advance from grade to grade."

This guidance is grounded in the statutory definition of a FAPE. One of the components of a FAPE is "special education," defined as "specially designed instruction . . . to meet the unique needs of a child with a disability." In determining what it means to "meet the unique needs" of a child with a disability, the provisions governing the IEP development process are a natural source of guidance: It is through the IEP that "[t]he 'free appropriate public education' required by the Act is tailored to the unique needs of" a particular child.

Rowley had no need to provide concrete guidance with respect to a child who is not fully integrated in the regular classroom and not able to achieve on grade level. That case concerned a young girl who was progressing smoothly through the regular curriculum. If that is not a reasonable prospect for a child, his IEP need not aim for grade-level advancement. But his educational program must be appropriately ambitious in light of his circumstances, just as advancement from grade to grade is appropriately ambitious for most children in the regular classroom. The goals may differ, but every child should have the chance to meet challenging objectives. Of course, this describes a general standard, not a formula. But whatever else can be said about it, this standard is markedly more demanding than the "merely more than *de minimis*" test applied by the Tenth Circuit. It cannot be the case that the Act typically aims for grade-level advancement for children with disabilities who can be educated in the regular classroom, but is satisfied with barely more than *de minimis* progress for those who cannot.

When all is said and done, a student offered an educational program providing "merely more than *de minimis*" progress from year to year can hardly be said to have been offered an education at all. For children with disabilities, receiving instruction that aims so low would be tantamount to "sitting idly . . . awaiting the time when they were old enough to 'drop out.'" The IDEA demands more. It requires an educational program reasonably calculated to enable a child to make progress appropriate in light of the child's circumstances.

C

Endrew's parents argue that the Act goes even further. In their view, a FAPE is "an education that aims to provide a child with a disability opportunities to achieve academic success, attain self-sufficiency, and contribute to society that are substantially equal to the opportunities afforded children without disabilities."

This standard is strikingly similar to the one the lower courts adopted in *Rowley*, and it is virtually identical to the formulation advanced by Justice Blackmun in his separate writing in that case. Mindful that Congress (despite several intervening amendments to the IDEA) has not materially changed the statutory definition of a FAPE since *Rowley* was decided, we decline to interpret the

FAPE provision in a manner so plainly at odds with the Court's analysis in that case.

D

We will not attempt to elaborate on what "appropriate" progress will look like from case to case. It is in the nature of the Act and the standard we adopt to resist such an effort: The adequacy of a given IEP turns on the unique circumstances of the child for whom it was created. This absence of a bright-line rule, however, should not be mistaken for "an invitation to the courts to substitute their own notions of sound educational policy for those of the school authorities which they review."

At the same time, deference is based on the application of expertise and the exercise of judgment by school authorities. The Act vests these officials with responsibility for decisions of critical importance to the life of a disabled child. The nature of the IEP process, from the initial consultation through state administrative proceedings, ensures that parents and school representatives will fully air their respective opinions on the degree of progress a child's IEP should pursue. By the time any dispute reaches court, school authorities will have had a complete opportunity to bring their expertise and judgment to bear on areas of disagreement. A reviewing court may fairly expect those authorities to be able to offer a cogent and responsive explanation for their decisions that shows the IEP is reasonably calculated to enable the child to make progress appropriate in light of his circumstances.

The judgment of the United States Court of Appeals for the Tenth Circuit is vacated, and the case is remanded for further proceedings consistent with this opinion.

Questions for Discussion

1. The 2017 *Endrew F.* ruling rejected the "merely more than *de minimis*" educational benefit test for providing FAPE to students with disabilities. Under the 1982 Supreme Court's ruling in *Rowley*, the standard for achieving educational benefit for students with disabilities in general education classrooms is achieving passing grades and advancing from one grade level to the next. What about students with disabilities who are unable to participate in the general education classroom? In *Endrew F.*, the Supreme Court stated that a student's IEP "must be appropriately ambitious" in light of the child's individual's circumstances. Do you think this is

a more inclusive educational benefit standards capable of including a wider range of students with moderate to severe disabilities? Explain.

2. The Court in *Endrew F.* affords considerable deference to local school officials in defining "appropriate" student progress, including whether or not a student's IEP is "reasonably calculated to enable the child to make progress in light of their circumstances. Discuss how some of the following practices, including research-based instruction, challenging academic and functional goals, and progress monitoring of students with disabilities can facilitate the development of IEPs that satisfy the heightened FAPE expectations based on the recent *Endrew F.* ruling.

Summary of Important Legal Policies, Principles, and Practices

1. Educators, school leaders, and other professionals need a framework to deliver special education and related services that is grounded in the practice of including students with disabilities in the general education classroom environment.

2. Least restrictive environment (LRE) is often best determined by the educational setting that is best suited to the student to achieve their goals. In some cases, a separate school, homebound instruction, or hospital setting is the environment that least restricts the student's learning.

3. As in other provisions under the IDEA 2004, a least restrictive environment is based on the specific special education needs of each individual student. Students with a similar disability may have different goals; therefore, the setting to achieve those goals can potentially be different.

4. Both the Supreme Court's *Rowley* (1982) and *Endrew F.* (2017) decisions do not legally require schools to provide a FAPE that maximizes each individual student's educational or functional performance potential.

5. School officials need to understand that "the *new Endrew F.* standard is not a specific legal rubric for compliance and does not change IDEA provisions of due process and procedural safeguards." Equally important is the fact that the Supreme Court's "*Rowley* decision remains legally important because school district personnel must adhere to the procedures of the *Rowley* test" (Dieterich, Kucharczyk, & Brady, 2020).

Useful Online Resources

U.S. Department of Education
Link to the federal definition of FAPE: https://sites.ed.gov/idea/regs/b/b/300.101
Link to the federal definition of LRE requirements: https://sites.ed.gov/idea/regs/b/b/300.114

U.S. Department of Education, Office of Special Education and Rehabilitative Services (OSERS)
On December 7, 2017, the U.S. Department of Education's Office of Special Education and Rehabilitative Services (OSERS) released a document, "Questions and Answers (Q&A) on
U.S. Supreme Court Case Decision *Endrew F. v. Douglas County School District Re-1*." This well-written and useful document addresses important questions raised about the Supreme Court's *Endrew F. v. Douglas County School District Re-1*." This document is available online: https://sites.ed.gov/idea/files/qa-endrewcase-12-07-2017.pdf

OCALI
Overview video of LRE: www.ocali.org/project/least_restrictive_environment_video

IRIS Center
An information brief on LRE: https://iris.peabody.vanderbilt.edu/wp-content/uploads/misc_media/info_briefs/LRE_information_brief.pdf

Recommended Reading

Brock, M. E., & Schaefer, J. M. (2015). Location matters: Geographic location and educational placement of students with developmental disabilities. *Research and Practice for Persons with Severe Disabilities, 40*(2), 154–164.

Hammel, A. M. (2018). Amy and Drew: Two children who helped determine what free appropriate public education means. *General Music Today, 31*(2), 29–32.

Prager, S. (2015). An "IDEA" to consider adopting: Applying a uniform test to evaluate compliance with the IDEA's least restrictive environment mandate. *New York Law School Law Review, 59,* 653–678.

Underwood, J. (2018). Defining the least restrictive environment. *Phi Delta Kappan, 100*(3), 66–67. Retrieved from www.kappanonline.org/underwood-under-the-law-defining-least-restrictive-environment/

Wright, P., & Wright, P. (2017). *Who is responsible for providing FAPE? How to document your concerns when you disagree with the IEP team.* Retrieved from www.wrightslaw.com/info/fape.sped.failed.htm

Yell, M., Smith, C., Katsiyannis, A., & Losinski, M. (2018). Mental health services, free appropriate public education, and students with disabilities: Legal considerations in identifying, evaluating, and providing services. *Journal of Positive Behavior Interventions, 20*(2), 67–77.

References

A.L. v. Jackson County School Board, 635 F. App'x 774 (11th Cir. 2015).

Anderson v. Thompson, 658 F.2d 1205 (7th Cir. 1981).

Barnett v. Fairfax County School Board, 927 F.2d 146 (4th Cir. 1991).

Barwacz v. Michigan Department of Education, 681 F. Supp. 427 (W.D. Mich. 1988).

Beth B. v. Van Clay, 282 F.3d 493 (7th Cir. 2002).

Blackmon v. Springfield R-XII School District, 198 F.3d 648 (8th Cir. 1999).

Board of Education of East Windsor Regional School District v. Diamond, 808 F.2d 987 (3d Cir. 1986).

Board of Education of Hendrick Hudson Central School District v. Rowley, 458 U.S. 176 (1982).

Bonadonna v. Cooperman, 619 F. Supp. 401 (D.N.J. 1985).

Brimmer v. Traverse City Area Public Schools, 872 F. Supp. 447 (W.D. Mich. 1994).

Brown v. Board of Education, 347 U.S. 483 (1954).

B.S. ex rel. R.S. and P.S. v. Placentia-Yorba Linda Unified School District, 306 F. App'x 397 (9th Cir. 2009).

Burke County Board of Education v. Denton, 895 F.2d 973 (4th Cir. 1990).

Burlington School Committee v. Department of Education of the Commonwealth of Massachusetts, 471 U.S. 359 (1985).

Campbell v. Talladega County Board of Education, 518 F. Supp. 47 (N.D. Ala. 1981).

Capistrano Unified School District v. Wartenberg, 59 F.3d 884 (9th Cir. 1995).

Clyde K. v. Puyallup School District, 35 F.3d 1396 (9th Cir. 1994).

Colker, R. (2018). *Special education law in a nutshell.* St. Paul, MN: West Academic.

Daniel R.R. v. State Board of Education, 874 F.2d 1036 (5th Cir. 1989).

David D. v. Dartmouth School Committee, 775 F.2d 411 (1st Cir. 1985).

DeVries v. Fairfax County School Board, 882 F.2d 876 (4th Cir. 1989).

Dick-Friedman ex rel. Friedman v. Board of Education of West Bloomfield Public Schools, 427 F. Supp.2d 768 (E.D. Mich. 2006).

Dieterich, C. A., Kucharczyk, S., & Brady, K. P. (2020). *Endrew v. Douglas:* Beyond De Minimis progress for students with Autism. *Journal of Special Education Leadership, 32*(2), 72–85.

Dong v. Board of Education of the Rochester Community Schools, 197 F.3d 793 (6th Cir. 1999).

Endrew F. v. Douglas County School District, 137 S. Ct. 988 (2017).

E.S. v. Independent School District, No 196, 135 F.3d 566 (8th Cir. 1998).

Flour Bluff Independent School District v. Katherine M., 91 F.3d 689 (5th Cir. 1996).

Geis v. Board of Education of Parsippany-Troy Hills, 774 F.2d 575 (3d Cir. 1985).

Gladys J. v. Pearland Independent School District, 520 F. Supp. 869 (S.D. Tex. 1981).

Greer v. Rome City School District, 950 F.2d 688, (11th Cir. 1991).

Hall v. Vance County Board of Education, 774 F.2d 629 (4th Cir. 1985).

Hartman v. Loudoun County Board of Education, 118 F.3d 996 (4th Cir. 1997).

Hazelkorn, M. (2004). Reasonable v. reasonableness: The Littlegeorge standard. *Education Law Reporter, 182,* 655–682.

Individuals with Disabilities Education Act, 20 U.S.C. §§ 1400–1482 (2004).

In re Conklin, 946 F.2d 306 (4th Cir. 1991).

J.H. ex rel. A.H. and S.H. v. Fort Bend Independent School District, 482 F. App'x 915 (5th Cir. 2012).

Johnston v. Ann Arbor Public Schools, 569 F. Supp. 1502 (E.D. Mich. 1983).

J.S.K. v. Hendry County School Board, 941 F.2d 1563 (11th Cir. 1991).

Kevin G. by Jo-Ann G. v. Cranston School Committee, 130 F.3d 481 (1st Cir. 1997).

Lachman v. Illinois State Board of Education, 852 F.2d 290 (7th Cir. 1988).

Lagares v. Camdenton R-III School District, 68 S.W.3d 518 (Mo. Ct. App. 2001).

Laura M. v. Special School District, EHLR 552:152 (D. Minn. 1980).

L.H. v. Hamilton County Department of Education, 900 F.3d 779 (6th Cir. 2018).

Logue v. Shawnee Mission Public School Unified School District, 153 F.3d 727 (10th Cir. 1998).

Murray v. Montrose County School District, 51 F.3d 921 (10th Cir.1995).

Norris v. Massachusetts Department of Education, 529 F. Supp. 759 (D. Mass. 1981).

Oberti v. Board of Education of the Borough of Clementon School District, 995 F.2d 1204 (3d Cir. 1993).

O'Hara, J. (1985). Determinants of an appropriate education under 94–142. *Education Law Reporter, 27,* 1037–1045.

Osborne, A. G. (1992). Legal standards for an appropriate education in the post-Rowley era. *Exceptional Children, 58,* 488–494.

O'Toole v. Olathe District Schools Unified School District No. 233, 144 F.3d 692 (10th Cir. 1998).

P. ex rel. Mr. P. v. Newington Board of Education, 546 F.3d 111 (2d Cir. 2008).

Pink v. Mt. Diablo Unified School District, 738 F. Supp. 345 (N.D. Cal. 1990).

Poolaw v. Bishop, 67 F.3d 830 (9th Cir. 1995).

Prince, A. M. T., Yell, M. L., & Katsiyannis, A. (2018). Endrew v. Douglas County School District. *Intervention of School and Clinic, 53*(5), 321–324.

Remis v. New Jersey Department of Human Services, 815 F. Supp. 141 (D.N.J. 1993).

Renner v. Board of Education of the Public Schools of the City of Ann Arbor, 185 F.3d 635 (6th Cir. 1999).

Rettig v. Kent City School District, 788 F.2d 328 (6th Cir. 1986).

Roncker v. Walter, 700 F.2d 1058 (6th Cir. 1983).

Rozalski, M., Steward, A., & Miller, J. (2010). How to determine the least restrictive environment for students with disabilities. *Exceptionality, 18*(3), 151–163.

Sacramento City Unified School District, Board of Education v. Rachel H., 14 F.3d 1398 (9th Cir. 1994).

School District of Wisconsin Dells v. Z.S. ex rel. Littlegeorge, 295 F.3d 671 (7th Cir. 2002).

Schuldt v. Mankato Independent School District No. 77, 937 F.2d 1357 (8th Cir. 1991).

Springdale School District v. Grace, 656 F.2d 300 (8th Cir. 1981).

St. Louis Developmental Disabilities Center v. Mallory, 591 F. Supp. 1416 (W.D. Mo. 1984).

T.M. ex rel. A.M. v. Cornwall Central School District, 752 F.3d 145 (2d Cir. 2014).

Travis G. v. New Hope-Solebury School District, 544 F. Supp.2d 435 2008).

Tucker v. Calloway County Board of Education, 136 F.3d 495 (6th Cir. 1998).

Turnbull, H. R., Stowe, M. J., & Huerta, N. E. (2007). *Free appropriate public education: The law and children with disabilities.* Denver, CO: Love Publishing.

T.W. ex rel. McCullough v. Unified School District No. 259, 136 Fed. Appx. 122 (10th Cir. 2005).

Watson ex rel. Watson v. Kingston City School District, 142 Fed. Appx. 9 (2d Cir. 2005).

White v. Ascension Parish School Board, 343 F.3d 373 (5th Cir. 2003).

Wilson v. Marana Unified School District, 735 F.2d 1178 (9th Cir. 1984).

8

Related Services, Assistive Technology, and Student Transition Services

---

Key Concepts and Terms in This Chapter

- Related services
- When related services must be provided
- Assistive technology services
- Transition services

In addition to providing students with a FAPE in the LRE, the Individuals with Disabilities Education Act (IDEA) of 2004 requires states, through local school boards, to provide related, or supportive, services to students with disabilities that students need to benefit from their special education programs (20 U.S.C. § 1401(26)). For example, transportation gives a student access to their program; therefore, it is a related service that allows the student to benefit from special education. In addition to transportation, the IDEA defines examples of *related services* to include the following: developmental, corrective, and other supportive services such as speech-language pathology, audiology, interpreting services, psychological services, physical therapy, occupational therapy, recreation (including therapeutic recreation), social work services, school nurse services, counseling services (including rehabilitation counseling), and orientation and mobility services. Medical services are permitted, but only for diagnostic or evaluative purposes. School officials are exempt from providing medical services that go beyond those parameters. In addition, the 2004 IDEA amendments clarified that a medical service does not include a medical device that is surgically implanted or the replacement of such a device (20 U.S.C. § 1401(20)(B)).

This is not an exhaustive list, given that the individual needs of students vary and other related services may be considered if they help students with disabilities to benefit from special education. For instance, through services such as artistic and cultural programs or art, music, and dance therapy students can express ideas through art and work with other students on collaborative projects (*A ex rel. D.A. v. New York City Department of Education*, 2011). Thus, related services may be provided by persons of varying professional backgrounds with a variety of occupational qualifications.

Required Related Services

Related services must be provided to students with a disability who are receiving special education services. By definition, children have a disability under the IDEA *only* if they require special education and related services. In other words, there is no requirement to provide related services to students who are not receiving special education. However, since many special education services could qualify as accommodations under Section 504 of the Rehabilitation Act of 1973 (Section 504) (29 U.S.C § 794), it is not uncommon for school boards to provide related services to students who are qualified to receive assistance under Section 504, but do not qualify for help under the IDEA. For example, a student has autism, but it does not "adversely affect" their education, which is the requirement to qualify for special education and related services. On the other hand, their disability does "substantially limit" one or more major life activities such as learning which is the qualifying definition for assistance under Section 504.

When Congress amended the IDEA in 1990 it added definitions of assistive technology devices and services with the most recent version of the IDEA clarifying and expanding these definitions. An *assistive technology device* (AT) is defined as any item, piece of equipment, or product system whether acquired commercially off the shelf, modified or customized, that is used to increase, maintain, or improve the functional capabilities of individuals with disabilities (20 U.S.C. § 1401(1)(A)), but, as with related services, does not include surgically implanted medical devices (20 U.S.C. § 1401(1)(B)). The objective of assistive technology services is to assist students in the selection, acquisition, or use of assistive technology devices. In addition, assistive technology services include evaluations of the needs of children, provision of assistive technology devices, training in the use of these devises, coordination of other services with assistive technology, and maintenance and repair of devices (20 U.S.C. § 1401(2)).

Curiously, assistive technology is not explicitly included in either the definition of special education or related services, yet it does fit within the definition of special education, as specially designed instruction, and within the definition of related services, as a developmental, corrective, or supportive service. Rather than include assistive technology within either of these two definitions, Congress chose to create assistive technology as a category separate from both special education and related services. Assistive technology can thus be a special education service, a related service, or simply a supplementary aid or service (34 C.F.R. § 300.105(a)(1)). School boards are required to provide supplementary aids and services to students with disabilities to allow them to be educated in the least restrictive environment (LRE) (20 U.S.C. §§ 1401(33), 1412(a)(5)).

Increasing, maintaining, or improving the functional capabilities of individuals with disabilities is also the intent of *transition services* for students with disabilities to promote their movement from school to post-school activities such as employment, vocational training, and/ or independent living. Since the 1990 reauthorization of IDEA, educators are required to put in place, by the time a child is sixteen, a transition plan that includes related services, instruction, community experiences, and the acquisition of daily living skills (20 U.S.C. § 1401(34)). School personnel must include a statement of needed transition services in student individualized education plans (IEPs) beginning no later than the age sixteen (20 U.S.C. § 1414(d)(1)(A)(i)(VIII)). However, the plan can be initiated at an earlier age as is the case in some states.

As with special education, the provision of related services, assistive technology, and transition services must be done on an individual basis according to each student's unique needs. Not surprisingly, there have been many disputes between parents and school boards over whether some of the programs and devices that students with disabilities need qualified as required related services under the IDEA. Although each of the categories of related services listed in the IDEA is defined in the regulations, the precise parameters of some categories are subject to dispute. Moreover, where the list is not exhaustive, parents have filed suit seeking services that are not expressly mentioned in the IDEA. The first part of this chapter reviews pertinent litigation under the IDEA's related services provision. The next two sections address assistive technology and transition services directives.

As previously indicated, the list of required related services in the IDEA is not exhaustive. Thus, any developmental, supportive, or corrective service could be a required related service. In spite of the IDEA's fairly clear definition of related services, questions have often arisen as to what services are required and which students are entitled to related services. The following sections detail the most frequently litigated issues.

Counseling, Psychological, and Social Work Services

The IDEA's regulations define counseling as a service that is provided by a qualified social worker, psychologist, guidance counselor, or other qualified person (34 C.F.R. § 300.34(c)(2)). The definition of psychological services includes psychological counseling (34 C.F.R. § 300.34(c)(10)), while the definition of social work services includes group and individual counseling (34 C.F.R. § 300.34(c)(14)).

One related services controversy includes the use of psychotherapy. Services such as counseling, psychological, and social work services are defined in the IDEA's regulations—they clearly are required related services when students with disabilities need them in order to benefit from their special education placements. On the other hand, psychotherapy is not defined.

The distinguishing criterion regarding whether psychotherapy is a related service or an exempted medical service is how it is defined by state law, not by who actually provides services. For example, a federal trial court in Illinois ruled that a school board was responsible for the costs of psychotherapy even though it was actually provided by a psychiatrist (*Max M. v. Illinois*, 1986); however, a school district is only required to pay for the services to the extent of the costs of their being performed by non-physicians.

In many situations students with emotional difficulties may not be able to benefit from their special education programs until professionals address the underlying emotional problems. Under these circumstances, counseling, psychotherapy, or social work services may be required as related services. In *K.E. v. Independent School District No. 15* (2011) the Eight Circuit concluded that psychological and social work services were necessary to monitor the student's mental health and address issues arising from the cyclical nature of bipolar disorder. The court found that these related services were necessary for the student to advance appropriately toward attaining the annual goals" and "to be involved in and make progress in the general education curriculum" 20 U.S.C. § 1414(d)(1)(A)(i)(IV).

A requirement to provide related services is that they must be necessary for the student to benefit from special education services. In such a case, the Fourth Circuit reasoned that counseling services were unnecessary for a student who made great improvement under an IEP that did not include counseling (*Tice v. Botetourt County School Board*, 1990). On the other hand, as reflected by a judgment of a federal trial court in Illinois, when therapeutic services are classified as psychiatric services, courts will declare that they fall within the medical exception. Here, since the court was convinced that psychiatric services are medical because psychiatrists are licensed physicians, it declared that they were not related services (*Darlene L. v. Illinois Board of Education*, 1983).

Whether placements in facilities that provide psychiatric services are primarily for medical or educational reasons may determine the costs that school boards must pay. Two Ninth Circuit cases, which were months apart, illustrate this determination. In the first case, a student was admitted to an acute care psychiatric hospital when the residential school she attended could no longer control her behavior. The court compared the placement to one for a student suffering from a physical illness and declared that it had been made for medical reasons. The court decided that room and board costs were medically related, not educationally related, because the hospital did not provide educational services (*Clovis Unified School District v. California Office of Administrative Hearings*, 1990). In the second case, the student was placed in a residential school and psychiatric hospital after he assaulted a family member. In this instance the court affirmed that the residential facility was a boarding school that had the capacity to offer necessary medical services. The court observed that since the placement was made primarily for educational reasons, it was appropriate under the IDEA (*Taylor v. Honig*, 1990).

School Health, School Nurse, and Medical Services

The IDEA's regulations define school health and school nurse services as those designed to enable students with disabilities to receive a free appropriate public education (FAPE) (34 C.F.R. § 300.34(c)(13)). The two services are distinguished by virtue of the fact that school nurse services are performed by qualified school nurses, while school health services can be performed by other qualified persons. A great deal of controversy has developed over the provision of health-related services in the schools because of the debate of whether they are medical services (i.e., for diagnostic or evaluative purposes only) permitted under IDEA. To the extent that a number of medical procedures can be performed by registered nurses, questions have arisen as to whether certain nursing services fall within the definition of school health services or are exempted medical services.

In one of its first special education cases, the United States Supreme Court, in *Irving Independent School District v. Tatro* (1984), ruled that catheterization was a required related service. In this case, since the student could not voluntarily empty her bladder due to spina bifida, she had to be catheterized every three to four hours. According to the Court, services that allow a student to remain in class during the school day, such as catheterization, are no less related to the effort to educate than services that allow the student to reach, enter, or exit the school. Considering that the catheterization procedure could be performed by a school nurse or trained health aide, the Court was of the opinion that Congress did not intend to exclude these services as medical services.

The Ninth Circuit affirmed that school boards are required to attend to such matters as a student's tracheotomy tube (*Department of Education, State of Hawaii v. Katherine D.*, 1983). Insofar as procedures such as reinserting the tube or suctioning students' lungs can be performed by school nurses or trained laypersons, the court treated them as required related services. In addition, services of this type can be required while students are being transported (*Skelly v. Brookfield LaGrange Park School District*, 1997). In one case, a federal trial court in Michigan specifically commented that the provision of an aide or other health professional on a school bus to attend to a medically fragile student did not constitute an exempted medical service (*Macomb County Intermediate School District v. Joshua S.*, 1989).

These cases reveal that services that may be provided by school nurses, health aides, or even trained laypersons fall within the IDEA's mandated related services provision. However, the fragile medical conditions of some students require the presence of full-time nurses. In its second case dealing with the IDEA's related services provision, the Supreme Court, in *Cedar Rapids Community School District v. Garret F.* (1999), affirmed that a school board was required to provide full-time nursing services for a student who was quadriplegic. The Court ruled that even though continuous services may have been more costly and may have required additional school personnel, this did not render them more medical. Emphasizing that cost was not a factor in the definition of related services, the Court asserted that even costly related services must be provided to help guarantee that students with significant medical needs are integrated into the public schools. This is consistent with one of the earliest medically related cases whereby the court ruled that Timothy, regardless of the severity of a disability (i.e., severe intellectual disability, spastic quadriplegia, cerebral palsy, seizure disorder and cortical blindness), was entitled to a public education(*Timothy W. v. Rochester, School District*, 1989).

Diagnostic and Evaluative Services

The IDEA makes it clear that medical services can be related services when used for diagnostic and evaluative purposes (34 C.F.R. § 300.34(a)). To this end, medical evaluations are often part of the proper diagnosis and evaluation of students suspected of having disabilities since this is an important component of the special education process. In some instances, a school district may seek an independent medical reevaluation of a student and lack of parental consent will not bar it from doing so (*Shelby S. v. Conroe Independent School District*, 2006).

An interesting case out of Tennessee illustrates many facets of a school board's responsibility in this regard. A federal trial court directed a school board to pay for neurological and psychological evaluations ordered by a student's pediatrician (*Seals v. Loftis*, 1985). School personnel had requested an evaluation by a pediatrician for a student who had a seizure disorder, visual difficulties, and learning disabilities, and whose behavior and school performance had deteriorated. The pediatrician referred the student to a neurologist who subsequently referred him to a psychologist. A dispute arose over who was responsible for paying for the neurological and psychological evaluations. The court pointed out that since the student's needs were intertwined, the evaluations were necessary for him to benefit from his special education. The court added that the student's parents could have been required to use their health insurance to pay for the evaluations if doing so did not incur a cost to them. However, since the parents' policy placed a lifetime cap on psychological services that would have been reduced by the amount of the evaluation bill, the court concluded that the board was responsible for payment. Where no such cap existed for neurological services, the court suggested that parents would have to use their insurance to pay for an evaluation.

School boards may even be responsible for hospitalization costs when they are an integral part of a child's overall evaluation for special needs. In such a case, the federal trial court in Hawaii ordered the Department of Education to reimburse parents for the cost of a hospital stay that it considered to be a significant part of the student's diagnosis and evaluation. The student was identified as having an emotional impairment and oppositional defiant disorder as a result of her hospitalization (*Department of Education, State of Hawaii v. Cari Rae S.*, 2001).

The phrase *diagnostic and evaluative services* does not refer only to assessments that may be conducted as part of an initial evaluation. An order of a federal trial court in Tennessee illustrates that ongoing monitoring of a student's condition could fall within the realm of diagnostic and evaluative services (*Brown v. Wilson County School Board*, 1990). The court wrote that since medical services that are provided to monitor and adjust a student's medication are medical services for diagnostic and evaluation purposes, they are the responsibility of the school board.

Physical, Occupational, and Speech Therapy

The IDEA's regulations simply define physical therapy as the services provided by a qualified physical therapist (34 C.F.R. § 300.34(c)(9)). Occupational therapy refers to services that improve, develop, or restore functions impaired or lost through illness, injury, or deprivation; improve a student's ability to perform tasks for independent functioning; and prevent initial or further loss of function (34 C.F.R. § 300.34(c)(6)). Speech pathology includes the identification, diagnosis, and appraisal of speech or language impairments and the provision of appropriate services for the habilitation or prevention of communication impairments (34 C.F.R. § 300.34(c)(15)). Students with disabilities often need these services in order to benefit from special education, since they facilitate the remediation of impediments to learning.

Improving the physical abilities of students frequently expedites their ability to benefit from their special education placements. The Third Circuit explained that for some children physical therapy is an important facilitator of classroom learning (*Polk v. Central Susquehanna Intermediate Unit 16*, 1988). Emphasizing that the IDEA requires boards to provide children with education services that provide meaningful benefit, the court was of the view that physical therapy is an essential prerequisite for learning for some children with severe disabilities.

A federal trial court in New York ordered a school board to provide occupational therapy to a student with disabilities over the summer months, recognizing that his regression in the areas of upper body strength and ambulation skills would have adversely affected his classroom performance in the fall (*Holmes v. Sobol*, 1988). In like manner, the federal trial court for the District of Columbia posited that a proposed placement for a student with multiple disabilities was inappropriate since it did not provide for an integrated occupational therapy program as called for in her IEP (*Kattan v. District of Columbia*, 1988). The court contended that the student would not have benefited from her special education program without this service. Accordingly, it is important to keep in mind that the term *education* for many students with severe disabilities encompasses instruction in daily living skills. For this reason, occupational therapy can be a necessary part of overall student programs because it may address deficits in skills related to dressing and eating (*Glendale Unified School District v. Almasi*, 2000).

Insofar as an inability to communicate effectively may interfere with a student's learning, speech and language therapy, when needed, generally is considered to be a related service. If a school district provides speech services they must be adequately designed to address and improve speech-language needs. In *L.O. v. N.Y. City Department of Education* (2016) a student with autism received twice weekly speech-language services in groups of three, yet the student's verbal communication skills were not improving with this schedule. The Second Circuit court ruled that the student needed greater support services in his learning environment related to his speech-language capabilities; that services were inadequately addressing the student's needs; were not reasonably calculated to provide an educational benefits;and that the school district did not provide the student with a FAPE.

In providing various therapeutic services, school systems often employ qualified assistants who work under the direction of the therapist. In light of a judgment from a federal trial court in Tennessee, such a practice is acceptable. The court approved an IEP that called for occupational therapy assistants to provide services to a student with autism (*Metropolitan Nashville and Davidson County School System v. Guest*, 1995). The court was convinced that since the assistants were well trained and the student made progress working with them, the board could continue to use them to assist the child.

Transportation

It almost goes without saying that students cannot benefit from educational programs if they cannot get to school. As such, school boards must provide special transportation arrangements for students who are unable to access standard transportation provisions. As used in the IDEA's regulations, the term *transportation* encompasses travel to and from school, between schools, and around school buildings. Moreover, boards must provide students with disabilities with specialized equipment, such as adapted busses, lifts, and ramps, if needed to provide the transportation (34 C.F.R. § 300.34(c)(16)).

The First Circuit, in a dispute from Rhode Island, affirmed that transportation may encompass transport from a student's house to a vehicle (*Hurry v. Jones*, 1984). The student challenged the denial of his request for assistance in getting from his house to a school bus. Insofar as the child could not get to the vehicle without assistance, his father transported him to school for a time. When the father was unable to transport his son to school, the student was unable to attend classes. The situation was finally resolved but the court awarded the parents compensation for their efforts in transporting him to school after insisting that transportation clearly was the responsibility of the school board. In a similar situation, the federal trial court for the District of Columbia ordered the school board to provide an aide to convey a student from his apartment to the school bus (*District of Columbia v. Ramirez*, 2005). Even so, door-to-door transportation is required only when a student cannot get to school without such assistance (*Malehorn v. Hill City School District*, 1997).

Students whose IEP teams place them in private schools are entitled to transportation (*Union School District v. Smith*, 1994). However, if parents unilaterally place their children in private schools, public school boards are not required to provide transportation (*A.A. v. Cooperman*, 1987; *McNair v. Oak Hills Local School District*, 1989; *Work v. McKenzie*, 1987).

If students attend residential schools, they are entitled to transportation between their homes and schools for usual vacation periods. On the other hand, a state court in Florida ruled that a student was not entitled to additional trips home for therapeutic purposes even though improved family relations was a goal of his IEP (*Cohen v. School Board of Dade County*, 1984).

Transportation arrangements must be reasonable. Still, courts recognize that alterations to transportation plans for students may need to be made from time to time. The Third Circuit affirmed that a minor change in a student's transportation plan did not constitute a change in placement under the IDEA (*DeLeon v. Susquehanna Community School District*, 1984). The court realized that transportation could have an effect on the child's learning but found that a change that added ten minutes to his return trip home would not have had much of an impact. On the other hand, a federal trial court in Virginia ordered a school board to develop better arrangements for a student whose transportation took more than thirty minutes even though she lived only six miles from school (*Pinkerton v. Moye*, 1981).

In this day and age many students do not return home after school, but go to caretakers. While courts have reached mixed results as to whether school boards are required to provide transportation to the homes or locations of caretakers, they generally agree that boards are not required to accommodate parents' personal or domestic circumstance. Yet, the Fifth Circuit affirmed that students with disabilities are entitled to transportation to caretakers even if the caretakers reside out of a school's attendance boundaries (*Alamo Heights Independent School District v. State Board of Education*, 1986). The court noted that the parents' request for transportation to a caretaker was reasonable and would not place any burden on the board. Conversely, the Eighth Circuit was of the opinion that a special education student was not entitled to be dropped off at a day-care center that was outside of a school's attendance area. In this instance, the board's policy for all students dictated that children could be dropped off only within their school's attendance boundary. As such, the court was satisfied that the board did not violate the IDEA by refusing to transport the child to his daycare center because the policy was facially neutral and the parent's request was based on her personal convenience, not her daughter's educational needs (*Fick ex rel. Fick v. Sioux Falls School District*, 2003). The federal trial court in Maine reached the same outcome, denying the request of a mother that the bus driver ensure that an adult was present at the bus stop to meet her son, and if one was not, to then drop the student off at an alternative location (*Ms. S. ex rel. L.S. v. Scarborough School Committee*, 2005). In its analysis, the court specified that the mother was not entitled to have her request granted because it was motivated by her child care arrangements with her ex-husband, with whom she shared joint custody, rather than her son's educational needs. Similarly, a state court in Pennsylvania refused to require a board to provide transportation on weeks a student stayed with his father, who had joint custody but lived out of the district's boundaries (*North Allegheny School District v. Gregory P.*, 1996). The court acknowledged that the request did not address any of the student's educational needs but served only to accommodate the parents' domestic situation.

School boards may not be required to provide transportation when parents send their children to schools other than the ones recommended by school personnel. A state court in Florida determined that a school board was not required to transport a student to a geographically distant facility after she was enrolled there at her parents' request. The court found that transportation was unnecessary since the student could have received an appropriate education at a closer facility (*School Board of Pinellas County v. Smith*, 1989).

In addition to providing specialized equipment, if needed, to transport students safely, school boards may be required to provide aides on the transportation vehicle. A federal trial court in Michigan ordered a school board to provide a trained aide to attend to a medically fragile student during transport (*Macomb County Intermediate School District v. Joshua S.*, 1989). The court asserted that under the IDEA students with disabilities were entitled to transportation and incidents thereto.

Extracurricular Activities

The IDEA specifically includes recreation and therapeutic recreation as related services (20 U.S.C. § 1402(22)). The definition of *recreation* indicates that it includes assessment of leisure function, recreation programs in schools and community agencies, and leisure education, along with therapeutic recreation (34 C.F.R. § 300.34(c)(11)). In addition, the IDEA's regulations require school boards to provide nonacademic and extracurricular services and activities to the extent necessary to afford students with disabilities equal opportunities for participation (34 C.F.R. § 300.107). Nonacademic and extracurricular services and activities may include athletics, recreational activities, special interest groups or clubs, employment, and many of the services listed as related services. School officials must offer these activities in inclusive settings the maximum extent appropriate (34 C.F.R. § 300.117).

If students with disabilities are unable to participate in general extracurricular programs, the regulations dictate that school boards may be required to develop special extracurricular programs for these children. Students who meet the eligibility requirements for participation in general extracurricular programs cannot be denied access to them under Section 504. School officials may have to provide reasonable accommodations to allow students with disabilities to participate in general extracurricular programs (Osborne & Battaglino, 1996; Rose & Huefner, 2005). For example, eligibility rules, particularly those dealing with age restrictions, that would prevent students with disabilities from participating due to their conditions, may have to be waived (*Metropolitan Government of Nashville and Davidson County v. Crocker*, 1990; *Texas Education Agency v. Stamos*, 1991; *University Interscholastic League v. Buchanan*, 1993).

A state court in Michigan ordered a school board to provide a summer enrichment program to a student who was autistic (*Birmingham and Lamphere School Districts v. Superintendent of Public Instruction*, 1982). Where the testimony at trial revealed that the student needed a program that included outdoor activities, the court thought that the requested program fell within the parameters of special education and related services because physical education was included in the definition of special education and recreation was a related service. Further, a federal trial court in Ohio issued a preliminary injunction requiring a school board to include participation in interscholastic athletics in a student's IEP. The court was persuaded by evidence that the student's participation in sports resulted in academic, physical, and personal progress (*Kling v. Mentor Public School District*, 2001). Conversely, a state court in New York declared that a board was not required to provide an afterschool program when such participation was unnecessary for a student to receive a FAPE (*Roslyn Union Free School District v. University of the State of New York, State Education Department*, 2000).

Assistive Technology

Assistive technology may be provided as a special education service, a related service, or as a supplementary aid and service. Assistive technology must be included in student IEPs when it is needed for children to receive a FAPE under the standard established by the United States Supreme Court in *Board of Education of the Hendrick Hudson School District v. Rowley* (1982). Additionally, since AT may permit many students with disabilities to benefit from education in less restrictive settings, it may be required under the IDEA's least restrictive environment provision.

IEP teams must consider whether children require AT devices and services in order to receive an appropriate education (34 C.F.R. § 300.324(a)(2)(v)). If teams determine that AT is required as a result of the assessment process, it must be written into IEPs. At the same time, if the AT assessment was not optimum, but the student receives services (i.e., sign language, picture cards, and voice communication devices) that permit the student to benefit from the instruction and progress toward annual goals, then the courts found that the school district provided a FAPE (*R.P. v. Alamo Heights Independent School District*, 2012). Table 8.1 provides a useful checklist of possible AT when determining if a student needs a device to meet their IEP goals.

At the same time the IDEA's regulations specifically mandate that school boards ensure that assistive technology devices and services are made available to students if either or both are required as part of their special education, related services, or supplementary aids and services (34 C.F.R. § 300.105(a)). Schools must also provide students with the use of school-provided assistive technology devices in their homes if IEP teams believe that children need access to these devices in order to receive a FAPE (34 C.F.R. § 300.105(a)(2)).

In one of the first cases involving assistive technology, a federal trial court in Pennsylvania reasoned that a school board's provision of assistive technology to a student with multiple disabilities was inadequate

Table 8.1 Sampling of Technology to Support Instructional Needs

Assistive Technology Worksheet	Explore	Consider	Not at This Time
Low Tech			
Plastic reading guides	☐	☐	☐
Teacher guided notes	☐	☐	☐
Graphic organizers	☐	☐	☐
Enlarged printed text materials	☐	☐	☐
Manual communication board	☐	☐	☐
Magnifying glass	☐	☐	☐
Timers—transitions	☐	☐	☐
Brailler	☐	☐	☐
Braille text and materials	☐	☐	☐
High Tech			
Frequency modulation (FM) system	☐	☐	☐
Calculator (basic, large screen, or talking)	☐	☐	☐
Large screen	☐	☐	☐
i-Pad or tablet	☐	☐	☐
Audio recorded instructions	☐	☐	☐
Audio books and publications	☐	☐	☐
Orbit Reader 20	☐	☐	☐
Tactile Braille Tablet insideONE	☐	☐	☐
Text-to-speech software (e.g., Kurzweil, Natural Reader, Voice Dream Reader)	☐	☐	☐
Screen Reader (e.g., JAWS, VoiceOver)	☐	☐	☐
Speech-to-text software (e.g., Dragon Naturally Speaking)	☐	☐	☐
Electronic communication board (e.g., tobii dynavox)	☐	☐	☐
Alternative Input Devices			
On-screen keyboards	☐	☐	☐
Head pointer	☐	☐	☐
Hand pointer/splints	☐	☐	☐
Chin pointer	☐	☐	☐
Joystick	☐	☐	☐
Lever	☐	☐	☐
Head switch	☐	☐	☐
Wobble	☐	☐	☐
Rocker	☐	☐	☐
Sip/puff	☐	☐	☐
Pencil grip	☐	☐	☐
Positioning			
Seat cushions (allows for movement without getting up to walk around)	☐	☐	☐
Pelvic belt or footrest	☐	☐	☐
Adapted chair	☐	☐	☐
Manual wheelchair	☐	☐	☐
Power wheelchair	☐	☐	☐

Assistive Technology Worksheet	Explore	Consider	Not at This Time
Standing frame	☐	☐	☐
Beanbag chair	☐	☐	☐
Floor mats	☐	☐	☐
Tumbleform chair	☐	☐	☐
Adapted table	☐	☐	☐

(*East Penn School District v. Scott B.*, 1999). The court observed that the student required a laptop computer with appropriate software, but that school personnel failed to obtain and set up the device for nearly a year. The court found fault with the school's chosen software program and keyboarding instruction. In like manner, the federal trial court in Maryland supported a hearing officer's order for a school board to provide a student with appropriate software to use at home and school while providing instruction in how to use the software (*Board of Education of Harford County v. Bauer*, 2000).

A case originating in the Second Circuit exemplifies the point that an assistive technology device should assist students in receiving a FAPE by mitigating the effects of their disability, but should not compromise the learning process. The dispute involved a student at the Mamaroneck School District in New York State who was allowed to use a calculator because he had learning disability in mathematics. School personnel denied the student's request to use a more advanced calculator on the basis that it would have circumvented the learning process. A hearing officer determined that school officials provided the student with an appropriate assistive technology and that the more advanced calculator was not needed, and a trial court ruled in his favor. The Second Circuit agreed with the hearing officer that denying the use of an advanced calculator did not deprive him of a FAPE. Evidence showed that he was capable of passing the class using a basic calculator in a manner consistent with the education goals of the curriculum and his own lack of effort contributed to his failing grade (*Sherman v. Mamaroneck Union Free School District*, 2003).

Under the IDEA, assistive technology does not "include a medical device that is surgically implanted, or the replacement of such device" (20 U.S.C.S. § 1401(26)(B), (1)(B)). In addition, school districts "are not responsible for selecting, designing, fitting, customizing, adapting, applying, maintaining, repairing, or replacing surgically implanted medical devices" (20 U.S.C.S. § 1401(2)(C)). Furthermore, the United States District Court for the District of Columbia in *Petit v. USDE* (2012) explained that school districts are also not required to maintain devices such as providing cochlear implant mapping as audiology services (i.e., calibrating a cochlear implant so that an individual with profound hearing loss can receive and interpret auditory signals).

Regardless of whether an AT is or is not a medical device (i.e., myoelectric prosthetic arm) even though it appears medical in nature is not necessarily relevant if the device was not included in the IEP as seen in *J. C. v. New Fairfield Board of Education* (2011). Furthermore, since the student successfully completed tasks with and without the myoelectric arm, it demonstrated that the arm was not necessary to provide a FAPE. In the same fashion as *Rowley*, the IDEA does not require the ideal circumstances for a student to reach their optimal potential. Finally, the court also ruled that even though an AT device was accepted as necessary in an early intervention program (i.e., Part C) it does not necessarily translate to a required AT under Part B of the IDEA.

Transition Services

The IDEA requires school boards to provide transition services to students with disabilities in order to facilitate their passage from school to post-school activities. A student's transition service is a coordinated set of activities that are purposeful and

(A) is designed to be within a results-oriented process, that is focused on improving the academic and functional achievement of the child with a disability to facilitate the child's movement from school to post-school activities, including post-secondary education, vocational education, integrated employment (including supported employment), continuing and adult education, adult services, independent living, or community participation; (B) is based on the individual child's needs, taking into account the child's strengths, preferences, and interests; and (C) includes instruction, related services, community experiences, the development of employment and other post-school adult living objectives, and, when appropriate, acquisition of daily living skills and functional vocational evaluation.

(20 U.S.C. § 1401(34))

A major goal of transition services is to provide "the basic structure for preparing an individual to live, work and play in the community, as fully and independently as possible" (PACER, 2001). This requires a transition plan to prepare the student to "move from the world of school to the world of adulthood" (Center for Parent Information & Resources, 2017) to make meaningful transitions from school to whatever they may face in the future (Ray, 2002).

Not surprisingly, the courts disagree on whether school boards have provided appropriate transition services for students with disabilities. On the one hand, the federal trial court in Connecticut maintained that a twenty-year-old student was entitled to instruction in community and daily living skills as these skills fell within the scope of transition services (*J.B. v. Killingly Board of Education*, 1997). Similarly, a federal trial court in Pennsylvania ruled that to only provide vocational evaluations and training was insufficient and that transition services should be designed to prepare a student for life outside the school system (*East Penn School District v. Scott B.*, 1999).

A school district in Alabama was also found to deny a student a FAPE by the Eleventh Circuit when they generated a generic postsecondary transition plan that merely was an IEP boilerplate where the student's name had been handwritten on several pages of the IEP above the name of another child, which had been crossed out. Furthermore, there was no evidence of a transition assessment which might account for the transition plan that included the same vocational and career-based training available to all students even though the student goals called for participation in postsecondary education and not an occupational track. (*Jefferson County Board of Education v. Lolita*, 2014). Additionally, not only are school districts expected to provide a meaningful transition assessment, but to provide for training and other services needed to help students achieve goals recognized as appropriate in the assessments. In *Gibson v. Forest Hills School District Board of Education* (2014) by omitting an appropriate transition assessment and training for a student with multiple disabilities a district court in Ohio ruled that the school must pay for up to $35,398 in postsecondary transition services. Nonetheless, the Sixth Circuit vacated the fees awarded, but affirmed the district court judgment that the school district denied the student a FAPE by failing to adequately plan for her postsecondary future (*Gibson v. Forest Hills Local School District Board of Education*, 2016).

Lacking clarity in a transition plan was evident in *Yankton School District v. Schramm* (1996) for a South Dakota high school student with a cerebral palsy. School leaders assumed that the student's successful completion of physical education requirements no longer qualified her for special education or other services such as a transition plan under IDEA since her last IEP only included adaptive physical education, physical therapy, and transportation. They then shifted responsibility for transition planning to the student's parents. Her parents disagreed, filed suit, and prevailed in an Eighth Circuit court decision. In their ruling, the court recognized that the student remained eligible as having an orthopedic impairment under IDEA that requires specially designed instruction in the classroom and mobility assistance and other related services that allow her to benefit from that education. Therefore, the school district was obligated to design an IEP that included necessary transition services with specific goals and objectives to enable the student to attend college.

On the other hand, the federal trial court in Hawaii approved a coordinated set of activities that were clearly designed to promote a student's movement from school to post-school activities. The court ruled that these activities, which were included as part of the student's IEP, were aimed at assisting him in completing high school, becoming part of his community, exploring careers and colleges, and meeting with vocational counselors (*Browell v. LeMahieu*, 2000). Subsequently, a federal trial court in Louisiana, affirmed by the Fifth Circuit, agreed that transition plans that detailed desired adult outcomes, and included school action steps and family action steps, were appropriate (*Pace v. Bogulusa City School Board*, 2003). Recently, the Ninth Circuit recognized that even though a school district did not conduct an age-appropriate transition assessment, this did not rise to a denial of a FAPE because the transition plans that were in place were years from a student's graduation date and sufficiently focused on the development of postsecondary skills (*Forest Grove School District v. Student*, 2016).

A number of resources are available to support school districts to create and implement legally sound transition plans that meet the unique needs of students regardless of the severity of the disability. In an effort to ensure "all students and youth with disabilities are equipped with the skills and knowledge to be engaged in the 21st Century workforce" (U.S. Department of Education, Office of Special Education and Rehabilitative Services (OSERS), 2017, p. iv), OSERS developed a transition guide to "assist families and their students and youth with disabilities in developing and pursuing their goals for adult life" (p. iv). Table 8.2 includes a flow chart that is part of this guide "to facilitate a seamless transition from school to post-school activities" (p. iv).

Table 8.2 Sample Flow Chart of Key Points in the Transition Process

	KEY POINTS IN THE TRANSITION PROCESS **Alignment: IEP and IPE alignment facilitates a seamless service delivery process**.	
#1	**Individualized Education Program**	Participate in your IEP or child's IEP development to **ensure** that transition services are addressed in your child's IEP by age 16 (or earlier, depending on your state's laws). Students with disabilities and their representative are critical members of the IEP Team and have valuable information that is needed for quality transition planning.
#2	**Be Familiar with the Steps to Transition Planning**	Schools should: 1. **Invite** student; 2. **Administer** age appropriate transition assessments; 3. **Determine** needs, interests, preferences, and strengths; 4. **Develop** postsecondary goals; 5. **Create** annual goals consistent with postsecondary goals; 6. **Determine** transition services, including course of study needed to assist your student in reaching those goals; 7. **Consult** other agencies, in particular, the VR agency; and 8. **Update** annually.
#3	**Implementation of Transition Services**	Provide transition services as identified in the IEP. Pre-employment transition services are provided under the Rehabilitation Act. Alignment of the IEP and IPE facilitates a seamless service delivery process.
#4	**Referral to VR and/or Other Adult Agencies**	1. Pre-employment transition services provided under the *Rehabilitation Act*, as appropriate; 2. Familiarize yourself with laws relating to other programs; and 3. Learn about community agencies that provide services to support students, such as travel training and daily living skills.
#5	**VR Application Process**	1. Share employment interests and capabilities during the intake interview. 2. Focus on assessment(s) to lead to the student's postsecondary goals.
#6	**Individualized Plan for Employment**	Once a student has been determined eligible for VR services, the IPE must be developed and approved within 90 days, and no later than the time student leaves the school setting.
#7	**Common VR Services Available under the *Rehabilitation Act***	1. Transition services; 2. Vocational counseling; 3. Vocational training; 4. Postsecondary education; 5. Supported employment services; 6. Career development; and 7. Job placement.
#8	**VR Service Record Closure**	As a result of the student or youth with disability: 1. Achieving an employment outcome; or 2. No longer pursuing an employment outcome and, therefore, determined ineligible for VR services.

Source: U.S. Department of Education (Department), Office of Special Education and Rehabilitative Services (2017). *A Transition guide to postsecondary education and employment for students and youth with disabilities*, Washington, D.C., 2017 Retrieved from https://sites.ed.gov/idea/files/postsecondary-transition-guide-may-2017.pdf

⚖️

SPECIAL EDUCATION LAW IN PRACTICE

Legal Case No. 10—Postsecondary Transition Needs of a Student With Multiple Disabilities

GIBSON V. FOREST HILLS SCHOOL DISTRICT

655 Fed. Appx. 423 (6th Cir. 2016)

BOGGS, Circuit Judge

I

A

The Individuals with Disabilities Education Act ("IDEA"), *20 U.S.C. §§ 1400–1482*, offers state governments federal funding to help educate children with disabilities *§ 1411(a)(1)*. In exchange for those funds, participating states must adopt policies and procedures that implement the Act's promise of making a FAPE available to every eligible child *§ 1412(a)(1)(A)*. Like every state in this circuit, Ohio has opted to receive IDEA funds.

The lynchpin of the IDEA is a document known as the "individualized educational program" ("IEP"). The IEP also specifies the services that the school will provide to help the child to accomplish her goals, and sets forth the criteria that the IEP Team will use to evaluate the child's progress over the course of the coming year.

By the time a child is sixteen years old, her IEPs must set "postsecondary goals" based on "age appropriate transition assessments related to training, education, employment, and, where appropriate, independent living skills." The IEPs must also list the "transition services" that the *school district* will provide to help the child achieve those transition-related goals.

B

In 1998, Jim and Laurie Gibson enrolled their daughter, Chloe, in first grade in the Forest Hills Local School District. Chloe had a developmental disability that adversely impacted her motor skills with adaptive and cognitive delays, seizure disorder, IQ of between forty-three and fifty-seven, and difficulty with simple math and reasoning tasks, such as counting and telling time. Nevertheless, she was able to read at a third-grade level, learned basic routines and complete repetitive tasks, such as bussing tables and unpacking boxes.

As Chloe approached middle school, the Gibsons and Forest Hills began to disagree about Chloe's future. Observing that Chloe remained dependent on others for safety, support, and prompting, Forest Hills's staff contemplated that Chloe would move on to a "recreational/leisure" setting after leaving the public school system, and promoted an educational program that focused on improving Chloe's functional life skills. The Gibsons, however, hoped that Chloe would ultimately find competitive work and began to worry that Forest Hills's "functional" approach would deprive their daughter of an opportunity to "develop some basic employability skills."

Chloe made substantial progress in elementary and middle school, where her education focused on improving basic life skills, such as personal care, food preparation, and communication; however, her progress was inconsistent. Forest Hills sought to place Chloe in Anderson High School, where she would learn in a multi-disabilities classroom and focus on improving basic living skills. The Gibsons, on the other hand, wanted Chloe to study at Turpin High School, where she would enroll in a program "designed for students with disabilities who have the capability to obtain and maintain competitive employment and live independently on their own."

Chloe made progress at Anderson High School, improving behavior, motor skills, communication, and reading skills. But she continued to struggle in other areas, such as problem solving and personal care, and remained dependent on others for prompting and safety. Gibsons focused on her progress and faulted Forest Hills for failing to provide IEP goals that would enable a transition into the workplace. Forest Hills, however, believed that Chloe was not ready for such advanced goals and continued to insist that she was better suited for a future in a nonvocational adult program.

After a series of "numerous long IEP [Team] meetings, the Gibsons finally gave up and filed a written request for a due process hearing." The Gibsons complained that Forest Hills had failed to fulfill its IDEA obligations in more than twenty ways, including the district's failure to provide Chloe with adequate math and reading IEP goals, an appropriate vocational assessment, or an adequate IEP transition plan. The Gibsons also complained that Forest Hills had failed to consider Chloe's transition-related goals, interests, and preferences when devising IEPs.

While waiting on the IHO decision, Forest Hills and the Gibsons agreed that Goodwill Industries would conduct a vocational assessment of Chloe's job-related abilities. A job coach assessed Chloe while she unpacked boxes at a local department store, bussed tables at a restaurant, and collected shopping carts from a parking lot. The assessment was mixed, showing that while Chloe had a positive attitude, responded to prompts, and was able to follow routines, she also required constant supervision, took a long time to complete basic tasks, and lacked awareness of safety.

IHO concluded that Forest Hills denied Chloe a FAPE by failing to provide her with adequate reading and math goals and programming, and ordered Forest Hills to provide Chloe with a total of 480 hours of compensatory math and reading education. However, the IHO agreed with Forest Hills that Chloe "will not be living independently" after leaving Forest Hills and, with this in mind, concluded that Forest Hills's transition planning had been adequate. The IHO also rejected the Gibsons remaining claims that Forest Hills had denied Chloe a FAPE.

Forest Hills declined to appeal the IHO's decision; however, the Gibsons apparently filed an appeal with the Ohio Department of Education, which then appointed an SLRO. The SLRO rejected all of the Gibsons' claims and held that, reading and math goals aside, Forest Hills had provided Chloe a FAPE and adequate transition services in light of the severity of her disability, the transition planning and services satisfied the IDEA. Despite having rejected all of the Gibsons' claims on appeal, the SLRO did not reverse the IHO's order requiring Forest Hills to provide Chloe with compensatory math and reading education, reasoning that Forest Hills had forfeited its claim by "cho[osing] not to appeal the IHO['s] decision."

C

Before the SLRO's decision the Gibsons went to the federal district court alleging that they were prevailing parties who could collect attorney's fees. After the SLRO issued her decision, Forest Hills then filed a separate federal action against the Gibsons, asserting that the SLRO erred when she declined to reverse the IHO's ruling as it pertained to Chloe's math and reading education. Gibsons responded

with a motion to dismiss arguing that Forest Hills's failure to appeal the IHO's decision meant that it had failed to exhaust administrative remedies. In addition, the Gibsons filed five counterclaims against Forest Hills, asserting, inter alia, that Forest Hills failed to properly plan for Chloe's transition into adult life. The Gibsons also repeated their claim for attorney's fees.

The district court rejected four of the Gibsons' counterclaims, reasoning that in most respects, the SLRO correctly concluded that Forest Hills had provided Chloe with a FAPE. But with respect to transition planning, the district court held that Forest Hills had failed to comply with three of the IDEA's transition-related procedural requirements, and concluded that these failures denied Chloe a FAPE.

In particular, the district court found that Forest Hills never invited Chloe to transition-related meetings, in violation of federal and Ohio regulations. Further the court found that Forest Hills compounded this error by failing to take other steps to consider Chloe's transition-related preferences and interests, as required by 34 C.F.R. § 300.321(b)(2). The court also found that until Goodwill Industries conducted its vocational assessment, at which time Chloe was nineteen years old, Forest Hills had failed to conduct any age-appropriate assessments related to Chloe's transition into adult life. The court concluded that without information about Chloe's preferences, interests, or abilities, Forest Hills could not properly plan for Chloe's transition and therefore denied her a FAPE.

In order to remedy Forest Hills's failures, the court ordered the school district to provide Chloe with 425 hours of transition-related services. In addition, the district court also concluded that the Gibsons were prevailing parties and awarded them $300,000.

Both parties appealed.

HOLDINGS

In an IDEA case, (1) school district's decision to forego an appeal of an impartial hearing officer's decision requiring the district to provide the disabled student at issue with compensatory math and reading education meant that it had not exhausted administrative remedies; (2) district court properly found that school district's failure to consider the disabled student's transition-related preferences or to conduct age-appropriate transition assessments resulted in a loss of educational opportunity that denied the student a FAPE and entitled her to relief; (3) failure to invite student to transition-related IEP team meetings, or even notify parents that student would be welcome at such meetings if she wanted to attend, was a procedural violation of IDEA, but student was not denied a FAPE by failure of school district to invite student to transition-related IEP team meetings; and (4) while it was clear that plaintiffs did not prevail on many of their contentions, the district court's decision to choose a 62.5 percent reduction in attorneys' fees was not sufficiently explained and therefore necessitated that the award be vacated and REMAND this case for further proceedings consistent with this opinion.

Questions for Discussion

1. Recognizing the expense related to litigation, how could the school district meet the needs of the family and student prior to high school? How could they use the materials noted in Useful Online Resources to address the family's concern early in the student's academic career?
2. Based on this case, federal law, regulations, and other case law, what procedures can the school district put in the place to minimize future litigation related to transition assessment and planning?

Summary of Important Legal Policies, Principles, and Practices

Central to related services provided under the IDEA is to deliver services that support the student to benefit from their special education program. This requires a collaborative effort within the district between various professionals, but at times, also requires outreach to individuals in the greater community. Below are suggestions for best practice based on the law, regulations, and litigation to support the school leader to design and deliver an appropriate special education program.

1. Create an environment that encourages collaboration particularly since individuals of varying professional backgrounds with a variety of occupational qualifications will need to work together to meet the needs of individual students. Implementation of any successful school program requires leaders "to understand and collaborate with colleagues guided by relationship-enhancing communication" (Alsbury, 2015, p. 55). A framework of collaboration supports the delivery of special education and related services.
2. A service for one student might be provided under IDEA, but another student is only eligible for the service under Section 504. Do not assume that ALL students with disabilities are serviced under IDEA. It is all about the degree a disability adversely affects a student's education.
3. Recognize that the related services indicated in IDEA is not an exhaustive list. With the ever-changing landscape of technology and service delivery, a service that is not available today may be on the horizon. Therefore, do not assume because a service is not listed under IDEA that the district is exempt from providing the service.
4. Actively involve the parent and student (if feasible) throughout the process when determining the nature of a student's services. School districts are likely to be found in violation of IDEA when they did not invite families and students to participate in the assessment and design of a program that meets the unique needs of the student.
5. Regularly evaluate school district polices to ensure that procedures to deliver services align with IDEA requirements. As noted in the preceding case law, school districts are often found to deny a FAPE if they neglected to follow procedures established under IDEA and further delineated in federal regulations.

Useful Online Resources

Related Services
The IRIS Center (2011). Related Services: Common Supports for Students with Disabilities.
Online module produced by the IRIS Center that offers an overview of related services under IDEA.
https://iris.peabody.vanderbilt.edu/module/rs/

Technology
Assistive Technology (AT) & Accessible Educational Materials (AEM) Center provides accessible educational materials, access to assistive technologies, technical assistance and professional development support.
https://ataem.org/at-assessment-guides?slug=project&slug2=at_resource_guide_A

Center for Applied Special Technology (CAST) Free Learning Tools is a nonprofit education research and development organization that works to expand learning opportunities for all individuals through Universal Design for Learning.
www.cast.org/our-work/learning-tools.html#.XMBqIqR7mcL

Early Childhood Technical Assistance Center (ecta) provides a wealth of resources for infants, toddlers, and young children across a variety of topics.
http://ectacenter.org/topics/atech/atech.asp

National Center on Accessible Educational Materials—Accessible Educational Materials (AEM) includes accessible digital materials and accessible technologies to support learners in K–12, as well postsecondary education and workforce development.
http://aem.cast.org/supporting/k-12-aem.html#.XLI7WqR7k2x

National Center on Accessible Educational Materials—Early Learning Resources accessible digital materials and accessible technologies to support early learning.
http://aem.cast.org/supporting/early-learning-resources.html#.XMBpCaR7nb2

Ohio Center for Autism and Low Incidence (OCALI) Assistive Technology Resource Guide
Complete assistive technology resource guide with a range of topics associated with AT including useful forms and checklist. This is a resource that is useful for students with all disabilities.
www.ocali.org/up_doc/AT_Resource_Guide_2013.pdf

TechMatrix is a resource that allows the user to input a content area, grade level, and IDEA disability category that searches for AT products or research associated with that criteria.
https://techmatrix.org/

Transition
National Parent Center on Transition and Employment
www.pacer.org/transition/learning-center/laws/idea.asp

National Technical Assistance Center on Transition provides a comprehensive transition resources for all students with disabilities.
https://transitionta.org/transitionplanning

National Technical Assistance Center on Transition (NTACT) provides a case study of a student, including an example of the information that might be captured in the student's Present Levels of Academic and Functional Performance (PLAFP) in the IEP. Additionally the background information is transposed into each of the eight elements that are measured for Part B Indicator 13 (compliance with the transition mandate of IDEA, 2004).
https://transitionta.org/node/1699

National Secondary Transition Technical Assistance Center (NSTTAC) Indicator 13 Checklist: Form B (Enhanced for Professional Development) is a checklist that includes a series of questions related to creating and assessing postsecondary transition goals across training, education, employment, and independent living skills.
https://transitionta.org/sites/default/files/transitionplanning/NSTTAC_ChecklistFormB.pdf

National Collaborative on Workforce and Disability for Youth (NCWD/Youth) assists state and local workforce development systems to better serve youth with disabilities.
www.ncwd-youth.info/

Secondary Transition Modules Alternate Access is a set of modules that foster an understanding the transition process and improve outcomes. Even though an Ohio resource, content is relevant for user across states.
http://education.ohio.gov/Topics/Special-Education/Federal-and-State-Requirements/Secondary
-Transition-and-Workforce-Development/Secondary-Transition-for-Students-with-Disabilitie/
Secondary-Transition-Modules-Alternate-Access

Transition Plan Worksheet is a sample form to guide the IEP team.
www.understood.org/~/media/2d264b8c58dd4e11b45586a8fa847355.pdf

Recommended Reading

Agran, M., Spooner, F., Brown, F., Morningstar, M., Singer, G. H. S., & Wehman, P. (2018). Perspectives on the state of the art (and science) of selected life-span services. *Research and Practice for Persons with Severe Disabilities*, *43*(2), 67–81. doi:10.1177/1540796918769566

Bouck, E. C., Working, C., & Bone, E. (2018). Manipulative apps to support students with disabilities in mathematics. *Intervention in School and Clinic, 53*(3), 177–182. doi:10.1177/1053451217702115

Center for Parent Information and Resources. (2017). *Related services.* Retrieved on May 5, 2017 from www.parentcenterhub.org/iep-relatedservices/

Coleman, M. B. (2011). Successful implementation of assistive technology to promote access to Curriculum and instruction for students with physical disabilities. *Physical Disabilities: Education and Related Services, 30*(2), 2–22.

Onaga, A. K. (2017). *Postsecondary transition services: An IDEA compliance guide for IEP teams.* Palm Beach Gardens, FL: LRP Publications.

Schaaf, D. N. (2018). Assistive technology instruction in teacher professional development. *Journal of Special Education Technology, 33*(3), 171–181. doi.org/10.1177/0162643417753561

Shogren, K. A., & Plotner, A. J. (2012). Transition planning for students with intellectual disability, autism, or other disabilities: Data from the National Longitudinal Transition Study-2. *Intellectual and Developmental Disabilities, 50*(1), 16–30. doi:10.1352/1934-9556-50.1.16

Simonsen, M. L., Novak, J. A., & Mazzotti, V. L. (2018). Status of credentialing structures related to secondary transition: A state-level policy analysis. *Career Development and Transition for Exceptional Individuals, 41*(1), 27–38. doi:10.1177/2165143417742109

Sinclair, J. S., Unruh, D. K., Griller Clark, H., & Waintrup, M. G. (2017). School personnel perceptions of youth with disabilities returning to high school from the juvenile justice system. *Journal of Special Education, 51*(2), 95–105. doi:10.1177/0022466916676089

Wise, P. H. (2012). Emerging technologies and their impact on disability. *Future of Children, 22*(1), 169–191.

References

A.A. v. Cooperman, 526 A.2d 1103 (N.J. Super. Ct. App. Div. 1987).

A ex rel. D.A. v. New York City Department of Education, 769 F. Supp.2d 403, (S.D.N.Y. 2011).

Alamo Heights Independent School District v. State Board of Education, 790 F.2d 1153 (5th Cir. 1986).

Alsbury, T. (2015). Hitting a moving target: How politics determines the changing roles of superintendents and school boards. In B. S. Cooper, J. G. Cibulka, & L. D. Fusarelli (Eds.), *Handbook of education politics and policy* (2nd ed., pp. 126–148). New York: Routledge.

Birmingham and Lamphere School Districts v. Superintendent of Public Instruction, 328 N.W.2d 59 (Mich. Ct. App. 1982).

Board of Education of Harford County v. Bauer, 2000 WL 1481464 (D. Md. 2000).

Board of Education of Hendrick Hudson Central School District v. Rowley, 458 U.S. 176 (1982).

Browell v. LeMahieu, 2000 WL 1117 (D. Haw. 2000).

Brown v. Wilson County School Board, 747 F. Supp. 436 (M.D. Tenn. 1990).

Cedar Rapids Community School District v. Garret F., 526 U.S. 66 (1999).

Center for Parent Information & Resources. (2017, June 21) *Transition to adulthood.* Retrieved from www.parentcenterhub.org/transitionadult/

Clovis Unified School District v. California Office of Administrative Hearings, 903 F.2d 635 (9th Cir. 1990).

Cohen v. School Board of Dade County, 450 So. 2d 1238 (Fla. Dist. Ct. App. 1984).

Darlene L. v. Illinois Board of Education, 568 F. Supp. 1340 (N.D. Ill. 1983).

DeLeon v. Susquehanna Community School District, 747 F.2d 149 (3d Cir. 1984).

Department of Education, State of Hawaii v. Cari Rae S., 158 F. Supp.2d 1190 (D. Haw. 2001).

Department of Education, State of Hawaii v. Katherine D., 727 F.2d 809 (9th Cir. 1983).

District of Columbia v. Ramirez, 377 F. Supp.2d 63 (D.D.C. 2005).

East Penn School District v. Scott B., 1999 WL 178363 (E.D. Pa. 1999).

Fick ex rel. Fick v. Sioux Falls School District, 337 F.3d 968 (8th Cir. 2003).

Forest Grove School District v. Student, 665 Fed. Appx. 612 (9th Circ. 2016).

Gibson v. Forest Hills Local School District Board of Education, 655 Fed. Appx. 423 (6th Circ. 2016).

Gibson v. Forest Hills School District Board of Education, Case No. 1:11-cv-329 (S.D. Ohio February 11, 2014).

Glendale Unified School District v. Almasi, 122 F. Supp.2d 1093 (C.D. Cal. 2000).

Holmes v. Sobol, 690 F. Supp. 154 (W.D.N.Y. 1988).

Hurry v. Jones, 734 F.2d 879 (1st Cir. 1984).

Individuals with Disabilities Education Act, 20 U.S.C. §§ 1400–1482 (2004).

Irving Independent School District v. Tatro, 468 U.S. 883 (1984).

J.B. v. Killingly Board of Education, 900 F. Supp.2d 57 (D. Conn. 1997).

J. C. v. New Fairfield Board of Education, 56 IDELR 207 (D.C. Conn 2011).

Jefferson County Board of Education, v. Lolita, 581 Fed. Appx. 760 (11th Cir. 2014).

Kattan v. District of Columbia, 691 F. Supp. 1539 (D.D.C. 1988).

K.E. v. Independent School District. No. 15, 647 F.3d 795 (8th Circ. 2011).

Kling v. Mentor Public School District, 136 F. Supp.2d 744 (N.D. Ohio 2001).

L.O. v. N.Y. City Department of Education, 822 F.3d 95 (2d Cir. 2016).

Macomb County Intermediate School District v. Joshua S., 715 F. Supp. 824 (E.D. Mich. 1989).

Malehorn v. Hill City School District, 987 F. Supp.2d 772 (D.S.D. 1997).

Max M. v. Illinois State Bd. of Educ., 629 F. Supp. 1504 (N.D. Ill. 1986).

McNair v. Oak Hills Local School District, 872 F.2d 153 (6th Cir. 1989).

Metropolitan Government of Nashville and Davidson County v. Crocker, 908 F.2d 973 (6th Cir. 1990).

Metropolitan Nashville and Davidson County School System v. Guest, 900 F. Supp.2d 905 (M.D. Tenn. 1995).

Ms. S. ex rel. L.S. v. Scarborough School Committee, 366 F. Supp.2d 98 (D. Me. 2005).

North Allegheny School District v. Gregory P., 687 A.2d 37 (Pa. Comm. Ct. 1996).

Osborne, A. G., & Battaglino, L. (1996). Eligibility of students with disabilities for sports: Implications for policy. *Education Law Reporter, 105,* 379–388.

PACER Center. (2001). *Parent tips for transition planning.* Retrieved from www.asec.net/Archives/Transitionresources/ Parent%20tips%20for%20transition.pdf

Pace v. Bogulusa City School Board, 325 F.3d 609 (5th Cir. 2003).

Petit v. USDE, 675 F.3d 769 (D.C. Cir. 2012).

Pinkerton v. Moye, 509 F. Supp. 107 (W.D. Va. 1981).

Polk v. Central Susquehanna Intermediate Unit 16, 853 F.2d 171 (3d Cir. 1988).

Ray, J. M. (2002). Components of legally sound, high quality transition services planning under the IDEA. *Education Law Reporter, 170,* 1–13.

Rose, T. E., & Huefner, D. S. (2005). High school athletic age-restriction rules continue to discriminate against students with disabilities. *Education Law Reporter, 196,* 385–401.

Roslyn Union Free School District v. University of the State of New York, State Education Department, 711 N.Y.S.2d 582 (N.Y. App. Div. 2000).

R.P. v. Alamo Heights Independent School District, 703 F.3d 801 (5th Cir. 2012).

School Board of Pinellas County v. Smith, 537 So. 2d 168 (Fla. Dist. Ct. App. 1989).

Seals v. Loftis, 614 F. Supp. 302 (E.D. Tenn. 1985).

Section 504 of the Rehabilitation Act of 1973, 29 U.S.C. § 794.

Shelby S v. Conroe Independent School District, 454 F.3d 450 (5th Cir. 2006).

Sherman v. Mamaroneck Union Free School District, 340 F.3d 87 (2d Cir. 2003).

Skelly v. Brookfield LaGrange Park School District, 968 F. Supp. 385 (N.D. Ill. 1997).

Taylor v. Honig, 910 F.2d 627 (9th Cir. 1990).

Texas Education Agency v. Stamos, 817 S.W.2d 378 (Tex. Ct. App. 1991).

Tice v. Botetourt County School Board, 908 F.2d 1200 (4th Cir. 1990).

Timothy W. v. Rochester, School District, 875 F.2d 954 (1st Cir. 1989).

Union School District v. Smith, 15 F.3d 1519 (9th Cir. 1994).

University Interscholastic League v. Buchanan, 848 S.W.2d 298 (Tex. Ct. App. 1993).

U.S. Department of Education (Department), Office of Special Education and Rehabilitative Services. (2017). *A transition guide to postsecondary education and employment for students and youth with disabilities.* Washington, DC. Retrieved from https://sites.ed.gov/idea/files/postsecondary-transition-guide-may-2017.pdf

Work v. McKenzie, 661 F. Supp. 225 (D.D.C. 1987).

Yankton School Dist. v. Schramm, 93 F.3d 1369 (8th Cir. 1996).

9
Student Discipline

Key Concepts and Terms in This Chapter

- Suspensions
- Expulsions
- Racial disproportionality in disciplining students with disabilities
- Interim Alternative Educational Settings (IAES)
- Functional Behavioral Assessments (FBA)
- Behavior Intervention Plans (BIP)
- Manifestation Determination Review (MDR)
- Physical restraint and seclusion

Recently, legal issues related to discipling students with disabilities have received notable attention (Colker, 2018). Much of this attention is not favorable to students with disabilities. For example, research reveals that the suspension rates for students with disabilities are twice as high compared to their student peers without disabilities (Williams, Pazey, Shelby, & Yates, 2013). In 2016, for example, the Executive Office of former President Barack Obama released a detailed report addressing issues of disciplinary student suspensions and expulsions as well as the physical restraint and seclusion of students (Executive Office of the President, 2016). Some of the report's major findings were alarming, especially those involving the discipline of students with disabilities. While students with disabilities nationwide comprise approximately 12 percent of the overall K–12 student population, statistics reveal disproportionately higher suspension and expulsion rates for students with disabilities compared to their nondisabled student peers. For instance, 25 percent of students with disabilities had experienced one or more out-of-school suspensions; 76 percent of students with disabilities were reported to be subject to physical restraints; and 59 percent of students with disabilities were subject to seclusion (Executive Office of the President, 2016).

Unfortunately, another issue that has generated national attention is the significantly high rate of physical restraint and seclusion used by educators and other school personnel, including school resource officers (SROs) on students with disabilities. A 2014 report found that approximately three-fourths of students subjected to physical restraint and seclusion practices were identified with disabilities (Vogell, 2014). Despite the national media attention and serious injuries and reported deaths from these practices, physical restraint and seclusion practices are still legal in a majority of states (ProPublica, 2014). The Council for Children with Behavioral Disorders (CCBD) developed a policy position paper in 2009 indicating that physical restraint and seclusion practices and procedures should occur only in emergencies and not when the primary purpose is to solely manage student behavior (Huefner & Herr, 2012). Based on existing research, many professional organizations and advocacy groups for students with disabilities strongly encourage schools in lieu of physical restraint and seclusion policies and practices to develop positive behavior support plans, pre-established emergency procedures, and continuous adult supervision during any period of seclusion involving students with disabilities (Council for Children with Behavioral Disorders, 2009).

As important a topic as school discipline is, the IDEA did not address how disciplinary policies and practices impact students with disabilities until the IDEA reauthorization of 1997 (Russo, 2018). As complex as the IDEA's discipline requirements are, educational practitioners can still extract guiding principles from the laws, regulations, and numerous court cases on this topic (Dayton, 2002). This chapter details specific legal requirements for administering discipline to IDEA–eligible students. The next sections review the specific requirements of the 2004 version of the IDEA and its accompanying regulations, as well as recent litigation involving the disciplining of students with disabilities. Interestingly, as complicated and contentious as this topic is, there are, as of yet, apparently no reported cases involving disputes over the discipline provisions in the 2004 IDEA and its regulations.

The original version of the IDEA, initially known as the Education for All Handicapped Children's Act (EAHCA), did not directly address the discipline of students with disabilities. Yet, however, since courts were often asked to resolve disputes involving discipline, a large body of case law emerged. Even though the IDEA now contains disciplinary provisions, a brief review of the early case law is instructive because it provides the necessary background to understand the current version of the law.

Early Legal Decisions

In apparently the first case involving discipline under the IDEA, *Stuart v. Nappi* (1978), school officials in Connecticut unsuccessfully tried to expel a student with disabilities who had been involved in several school-wide disturbances. The student's attorney requested a due process hearing under the IDEA while obtaining an order from the federal trial court that prevented the school board from conducting an expulsion hearing. In addressing the issues, the court proclaimed that an expulsion was a change in placement that was inconsistent with the IDEA procedures that existed at that time, which required written prior notice before any proposed change in a student's educational placement occurred (20 U.S.C. § 1415(b)(3)). At the same time, the court added that school officials could temporarily suspend a disruptive special education student or change his or her placement to a more restrictive setting as long as they followed the statutory procedures.

A year later, a federal trial court in Indiana, in *Doe v. Koger* (1979), overturned the expulsion of a student who had a mild intellectual disability. The court declared that school officials could not expel students whose disruptive conduct was caused by their disabilities. The court implied that students with disabilities could be expelled when there was no relationship between their misconduct and their disabilities, a standard subsequently referred to as the manifestation of the disability doctrine. Additionally, the court reasoned that a disruptive student in a special education setting could be transferred to a more restrictive placement as long as school officials followed the proper change in placement procedures.

The Fifth Circuit expanded the manifestation of disability doctrine in *S-1 v. Turlington* (1981) after one of at least seven students who were expelled from high school for a variety of acts of misconduct unsuccessfully requested a hearing. In rejecting the student's requests, the superintendent concluded that because the plaintiff was not classified as emotionally disturbed, the misconduct was not a manifestation of his disability. In overturning the expulsion, the court decided that a manifestation determination must be made by a specialized and knowledgeable group of persons. Moreover, the court explained that officials could not completely cease the delivery of services, even where there was no relationship between the student's misconduct and disability, and he was properly expelled in accord with the IDEA's procedures.

A case from the Fourth Circuit, affirming an earlier legal ruling from Virginia, illustrates that it is not always difficult to make the connection between a child's disability and misconduct. *School Board of the County of Prince William v. Malone* (1985) involved a student with a learning disability who participated in drug transactions. After a committee of special educators was satisfied that there was no causal relationship between the student's disability and his involvement in the drug transactions, he was expelled. Yet, on judicial review, a federal trial court found that a relationship did in fact exist, because the student's learning disability caused him to have a poor self-image, which in turn led him to seek peer approval by becoming involved in the drug transactions. The court maintained that since the student's learning disability prevented him from understanding the long-term consequences of his actions, officials acted improperly in expelling him from school.

In a topic of great importance, the courts generally agreed that educators can exclude students who pose a danger to others as long as they follow proper procedures. In *Jackson v. Franklin County School Board* (1985), the Fifth Circuit supported a school board's exclusion of a student who was diagnosed as having a psychosexual disorder. After the court committed the student to a hospital for treatment, school officials refused to admit him when he tried to return to school following his release from the hospital. The court agreed with the recommendation of school officials that the student had to be placed in a private facility on the basis that his presence may have endangered him and others while threatening to disrupt the overall safety of the school environment.

Honig v. Doe: The Stay-Put Provision

In 1988, the United States Supreme Court addressed its only dispute involving discipline of students with disabilities under the IDEA in *Honig v. Doe*. *Honig* concerned two students with disabilities, who were identified in court documents as John Doe and Jack Smith. Doe, a student with an emotional disturbance and aggressive tendencies, attended a developmental center for children with disabilities. Soon after Doe enrolled at the school, he assaulted a peer and broke a school window. Initially, Doe was suspended for five days, but he was later placed on an indefinite suspension pending an expulsion hearing. Doe's counsel unsuccessfully requested that school officials cancel his expulsion hearing and that his individualized education program (IEP) team be reconvened to assess his situation. Judicial review began after school board representatives ignored the attorney's request. A federal trial court eventually canceled the expulsion hearing, ordered Doe readmitted to school, and prevented officials from excluding him while they sought an alternative placement where he could attend classes.

Smith was also emotionally disturbed and displayed aggressive tendencies. Educators placed Smith in a special education program within a regular school on a trial basis. After he committed acts of misconduct, school authorities reduced Smith's program to a half-day schedule. Although his grandparents agreed to this reduction, they were not advised of their rights or options regarding Smith's IEP. Following an incident wherein he made sexual comments to female students, Smith was suspended for five days and recommended for expulsion. School officials continued Smith's suspension pending resolution of expulsion proceedings. When Smith's attorney objected to the expulsion hearing, the school board canceled it and offered to either restore the half-day program or provide home tutoring. Smith's grandparents chose the home tutoring option.

A federal trial court in California, the Ninth Circuit, and the Supreme Court all agreed that students with disabilities could not be expelled for behavior that was a manifestation of, or related to, their disabilities. The Supreme Court acknowledged that in passing the IDEA, Congress intended to limit the authority of school officials to exclude students with disabilities, even for disciplinary purposes:

> We think it clear, however, that Congress very much meant to strip schools of the unilateral authority they had traditionally employed to exclude disabled students, particularly emotionally disturbed students, from school. In so doing, Congress did not leave school administrators powerless to deal with dangerous students; it did, however, deny school officials their former right to "self help," and directed that in the future the removal of disabled students could be accomplished only with the permission of the parents or, as a last resort, the courts.
>
> (*Honig v. Doe*, 1988, pp. 323–324)

The Court did not leave school officials without recourse because it added that they could suspend students with disabilities for up to ten days if they posed immediate threats to the safety of others. During the ten-day "cooling off" period, the Court suggested that educators could seek to reach agreements with parents for alternate placements. In the event that parents adamantly refused to consent to changes in the placements of their children, the Court explained that school officials could seek judicial assistance. Under such circumstances, the Court specified that school officials would not be required to exhaust administrative remedies prior to filing court action if they could show that administrative review would be futile or inadequate. The Court indicated that in appropriate cases the judiciary could temporarily prevent dangerous children from attending school.

The *Honig* ruling emphasized the IDEA's "stay-put" rule, a requirement indicating that while administrative or judicial proceedings were pending, an IDEA–eligible student is required to "remain in the then current educational placement unless the parents and state or local education agency agreed otherwise" (20 U.S.C. § 1415(j)). More specifically, the stay-put provision expressly prohibits either state or local educational agencies from altering a student's existing educational placement during a due process proceeding, including those proceedings involving student disciplinary actions or appeals. Initially, the stay-put provision was a means for ensuring relative stability that an IDEA–eligible students was not being moved back and forth between or among classrooms during a student placement dispute (Huefner & Herr, 2012). However, prior to the 1988 *Honig* ruling the IDEA's stay-put provision caused controversy among school officials, especially in the case of perceived dangerous or highly disruptive students with disabilities. Some school officials argued that the stay-put provision prevented school officials from protecting and maintaining the overall safety of other students and staff. The Supreme Court's *Honig* ruling addressed this controversy by affording special education hearing officers the legal authority to order a placement of a student with disabilities in an interim alternative educational setting (IAES) of not more than forty-five days "if the hearing officer determines that maintaining the current placement of such child is substantially likely to result in injury to the child or others" (20 U.S.C. § 1415(k)(3)(B)(ii)(II)). As expressly stated in the *Honig* decision:

> [The stay-put rule] effectively creates a presumption in favor of the child's current educational placement which school officials can overcome only by showing that maintaining the child in his or her current placement is substantially likely to result in injury either to himself or herself, or to others.
>
> (*Honig*, 1988, p. 328)

Post-*Honig* Reactions From the Lower Courts

The Supreme Court's *Honig* decision addressed a majority of, but not all, legally related issues involving the discipline of students with disabilities in acknowledging that they could not be expelled for misbehavior related to their disabilities. At the same time, *Honig* suggested that educators could employ other disciplinary sanctions that did not cause changes in student placements, such as short-term suspensions. Not surprisingly, litigation continued.

The Tenth Circuit affirmed that short-term disciplinary measures were not changes in placements under the IDEA (*Hayes v. Unified School District No. 377*, 1989). The dispute began when the parents of two students with histories of academic and behavior problems objected to the use of in-school suspensions and time-outs. The court found that while these short-term measures did not amount to changes in placements, since they related to the education of the students, they were subject to the IDEA's due process procedures.

In sanctioning suspensions of up to ten school days, *Hoing* envisioned that "cooling off" periods would give school officials and parents time to work together to devise other placements for students if they were needed. Unfortunately, since educators and parents do not always agree, sometimes other options cannot be worked out during the ten-day suspension periods. When parents and school officials cannot agree, their disputes are subject to the often-lengthy, and contentious, administrative and judicial processes.

Honig granted school officials the ability to seek injunctions to remove students with disabilities who are dangerous or create serious disruptions in schools while administrative and judicial proceedings proceed. In these situations, the burden is on school officials to demonstrate that students are truly dangerous and that removing them from their current educational placements is the only feasible option.

In the face of disruptive behavior by children with disabilities, school boards began, with mixed results, seeking *Honig* injunctions to remove students who were dangerous. A court in Virginia granted a board's request to enjoin a twelve-year-old student who was involved in fights, struck and yelled obscenities at school officials, and had to be restrained by the police on several occasions from attending classes (*School Board of the County of Prince William v. Wills*, 1989). A year later another court in Virginia granted the request of school officials for an injunction to exclude a student who set a fire in a school locker among other infractions (*School Board of the County of Stafford v. Farley*, 1990). Similarly, a federal trial court in Illinois enjoined a student from attending class who had violently struck other children and threatened to kill students and staff (*Board of Education of Township High School District v. Kurtz-Imig*, 1989). Finally, a state court in New York asserted that educators met their burden of showing that a student, who ran out of the school waving an iron bar while threatening to kill someone, was likely to endanger other students if he returned to class (*East Islip Union Free School District v. Andersen*, 1994).

Courts have ordered alternative placements when granting *Honig* injunctions. A federal trial court in Texas prohibited a student who assaulted classmates and teachers, destroyed school property, used profanity, and threatened to kill himself and others from attending general education classes (*Texas City Independent School District v. Jorstad*, 1990). In addition, the court decreed that pending the completion of the administrative review process, the student could either attend a behavioral class recommended by school officials or receive home tutoring. In a dispute from New York, a federal trial court ordered school officials to place a student in a special education class pending completion of a due process hearing (*Binghampton City School District v. Borgna*, 1991). The student frequently exhibited aggressive behavior such as punching other children, sticking a pencil in another student's ear, throwing his shoes at staff, hitting faculty, tipping over desks, and throwing chairs. In like manner, a federal trial court in Florida allowed a school board to transfer a student who was involved in forty-three instances of aggressive behavior to a special education center (*School Board of Pinellas County v. J.M. by L.M.*, 1997).

As important as it is to place dangerous students in appropriate placements, not all courts have agreed that school boards were entitled to *Honig* injunctions. A federal trial court in Missouri refused to allow officials to remove a middle school student who made numerous threats to students and school officials, repeatedly exploded in anger, and threw furniture (*Clinton County R-III School District v. C.J.K.*, 1995). Although another child was injured during one of these incidents, and teachers testified that they were afraid of him, the court did not think that this was enough to establish that serious personal injury was likely to occur if he remained in his current placement. In another case, a federal trial court in Pennsylvania refused to issue an injunction in declaring that school officials failed to show that they took every reasonable measure to mitigate the dangers that the student posed (*School District of Philadelphia v. Stephan M. and Theresa M.*, 1997).

The Eighth Circuit provided school administrators with practical guidance on the removal of students with disabilities from their current educational settings in *Light v. Parkway C-2 School District* (1994). The court allowed officials to remove a student with mental disabilities, who exhibited a steady stream of aggressive and disruptive behaviors, from her then-current special education placement. In doing so, the court was of the opinion that even a child whose behaviors flowed directly from her disability was subject to removal if she posed a substantial risk of injury to herself or others. In addition to showing that the student presented such a danger, the court declared that school officials must also demonstrate that they had made a reasonable effort to accommodate the student's disabilities so as to minimize the likelihood that she would injure herself or others. The court emphasized that only a showing of the likelihood of injury was required and that serious harm need not be inflicted before a child could be considered likely to cause injury. The court added that injury is not defined solely as an infliction that draws blood or sends a victim to an emergency room but also includes bruises, bites, and poked eyes.

Another post-*Honig* issue that emerged was whether students who were not yet identified as disabled were entitled to the IDEA's protections if they claimed to be disabled. The Ninth Circuit, in *Hacienda La Puente Unified School District of Los Angeles v. Honig* (1992), interpreted *Honig v. Doe* as suggesting that all students with disabilities, regardless of whether they were previously identified, are entitled to the procedural protections of the IDEA. Similarly, in *M.P. by D.P. v. Governing Board of the Grossmont Union High School District* (1994) a federal trial court in California held that the IDEA's procedural safeguards must be applied regardless of whether a student was previously diagnosed as having a disability. The court recognized that a student who is not disabled could attempt to be labeled as disabled solely to gain the benefits of the IDEA, but it responded that the IDEA did not address this possibility. On the other hand, a federal trial court in Virginia decided that a student who was suspended on a weapons violation was not entitled to the protections of the IDEA because the question of her disability was raised well after she committed her infraction (*Doe v. Manning*, 1994).

A related issue is whether former special education students who were not receiving services at the time of their disciplinary infractions were entitled to the IDEA's protections. A federal trial court in Wisconsin answered this question in the affirmative where a student was removed from special education at the request of his mother. In *Steldt v. School Board of the Riverdale School District* (1995), the student was expelled for a series of acts including assaults on peers and school personnel. Previously, officials removed the student from a special education class for children with emotional disturbances at his mother's request, but contrary to his teacher's recommendation. The court, noting that the mother's request for her son to be removed from special education did not change his status as a student in need of special education, insisted that he was entitled to the protections of the IDEA.

Another similar issue was how school officials should treat students who were evaluated but not classified as disabled. As with most issues, the answer was based on the unique facts of each case. In one instance, a school's IEP team was convinced that a student did not require special education, but his mother contested its action. The Seventh Circuit maintained that the student was not entitled to an injunction barring his expulsion while administrative proceedings were pending (*Rodiriecus L. v. Waukegan School District No. 60*, 1996). In a circumstance such as this, the court stated, educators needed to employ a flexible approach when applying the IDEA's stay-put provision and should not have applied it automatically to every student who was referred for a placement in special education.

The *Honig* Court reasoned that students in special education placements could be suspended for up to ten days. Insofar as the Court failed to specify whether the ten-day limit was consecutive or cumulative, litigation ensued. The Ninth Circuit, in *Parents of Student W. v. Puyallup School District* (1994), interpreted *Honig* as not supporting the proposition that the ten-day limit referred to ten total days. The court affirmed that the school board's suspension guidelines, wherein each suspension triggered an evaluation to consider whether a student was receiving an appropriate education, were lawful. On the other hand, in *Manchester School District v. Charles M.F.* (1994), the federal trial court in New Hampshire held that cumulative suspensions that totaled more than ten days constituted a pattern of exclusion which resulted in a change of placement.

In *S-1 v. Turlington* (1981), discussed earlier, the Fifth Circuit asserted that even when a special education student was properly expelled by following all of the IDEA's due process procedures, a complete cessation of services was not authorized. According to *Turlington*, a school board would still have to provide special education and related services to an expelled student with disabilities.

This issue arose again in Virginia in 1992 when the commonwealth officials submitted their three-year plan for special education to the U.S. Department of Education. A regulation declaring that students with disabilities could be disciplined in the same manner as students who were not disabled, if there was no causal relationship between the misconduct and the disability, was included in that plan. The Department of Education responded by informing officials in Virginia that they could not discontinue educational services to expelled special education students, even if the discipline resulted from behavior unrelated to the students' disabilities. The officials in Virginia failed to change the regulation, and the dispute eventually ended up in the courts. Following years of litigation, the Fourth Circuit, in *Commonwealth of Virginia Department of Education v. Riley* (Riley) (1997), pointed out that the IDEA did not require local school boards to discipline disabled students differently from peers who were not disabled when their misconduct was unrelated to their disabilities. The court found that the IDEA only required states to provide disabled students with access to a free appropriate public education, which, as with any right, could be forfeited by conduct antithetical to the right itself. The court concluded that school boards were not required to provide educational services to students with disabilities who forfeited their right to a FAPE by willfully engaging in conduct so serious as to warrant the ultimate penalty of expulsion.

Later in the same year that the Fourth Circuit resolved *Riley*, the Seventh Circuit reached a similar outcome in *Doe v. Board of Education of Oak Park & River Forest High School District 200* (Oak Park) (1997). When school officials expelled a student for possession of a pipe and a small amount of marijuana, the board's evaluation team did not think that there was a causal relationship between his disability and misconduct. Under the circumstances, a federal trial court was of the opinion that the school board was not required to provide alternative educational services during the expulsion period. The appeals court agreed that the IDEA was not intended to shield special education students from the usual consequences of their misconduct when it is unrelated to their disabilities.

Riley and *Oak Park* can be compared to the order of the federal trial court in Arizona. In *Magyar v. Tucson Unified School District* (1997) school officials expelled a student with a learning disability after he gave an assault-style knife to another child. In reinstating the student, the court decided that the IDEA requires school boards to provide an appropriate education for all students with disabilities. The court thought that since the use of the word "all" in the IDEA was clear and unequivocal, it did not include an exception for misbehaving students.

IDEA 2004 Disciplinary Provisions

The current IDEA 2004 addresses the following issues regarding disciplining students with disabilities:

Authority of School Personnel

The IDEA now details the authority and obligations of school personnel regarding the discipline of students with disabilities. The current disciplinary language provides school officials with more guidance than at any time in the past. Still, questions do arise that need to be resolved by the courts.

Case-by-Case Determinations for Student Short-Term Suspensions

Recognizing that disciplinary infractions may present educators with some very unique situations, Congress inserted a clause into the IDEA 2004 allowing school officials some flexibility. The IDEA 2004 and its regulations permit educators to consider unique circumstances on case-by-case bases when evaluating whether changes in placement are necessary for students with disabilities who violate school rules (20 U.S.C. § 1415(k)(1)(A); 34 C.F.R. § 300.530(a)).

For instance, school officials may remove children with disabilities from their current settings to alternative interim educational placements or other locations or suspend them for no more than ten consecutive school days for violating school disciplinary rules. Further, such students can be removed for up to ten additional consecutive school days in the same academic year for separate disciplinary infractions as long as these moves do not constitute changes in placements. If children with disabilities are removed from their current placements for ten school days in an academic year, then educators must provide them with services (34 C.F.R. § 300.530(b)). At the same time, if misbehaviors that are not a manifestation of a student's disabilities lead to a change in placements that exceeds ten days, then the IDEA and its regulations afford officials the authority to make such a change as long as the same procedures would apply to students who are not disabled (20 U.S.C. § 1415(k)(1)(C); 300 C.F.R. § 300.53(c)). This means that students with disabilities who are removed from school must continue to receive services that enable them to continue to participate in the general education curriculum, even in other settings, and to progress toward meeting the goals established in their IEPs (34 C.F.R. § 300.530(d)(1)).

The regulation also requires educators to perform functional behavioral assessments, discussed later in this chapter, along with behavioral intervention services and modifications that are designed to address the misbehavior of students so that they do not reoccur (34 C.F.R. § 300.530(d)(2)). However, the regulation only requires educators to provide services to students who are removed for less than ten days only if they do so for students who do not have disabilities and are removed from school for misconduct (34 C.F.R. § 300.530(d)(3)). Further, the regulation neither indicates that school systems may deny services to students who are removed for more than ten days in an academic year nor require that they receive assistance when they are out of class for shorter periods of time (34 C.F.R. § 300.530(d)(4)). Of course, nothing prevents school systems from providing services under these circumstances. If removals constitute changes in placements, then the IEP teams of these children must determine what appropriate services they are entitled to receive (34 C.F.R. § 300.530(d)(5)).

Suspensions and Placements in Interim Alternative Educational Settings (IAES)

The IDEA 2004 clearly stipulates that school officials may remove students with disabilities who violate school rules to appropriate interim alternative settings, or other settings, or can suspend them for not more than ten school days (20 U.S.C. § 1415(k)(1)(B); 34 C.F.R. § 300.530(b)). Even so, educators can implement such measures only to the extent that they use similar punishments when disciplining students who are not disabled. In addition, students may be removed to interim alternative educational settings for up to forty-five days under specified circumstances, discussed ahead, without regard for whether their misbehavior is a manifestation of their disabilities (20 U.S.C. § 1415(k)(1)(G); 34 C.F.R. § 300.530(g)).

Short-Term Student Suspensions (The Ten-Day Rule)

The so-called "ten-day rule" authorizes school officials to unilaterally remove a student with a disability who violates a disciplinary code of conduct from the student's current placement for not more than ten school days in a school year (34 C.F.R. §300.530(b)). Thus, the IDEA 2004 affords school personnel the legal authority to suspend special education students for not more than ten school days as long as similar sanctions would apply to children who are not disabled (20 U.S.C. § 1415(k)(1)(B); 34 C.F.R. § 300.530(b)(1)). Under these circumstances, school officials not only must conduct functional behavioral assessments (FBAs) for students if they have not already been completed but must also take active steps to address their misconduct (20 U.S.C. § 1415(k)(1)(D)(ii); 34 C.F.R. § 300.530(d)(1)(ii)).

Change of Student Placement—More Than Ten-Day Rule

The IDEA's Part B regulations define "change of placement" for disciplinary removals based on two situations involving the student with a disability, including:

1. change of placement occurs if a removal is for more than 10 consecutive school days;
2. a change of student placement occurs if a student is subjected to a series of short-term constancy pattern because:
    a. the series of removals total more than 10 school days in a school year;
    b. this student's behavior is substantially similar to the student's behavior and previous incidents that resulted in the series of removals; and
    c. additional factors, such as the length of each removal, total amount of time removed, and proximity of removals to one another

(34 C.F.R. § 300.536)

The IDEA's regulations maintain that a series of student removals resulting in a pattern of exclusions that cumulate to more than ten school days constitutes a change in placement (34 C.F.R. § 300.356(a)(2)(i)). The regulation on changes of placements due to disciplinary removals includes the significant modification that if students are suspended for misbehavior that was "substantially similar" to past infractions that were viewed as manifestations of their disabilities, then a change in placement also would have occurred (34 C.F.R. § 300.536(a)(2)(ii)). Moreover, where students have been subject to a series of removals that constitute a pattern, hearing officers and courts will consider the length of each removal, the total amount of time that students are removed, and the proximity of the exclusions to one another in evaluating whether changes in placements occurred (34 C.F.R. § 300.536(a)(2)(iii)).

Table 9.1 summarizes the major disciplinary requirements under the IDEA 2004. Presently, educators have the authority to remove children with disabilities who violate school codes of conduct in their current placements to what are considered appropriate interim alternative educational settings, other settings, or

Table 9.1 Summary of Major Disciplinary Provisions Under IDEA 2004

Rule	*IDEA 2004 Requirements*
Ten-Day Rule No change in student placement	• In-school or out-of-school suspensions of ten school days or less within a school year are not considered changes in placement for students with disabilities. • School officials can impose out-of-school suspensions of up to ten days without having to convene IEP teams. • The student is disciplined in the same manner as their nondisabled peers.

(Continued)

Table 9.1 (Continued)

Rule	IDEA 2004 Requirements
Required change(s) in student placement Based on student suspensions/expulsions greater than ten school days	A student change of placement occurs if: • If a student removal is for more than ten consecutive school days; or • The student is subjected to a series of removals that constitute a pattern because they result in more than ten school days in a school year and because of additional factors (length of removal, total amount of time removed, proximity of removals) (*See:* 34 C.F.R. §300.536). Requirements for a student change of placement include: • Notice; • Provision of appropriate services, as determined by IEP team; • IEP team determines interim alternative educational setting (IAES) and appropriate behavioral interventions and modifications; • Within ten days, the IEP team must determine whether the student's conduct is a manifestation of the disability(ies); • Within ten days, there must be a manifestation determination review (MDR) meeting (*See:* 34 C.F.R. §300.530).
Forty-Five -Day Rule Special Circumstances/ Exceptions to the manifestation determination rule	If educators encounter IDEA–eligible students identified as dangerous and presenting a threat(s) to school safety, educators are allowed to remove such students to an interim alternative educational setting, or IAES for up to forty-five days without addressing whether their behaviors are manifestations of their disabilities. Forty-five-day requirements include: • Schools may remove IDEA-eligible student for up to forty-five school days to an interim alternative educational setting (IAES) for possession of weapons, drugs, or infliction of serious bodily injury; or • A special education hearing officer may remove a student to an IAES for up to forty-five school days if the student's behavior is substantially likely to result in injury to others in current placement (*See:* 34 C.F.R. §300.530(g), 34 C.F.R. §300.532(b)(ii)).
Disciplinary appeals and the stay-put provision	• During any student disciplinary appeals, the student must remain in their interim alternative educational setting (IAES) pending a special education hearing officer's decision or until the required time period for disciplinary action expires, whichever takes place first, unless the student's parents agree otherwise (*See:* 34 C.F.R. §300.530).

suspend them for not more than ten consecutive school days to the extent those alternatives are applied to children without disabilities (34 C.F.R. § 300.530(b)(1)). Under this provision, school officials can impose additional removals of not more than ten consecutive school days in the same academic year for separate incidents of misconduct as long as these removals do not constitute a change of placement. If subsequent suspensions exceed ten cumulative school days in one year, services must begin after the tenth day (34 C.F.R. § 300.356(b)(2)). Figure 9.1 provides a useful flowchart detailing the IDEA 2004's disciplinary procedures for students with disabilities.

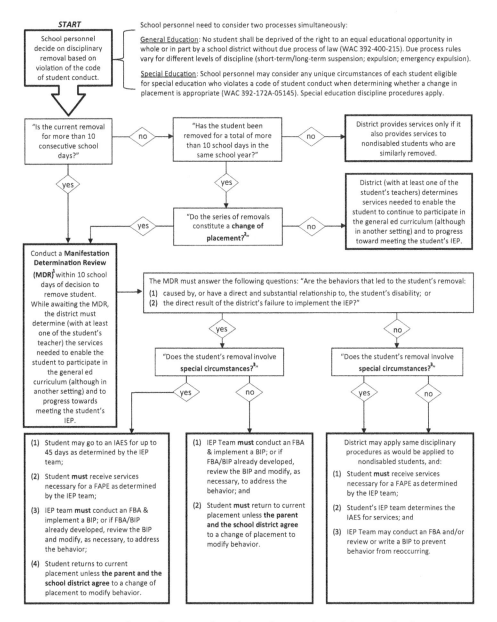

Figure 9.1 Overview of Discipline Procedures for Students With Disabilities Under the IDEA 2004

Source: State of Washington Office of Superintendent of Public Education. *Additional resources and information about behavior and discipline: Special education discipline flowchart.* Retrieved from www.k12.wa.us/SpecialEd/Families/pubdocs/SpEd_DisciplineFlowchart.pdf

Transfers to Other Settings for Disciplinary Reasons (The Forty-Five -Day Rule)

Beginning with its 1997 amendments, the IDEA allows for the placement of students with disabilities to interim alternative educational settings (IAES) for up to forty-five school days for weapons, drug violations, or serious bodily injury. In an important clarification, the regulations permit students to be removed for up to forty-five school days, as opposed to calendar, days, a timeframe that grants educators more latitude (34 C.F.R. § 300.530(g)(1)).

The IDEA and its regulations now authorize school officials to transfer students to alternative settings if they carry or possess weapons at school, on school premises, or at school functions (20 U.S.C. § 1415(k)(1)(G)(i); 34 C.F.R. § 300.530(g)(1)). Similarly, educators can transfer students who knowingly possess, use, sell, or solicit drugs under those same circumstances (20 U.S.C. § 1415(k)(1)(G)(ii); 34 C.F.R. § 300.530(g)(2)). When it comes to drugs, their mere possession is not enough for exclusions. Instead, students must "knowingly" possess drugs before they can be excused. Perhaps this difference can be explained by anecdotal reports that drug dealing and using students often ask children with disabilities, with whom they would not otherwise associate, to unknowingly transport their caches of drugs as a sign of friendship or as favors. Finally, officials can transfer students if they have inflicted bodily injury on other persons (20 U.S.C. § 1415(k)(1)(G)(iii); 34 C.F.R. § 300.530(g)(3)). The regulation eliminated any specific requirements that IEP teams must consider in selecting interim alternative placements, thereby affording them greater authority and discretion.

When students are placed in interim settings for possession of drugs, weapons, or having caused bodily harm, the duties of school officials are relaxed to the extent that they are no longer required to conduct functional behavioral assessments and implement behavioral intervention plans in doing so. Rather, on the date on which educators make removals that constitute changes in placement of children with disabilities due to violations of student codes of conduct, they must inform the parents of their doing so and provide them with notice of their procedural safeguards (34 C.F.R. § 300.530(h)).

If parents disagree with the placements of their children in interim alternative settings and request hearings, students must remain in these locations pending the outcomes of hearings, until the expiration of the forty-five-day period, or the parties agree otherwise (20 U.S.C. § 1415(k)(4)(A); 34 C.F.R. § 300.533). The new regulation on placements during appeals introduced an important new change, replacing a lengthier, more detailed rule, with its streamlined provisions. Under this regulation, children must remain in their alternative settings for all disciplinary appeals, not just those relating to challenges of forty-five-day placements or where school officials sought hearings under the IDEA's "dangerousness" provisions (34 C.F.R. § 300.533). Additionally, school officials are required to arrange for expedited hearings within twenty school days of when they receive requests for one and must render decisions within ten school days after hearings are completed (20 U.S.C. § 1415(k)(4)(B); 34 C.F.R. § 300.532 (c)(2)). At the expiration of the forty-five-day period, students are entitled to return to their former placements even if hearings about school board proposals to change their placements are pending (20 U.S.C. § 1415(k)(4)(A)).

Weapons, Alcohol, and Drugs

School officials have the explicit authority to transfer students with disabilities to appropriate interim alternative placements for up to forty-five school days for weapon, drug, and alcohol violations (20 U.S.C. §§ 1415(k)(1)(G)(i)-(ii); 34 C.F.R. §§ 300.530(g)(1), (2), (4)). This clause expands the authority that the Gun-Free Schools Act of 1994 granted school officials to exclude students from schools for drug violations. The IDEA defines weapons and illegal drugs by referencing other federal legislation (20 U.S.C. §§ 1415(k)(7)(A), (B); 34 C.F.R. § 300.530(i)(1), (2)). In this regard, the definition of a dangerous weapon is expanded beyond the previous definition enunciated in the Gun-Free Schools Act. Under the new definition, what can be considered a dangerous weapon includes other instruments, devices, materials, and substances capable of inflicting harm in addition to firearms, but it does not include small pocket knives (18 U.S.C. § 930(g)(2)). The IDEA defines illegal drugs as controlled substances, but it excludes controlled substances that may be legally prescribed by physicians (20 U.S.C. § 1415(k)(7)(B); 34 C.F.R. § 300.530(i)(1)). The Controlled Substances Act (21 U.S.C. § 812 (c)), which is too lengthy to repeat here, specifies the full list of controlled substances.

Infliction of Serious Bodily Injury

The IDEA also now allows school personnel to remove students to interim alternative settings for up to forty-five school days for inflicting serious bodily injuries (20 U.S.C. § 1415(k)(1)(G)(iii); 34 C.F.R. § 300.530(g)(3)). The IDEA's definition of serious bodily injury, which refers to another section of the United States Code (20 U.S.C. § 1415(k)(7)(C); 34 C.F.R. § 300.530(I)(3)), is that which may involve a substantial risk of death; extreme physical pain; protracted and obvious disfigurement; or protracted loss or impairment of the function of a bodily member, organ, or mental faculty (18 U.S.C. § 1365(h)(3)). Serious bodily injury may be contrasted with bodily injury, which generally involves only cuts, abrasions, bruises, burns, or other temporary injuries (18 U.S.C. § 1365(h)(4)).

Other Infractions

The IDEA's disciplinary provisions permit school officials to remove students from fully inclusive settings and place them in interim alternative placements for infractions other than those specifically listed in its text as long as they are doing so under "unique circumstances" (20 U.S.C. § 1415(k)(1)(A); 34 C.F.R. § 300.530(a)). When exercising this case-by-case authority, it is likely that school officials will be faced with parental challenges. Even so, prior case law suggests that officials will be upheld as long as they can reasonably justify their actions.

As illustrated by a case from Texas that was resolved prior to the IDEA's reauthorization, a circumstance justifying a student's exclusion may be an act of sexual harassment. In *Randy M. v. Texas City ISD* (2000) educators recommended that a special education student be transferred to an alternative education program for the remainder of a school year after he, in consort with another child, ripped the pants off of a female student. Prior to making this recommendation, the IEP team agreed that the student's misconduct was not a manifestation of his disability. When the student's parents sought to prevent the transfer, a federal trial court refused their request to do so. The court expressed its view that the disciplinary actions of the school officials were entirely appropriate under the facts of the case. The court explained that school officials were justified in taking stern and aggressive remedial action when faced with such conduct.

Another circumstance that can lead to a student's removal is behavior that may not necessarily have caused serious bodily injury but which, if repeated, has the potential to do so. In such a case, an appellate court in New York approved the removal of a student who hit other children and teachers in conceding that educators demonstrated that allowing him to return to school would have been likely to have resulted in injuries to the child and/or others (*Roslyn Union Free School District v. Geffrey W.*, 2002).

Functional Behavioral Assessments (FBAs) and Behavioral Intervention Plans (BIPs)

The IDEA 2004 requires school personnel to conduct functional behavioral assessments (FBAs) and implement behavioral intervention plans (BIPs), if they are not already in place, or review such assessments and plans if they have been implemented under certain circumstances. Specifically, officials must perform FBAs and implement BIPs whenever students with disabilities are removed from their current placements for disciplinary reasons for more than ten school days (20 U.S.C. § 1415(k)(1)(D)(ii); 34 C.F.R. § 300.530(d)(ii)). Further, educators must complete FBAs and BIPs it they determine that misbehavior is a manifestation of students' disabilities (20 U.S.C. § 1415(k)(1)(F)(i); 34 C.F.R. § 300.530(f)(1)). Surprisingly, since the IDEA is generally prescriptive about such concerns, the statute and its regulations are silent about the form that BIPs must take. Even though the Eighth Circuit, relying on the IDEA's facial language, ruled that there was no requirement that a BIP be in writing (*School Board of Independent School District No. 11 v. Renollett*, 2006), educators would be wise to reduce their agreements to writing both to avoid potential problems down the line and to be consistent with the statute's overall stance with regard to record keeping.

Neither the IDEA nor its regulation provides much guidance as to what should be included in FBAs or BIPs. As of this writing, there have been few reported judicial decisions or due process hearings dealing with the contents of either FBAs or BIPs. In one dispute over a school's BIP, the Seventh Circuit affirmed that since there are no substantive requirements for a BIP, the challenged BIP could not have fallen short of criteria that did not exist (*Alex R. v. Forrestville Valley Community Unit School District*, 2004). Yet, the fact that substantive criteria for FBAs and BIPs do not exist, does not mean that developing them is unimportant. To this end, a federal trial court in New York overturned a school's manifestation determination, in part, because school personnel had not conducted an FBA prior to acting (*Coleman v. Newburgh Enlarged City School District*, 2004).

Expulsions

The IDEA permits educators to expel students with disabilities as long as the behaviors that gave rise to the violations of school rules are not a manifestation of their disabilities. Again, though, under these circumstances expulsions must be treated in the same manner and for the same duration as they would be for students who are not disabled (20 U.S.C. § 1415(k)(1)(C); 300 C.F.R. § 300.530(c)).

Provision of Special Education Services During Expulsions

The IDEA makes it clear that special education services must continue during expulsions (20 U.S.C. §§ 1412(a)(1)(A), 1415(k)(1)(D)(i); 34 C.F.R. § 530(d)(i)). This provision essentially codifies the position of the United States Department of Education and effectively reversed judicial orders to the contrary (*Commonwealth of Virginia Department of Education v. Riley*, 1997; *Doe v. Board of Education of Oak Park & River Forest High School District 200*, 1997). The addition of this section to the IDEA ended a controversy that existed among the federal circuits prior to the enactment of the 1997 amendments.

Manifestation Determination

As noted earlier, the courts have long recognized that expulsions of students in special education settings constitute changes in placements. Expelling students for misconduct that was a manifestation of their disabilities, the courts reasoned, would have been the equivalent of punishing children for behavior over which they had no control. Additionally, the courts agreed that expulsion would result in the denial of the FAPEs the students are entitled to under federal law.

When school officials contemplate the expulsion of special education students, the IDEA requires educators to first ascertain whether their misbehaviors are manifestations of their disabilities. If officials agree that there is no connection between disabilities and misconduct, they may expel students (20 U.S.C. § 1415(k)(1)(C); 34 C.F.R. § 300.530(c)). However, even if students with disabilities are expelled, they must continue to receive educational services that will permit them to make progress toward meeting the goals set out in the IEPs (34 C.F.R. § 300.530d(1)(I)). Insofar as it is highly likely that expulsions will be challenged, it is imperative for school officials to follow proper procedures when making manifestation determinations.

Timeline of Manifestation Determinations

Manifestation determinations must be made within ten school days of any decision to change the placements of children with disabilities who violated school codes of conduct (20 U.S.C. § 1415(k)(1)(E)(i); 34 C.F.R. § 300.530(e)(1)). As explicit as this language is, the federal trial court in Maine pointed out that a delay in conducting a manifestation hearing was of no consequence because the parents had the opportunity to participate and the delay did not affect its outcome (*Farrin v. Maine School Administrative District No. 59*, 2001). The court observed that the delay in convening the meeting was understandable because the school board's special education director made several unsuccessful attempts to contact the parents in trying to schedule the hearing within the ten-day time period.

Manifestation as Defined in the IDEA

Prior to 2004 the IDEA did not provide a precise definition of the term "manifestation." Yet, as indicated, the IDEA now specifies the criteria that IEP teams should consider in evaluating whether misconduct is a manifestation of a disability. More specifically, IEP teams must review all relevant information in student files, including IEPs, teacher observations, and other relevant information from parents that can be used to evaluate whether students' conduct was caused by, or had a direct and substantial relationship to, their disabilities or whether it was a direct result of a school board's failure to implement an IEP (20 U.S.C. § (k)(1)(E); 34 C.F.R. § 300.530(e)(1)). Earlier case law can provide some guidance on how this new language can be interpreted.

The IDEA's definition of manifestation is identical to the wording that the Ninth Circuit used in *Doe v. Maher* (1986), the case that became known as *Honig v. Doe* (1988) once it reached the Supreme Court. The court held that manifestation of a disability refers to "conduct that is caused by, or has a direct and substantial relationship" to the student's disability (pp. 1480–1481, n. 8). The court further clarified this by explaining that disabilities must significantly impair the ability of students' behavioral controls and that the term does not embrace conduct that "bears only an attenuated relationship" to the disabilities (pp. 1480–1481, n. 8).

In a judgment that was handed down before the current definition of manifestation took effect, a federal trial court in New York overturned a school panel's finding that a student's misconduct was not a manifestation of his disability. Although it is a pre–2004 amendment opinion, this case illustrates one way that a disability may be deemed to have a direct relationship to a student's misconduct. After the student was disciplined following an altercation with another child, he claimed that he was merely responding to taunting about his status as being in special education. Under the circumstances, the court was satisfied that the student's disability was directly involved in the altercation (*Coleman v. Newburgh Enlarged City School District*, 2004).

On the other hand, in another pre–2004 amendment case, the Fourth Circuit upheld a school board's manifestation determination where a student coerced another child into putting a threatening note in the computer file of a third child. The court decided that the student was aware of the consequences of sending the threatening note, and even anticipated them by enlisting the services of another student. Uncovering nothing in the student's records indicating that he could not manage his emotional problems, the court agreed that his misconduct was not a manifestation of his disability (*AW ex rel. Wilson v. Fairfax County School Board*, 2004).

Decisions the Manifestation Team Must Make

Along with evaluating whether misconduct was caused by or had a direct and substantial relationship to a student's disability, an IEP team must consider whether it was due to an IEP that was not properly implemented (20 U.S.C. § 1415(k)(1)(E)(i)(II); 34 C.F.R. § 300.530(e)(1)(ii)). In reviewing whether a placement was inappropriate, an IEP team should use the same standards that apply when prospectively determining whether a proposed placement is appropriate. Unless state law dictates otherwise, the basic criterion of an appropriate placement is whether it resulted in educational benefit to the student (*Board of Education of the Hendrick Hudson Central School District v. Rowley*, 1982).

If IEP teams decide that misconduct either is a manifestation of student disabilities or results from inappropriate placements or IEPs, the children may neither be expelled nor suspended for more than ten days and school officials must reconsider their current placements. Nonpunitive changes in placement may be appropriate and should be implemented subject to the applicable procedural safeguards and the IDEA's least restrictive environment provision. Students may be suspended for more than ten days, or expelled, if the misconduct was not caused by their disabilities or did not result from inappropriate IEPs or placements.

As reflected by a case from Michigan, one circumstance that requires an earlier evaluation is whenever an IEP team is considering a significant change in placement (*Brimmer v. Traverse City Area Public Schools*, 1994). A reevaluation should include a psychological assessment designed specifically to elicit data relative to the behavior which led to the disciplinary action. If those who conducted the most recent assessments are not part of the group making the manifestation determination, they should be consulted regarding the specific incident in question. If available evaluation data is more than one year old, a reevaluation should be completed before the manifestation decision is undertaken.

Making a Manifestation Determination

In making a manifestation determination, IEP teams must consider all relevant information, including all evaluation and diagnostic results and observations of children (20 U.S.C. § 1415(k)(1)(E)(i); 34 C.F.R. § 300.530(e)(1)). After IEP teams have considered all relevant information, they should proceed as they would have in making any other identifications, classifications, or placement decisions. IEP teams must thus exercise sound professional judgment. Members of IEP teams must rely on their professional knowledge, knowledge of the students, and understanding of the circumstances that led to the misconduct in making this critical decision.

Appeals

As are any matters related to special education programs, manifestation determinations are subject to the IDEA's administrative appeals process. In the case of a manifestation determinations, hearings must be expedited (20 U.S.C. § 1415(k)(4)(B); 34 C.F.R. § 300.532 (c)), meaning that they must take place within twenty school days of the date on which they were requested and decisions must be issued within ten days of hearings. If parents contest manifestation determinations, school officials must postpone any long-term suspensions or expulsions until hearings are completed, even though students must remain in their interim alternative educational settings (20 U.S.C. § 1415(k)(4)(A); 34 C.F.R. § 300.533).

Authority of Special Education Hearing Officers

The IDEA affords hearing officers the authority to issue change in placement orders (20 U.S.C. § 1415(k)(3)(B); 34 C.F.R. § 300.532(b)(2)(ii)). Essentially, when hearing appeals, officers have two options: they may either return students to the placements from which they were removed or order that they be placed in interim alternative settings. If hearing officers choose the latter option, placements may not be for any more than forty-five school days.

Student Placement Pending Appeals

Whenever parents challenge a placement made by their school boards, the IDEA requires children to remain in their then-current placements pending the outcome of hearings (20 U.S.C. § 1415(j)). An exception exists when parents challenge a school board's wish to place children in interim alternative settings for disciplinary reasons. The IDEA declares that while such appeals are pending, students are to remain in interim alternative settings until a hearing officer renders judgments or the forty-five-day limit has expired (20 U.S.C. § 1415(k)(3)(4)(A); 34 C.F.R. § 300.533). In these circumstances, hearings must take place within twenty days and orders must be rendered within another ten days (20 U.S.C. § 1415(k)(3)(4)(B); 34 C.F.R. § 300.532(c)).

Injunctions Allowing School Districts to Exclude Dangerous Students With Disabilities

In *Honig*, the Supreme Court gave school officials the authority to seek injunctions to exclude dangerous students with disabilities from the regular education environment. Although hearing officers have the authority to order changes in placements to appropriate interim alternative educational settings (IAES) for periods of up to forty-five days, when school officials can demonstrate that maintaining students in their then-current placements is substantially likely to result in injury to them or other children (20 U.S.C. § 1415(k)(3)(B)(ii); 34 C.F.R. § 300.532(b)(2)(ii)), they may still seek injunctive relief to bar students from attending school.

⚖️

SPECIAL EDUCATION LAW IN PRACTICE
Legal Case No. 11—IDEA's Stay-Put Provision Involving Disciplinary Proceedings

HONIG V. DOE
Supreme Court of the United States, 1988
484 U.S. 305

Justice Brennan delivered the opinion of the Court.

As a condition of federal financial assistance, the Education of the Handicapped Act requires States to ensure a "free appropriate public education" for all disabled children within their jurisdictions. In aid of this goal, the Act establishes a comprehensive system of procedural safeguards.... Among these safeguards is the so-called "stay-put" provision, which directs that a disabled child "shall remain in [his or her] then current educational placement" pending completion of any review proceedings, unless the parents and state or local educational agencies otherwise agree. Today we must decide whether, in the face of this statutory proscription, state or local school authorities may nevertheless unilaterally exclude disabled children from the classroom for dangerous or disruptive conduct growing out of their disabilities.

. . .

I

. . .

The present dispute grows out of the efforts of certain officials of the San Francisco Unified School District (SFUSD) to expel two emotionally disturbed children from school indefinitely for violent and disruptive conduct related to their disabilities. In November 1980, respondent John Doe assaulted another student at the Louise Lombard School, a developmental center for disabled children. Doe's April 1980 IEP identified him as a socially and physically awkward 17-year-old who experienced considerable difficulty controlling his impulses and anger. Among the goals set out in his IEP was "[i]mprovement in [his] ability to relate to [his] peers [and to] cope with frustrating situations without resorting to aggressive acts." Frustrating situations, however, were an unfortunately prominent feature of Doe's school career: physical abnormalities, speech difficulties, and poor grooming habits had made him the target of teasing and ridicule as early as the first grade; his 1980 IEP reflected his continuing difficulties with peers, noting that his social skills had deteriorated and that he could tolerate only minor frustration before exploding.

On November 6, 1980, Doe responded to the taunts of a fellow student in precisely the explosive manner anticipated by his IEP: he choked the student with sufficient force to leave abrasions on the child's neck, and kicked out a school window while being escorted to the principal's office afterwards. Doe admitted his misconduct and the school subsequently suspended him for five days. Thereafter, his principal referred the matter to the SFUSD Student Placement Committee (SPC or Committee) with the recommendation that Doe be expelled. On the day the suspension was to end, the SPC notified Doe's mother that it was proposing to exclude her child permanently from SFUSD and was therefore extending his suspension until such time as the expulsion proceedings were completed. The Committee further advised her that she was entitled to attend the November 25 hearing at which it planned to discuss the proposed expulsion.

After unsuccessfully protesting these actions by letter, Doe brought this suit . . . [a]lleging that the suspension and proposed expulsion violated the EHA, he sought a temporary restraining order canceling the SPC hearing and requiring school officials to convene an IEP meeting. The District Judge granted the requested injunctive relief and further ordered defendants to provide home tutoring for Doe on an interim basis; shortly thereafter, she issued a preliminary injunction directing defendants to return Doe to his then current educational placement at Louise Lombard School pending completion of the IEP review process. Doe reentered school on December 15, 5 1/2 weeks, and 24 school-days, after his initial suspension.

Respondent Jack Smith was identified as an emotionally disturbed child by the time he entered the second grade in 1976. School records prepared that year indicated that he was unable "to control verbal or physical outburst[s]" and exhibited a "[s]evere disturbance in relationships with peers and adults." Further evaluations subsequently revealed that he had been physically and emotionally abused as an infant and young child and that, despite above average intelligence, he experienced academic and social difficulties as a result of extreme hyperactivity and low self-esteem. Of particular concern was Smith's propensity for verbal hostility; one evaluator noted that the child reacted to stress by "attempt[ing] to cover his feelings of low self worth through aggressive behavior . . . primarily verbal provocations."

Based on these evaluations, SFUSD placed Smith in a learning center for emotionally disturbed children. His grandparents, however, believed that his needs would be better served in the public school setting and, in September 1979, the school district acceded to their requests and enrolled him at A.P. Giannini Middle School. His February 1980 IEP recommended placement in a Learning Disability Group, stressing the need for close supervision and a highly structured environment. Like earlier evaluations, the February 1980 IEP noted that Smith was easily distracted, impulsive, and anxious; it therefore proposed a half-day schedule and suggested that the placement be undertaken on a trial basis.

At the beginning of the next school year, Smith was assigned to a full-day program; almost immediately thereafter he began misbehaving. School officials met twice with his grandparents in October 1980 to discuss returning him to a half-day program; although the grandparents agreed to the reduction, they apparently were never apprised of their right to challenge the decision through EHA procedures. The school officials also warned them that if the child continued his disruptive behavior—which included stealing, extorting money from fellow students, and making sexual comments to female classmates—they would seek to expel him. On November 14, they made good on this threat, suspending Smith for five days after he made further lewd comments. His principal referred the matter to the SPC, which recommended exclusion from SFUSD. As it did in John Doe's case, the Committee scheduled a hearing and extended the suspension indefinitely pending a final disposition in the matter. On November 28, Smith's counsel protested these actions on grounds essentially identical to those raised by Doe, and the SPC agreed to cancel the hearing and to return Smith to a half-day program at A.P. Giannini or to provide home tutoring. Smith's grandparents chose the latter option and the school began home instruction on December 10; on January 6, 1981, an IEP team convened to discuss alternative placements.

After learning of Doe's action, Smith sought and obtained leave to intervene in the suit. The District Court subsequently entered summary judgment in favor of respondents on their EHA claims and issued a permanent injunction. In a series of decisions, the District Judge found that the proposed expulsions and indefinite suspensions of respondents for conduct attributable to their disabilities deprived them of their congressionally mandated right to a free appropriate public education, as well as their right to have that education provided in accordance with the procedures set out in the EHA. The District Judge therefore permanently enjoined . . . any disciplinary action other than a 2- or 5-day suspension against any disabled child for disability-related misconduct, or from effecting any other change in the educational placement of any such child without parental consent pending completion of any EHA proceedings. In addition, the judge barred the State from authorizing unilateral placement changes and directed it to establish an EHA compliance-monitoring system or, alternatively, to enact guidelines governing local school responses to disability-related misconduct. Finally, the judge ordered the State to provide services directly to disabled children when, in any individual case, the State determined that the local educational agency was unable or unwilling to do so.

. . . the Ninth Circuit affirmed the orders with slight modifications. Agreeing with the District Court that an indefinite suspension in aid of expulsion constitutes a prohibited "change in placement" under [the EHA], the Court of Appeals held that the stay-put provision admitted of no "dangerousness" exception and that the statute therefore rendered invalid those provisions of the California Education Code permitting the indefinite suspension or expulsion of disabled children for misconduct arising out of their disabilities. The court concluded, however, that fixed suspensions of up to 30 school days did not fall within the reach of [the EHA], and therefore upheld recent amendments to the state Education Code authorizing such suspensions. . .

Petitioner Bill Honig, California Superintendent of Public Instruction, sought review in this Court, claiming that the Court of Appeals' construction of the stay-put provision conflicted with that of several other Courts of Appeals which had recognized a dangerousness exception. . . . We granted certiorari to resolve these questions and now affirm.

II

. . .

III

The language of [the EHA] is unequivocal. It states plainly that during the pendency of any proceedings initiated under the Act, unless the state or local educational agency and the parents or guardian of a disabled child otherwise agree, "the child shall remain in the then current educational placement." (emphasis added). Faced with this clear directive, petitioner asks us to read a "dangerousness" exception into the stay-put provision on the basis of either of two essentially inconsistent assumptions: first, that Congress thought the residual authority of school officials to exclude dangerous students from the classroom too obvious for comment; or second, that Congress inadvertently failed to provide such authority and this Court must therefore remedy the oversight. Because we cannot accept either premise, we decline petitioner's invitation to rewrite the statute.

Petitioner's arguments proceed, he suggests, from a simple, commonsense proposition: Congress could not have intended the stay-put provision to be read literally, for such a construction leads to the clearly unintended, and untenable, result that school districts must return violent or dangerous students to school while the often lengthy EHA proceedings run their course. We think it clear, however, that Congress very much meant to strip schools of the unilateral authority they had traditionally employed to exclude disabled students, particularly emotionally disturbed students, from school. In so doing, Congress did not leave school administrators powerless to deal with dangerous students; it did, however, deny school officials their former right to "self-help," and directed that in the future the removal of disabled students could be accomplished only with the permission of the parents or, as a last resort, the courts.

As noted above, Congress passed the EHA after finding that school systems across the country had excluded one out of every eight disabled children from classes. In drafting the law, Congress was largely guided by the recent decisions in Mills v. Board of Education of District of Columbia and PARC, both of which involved the exclusion of hard-to-handle disabled students. Mills in particular demonstrated the extent to which schools used disciplinary measures to bar children from the classroom. . . .

Congress attacked such exclusionary practices in a variety of ways. It required participating States to educate all disabled children, regardless of the severity of their disabilities, and included within the definition of "handicapped" those children with serious emotional disturbances. It further provided for meaningful parental participation in all aspects of a child's educational placement, and barred schools, through the stay-put provision, from changing that placement over the parent's objection until all review proceedings were completed. Recognizing that those

proceedings might prove long and tedious, the Act's drafters did not intend to operate inflexibly and they therefore allowed for interim placements where parents and school officials are able to agree on one. Conspicuously absent from [the EHA], however, is any emergency exception for dangerous students. This absence is all the more telling in light of the injunctive decree issued in PARC, which permitted school officials unilaterally to remove students in "'extraordinary circumstances.'" Given the lack of any similar exception in Mills, and the close attention Congress devoted to these "landmark" decisions, we can only conclude that the omission was intentional; we are therefore not at liberty to engraft onto the statute an exception Congress chose not to create.

Our conclusion that [the EHA] means what it says does not leave educators hamstrung. The Department of Education has observed that, "[w]hile the [child's] placement may not be changed [during any complaint proceeding], this does not preclude the agency from using its normal procedures for dealing with children who are endangering themselves or others." Such procedures may include the use of study carrels, time-outs, detention, or the restriction of privileges. More drastically, where a student poses an immediate threat to the safety of others, officials may temporarily suspend him or her for up to 10 school days. This authority, which respondent in no way disputes, not only ensures that school administrators can protect the safety of others by promptly removing the most dangerous of students, it also provides a "cooling down" period during which officials can initiate IEP review and seek to persuade the child's parents to agree to an interim placement. And in those cases in which the parents of a truly dangerous child adamantly refuse to permit any change in placement, the 10-day respite gives school officials an opportunity to invoke the aid of the courts under, which empowers courts to grant any appropriate relief.

Petitioner contends, however, that the availability of judicial relief is more illusory than real, because a party seeking review under [the EHA] must exhaust time-consuming administrative remedies, and because under the Court of Appeals' construction of [the EHA's due process procedures], courts are as bound by the stay-put provision's "automatic injunction," as are schools. It is true that judicial review is normally not available under [the EHA] until all administrative proceedings are completed, but as we have previously noted, parents may bypass the administrative process where exhaustion would be futile or inadequate. While many of the EHA's procedural safeguards protect the rights of parents and children, schools can and do seek redress through the administrative review process, and we have no reason to believe that Congress meant to require schools alone to exhaust in all cases, no matter how exigent the circumstances. The burden in such cases, of course, rests with the school to demonstrate the futility or inadequacy of administrative review, but nothing in [the EHA] suggests that schools are completely barred from attempting to make such a showing. Nor do we think that [the EHA] operates to limit the equitable powers of district courts such that they cannot, in appropriate cases, temporarily enjoin a dangerous disabled child from attending school. As the EHA's legislative history makes clear, one of the evils Congress sought to remedy was the unilateral exclusion of disabled children by schools, not courts, and one of the purposes of [the EHA's procedural protections], therefore, was "to prevent school officials from removing a child from the regular public school classroom over the parents' objection pending completion of the review proceedings." The stay-put provision in no way purports to limit or preempt the authority conferred on courts by [the EHA]; indeed, it says nothing whatever about judicial power.

In short, then, we believe that school officials are entitled to seek injunctive relief under [the EHA] in appropriate cases. In any such action, [the EHA's procedural protections] effectively creates a presumption in favor of the child's current educational placement which school officials can overcome only by showing that maintaining the child in his or her current placement is substantially likely to result in injury either to himself or herself, or to others. In the present case, we are satisfied that the District Court, in enjoining the state and local defendants from indefinitely suspending respondent or otherwise unilaterally altering his then current placement, properly balanced respondent's interest in receiving a free appropriate public education in accordance with the procedures and requirements of the EHA against the interests of the state and local school officials in maintaining a safe learning environment for all their students.

IV

We believe the courts below properly construed and applied [the EHA], except insofar as the Court of Appeals held that a suspension in excess of 10 school-days does not constitute a "change in placement." We therefore affirm the Court of Appeals' judgment on this issue as modified herein. . . . Affirmed.

Questions for Discussion

1. In *Honig* the Court did not mention or address whether school officials must determine whether a student's misbehavior is a manifestation of a disability. Perhaps because the students in this case were identified as having behavior problems, it was automatically assumed that their misbehavior was a manifestation of their disabilities. Recent amendments to the IDEA make it clear that the manifestation doctrine is alive and well. Is it appropriate to assume that behavior is a manifestation of a student's disability based on a disability classification?

2. As *Honig* indicated, suspensions of up to ten school days can be handed out in the same manner for students with disabilities as they are for those who are not disabled. However, serial suspensions that, when taken together, exceed ten days can be problematic if they create a pattern of exclusion. What factors need to be considered when a student's total suspension days in a year exceed ten days?

3. School officials can sometimes be heard to lament that the IDEA creates a different standard of discipline for students with disabilities. Yet, commentators insist that the IDEA only creates different procedures. Does the IDEA's process for disciplining students with disabilities result in different codes of conduct? How would you explain this to the parents of a student who was not disabled but was disciplined for hitting back after being struck by a student with disabilities?

Summary of Important Legal Policies, Principles, and Practices

1. The IDEA statute and accompanying regulations did not address the topic of disciplining students with disabilities until the 1997 reauthorization.
2. Current research reveals that students with disabilities, especially students of color, are disproportionately suspended and expelled from school compared to their nondisabled student peers. Additionally, today's students with disabilities are at a substantially greater risk of experiencing physical restraints or seclusion in school settings.

3. *Honig v. Doe* (1988) remains the only U.S. Supreme Court case involving discipline and students with disabilities. In *Honig*, the Court affirmed the IDEA's stay-put provision, which prevents state or local educational agencies from changing a student's placement during any due process proceeding, including disciplinary proceedings and appeals.

4. The IDEA 2004 contains specific procedures involving the discipline of students with disabilities, including no change in student placement (i.e., ten-day rule); required changes in student placement based on suspensions/expulsions in excess of ten school days; and special circumstances, including possession of weapons, drugs, or infliction of serious bodily injury where IDEA–eligible students may be removed from the classroom for up to forty-five school days to an interim alternative educational setting (IAES).

5. School officials must complete functional behavioral assessments (FBAs) or behavior intervention plans (BIPs) if they believe based on data and other assessments that a particular student's disciplinary infractions are manifestations of students' disabilities.

6. A manifestation determination review (MDR) requires schools to determine if a student's problematic behavior was caused by or related to the student's disability or due to the district's failure to properly implement the IEP.

7. Consider implementing FBAs and BIPs across a broad spectrum of behavior problems (Dieterich, Villani, & Bennett, 2003) which is "the intent of FBA and BIP practices within social sciences; that is, to systematically identify the underlying cause of problematic behaviors and to create positive behavioral interventions to develop socially appropriate responses" (Dieterich, Snyder, & Villani, 2017, p. 197).

8. Recognize that even though the law does not provide specificity related to FBA that the "FBA is a specific approach identifying behavior problems. This is not a vague term, but a distinctive process" (Dieterich & Villani, 2000). School leaders then need to identify a specific protocol for conducting a FBA that demonstrates to the court, that in good faith, they considered behaviors that might impede a student's learning.

9. Recognize that schools may prevail without an active FBA or BIP, because they met procedural requirements, they unnecessarily exhausted time and financial resources to resolve issues that could have been avoided. Hence, school districts would be well suited to follow procedures to conduct an appropriate FBA and BIP with trained staff; otherwise schools are risking that parents will seek relief on the basis of procedural violations" (Dieterich, Snyder, & Villani, 2017, p. 215).

Useful Online Resources

U.S. Department of Education, Office of Special Education and Rehabilitative Services (OSERS)
IDEA: Questions and Answers on Discipline Procedures
   The U.S. Department of Education's Office of Special Education and Rehabilitative Services (OSERS) issued this Q&A document as guidance on the IDEA 2004's disciplinary provisions.
   Website: www2.ed.gov/policy/speced/guid/idea/discipline-q-a.pdf
U.S. Department of Education, Restrain and Seclusion Resource Document
   In 2012, the U.S. Department of Education published a report detailing fifteen principles and practices for school officials, parents, and other stakeholders to consider when developing policies and procedures on the use of restraint and seclusion in schools.
   Website: www2.ed.gov/policy/seclusion/restraints-and-seclusion-resources.pdf

Recommended Reading

Brady, K. P. & Dietrich, C. A. (2016). Video surveillance of special education classrooms: Promotion of student safety or violation of student privacy? *Education Law Reporter, 325*(2), 573–588.

Brady, K. P., & Russo, C. J. (2018, November). Balancing school safety and the rights of children with special needs. *School Business Affairs*, 37–39.

Johns, B. H. (2018). *Reduction of school violence: Alternatives to suspension.* Palm Beach, FL: LRP Publications.

Morrow, E. A. (2017). *Dangerous conduct by students with disabilities: Legal guidelines for appropriate responses.* Palm Beach, FL: LRP Publications.

Pfrommer, J. L. (2017). *Roadmap to IDEA/504 compliance: Manifestation determinations.* Palm Beach, FL: LRP Publications.

Ryan, J. B., Katsiyannis, A., Peterson, R., & Chelar, R. (2007, June). IDEA 2004 and disciplining students with disabilities. *NASSP Bulletin, 91*(2), 130–140.

Shaver, E. A., & Decker, J. R. (2017). Handcuffing a third grader? Interactions between school resource officers and students with disabilities. *Utah Law Review, 2,* 229–282.

Strassfeld, N. M. (2017). The future of IDEA: Monitoring disproportionate representation of minority students in special education and intentional discrimination claims. *Case Western Reserve University Law Review, 67*(4), 1121–1151.

Strassfeld, N. M. (2019). Education federalism and minority disproportionate representation monitoring: Examining IDEA provisions, regulations, and judicial trends. *Journal of Disability Policy Studies,* 1–10.

Sullivan, A. L., & Osher, D. (2019). IDEA's double bind: A synthesis of disproportionality policy interpretations. *Exceptional Children, 85*(4), 395–412.

References

Alex R. v. Forrestville Valley Community Unit School District, 375 F.3d 603 (7th Cir. 2004), *cert. denied,* 543 U.S. 1009 (2004).

AW ex rel. Wilson v. Fairfax County School Board, 372 F.3d 674 (4th Cir. 2004).

Binghampton City School District v. Borgna, 17 EHLR 677 (N.D.N.Y. 1991).

Board of Education of the Hendrick Hudson Central School District v. Rowley, 458 U.S. 176 (1982).

Board of Education of Township High School District v. Kurtz-Imig, 16 EHLR 17 (N.D. Ill. 1989).

Brimmer v. Traverse City Area Public Schools, 872 F. Supp. 447 (W.D. Mich. 1994).

Clinton County R-III School District v. C.J.K., 896 F. Supp. 948 (W.D. Mo. 1995).

Coleman v. Newburgh Enlarged City School District, 319 F. Supp.2d 446 (S.D.N.Y. 2004).

Colker, R. (2018). *Special education law in a nutshell.* St. Paul, MN: West Academic.

Commonwealth of Virginia Department of Education v. Riley, 106 F.3d 559 (4th Cir. 1997).

Controlled Substances Act, 21 U.S.C. § 812 (2006).

Council for Children with Behavioral Disorders. (2009). *CCBD'S Position summary on physical restraint & seclusion procedures in school settings.* Available at https://www.cec.sped.org/~/media/Files/Policy/Restraint%20and%20Seclusion/CCBD_on_Use_of_Restraint_7809.pdf

Dayton, J. (2002). Special education discipline law. *Education Law Reporter, 163,* 17–35.

Dieterich, C. A., Snyder, N. D., & Villani, C. J. (2017). Functional behavioral assessments and behavioral intervention plans: Review of the Law and Recent Cases. *Brigham Young University Education and Law Journal, 2,* 195–217.

Dieterich, C. A., & Villani, C. J. (2000). Functional behavioral assessment: Process without procedures. *Brigham Young University Education and Law Journal, 2,* 209–219.

Dieterich, C. A., Villani, C. J., & Bennett, P. T. (2003). Functional behavioral assessments: Beyond student behavior. *Journal of Law & Education, 34*(3), 357–368.

Doe v. Board of Education of Oak Park & River Forest High School District 200, 115 F.3d 1273 (7th Cir. 1997).

Doe v. Koger, 480 F. Supp. 225 (N.D. Ind. 1979).

Doe v. Maher, 793 F.2d 1470 (9th Cir. 1986), *affirmed Honig v. Doe,* 484 U.S. 305 (1988).

Doe v. Manning, 1994 WL 99052, 21 IDELR 357 (W.D. Va. 1994).

East Islip Union Free School District v. Andersen, 615 N.Y.S.2d 852 (N.Y. Sup. Ct. 1994).

Executive Office of the President. (2016, December). *Report: The continuing need to rethink discipline.* Retrieved from www.aclupa.org/files/9514/8493/3029/WH__Continuing_Need_to_Rethink_Discipline.pdf

Farrin v. Maine School Administrative District No. 59, 165 F. Supp.2d 37 (D. Me. 2001).

Gun-Free Schools Act of 1994, 20 U.S.C. § 8921 (1994).

Hacienda La Puente Unified School District of Los Angeles v. Honig, 976 F.2d 487 (9th Cir. 1992).

Hayes v. Unified School District No. 377, 877 F.2d 809 (10th Cir. 1989).

Honig v. Doe, 484 U.S. 305 (1988).

Huefner, D. S., & Herr, C. M. (2012). *Navigating special education law and policy.* Verona, WI: Attainment Company, Inc.

Jackson v. Franklin County School Board, 765 F.2d 535 (5th Cir. 1985).

Light v. Parkway C-2 School District, 41 F.3d 1223 (8th Cir. 1994).

Magyar v. Tucson Unified School District, 958 F. Supp. 1423 (D. Ariz. 1997).

Manchester School District v. Charles M.F., 1994 WL 485754, 21 IDELR 732 (D.N.H. 1994).

M.P. by D.P. v. Governing Board of the Grossmont Union High School District, 858 F. Supp. 1044 (S.D. Cal. 1994).

Parents of Student W. v. Puyallup School District, 31 F.3d 1489 (9th Cir. 1994).

Randy M. v. Texas City ISD, 93 F. Supp.2d 1310 (S.D. Tex. 2000).

Rodiriecus L. v. Waukegan School District No. 60, 90 F.3d 249 (7th Cir. 1996).

Roslyn Union Free School District v. Geffrey W., 740 N.Y.S.2d 451 (N.Y. App. Div. 2002).

Russo, C. J. (2018). *Russo's the Law of Public Education* (10th ed.). St. Paul, MN: West Academic.

S-1 v. Turlington, 635 F.2d 342 (5th Cir. 1981).

School Board of the County of Prince William v. Malone, 762 F.2d 1210 (4th Cir. 1985).

School Board of the County of Prince William v. Wills, 16 EHLR 1109 (Va. Cir. Ct. 1989).

School Board of the County of Stafford v. Farley, 16 EHLR 1119 (Va. Cir. Ct. 1990).

School Board of Independent School District No. 11 v. Renollett, 440 F.3d 1007 (8th Cir. 2006).

School Board of Pinellas County v. J.M. by L.M., 957 F. Supp. 1252 (M.D. Fla. 1997).

School District of Philadelphia v. Stephan M. and Theresa M., 1997 WL 89113 (E.D. Pa. 1997).

Steldt v. School Board of the Riverdale School District, 885 F. Supp. 1192 (W.D. Wis. 1995).

Stuart v. Nappi, 443 F. Supp. 1235 (D. Conn. 1978).

Texas City Independent School District v. Jorstad, 752 F. Supp. 231 (S.D. Tex. 1990).

Vogell, H. (2014, June). Violent and legal: The shocking ways school kids are pinned down isolated against their will. *ProPublica*.Retrieved from www.tucsonsentinel.com/nationworld/report/062014_school_restraints/shocking-ways-school-kids-are-being-restrained-isolated/

Williams, J. L., Pazey, B., Shelby, L., & Yates, J. R. (2013). The enemy among us: Do school administrators perceive students with disabilities as a threat? *NASSP Bulletin, 97*(2), 139–165.

10
Dispute Resolution
Alternatives to Litigation

Key Concepts and Terms in This Chapter

- Mediation
- Due Process Dispute Resolution
- Administrative Due Process Hearings
- State Complaints

As discussed throughout this book, the Individuals with Disabilities Education Act (IDEA) was enacted, in part, to grant both parents and school officials opportunities to work collaboratively together to develop individualized educational programs (IEPs) for students with disabilities. Yet, in recognizing that parents and educators may not agree in all situations, Congress also included specific dispute resolution provisions in the IDEA (20 U.S.C. § 1415).

Under the IDEA 2004, due process hearings are actively encouraged as the primary method for resolving disputes between the parents of students with disabilities and school districts. Due process hearings address a wide range of special education conflicts, including the identification, evaluation, placement, or provision of FAPE to students with disabilities (34 C.F.R. § 300.507). Parents of students with disabilities may request mediation (20 U.S.C. § 1415(e)) or due process hearings (20 U.S.C. § 1415(f)) if they disagree with any actions of school officials regarding proposed IEPs or of the provision of a free appropriate public education (FAPE) for their children. Once they exhaust administrative remedies, parents may seek judicial review in federal or state courts (20 U.S.C. § 1415(i)(2)(A)). As discussed in the previous chapter on discipline, students with disabilities must remain in their then-current placements while administrative or judicial actions are pending unless school officials and parents agree to the contrary (20 U.S.C. § 1415(j)), hearing officers order changes (20 U.S.C. § 1415(k)(3)(B)), or judicial decrees call for new placements (*Honig v. Doe*, 1988).

Mediation

Part B of the IDEA 2004 "strongly encourages" the use of mediation as an alternative to litigation in the courts to resolve special education disputes between the parents of students with disabilities and school officials (34 C.F.R. § 300.506(a)). The language of the IDEA 2004's statute and regulations strongly reinforce a central theme of the IDEA, namely the need for parents and school districts to work collaboratively, cooperatively minimizing conflict, striving to resolve disputes early and quickly, and avoiding an adversarial process between parents and school officials. The mediation process is always preferred over the option of using the courts based on mediation's numerous benefits, including its cost-effectiveness as well as mediation's likelihood of resulting in more positive, collaborative relationships between parents and school officials as both parties work in the best interests of children and youth with disabilities.

The mediation process affords parents and school officials a viable alternative to litigation in the courts involving special education-related legal disputes. As such, the IDEA 2004 and its accompanying regulations (34 C.F.R. § 300.506(a)) directs both individual states and local educational agencies (LEAs) to offer mediation, at public expense (20 U.S.C. § 1415(e)(2)(D)), as an option when due process hearings may be possible. To date, these provisions have been subject to little litigation.

The IDEA specifies that mediation must be voluntary on the part of all the parties involved; the mediation process cannot be used to deny or delay parental rights to due process hearings or to deny any other rights under the IDEA 2004; and must be conducted by trained, qualified, impartial mediators (20 U.S.C. § 1415(e)(2)(A)(iii), 34 C.F.R. § 300.506(b)(1)) whose names are on state-maintained lists of qualified mediators in special education legal disputes (20 U.S.C. § 1415(e)(2)(C)). Mediation sessions must also be scheduled in a timely manner at locations convenient to all the parties involved (20 U.S.C. § 1415(e)(2)(E)). Agreements that the parties reach as a result of mediation must be formalized in writing (20 U.S.C. § 1415(e)(2)(F)). Discussions that occur during mediation must be kept confidential and cannot be used as evidence in subsequent due process hearings or civil proceedings; the parties may also be required to sign confidentiality pledges prior to initiating mediation (20 U.S.C. § 1415(e)(2)(G)). A new subsection in one of the IDEA regulations makes it clear that the results of mediation agreements can be enforced in federal or state courts (34 C.F.R. § 300.506(b)(7)).

To the extent that mediation is voluntary, parents may choose to bypass the process entirely. If parents choose not to participate in mediation, then states may establish procedures allowing the parties to meet at convenient times and locations with disinterested third parties who are under contract with parent training and information centers, community parent resource centers, or appropriate alternative dispute resolution entities to encourage the use of, and explain the benefits of, the process (20 U.S.C. § 1415(e)(2)(B)).

Due Process Hearings

Another option not involving litigation available to parents and school districts is a due process hearing. Either parents or the school district may request a due process hearing. An impartial hearing officer conducts a due process hearing based on a particular state's law. State law also determines the specific structure of the due process hearing appeals process. For due process decision appeals, state law establishes either a one- or two-tier appeals system. In a one-tier system, due process decisions are appealed directly to either a federal or state-level court; whereas in a two-tier system, due process appeals are made directly to the state education agency (SEA) before both parties can officially file an appeal in either a federal or state-level court (34 C.F.R. § 300.516; and 34 C.F.R. § 300.514).

As part of the dispute resolution process, school officials must convene meetings between parents and relevant members of the IEP teams of their children (34 C.F.R. § 300.510(a)(4)) within fifteen days of parental requests for due process hearings in an attempt to resolve student placement disputes (20 U.S.C. § 1415(f)(1)(B)(i); 34 C.F.R. § 300.510(a)). If educators do not convene requested resolution sessions within this fifteen-day timeframe, parents can seek the intervention of hearing officers to begin this process (34 C.F.R. § 300.510(b)(5)).

Each resolution session must include a school board representative with decision-making authority on its behalf (34 C.F.R. § 300.510(a)(i)) but may not involve a school board attorney, unless parents are also accompanied by counsel (34 C.F.R. § 300.510(a)(ii)). However, if school officials are unable to get parents to participate in resolution sessions and can document their reasonable efforts to do so within thirty days, hearing officers can dismiss complaints (34 C.F.R. § 300.510(b)(4)). The parties need not attend resolution sessions if they agree, in writing, to waive their meetings, or instead, agree to mediation (34 C.F.R. § 300.510(a)(3)).

If parties do not resolve their disputes within thirty days, they should schedule due process hearings (20 U.S.C. § 1415(f)(1)(B)(ii); 34 C.F.R. § 300.510(b)). If the parties do resolve their differences at resolution sessions, they must execute and sign legally binding settlement agreements (20 U.S.C. § 1415(f)(1)(B)(iii); 34 C.F.R. § 300.510(c)).

Parents have the right to request due process hearings on any matters concerning the delivery of any aspect of the special education that their children receive, including identification, evaluation, and placement (20 U.S.C. § 1415(f)). School officials may request hearings if parents refuse to consent to evaluations (34 C.F.R. § 300.300(a)(3)) and must provide parents with proper notice of their rights when they make requests for the evaluations of their children (34 C.F.R. § 300.503(a)). While administrative or judicial actions are pending, students must remain in their then-current placements unless parents and school officials agree to other settings (20 U.S.C. § 1415(j)), hearing officers order changes (20 U.S.C. § 1415(k)(3)(B)), or judicial decrees mandate changes in placements (*Honig v. Doe*, 1988).

The IDEA's regulations grant parents the right to choose whether to have their children present at hearings (34 C.F.R. § 300.512(c)(1)) and whether they should be open to the public (34 C.F.R. § 300.512(c)(2)). If parents cannot be identified, their whereabouts cannot be discovered, or children are wards of the state, surrogate parents who are appointed to safeguard the educational interests of children can request hearings (34 C.F.R. § 300.30(a)(5)). The IDEA's regulations specify that surrogate parents are employees of school boards or state educational agencies, cannot have personal or professional conflicts of interest with regard to the interests of the children involved, and have the knowledge and skill to act in this capacity (34 C.F.R. § 300.519(d)(2)). Otherwise, state laws and regulations govern other qualifications for surrogate parents, such as necessary educational preparation and background.

Parties who file due process complaints must forward copies of the materials to their state education agencies (34 C.F.R. § 300.508(a)(2)). Complaints must include the names and addresses of the children, their schools, and, if they are homeless, available contact information. In addition, complaints must include descriptions of the nature of the problems relating to the proposed or refused initiations or changes in the placements of the children, including facts relating to the problems and proposed resolutions to the extent known and available to the parties (34 C.F.R. § 300.508(b)).

Assuming, as is almost always the case, that parents requested due process hearings, school officials must respond within ten days of receiving complaints. Responses must include explanations of why school officials proposed or refused to take the actions raised in the complaints; descriptions of other options that IEP teams considered and the reasons why they were rejected; descriptions of each evaluation procedure, assessment, record, or report they relied on as the basis for the proposed or refused actions; and descriptions of the other factors that were relevant to their proposed or refused actions. The regulations add that responses cannot be interpreted as precluding school officials from asserting, if appropriate, that parental due process complaints are insufficient (34 C.F.R. § 300.508(e)).

Depending on the law in a given jurisdiction, either states or local school boards may conduct due process hearings (20 U.S.C. § 1415(f)(1)(A)). States are free to establish either one- or two-tiered administrative due process mechanisms. If local boards conduct initial hearings, either party may initiate state-level appeals (20 U.S.C. § 1415(g)). While procedures vary from one state to another, most jurisdictions created two-tiered systems that begin with hearings before individual hearing officers with appeals to review panels.

In the past, the IDEA did not contain a statute of limitations for requesting administrative due process hearings. Thus, time limitations needed to be either mandated by state law or borrowed from analogous state statutes. Congress remedied this situation with the passage of the 2004 IDEA amendments by instituting a two-year limitations period for requesting due process hearings (20 U.S.C. § 1415(f)(3)(C)). If state laws create other limitations periods, they prevail (34 C.F.R. § 300.507(a)(2)). Moreover, the federal timeline is to be stayed if parents can show that school officials misrepresented that they resolved the problems or if they withheld pertinent information from parents (20 U.S.C. § 1415(f)(3)(D)).

Subject Matter of Due Process Hearings

Parents can request due process hearings on any matters relating to the education of their children with disabilities (20 U.S.C. § 1415(f)(1)(A)). State laws and regulations may provide parents with additional rights over the content and structure of due process hearings.

If parents whose children are either enrolled in public schools or seeking to enroll them fail, or refuse, to respond to requests to provide consent for initial evaluations, school officials may, but are not required to, request due process hearings to pursue initial evaluations, if appropriate, except to the extent that doing so would be inconsistent with state laws relating to parental consent (34 C.F.R. § 300.300(a)(3)(i)). If school officials choose not to pursue evaluations under the circumstances, parents may not accuse them of violating their duties under the IDEA (34 C.F.R. § 300.300(a)(3)(ii)). School officials can request hearings if parents refuse to consent to evaluations (34 C.F.R. § 300.300(a)(3)), but not if parents refuse to consent to the provision of services for their children (34 C.F.R. § 300.300(b)(2)).

Parents can also request due process hearings after the eligibility of their children to receive special education ends because students may be entitled to compensatory educational services if courts agree that they were denied a FAPE.

Impartiality of Special Education Hearing Officers

Hearing officers, typically selected pursuant to provisions in state law (*Cothern v. Mallory*, 1983), must be impartial, meaning that they cannot be employees of the states or districts involved in the education of the children whose cases appear before them or have personal or professional interests in these students (20 U.S.C. § 1415(f)(3)(A); 34 C.F.R. § 300.511(c)). Individuals who otherwise qualify as hearing officers are not considered employees of states or local school boards solely by virtue of being paid to serve in this capacity (34 C.F.R. § 300.511(c)(2)). State education agencies are required to keep lists of qualified hearing officers along with explanations of their qualifications (34 C.F.R. § 300.511(c)(3)).

Authority of Hearing Officers

In due process hearings, hearing officers must sort out what took place and apply the law to the facts in a manner similar to that of trial court judges. Like judges, hearing officers are empowered to issue orders and grant equitable relief regarding the provision of a FAPE for students with disabilities.

The importance of their duties aside, the authority of hearing officers is limited. Hearing officers generally do not have the authority to provide remedies when parties challenge broad policies or procedures that affect a large number of students or to address matters of law since they lack the ability to consider a statute's constitutionality. Rather, the power of hearing officers is limited to the facts of the disputes at hand. In addition, the IDEA limits the awarding of attorney's fees to prevailing parents in special education disputes to the discretion of federal courts (20 U.S.C. §1415(i)(3)(B)).

An unresolved question remains over whether hearing officers can grant awards of compensatory services to students who were denied a FAPE. While the Third Circuit affirmed that hearing officers were powerless to address the question of compensatory education (*Lester H. v. Gilhool*, 1990), the Second Circuit reached the opposite result (*Burr v. Ambach*, 1988, 1989a, 1989b, 1990). Moreover, the federal trial court in New Hampshire asserted that a hearing officer erred in writing that he lacked the authority to award compensatory services. The court thought that in light of the importance Congress placed on the process, such power was coextensive with that of the judiciary (*Cocores v. Portsmouth, New Hampshire School District*, 1991). To the extent that hearing officers can grant awards of tuition reimbursement, it seems logical that they should have the authority to award compensatory educational services as well.

Burden of Proof

Until recently, the IDEA and its regulations were silent as to which party bore the burden of proof in due process hearings. As such, this important question was resolved based on state laws or judicial discretion, leading to a great deal of disagreement and inconsistency. Not surprisingly, two distinct perspectives emerged. On the one hand, the Fourth (*Weast v. Schaffer*, 2004), Fifth (*Alamo Heights Independent School District v. State Board of Education*, 1986), Sixth (*Doe v. Board of Education of Tullahoma City Schools*, 1993), and Tenth (*Johnson v. Independent School District No. 4*, 1990) Circuits agreed that the parties challenging IEPs bore the burden of proof. These courts assigned presumptions in favor of IEPs as long as they were developed according to the procedures outlined in the IDEA.

Conversely, the Second (*Grim v. Rhinebeck Central School District*, 2003), Third (*Carlisle Area School v. Scott P.*, 1995), Seventh (*Beth B. v. Van Clay*, 2002), Eighth (*Blackmon v. Springfield R-XII School District*, 1999), Ninth (*Seattle School District No. 1 v. B.S.*, 1996), and District of Columbia (*McKenzie v. Smith*, 1985) Circuits placed the burden of proof on school boards, regardless of whether they or parents wished to alter IEPs. These courts noted that since boards had the duty to provide a FAPE for students with disabilities, school officials should have been better able to meet the burden of proof due to their access to relevant information, coupled with parental lack of expertise in formulating an appropriate IEP.

The Supreme Court stepped into the fray and resolved this controversy over who bore the legal burden of proof in *Schaffer v. Weast* (Schaffer) (2005). In conceding that arguments could be made on both sides of the issue, the Court saw no reason to depart from the usual rule that the party seeking relief bears the burden of persuasion. In IDEA cases, this is generally the parents (Osborne & Russo, 2005). The issue was important since the assignment of the burden of proof can well impact the final outcome in close cases (Wenkart, 2004). Under *Schaffer*, parents who challenge proposed IEPs must now demonstrate that the IEPs are deficient unless state laws provide otherwise (Russo & Osborne, 2006). In the wake of *Schaffer*, at least two circuits placed the burden of proof on the party challenging the IEPs (*L.E. ex rel. E.S. v. Ramsey Board of Education*, 2006; *West Platte R-II School District v. Wilson ex rel. L.W.*, 2006).

Exhaustion of Administrative Remedies

As reflected by a case from New Mexico, "[t]he IDEA favors prompt resolution of disputes" (*Sanders v. Santa Fe Public Schools*, 2004, p. 1311) over the education of students with disabilities because Congress acknowledged the need to help children who may be at formative stages in their development. Courts can also excuse parental failure to exhaust administrative remedies if school officials deny their requests for due process hearings or frustrate their attempts to dispute the results of hearings (*Abney ex rel. Kantor v. District of Columbia*, 1988; *Independent School District No. 623 v. Digre*, 1990), or if it is impossible for parents to obtain adequate relief through hearings (*Padilla v. School District No. 1*, 2000).

Rights of Parties to a Hearing

Parties involved in due process hearings have the right to be accompanied and advised by legal counsel with special knowledge concerning the education of students with disabilities (20 U.S.C. § 1415(h)(1)). The parties at hearings may present evidence, compel the attendance of witnesses, and cross-examine witnesses during these quasi-judicial proceedings (20 U.S.C. § 1415(h)(1)(2)). The parties can prohibit the introduction of evidence that is not disclosed at least five business days prior to hearings (34 C.F.R. § 300.512(a)(3)). At the same time, the parties have the right to obtain written or, at the option of the parents, electronic verbatim records of hearings, as well as findings of fact and decisions (20 U.S.C. § 1415(h)(3)–(4)). Pursuant to the IDEA, hearing officers must render final orders within forty-five days of requests for hearings (34 C.F.R. § 300.515(a)). Even so, hearing officers can grant requests from the parties for extensions or continuances (34 C.F.R. § 300.515(c)). The results of hearings are final unless they are appealed (20 U.S.C. § 1415(i)(1)(A)).

Once administrative review is complete, aggrieved parties may file suit in federal or state courts (20 U.S.C. § 1415(i)(2)(A)). Aggrieved parties are generally considered to be the losing parties or the ones who did not obtain the relief sought. As mentioned earlier, under the IDEA, either party can appeal the results of due process hearings to federal or state courts once they have exhausted administrative remedies. As important as this issue is, the IDEA is silent about whether cases are to be submitted to juries. Insofar as due process hearings generate their own record, the courts generally do not conduct trials *de novo*. In other words, courts ordinarily do not repeat investigations as none had occurred administratively. Rather, the courts examine the records of hearings and hear new or additional testimony when necessary. Due to the importance Congress placed on the administrative process, the IDEA requires courts to give due weight to the results of due process hearings and overturn adjudications only when they are convinced that they were clearly erroneous. Given the Supreme Court's ruling in *Schaffer* that placed the burden of proof in due process hearings on the party challenging IEPs, courts in the future may very well keep the burden of proof on that party throughout the proceedings.

Judicial Deference

In line with the Supreme Court's position that judges should not substitute their views for those of school officials (*Board of Education of the Hendrick Hudson Central School District v. Rowley*, 1982), most jurists defer to educators on matters dealing with appropriate instructional methodologies as long as school officials followed procedural requirements. The Supreme Court (*Board of Education of the Hendrick Hudson Central School District v. Rowley*, 1982) and other federal courts (*Roncker v. Walter*, 1983; *Briggs v. Board of Education of Connecticut*, 1989; *Kerkham v. Superintendent, District of Columbia Schools*, 1991) agree that the IDEA's mandate requiring courts to review the records of due process hearings implies that their results must be given due weight. Still, it is unclear how much weight is due to these results.

Exchange of Information

Attorneys for the parties in IDEA proceedings generally exchange information prior to trials. Principles of fairness dictate that one side cannot withhold information that is crucial to one party's case because, just as in due process hearings, the goal is to have all possible evidence available to help measure the appropriateness of IEPs rather than prevail in disputes just for the sake of winning.

Res Judicata

Based on the principle of *res judicata*, courts cannot hear cases or render judgments on matters that they have already resolved. *Res judicata* stands for the proposition that a final judgment by a court of competent jurisdiction is conclusive and acts as an absolute bar to a subsequent action involving the same claim.

Settlement Agreements

During the course of disputes parents and school officials often negotiate settlement agreements that effectively end controversies. The parties sometimes reach settlement agreements as a result of resolution sessions or mediation before due process hearings started or during litigation. When the parties agree on settlements during litigation, hearing officers or courts may either approve or reject them if they deem their terms to be contrary to public policy or existing law.

Statutes of Limitations

The IDEA and its regulations now require parties to request impartial due process hearings within two years of the date they knew or should have known about the actions that form the bases of their complaints (20 U.S.C. § 1415(f)(3)(C); 34 C.F.R. § 300.511(e)). If states have explicit time limitations for requesting hearings, these limitations apply. Limitations periods may be set aside if school boards misrepresented that they resolved the problems forming the bases of complaints or if officials withheld information that they should have provided to parents (20 U.S.C. § 1415(f)(3)(D); 34 C.F.R. § 300.511(f)). After final administrative decisions are rendered, parties have ninety days to file judicial appeals (20 U.S.C. § 1415(g)(2)(B); 34 C.F.R. § 300.516(b)). Again, if state laws provide otherwise, they prevail.

State Administrative Complaints

In addition to the previously mentioned non-ligation dispute resolution options of mediation and due process hearings, there is another, more formal dispute resolution option available to either parents or school systems: a state administrative complaint. Every state must have a documented procedure allowing either an individual or organization to file a signed, written complaint involving an IDEA violation occurring no more than one year before the date the state received the formal complaint (Colker, 2018). Within sixty days of receiving the complaint, the state must initiate an investigation which can include an on-site investigation. Although no hearing is held, the state collects information to potentially resolve the dispute. An important difference between state administrative complaints and due process hearings is that state administrative complaints cannot be appealed to a federal or state court (34 C.F.R. § 300.516). Under the IDEA 2004 regulations, a description of the minimum procedures associated with a state administrative complaint include

1. Each state must include in its complaint procedures a time limit of sixty days after a complaint is filed;
2. Carry out an independent on-site investigation;
3. Give complainant an opportunity to submit additional information, either orally or in writing, about the allegations in the complaint;
4. Review all the relevant information and make an independent determination as to whether the local educational agency is violating a requirement of Part B of the IDEA 2004;
5. Issue a written decision to the complainant that addresses each allegation in the complaint;
6. Allow an extension of the time limit under exceptional circumstances;
7. Include procedures for effective implementation of the state education agencies (SEA's) final decision;
8. If an issue raised in the state complaint has previously been decided in a due process hearing involving the same parties, the due process hearing decision is legally binding on that issue(s).

(34 C.F.R. § 300.152)

Table 10.1 provides a comparison of the major dispute resolution processes, including mediation, due process complaints, resolution process, and state administrative complaints.

Table 10.1 IDEA 2004 Part B Dispute Resolution Options Comparison Chart

	Mediation	*Due Process Complaint*	*Resolution Process*	*State Administrative Complaint*
Who can initiate the process?	Parent or LEA/ Public Agency, but must be voluntary for both	Parent or LEA/Public Agency	LEA schedules the resolution meeting upon receipt of a due process complaint unless the parties agree to waive or use mediation	Any individual or organization, including those from out of state
What is the time limit for filing?	None specified	Two years from when the party knew or should have known of the problem (or a State law specified timeline) with limited exceptions	Triggered by a parent's due process complaint	Year from the date of the alleged violation
What issues can be resolved?	Any matter under Part 300 including matters arising prior to the filing of a due process complaint (there are exceptions)	Any matter relating to the identification, evaluation or educational placement or provision of a free appropriate public	Same as the issues raised in the parent's due process complaint	Alleged violations of Part B of IDEA or Part 300
What is the timeline for resolving the issues?	None specified	Forty-five days from the end of the resolution period	School district must convene a resolution meeting within fifteen days of the receipt of the parent/guardian's due process compliant, unless the parties agree in writing to waive the meeting or agree to use mediation	Sixty days from receipt of the complaint, unless an extension is permitted
Who resolves the issues?	Parent/guardian and school district with a mediator. The process is voluntary, and both parties must agree to a resolution	Hearing officer	Parent/guardian and school district. Both parties must agree to a resolution	State educational agency (SEA)

Source: The Center for Appropriate Dispute Resolution in Special Education (CADRE) (2013). Retrieved from www.cadreworks.org/sites/default/files/resources/OSEP%20Comparison%20Chart%20FINAL%2011-2013_0.pdf

⚖️

SPECIAL EDUCATION LAW IN PRACTICE
Legal Case No. 12—Burden of Proof at Due Process Hearings

SCHAFFER EX REL. SCHAFFER V. WEAST
Supreme Court of the United States, 2005
546 U.S. 49

Justice O'Connor delivered the opinion of the Court.

The Individuals with Disabilities Education Act (IDEA or Act) is a Spending Clause statute that seeks to ensure that "all children with disabilities have available to them a free appropriate public education." Under IDEA, school districts must create an "individualized education program" (IEP) for each disabled child. If parents believe their child's IEP is inappropriate, they may request an "impartial due process hearing." The Act is silent, however, as to which party bears the burden of persuasion at such a hearing. We hold that the burden lies, as it typically does, on the party seeking relief.

I

A

Congress first passed IDEA as part of the Education of the Handicapped Act in 1970 and amended it substantially in the Education for All Handicapped Children Act of 1975 . . . . {Unless otherwise noted, the Court applied . . . the pre—2004 version of the statute because this is the version that was in effect during the proceedings below}

. . .

Parents and guardians play a significant role in the IEP process. They must be informed about and consent to evaluations of their child under the Act. Parents are included as members of "IEP teams." They have the right to examine any records relating to their child, and to obtain an "independent educational evaluation of the[ir] child." They must be given written prior notice of any changes in an IEP, and be notified in writing of the procedural safeguards available to them under the Act. If parents believe that an IEP is not appropriate, they may seek an administrative "impartial due process hearing." School districts may also seek such hearings, as Congress clarified in the 2004 amendments. They may do so, for example, if they wish to change an existing IEP but the parents do not consent, or if parents refuse to allow their child to be evaluated. As a practical matter, it appears that most hearing requests come from parents rather than schools.

Although state authorities have limited discretion to determine who conducts the hearings, and responsibility generally for establishing fair hearing procedures, Congress has chosen to legislate the central components of due process hearings. It has imposed minimal pleading standards, requiring parties to file complaints setting forth "a description of the nature of the problem" and "a proposed resolution of the problem to the extent known and available at the time." At the hearing, all parties may be accompanied by counsel, and may "present evidence and confront, cross-examine, and compel the attendance of witnesses." After the hearing, any aggrieved party may bring a civil action in state or federal court. Prevailing parents may also recover attorney's fees. Congress has never explicitly stated, however, which party should bear the burden of proof at IDEA hearings.

B

This case concerns the educational services that were due, under IDEA, to petitioner Brian Schaffer. Brian suffers from learning disabilities and speech-language impairments. From prekindergarten through seventh grade he attended a private school and struggled academically. In 1997, school officials informed Brian's mother that he needed a school that could better accommodate his needs. Brian's parents contacted respondent Montgomery County Public Schools System (MCPS) seeking a placement for him for the following school year.

MCPS evaluated Brian and convened an IEP team. The committee generated an initial IEP offering Brian a place in either of two MCPS middle schools. Brian's parents were not satisfied with the arrangement, believing that Brian needed smaller classes and more intensive services. The Schaffers thus enrolled Brian in another private school, and initiated a due process hearing challenging the IEP and seeking compensation for the cost of Brian's subsequent private education.

In Maryland, IEP hearings are conducted by administrative law judges (ALJs). After a 3-day hearing, the ALJ deemed the evidence close, held that the parents bore the burden of persuasion, and ruled in favor of the school district. The parents brought a civil action challenging the result. The United States District Court for the District of Maryland reversed and remanded, after concluding that the burden of persuasion is on the school district. Around the same time, MCPS offered Brian a placement in a high school with a special learning center. Brian's parents accepted, and Brian was educated in that program until he graduated from high school. The suit remained alive, however, because the parents sought compensation for the private school tuition and related expenses.

Respondents appealed . . . . While the appeal was pending, the ALJ reconsidered the case, deemed the evidence truly in "equipoise," and ruled in favor of the parents. The Fourth Circuit vacated and remanded the appeal so that it could consider the burden of proof issue along with the merits on a later appeal. The District Court reaffirmed its ruling that the school district has the burden of proof. On appeal, a divided panel of the Fourth Circuit reversed. Judge Michael, writing for the majority, concluded that petitioners offered no persuasive reason to "depart from the normal rule of allocating the burden to the party seeking relief." We granted *certiorari*, to resolve the following question: At an administrative hearing assessing the appropriateness of an IEP, which party bears the burden of persuasion?

II

A

The term "burden of proof" is one of the "slipperiest member[s] of the family of legal terms." Part of the confusion surrounding the term arises from the fact that historically, the concept encompassed two distinct burdens: the "burden of persuasion," *i.e.*, which party loses if the evidence is closely balanced, and the "burden of production," *i.e.*, which party bears the obligation to come forward with the evidence at different points in the proceeding. We note at the outset that this case concerns only the burden of persuasion, as the parties agree, and when we speak of burden of proof in this opinion, it is this to which we refer.

When we are determining the burden of proof under a statutory cause of action, the touchstone of our inquiry is, of course, the statute. The plain text of IDEA is silent on the allocation of the burden of persuasion. We therefore begin with the ordinary default rule that plaintiffs bear the risk of failing to prove their claims.

Thus, we have usually assumed without comment that plaintiffs bear the burden of persuasion regarding the essential aspects of their claims. For example, Title VII of the Civil Rights Act of 1964, does not directly state that plaintiffs bear the "ultimate" burden of persuasion, but we have so concluded. In numerous other areas, we have presumed or held that the default rule applies . . . .

The ordinary default rule, of course, admits of exceptions. For example, the burden of persuasion as to certain elements of a plaintiff's claim may be shifted to defendants, when such elements can fairly be characterized as affirmative defenses or exemptions. Under some circumstances this Court has even placed the burden of persuasion over an entire claim on the defendant. But while the normal default rule does not solve all cases, it certainly solves most of them. Decisions that place the *entire* burden of persuasion on the opposing party at the *outset* of a proceeding—as petitioners urge us to do here—are extremely rare. Absent some reason to believe that Congress intended otherwise, therefore, we will conclude that the burden of persuasion lies where it usually falls, upon the party seeking relief.

B

Petitioners contend first that a close reading of IDEA's text compels a conclusion in their favor. They urge that we should interpret the statutory words "due process" in light of their constitutional meaning, and apply the balancing test established by *Mathews v. Eldridge*. Even assuming that the Act incorporates constitutional due process doctrine, *Eldridge* is no help to petitioners, because "[o]utside the criminal law area, where special concerns attend, the locus of the burden of persuasion is normally not an issue of federal constitutional moment."

Petitioners next contend that we should take instruction from the lower court opinions of *Mills v. Board of Education* and *Pennsylvania Association for Retarded Children v. Commonwealth* (hereinafter *PARC*). IDEA's drafters were admittedly guided "to a significant extent" by these two landmark cases. As the court below noted, however, the fact that Congress "took a number of the procedural safeguards from *PARC* and *Mills* and wrote them directly into the Act" does not allow us to "conclude that Congress intended to adopt the ideas that it failed to write into the text of the statute."

Petitioners also urge that putting the burden of persuasion on school districts will further IDEA's purposes because it will help ensure that children receive a free appropriate public education. In truth, however, very few cases will be in evidentiary equipoise. Assigning the burden of persuasion to school districts might encourage schools to put more resources into preparing IEPs and presenting their evidence. But IDEA is silent about whether marginal dollars should be allocated to litigation and administrative expenditures or to educational services. Moreover, there is reason to believe that a great deal is already spent on the administration of the Act. Litigating a due process complaint is an expensive affair, costing schools approximately $8,000—to-$12,000 per hearing. Congress has also repeatedly amended the Act in order to reduce its administrative and litigation-related costs. For example, in 1997 Congress mandated that States offer mediation for IDEA disputes. In 2004, Congress added a mandatory "resolution session" prior to any due process hearing. It also made new findings that "[p]arents and schools should be given expanded opportunities to resolve their disagreements in positive and constructive ways," and that "[t]eachers, schools, local educational agencies, and States should be relieved of irrelevant and unnecessary paperwork burdens that do not lead to improved educational outcomes."

Petitioners in effect ask this Court to assume that every IEP is invalid until the school district demonstrates that it is not. The Act does not support this conclusion. IDEA relies heavily upon the expertise of school districts to meet its goals. It also includes a so-called "stay-put" provision, which requires a child to remain in his or her "then current educational placement" during the pendency of an IDEA hearing. Congress could have required that a child be given the educational placement that a parent requested during a dispute, but it did no such thing. Congress appears to have presumed instead that, if the Act's procedural requirements are respected, parents will prevail when they have legitimate grievances.

Petitioners' most plausible argument is that "[t]he ordinary rule, based on considerations of fairness, does not place the burden upon a litigant of establishing facts peculiarly within the knowledge of his adversary." But this "rule is far from being universal, and has many qualifications upon its application." School districts have a "natural advantage" in information and expertise, but Congress addressed this when it obliged schools to safeguard the procedural rights of parents and to share information with them. As noted above, parents have the right to review all records that the school possesses in relation to their child. They

also have the right to an "independent educational evaluation of the[ir] child." The regulations clarify this entitlement by providing that a "parent has the right to an independent educational evaluation at public expense if the parent disagrees with an evaluation obtained by the public agency." IDEA thus ensures parents access to an expert who can evaluate all the materials that the school must make available, and who can give an independent opinion. They are not left to challenge the government without a realistic opportunity to access the necessary evidence, or without an expert with the firepower to match the opposition.

Additionally, in 2004, Congress added provisions requiring school districts to answer the subject matter of a complaint in writing, and to provide parents with the reasoning behind the disputed action, details about the other options considered and rejected by the IEP team, and a description of all evaluations, reports, and other factors that the school used in coming to its decision. Prior to a hearing, the parties must disclose evaluations and recommendations that they intend to rely upon. IDEA hearings are deliberately informal and intended to give ALJs the flexibility that they need to ensure that each side can fairly present its evidence. IDEA, in fact, requires state authorities to organize hearings in a way that guarantees parents and children the procedural protections of the Act. Finally, and perhaps most importantly, parents may recover attorney's fees if they prevail. These protections ensure that the school bears no unique informational advantage.

III

Finally, respondents and several States urge us to decide that States may, if they wish, override the default rule and put the burden always on the school district. Several States have laws or regulations purporting to do so, at least under some circumstances. . . . Because no such law or regulation exists in Maryland, we need not decide this issue today. Justice BREYER contends that the allocation of the burden ought to be left *entirely* up to the States. But neither party made this argument before this Court or the courts below. We therefore decline to address it.

We hold no more than we must to resolve the case at hand: The burden of proof in an administrative hearing challenging an IEP is properly placed upon the party seeking relief. In this case, that party is Brian, as represented by his parents. But the rule applies with equal effect to school districts: If they seek to challenge an IEP, they will in turn bear the burden of persuasion before an ALJ. The judgment of the United States Court of Appeals for the Fourth Circuit is, therefore, affirmed.

It is so ordered.

The Chief Justice took no part in the consideration or decision of this case.

Questions for Discussion

1. Do you agree or disagree with this decision and why?
2. Is it appropriate for individual states to set their own burdens of proof? Can this lead to inconsistent results among states, making the rights of children with disabilities depend on where their parents live?

Summary of Important Legal Policies, Principles, and Practices

1. It is clear that both the IDEA statute and regulations favor alternative dispute resolution processes, including mediation, due process hearings, resolution process, and state administrative complaints.
2. A parent or school official may request a due process hearing involving any IDEA–related matter relating to the identification, evaluation, or educational placement of the child, or the provision of free appropriate education (FAPE) to the student.
3. The resolution process is triggered by a parent's due process complaint. Local educational agency schedules the resolution meeting upon receipt of a due process complaint.
4. The most formal of the dispute resolution options is the state administrative complaint, which can be filed by any individual or organization up to one year from the date of the alleged IDEA violation. Unlike due process hearings, state administrative complaints cannot be appealed to either a federal or state court. Another important difference between a state administrative complaint and a due process hearing is that state administrative complaints can only involve issues that occurred within one year of filing the initial complaint.

Useful Online Resources

The Center for Appropriate Dispute Resolution in Special Education (CADRE)
> An organization that supports the prevention and resolution of special education disputes through collaboration and partnerships between parents and school officials
> Website: www.cadreworks.org/

Office of Special Education Programs (OSEP), U.S. Department of Education
Questions and Answers (Q&A) On IDEA Part B Dispute Resolution Procedures (2013)
> This useful document provides concise and well-written answers to major questions surrounding the IDEA 2004 Part B provisions on issues related to dispute resolution at www2.ed.gov/policy/speced/guid/idea/memosdcltrs/acccombinedosersdisputeresolutionqafinalmemo-7-23-13.pdf

U.S. Department of Education, Alternative Dispute Resolution (ADR)
> A useful site discussing the current options available for resolving IDEA-related disputes collaboratively and by avoiding time-consuming and costly litigation in the court system at www2.ed.gov/about/offices/list/ogc/adr-page.html

Recommended Reading

Mueller, T. G. (2015). Litigation and special education: The past, present, and future direction for resolving conflicts between parents and school districts. *Journal of Disability Policy Studies, 26*(3), 135–143.

Zirkel, P. A., & Scala, G. (2010). Due process hearing systems under the IDEA: A state-by-state survey. *Journal of Disability Policy Studies, 21*, 3–8.

References

Abney ex rel. Kantor v. District of Columbia, 849 F.2d 1491 (D.C. Cir. 1988).

Alamo Heights Independent School District v. State Board of Education, 790 F.2d 1153 (5th Cir. 1986).

Beth B. v. Van Clay, 282 F.3d 493 (7th Cir. 2002).

Blackmon v. Springfield R-XII School District, 198 F.3d 648 (8th Cir. 1999).

Board of Education of the Hendrick Hudson Central School District v. Rowley, 458 U.S. 176 (1982).

Briggs v. Board of Education of Connecticut, 882 F.2d 688 (2d Cir. 1989).

Burr v. Ambach, 863 F.3d 1071 (2d Cir. 1988), *vacated sub nom. Sobol v. Burr*, 492 U.S. 902 (1989a), *affirmed*, 888 F.2d 258 (2d Cir. 1989b), *cert. denied*, 494 U.S. 1005 (1990).

Carlisle Area School v. Scott P., 62 F.3d 520 (3d Cir. 1995).

Cocores v. Portsmouth, New Hampshire School District, 779 F. Supp. 203 (D.N.H. 1991).

Colker, R. (2018). *Special education law in a nutshell*. St. Paul, MN: West Academic.

Cothern v. Mallory, 565 F. Supp. 701 (W.D. M0.1983).

Doe v. Board of Education of Tullahoma City Schools, 9 F.3d 455 (6th Cir. 1993).

Grim v. Rhinebeck Central School District, 346 F.3d 377 (2d Cir. 2003).

Honig v. Doe, 484 U.S. 305 (1988).

Independent School District No. 623 v. Digre, 893 F.2d 987 (8th Cir. 1990).

Johnson v. Independent School District No. 4, 921 F.2d 1022 (10th Cir. 1990).

Kerkham v. Superintendent, District of Columbia Schools, 931 F.2d 84 (D.C. Cir. 1991).

L.E. ex rel. E.S. v. Ramsey Board of Education, 435 F.3d 384 (3d Cir. 2006).

Lester H. v. Gilhool, 916 F.2d 865 (3d Cir. 1990).

McKenzie v. Smith, 771 F.2d 1527 (D.C. Cir. 1985).

Osborne, A. G., & Russo, C. J. (2005). The burden of proof in special education hearings: *Schaffer v. Weast*. *Education Law Reporter*, *200*, 1–12.

Padilla v. School District No. 1, 233 F.3d 1268 (10th Cir. 2000).

Roncker v. Walter, 700 F.2d 1058 (6th Cir. 1983).

Russo, C. J., & Osborne, A. G. (2006). The Supreme Court clarifies the burden of proof in special education due process hearings: *Schaffer ex rel. Schaffer v. Weast*. *Education Law Reporter*, *208*, 705–717.

Sanders v. Santa Fe Pub. Schools, 383 F. Supp.2d 1305 (D.N.M. 2004).

Schaffer v. Weast, 546 U.S. 49 (2005).

Seattle School District No. 1 v. B.S., 82 F.3d 1493 (9th Cir. 1996).

Weast v. Schaffer, 377 F.3d 449 (4th Cir. 2004), *affirmed sub nom. Schaffer v. Weast*, 546 U.S. 49 (2005).

Wenkart, R. D. (2004). The burden of proof in IDEA due process hearings. *Education Law Reporter*, *187*, 817–823.

West Platte R-II School District v. Wilson ex rel. L.W., 439 F.3d 783 (8th Cir. 2006).

11
Legal Remedies Available Under the IDEA

Key Concepts and Terms in This Chapter

- Monetary Damages
- Tuition Reimbursement
- Compensatory Educational Services
- Attorneys' Costs and Fees

If school officials fail to provide students with disabilities with the free appropriate public education (FAPE) required in the Individuals with Disabilities Education Act (IDEA), the courts can grant appropriate relief based on the preponderance of evidence standard (20 U.S.C. § 1415(i)(2); 34 C.F.R. § 300.516(c)(3)). Courts typically award such relief as reimbursement for tuition and other costs that parents incur when they unilaterally place their children in the schools of their choice. Courts can also grant parents who cannot afford to pay prospectively for placing their children in private schools awards of compensatory educational services. Furthermore, courts can grant prevailing parents' reimbursement for their legal expenses. While courts are generally reluctant to award monetary, or punitive damages against school districts, recent litigation indicates that this attitude may potentially be changing.

A great deal of litigation has focused on legal remedies in special education, including significant cases that have made their way to the United States Supreme Court. Many of the legal remedies that exist to compensate for the failure of school officials to provide a free appropriate public education (FAPE) are based on case law. As such, in amending the IDEA 2004, Congress provided additional guidance about the types of remedies that are available to students and parents, along with establishing the circumstances under which they may be granted. In fact, some legislative changes occurred in response to judicial interpretations of the IDEA. This chapter provides information on the legal remedies available to parents and students, including those based on provisions in the IDEA and those that emerged from case law.

This chapter begins with an overview of the most common legal remedies fashioned by the courts: monetary damages, tuition reimbursement, compensatory educational services, and attorneys' costs and fees.

Monetary Damages

There has been significant litigation concerning whether courts have the authority to award monetary damages to plaintiffs who prevail in legal actions brought under the IDEA. However, the courts have generally not imposed monetary damages on school officials for failing to provide a free appropriate public education (FAPE) or services for students with disabilities, especially if other nonmonetary remedies are available under the IDEA (Russo, 2006). Relatedly, the courts have not awarded monetary damages for "pain and suffering" involving special education legal disputes (*Ft. Zumwalt School District v. Missouri*

State Board of Education (1994). Interestingly, the U.S. Circuit Court of Appeals for the Ninth Circuit decided a case awarding monetary damages under Section 504 of the Rehabilitation Act of 1973 (*Mark H. v. Lemahieu* (2008). This case awarded monetary damages because the parents were able to demonstrate that teachers engaged in intentional discrimination or egregiously disregarded the rights of children or youth with disabilities.

The term damages refers to monetary relief that is awarded to compensate aggrieved parties for their losses (Zirkel & Osborne, 1987). The term, as used in this chapter, is defined in a narrower context. Here, the term *damages* refers to monetary awards given to persons who were injured by the actions of another for punitive purposes (Garner, 1999). For the purposes of this chapter, compensatory awards, such as reimbursement for tuition and other out-of-pocket expenses, are not considered to be damages awards. In the context of special education cases, courts treated punitive damages as a separate entity from compensation for lost services.

Failure to Provide a FAPE

In general, courts historically agreed that damages are unavailable under the IDEA unless school boards flagrantly failed to comply with the IDEA's procedural requirements (Osborne & Russo, 2001). The Seventh Circuit, in a case where the parents actually sought tuition reimbursement, insisted that monetary awards were not available under the IDEA unless exceptional circumstances existed (*Anderson v. Thompson*, 1981). One of those exceptional circumstances occurs when school boards act in bad faith by failing to comply with the IDEA's procedural provisions in an egregious manner. Although this case involved an award of tuition reimbursement, other courts either cited the Seventh Circuit's judgment or used analogous reasoning to declare that damages are not available under the IDEA (*Marvin H. v. Austin Independent School District*, 1983; *Powell v. DeFore*, 1983; *Gary A. v. New Trier High School District No. 203*, 1986; *Barnett v. Fairfax County School Board*, 1991).

The Supreme Court specifically struck down the Seventh Circuit's treatment of reimbursement as a damages award in *Burlington School Committee v. Department of Education, Commonwealth of Massachusetts* (1985). Even so, the legal principle that courts can award damages only when school boards act in bad faith has survived (*Charlie F. v. Board of Education of Skokie School District 68*, 1996). The Fifth Circuit asserted that a damages award is inconsistent with the IDEA's goals and that appropriate relief does not include punitive damages when school boards act in good faith (*Marvin H. v. Austin Independent School District*, 1983). Similarly, the Fourth Circuit affirmed that damages are unavailable unless it can be shown that school boards acted in bad faith or committed intentional acts of discrimination (*Barnett v. Fairfax County School Board*, 1991). A trial court in New York decreed that while damages are allowed for bad faith or egregious failures to comply with the IDEA, they are unwarranted when officials make good faith efforts to provide appropriate placements but commit misjudgments (*Gerasimou v. Ambach*, 1986). On the other hand, a federal trial court in Michigan indicated that when a court finds that school board placements are inappropriate, they are limited to fashioning appropriate placements. The court held that damages were unavailable even if parents could show that school officials acted in bad faith or grossly misused their professional discretion.

Tuition Reimbursement

When administrative or judicial proceedings involving placement disputes are pending pursuant to the IDEA, students must remain in their then-current educational placements unless their parents and school officials or states agree otherwise (20 U.S.C. § 1415(j); 34 C.F.R. § 300.318(a)). Parents who are concerned that the current placements of their children are inappropriate may not wish to have the children remain in those placements for the length of time it takes to reach final settlements. In these situations, parents frequently remove their children from their current placements and enroll them in private facilities. Parents who prevail in their placement challenges can, under appropriate circumstances, be reimbursed for the costs of tuition and other expenses associated with unilateral private placements. While case law provided parents with this relief, the IDEA and its regulations now explicitly authorize tuition reimbursement (20 U.S.C. § 1412(a)(10)(C)(ii); 34 C.F.R. § 300.148).

Supreme Court and Tuition Reimbursement for Parents of Students in Private Schools

The United States Supreme Court rendered two important judgments regarding tuition reimbursement for parents who unilaterally placed their children in private schools. In *Burlington School Committee v. Department of Education, Commonwealth of Massachusetts (Burlington)* (1985) the Court affirmed that the IDEA allowed reimbursement as long as the parents' chosen placement was determined to be the appropriate placement for their child. The Court declared that when Congress empowered the judiciary to grant appropriate relief, it intended to include retroactive relief as an available remedy. The Court reasoned that reimbursement merely requires school boards to pay the expenses that they would have incurred all along if officials had initially developed proper individualized education programs (IEPs). If reimbursement were not available, the Court explained that the rights of students to a FAPE and parental rights to participate fully in developing appropriate IEPs pursuant to the IDEA's procedural safeguards would have been less than complete. The Court maintained that parental violations of the IDEA's status quo provision do not constitute waiver of the right to request tuition reimbursements. However, the Court cautioned parents who make unilateral placements that they do so at their own financial risk since they will not be reimbursed if school officials can show that they proposed, and had the capacity to implement, appropriate IEPs.

Eight years later, in *Florence County School District Four v. Carter (Carter)* (1993), the Supreme Court unanimously affirmed that parentally chosen placements need not be in state-approved facilities in order for them to obtain tuition reimbursements. In *Carter*, parents who were dissatisfied with the IEP that school officials developed for their daughter placed her in a private school that was not on the state's list of approved facilities. Eventually, a trial court found that insofar as the school board's proposed IEP was inadequate, it had to reimburse the parents for the cost of the private school placement. The Fourth Circuit affirmed, noting that the private school provided an educational program that met the Supreme Court's standard of appropriateness as enunciated in *Board of Education of the Hendrick Hudson Central School District v. Rowley* (1982), even though it was not state approved and did not fully comply with the IDEA. The Fourth Circuit asserted that when the board defaulted on its obligations under the IDEA, reimbursement for the parental placement at a facility that was not approved by the state was not forbidden as long as the educational program met the *Rowley* standard. The Supreme Court agreed, emphasizing that the IDEA is designed to ensure that all students with disabilities receive an education that is both appropriate and free. The Court pointed out that barring reimbursement under the circumstances in *Carter* would have defeated the IDEA's statutory purposes.

Tuition Reimbursement Ordered Under Burlington and Carter

Parents can be denied tuition reimbursement awards if courts find that school officials offered, and had the capacity to implement, appropriate IEPs (20 U.S.C. § 1412(a)(10)(C)(i); 34 C.F.R. § 300.148(a)). Once courts agree that proposed IEPs are appropriate, they do not need to examine the appropriateness of parentally chosen placements. Even so, courts often award tuition reimbursement when parents can demonstrate that their school boards failed to offer appropriate IEPs and that the facilities they selected provided their children with appropriate educational programs.

Parentally Chosen Placements Must Be Appropriate, Not Perfect

According to *Burlington*, parents can be reimbursed for private school costs when their chosen placements are appropriate and those of school board officials are inappropriate. Recognizing that parents are not experts when it comes to making educational placements, courts do not expect them to make the exact required placements. Rather, as long as hearing officers or courts are satisfied that parentally chosen placements are more appropriate than those proposed by school boards, the judiciary generally awards reimbursement, even when the settings are not identical to those that are finally judged to be appropriate. The courts grant parents such latitude because they are aware that when parents make unilateral placements, they may not have as many options available to them as do school boards. Consequently, parents may not necessarily make the exact appropriate placement decisions made by school officials. Not surprisingly, courts ruled that reimbursement is still an available remedy (*Garland Independent School District v. Wilks*, 1987).

On the other hand, parents are not entitled to full reimbursements if courts discern that their chosen placements exceed what was required and were more costly than necessary (*Alamo Heights Independent School District v. State Board of Education*, 1986). The amount of advice and counsel that school officials provide to parents who seek to make unilateral placements may influence the extent of reimbursement awards. The Eleventh Circuit agreed that a residential placement was required for an autistic child, but was troubled by the fact that the parents had chosen one in Tokyo, Japan (*Drew P. v. Clarke County School District*, 1987, 1989). The court affirmed that while the parents were entitled to some reimbursement, it did not think that a placement so far from home was necessary. Other courts denied full reimbursement to parents who chose residential placements when private day schools could provide an appropriate education (*Board of Education of Oak Park & River Forest High School District No. 200 v. Illinois State Board of Education*, 1988; *Lascari v. Board of Education of the Ramapo Indian Hills Regional High School District*, 1989). Under these circumstances, courts generally award reimbursement for educational expenses at schools but not for room and board.

Parents are not entitled to tuition reimbursement for unilaterally obtained placements if they are not appropriate, even when school boards fail to offer appropriate IEPs. For example, in Connecticut the federal trial court held that a school board's IEP was not appropriate because school personnel committed several procedural errors. The court denied the parental request for reimbursement because their chosen placement was inappropriate since the school was not staffed by professionals who could deliver the special education services the student needed (*P.J. v. State of Connecticut State Board of Education*, 1992). Similarly, the Second Circuit posited that reimbursement was unwarranted where a hearing officer determined that a board's proposed placement was inappropriate, but that the parents' chosen placement was also unacceptable (*M.S. ex rel. S.S. v. Board of Education of the City School District of the City of Yonkers*, 2000).

Courts can award parents reimbursement under *Carter* if their chosen facilities can deliver appropriate services, regardless of whether they or their staffs are certificated. The Ninth Circuit awarded reimbursement to the parents of an autistic student who unilaterally enrolled him in a private clinic that was not certified to provide special education services (*Union School District v. Smith*, 1994). The court affirmed that although school officials failed to offer a FAPE, the student received educational benefit from his placement at the private clinic. Likewise, the federal trial court in Maryland declared that parents were entitled to be reimbursed for tuition expenses at a private school that was not approved to provide special education services because evidence indicated that the student received a FAPE while there (*Gerstmyer v. Howard County Public Schools*, 1994). The Second Circuit affirmed that parents who enrolled their child in a program that was not staffed by certified individuals were entitled to reimbursement because the program still offered an appropriate education (*Still v. DeBuono*, 1996). The court concluded that the promise of the IDEA would have been defeated if reimbursement were barred when the parentally chosen providers were not certified and the reason the service was not provided by the state was that there was a shortage of qualified providers.

The Third Circuit affirmed a monetary award to compensate a mother for the time she spent providing services to her preschool-age daughter. After the mother unsuccessfully requested the addition of Lovaas therapy to her daughter's program, she received training to provide it herself and offered the services to her child. In finding that the child's program was inadequate, the court remanded to the hearing officer to consider an appropriate remedy. The hearing officer awarded reimbursement to compensate the parent for the time she spent providing therapy to her child. Subsequently, the federal trial court and the Third Circuit agreed with that award since the services that the mother provided were appropriate and the county's denial of those services constituted a violation of the IDEA (*Bucks County Department of Mental Health/ Mental Retardation v. Commonwealth of Pennsylvania*, 2004).

School Boards Must Be Given the Opportunity to Act

In *Burlington*, the Supreme Court ruled that parents who violated the status quo provision did not waive their right to tuition reimbursement. Yet, in post-*Burlington* cases, courts agreed that parents waived their right to reimbursement when they made unilateral placements before giving school board officials opportunities to address their concerns. To this end, parents must notify school officials that they are dissatisfied with the IEPs of their children and afford educators the opportunity to take appropriate corrective action.

This case law is now incorporated into the IDEA and its regulations (20 U.S.C. § 1412(a)(10)(C)(iii); 34 C.F.R. § 300.148(d)).

Pursuant to the IDEA and its regulations, reimbursement costs may be reduced or denied in three situations. First, costs can be reduced or denied if at the most recent IEP team meetings that parents attended prior to removal of their children from public schools, they did not inform the teams that they were rejecting the proposed placements of their children; notice must include a statement of parental concerns and their intent to enroll their children in private schools at public expense (20 U.S.C. § 1412(a)(10)(C)(iii)(I)(aa); 34 C.F.R. § 300.148(d)(1)(i)). Second, costs can be reduced or denied if at least ten business days (including any holidays that occur on business days), prior to the removal of children from public schools, parents do not provide school officials with written notice of their intent to do so (20 U.S.C. § 1412(a)(10)(C)(iii) (I); 34 C.F.R. § 300.148(d)(1)(ii)). Third, if, prior to parental removal of their children from public schools, educational officials informed parents of their intent to evaluate the students (along with statements of the purposes of the evaluations that were appropriate and reasonable), but the parents did not make them available (20 U.S.C. § 1412(a)(10)(C)(iii)(II); 34 C.F.R. § 300.148(d)(2)). Fourth, costs can be reduced or denied if courts find that parents acted unreasonably (20 U.S.C. § 1412(a)(10)(C)(iii)(III); 34 C.F.R. § 300.148(d)(3)).

A dispute from the Eighth Circuit, although litigated before these provisions were incorporated into the IDEA, provides an illustration of how parents can be denied reimbursement awards. The court affirmed that parents were not entitled to reimbursement rather than afford officials a chance to change their daughter's educational program (*Evans v. District No. 17 of Douglas County*, 1988). The court decided that insofar as there was no indication that the educators would have refused to change the student's program, they were entitled to have the opportunity to modify the child's IEP and placement. The court maintained that parents must put school officials on notice that they disagree with the educational programs of their children and must be given the opportunity to modify placements voluntarily before parents can take unilateral actions. Ten years later, the same court denied reimbursement to parents who removed their child from school after one day in the eighth grade, without any discussion of accommodations to meet his needs (*Schoenfield v. Parkway School District*, 1998).

Courts frequently deny reimbursement awards when parents take unilateral actions before giving school officials opportunities to intervene. Generally, courts reason that equity prevents reimbursement awards from accruing prior to the time school officials could evaluate students and make placement recommendations (*Ash v. Lake Oswego School District*, 1991, 1992; *Tucker v. Calloway County Board of Education*, 1998; *Johnson v. Metro Davidson County School System*, 2000; *L.K. ex rel. J.H. v. Board of Education for Transylvania County*, 2000). Parents may also forfeit their right to tuition reimbursement by failing to cooperate with school officials in the evaluation process (*Patricia P. v. Board of Education of Oak Park and River Forest High School District No. 200*, 2000). As stated earlier, the IDEA requires parents to provide school officials with written notification of their intent to enroll their child in private schools at public expense if they hope to obtain reimbursement awards. Parents who fail either to challenge the IEPs of their children or to provide school officials with the written notice required by the IDEA prior to making unilateral placements are not entitled to reimbursements (*Yancy v. New Baltimore City Board of School Commissioners*, 1998; *Nein v. Greater Clark County School Corporation*, 2000; *Greenland School District v. Amy N.*, 2004; *Ms. M. ex rel. K.M. v. Portland School Committee*, 2004).

Controversy has developed over new language in the IDEA that limits the obligation of school boards to reimburse parents. According to this language:

> If the parents of a child with a disability, who previously received special education and related services under the authority of a public agency, enroll the child in a private elementary school or secondary school without the consent of or referral by the public agency, a court or a hearing officer may require the agency to reimburse the parents for the cost of that enrollment if the court or hearing officer finds that the agency had not made a free appropriate public education available to the child in a timely manner prior to that enrollment.
>
> (20 U.S.C. § 1412(a)(10)(C)(ii))

The question has arisen as to whether that clause means that school boards are not required to reimburse the parents of students who have been unilaterally enrolled in private schools if the children never attended the public schools. The Supreme Court settled this issue in *Forest Grove School District v. T.A.* (2009) by declaring that parents are entitled to reimbursement even in situations where their children never attended the public schools.

Parents Entitled to Reimbursement If School Boards Commit Procedural Errors

The fact that school officials devised appropriate educational programs for students is insufficient to preclude reimbursement awards. IEP teams must spell out appropriate placements in properly executed IEPs. Procedural errors are sufficient grounds for awarding reimbursement for unilateral placements because, under *Rowley*, an educational placement is inappropriate if it is not contained in a properly executed IEP. For example, the Third Circuit held that reimbursement is warranted when a school board proposes an appropriate program but the IEP is defective on procedural grounds (*Muth v. Central Bucks School District*, 1988). Here school officials proposed a placement that was later deemed appropriate, but they failed to write an IEP for that proposal. In like fashion, the Fourth Circuit affirmed a reimbursement award in positing that school board officials failed to provide a FAPE for a child (*Board of Education of the County of Cabell v. Dienelt*, 1988). The trial court had decided that the board's program was inappropriate due to procedural defects since officials failed to conduct annual reviews and involve the parents in the IEP process.

If parents are unhappy with the education of their children, as noted, they must give school officials chances to evaluate students and propose appropriate placements. Boards may also be liable for tuition reimbursement if officials do not properly evaluate children. In one case, the Fourth Circuit affirmed that parents were justified in making a unilateral placement when school board officials failed to propose an appropriate placement due to an improper evaluation of the child (*Hudson v. Wilson*, 1987). The court maintained that the parents did not waive their right to reimbursement when they removed their child from the public schools before board personnel could conduct further assessments and propose a final IEP.

The IDEA requires parents to provide school officials with notice of their intent to place their children in private facilities in order to qualify for reimbursements. Even so, courts may excuse parental failure to notify officials if educators did not comply with proper procedures. For instance, the federal trial court in Maryland found that parents could not be denied reimbursement in failing to notify school board officials of their intent where educators failed to provide the parents with the notice of procedural requirements called for by state law and the IDEA (*Mayo v. Baltimore City Public Schools*, 1999).

As reflected by a case from Ohio, improperly written IEPs can serve as the bases for reimbursement awards. The Sixth Circuit, noting that flaws in an IEP were not harmless technical errors, awarded reimbursement to a parent who rejected an IEP that neither provided an objective means to measure progress nor adequately explained the services the student would have received (*Cleveland Heights–University Heights City School District v. Boss*, 1998). In addition, the Second Circuit approved a reimbursement award to parents who enrolled their child in a private school after school officials proposed a Section 504 accommodation plan instead of an IEP (*Muller v. Committee on Special Education of the East Islip Union Free School District*, 1998). The trial court decreed that the student qualified for special education as emotionally disturbed. Moreover, the Sixth Circuit awarded parents reimbursement in concluding that officials denied a child a FAPE because they predetermined his placement (*Deal ex rel. Deal v. Hamilton County Department of Education*, 2004). Previously, the Fourth Circuit was of the opinion that procedural errors must actually interfere with the provision of a FAPE before parents are entitled to reimbursement awards. When parents sought summer services and officials failed to consider their request properly, the court treated this as a harmless error since the evidence revealed that the student was not entitled to summer services (*DiBuo v. Board of Education of Worcester County*, 2002).

Parental Delays or Failure to Cooperate May Affect Reimbursement Awards

In New York, a federal trial court thought that nothing prohibited parents from being reimbursed even if they cause delays in the hearing process (*Eugene B. v. Great Neck Union Free School District*, 1986). The court decided that the parents could still be reimbursed because their choice of a private school was the appropriate placement. In response to a request for reimbursement, school officials responded that since the parents caused several delays in the proceedings, they should not have been compensated for the periods of each of the delays. The court disagreed, stating that the board was responsible for the private school tuition for the entire time period regardless of whether there were delays in the proceedings.

On the other hand, the parents can be denied reimbursement if they delay unreasonably in requesting hearings. The Third Circuit was of the view that parents waived their right to reimbursement if they did not initiate review proceedings within a reasonable period of time (*Bernardsville Board of Education v. J.H.*, 1994). When the parents waited two years before filing their claim, the court observed that such a delay, absent mitigating factors, was unreasonable. Echoing this rationale in another case, the same court subsequently remarked that parents who enrolled their children, gifted students with learning disabilities, in a private school, but waited sixteen months before requesting tuition reimbursement, were not entitled to recover the costs for the time period prior to their request for a hearing (*Warren G. v. Cumberland County School District*, 1999). State statutes of limitations may impose additional restrictions on the timeframes within which parents may file reimbursement claims.

Parents can lose awards or have them reduced if they frustrate attempts by school officials to develop IEPs. A federal trial court in California contended that a parent's failure to cooperate fully with attempts by school officials to design an educational program justified the reduction of a reimbursement award (*Glendale Unified School District v. Almasi*, 2000). In Wisconsin, where a parent refused a recommended evaluation but later placed the child in a residential facility, the school board refused to pay the tuition at the facility because it had not made the placement. The trial court agreed that since the board could not have been faulted for failing to act in the face of parental resistance, the parent was not entitled to reimbursement (*Suzawith v. Green Bay Area School District*, 2000).

Tuition Reimbursements for Related Services

Along with tuition, courts consistently award reimbursement for the costs of related services. The criteria for reimbursement of related services are the same as for tuition expenses: Parents must demonstrate that the services were required for their children to receive an appropriate education. In most cases, related services are provided at private schools in conjunction with special education services. However, courts award reimbursement for the costs of privately obtained related services when school boards fail to provide needed services in conjunction with public special education placements.

Parents have received reimbursement awards for the costs of psychotherapy or counseling services (*Max M. v. Thompson*, 1983, 1984, sub nom. *Max M. v. Illinois State Board of Education*, 1986; *Gary A. v. New Trier High School District No. 203*, 1986; *Doe v. Anrig*, 1987; *Vander Malle v. Ambach*, 1987; *Tice v. Botetourt County School District*, 1990; *Babb v. Knox County School System*, 1992; *Straube v. Florida Union Free School District*, 1992). In many of these cases, the therapeutic services were provided to students who were placed in private schools or psychiatric facilities due to emotional difficulties. In others, parents obtained the counseling services privately to supplement the services that their children received in public schools. Regardless of the setting where students receive special education services, parents seeking reimbursement awards must show that their children would not benefit from special education without psychotherapy or counseling.

School officials must provide needed transportation because children cannot benefit from special education services if they cannot get to class. Officials must even provide students who attend private schools at public expense with appropriate transportation. Frequently, tuition reimbursement awards include compensation for other necessary costs such as transportation.

Even when tuition reimbursement is not an issue, courts may make such awards to parents when school officials fail to provide appropriate transportation. For example, the First Circuit permitted the father of a child with physical disabilities who drove his son to school himself to reimbursement since school personnel failed to make appropriate arrangements (*Hurry v. Jones*, 1984). In another case, a trial court in New York reimbursed a care provider for costs associated with transporting a student to an educational facility for children with physical disabilities (*Taylor v. Board of Education of Copake-Taconic Hills Central School District*, 1986). The award in this case included reimbursement for hiring a babysitter to watch other children while the caretaker transported the child to the center. A trial court in South Dakota awarded reimbursement for transportation for a student who moved into the district with an IEP calling for door-to-door transportation (*Malehorn v. Hill City School District*, 1997). After officials in the new district determined that the student did not require special transportation, her mother appealed. While a hearing officer upheld the action of school officials, the court explained that the board was required to honor the terms of the previous IEP until such time as it could be reviewed.

Parents have recovered reimbursement awards for other related services, such as occupational therapy (*Rapid City School District v. Vahle*, 1990) and speech therapy (*Johnson v. Lancaster-Lebanon Intermediate Unit 13, Lancaster City School District*, 1991). The Ninth Circuit went so far as to affirm a reimbursement award for the cost of lodging for a student and his mother that was required because the facility he attended was not within daily commuting distance of the family's residence (*Union School District v. Smith*, 1994).

Hearing Officers and Reimbursement Awards

Although the courts granted all of the reimbursement awards cited in this section, parents do not necessarily have to seek judicial review in order to obtain reimbursements. Hearing officers have the authority to grant reimbursement awards along with other forms of appropriate equitable relief. In one such case, a trial court in North Carolina ruled that reimbursement was included within the IDEA's provision that a hearing may be conducted on any matter relating to a FAPE (*S-1 v. Spangler*, 1986, 1987, 1993, 1994). In addition, the court pointed out that Congress did not intend to give courts any greater powers of equity than those given to a hearing officer. The IDEA currently grants hearing officers the authority to grant reimbursement awards (20 U.S.C. § 1412(a)(10)(C)(ii); 34 C.F.R. § 300.148(b)).

Compensatory Educational Services

Courts grant awards of compensatory educational services when school officials fail to provide children with a free appropriate public education (FAPE) and their parents lack the financial means to obtain alternate services or for whatever reason have chosen not to obtain services privately. Students are thus forced to remain in inappropriate programs while administrative hearings are pending. As a result, children can lose several years of appropriate educational services during the often-lengthy appeals process. Generally, students are entitled to compensatory services during time periods when they would otherwise have been ineligible for services. In most cases involving the remedy of compensatory services, courts apply the *Burlington* rationale to evaluate whether services are warranted (Zirkel & Hennessy, 2001).

Awards of Compensatory Services

The courts acknowledge that they have had the authority to award compensatory services since Congress empowered them to fashion appropriate remedies to cure deprivations of rights secured by the IDEA. Courts agree that compensatory services, like reimbursement, merely compensate students for the inappropriate education they received while placement issues were in dispute or school board officials failed to act properly.

The theory behind compensatory educational services awards is that appropriate remedies are not limited to those parents who can afford to provide their children with alternate educational placements while litigation is pending (*Lester H. v. Gilhool*, 1990; *Todd D. v. Andrews*, 1991; *Manchester School District v. Christopher B.*, 1992; *Murphy v. Timberlane Regional School District*, 1992, 1993, 1994a). Generally, compensatory services must be provided for periods equal to the time students were denied services (*Valerie J. v. Derry Cooperative School District*, 1991; *Manchester School District v. Christopher B.*, 1992; *Big Beaver Falls Area School District v. Jackson*, 1993). In addition, plaintiffs can recover compensatory awards even after students pass the ceiling age for eligibility under the IDEA (*Pihl v. Massachusetts Department of Education*, 1993; *State of West Virginia ex rel. Justice v. Board of Education of the County of Monongalia*, 2000).

A case from the Eleventh Circuit illustrates the similarity between awards of tuition reimbursement and compensatory services. That court affirmed that an award of compensatory educational services was similar to one for tuition reimbursement insofar as it was necessary to preserve the student's right to a FAPE (*Jefferson County Board of Education v. Breen*, 1988). The court wrote that without compensatory services awards, the rights of students under the IDEA would depend on the ability of their parents to obtain services privately while due process hearings progressed. Along the same line, the Eighth Circuit found that compensatory educational services were available to the parent of a student with disabilities who could not afford to provide appropriate educational services himself during the lengthy court battle (*Miener v. Missouri*, 1986). In granting the award, the court added that Congress did not intend for the entitlements of children to a FAPE to rest on the ability of their parents to pay for the costs of placements up front. Yet another court agreed that if compensatory services were not available, the parents would have gained a Pyrrhic victory because their child's right to a FAPE would have been illusory (*Cremeans v. Fairland Local School District Board of Education*, 1993).

Students may receive compensatory services even after they earn valid high school diplomas. The federal trial court in Massachusetts awarded compensatory educational services to a student who earned a high school diploma after discovering that the school officials failed to follow proper procedures (*Puffer v. Raynolds*, 1988). The court reasoned that the fact that the student earned a diploma was not an indication that she had not required special education services, but rather, was evidence that she succeeded despite the shortcomings of her educational program. The court ordered the school board to provide services equal in scope to what it should have provided prior to the student's graduation. A federal trial court in New York also thought that a student who graduated was entitled to compensatory educational services while attending college, but not in the form of tuition (*Straube v. Florida Union Free School District*, 1992). Further, the federal trial court in New Hampshire ordered a board to provide compensatory services to a student for the time when he was denied educational services (*Valerie J. v. Derry Cooperative School District*, 1991).

Compensatory services awards accrue from the point that school officials know, or should have known, that IEPs were inadequate (*M.C. ex rel. J.C. v. Central Regional School District*, 1996; *Ridgewood Board of Education v. N.E.*, 1999). Generally, compensatory services are provided for a period of time equal to the length of the deprivation.

Hearing officers can grant awards of compensatory educational services. As with the power to confer tuition reimbursement, courts recognized that hearing officers may fashion appropriate relief, which sometimes requires an award of compensatory services (*Cocores v. Portsmouth, NH School District*, 1991; *Big Beaver Falls Area School District v. Jackson*, 1993).

Denials of Compensatory Services

Awards of compensatory services, as with tuition reimbursement, are available only when parents can demonstrate that their children were denied the FAPE mandated by the IDEA (*Timms v. Metropolitan School District*, 1982, 1983; *Martin v. School Board of Prince George County*, 1986; *Garro v. State of Connecticut*, 1994). Nevertheless, a federal trial court in Tennessee denied an award of compensatory education in positing that the homebound program that a student received was inappropriate, but the school board and the parents were unaware of the existence of an appropriate program (*Brown v. Wilson County School District*, 1990). Insofar as school officials had not taken any actions that resulted in the denial of a FAPE, the court maintained that the board was not required to provide compensatory services.

The Third Circuit pointed out that compensatory services are warranted only when parents can demonstrate that their children underwent prolonged or gross deprivations of the right to a FAPE (*Carlisle Area School District v. Scott P.*, 1995). Absent such evidence, the court denied an award of compensatory services where an administrative appeals panel ordered officials to include additional services in the student's IEP. The Eighth Circuit also affirmed that a student was not entitled to compensatory services absent a showing of egregious circumstances or culpable conduct on the part of school officials (*Yankton School District v. Schramm*, 1995, 1996).

In a case from New York, the Second Circuit affirmed that the parents of a student who was seriously injured in an automobile accident failed to demonstrate that he regressed as a result of the school board's failure to provide special education services in a timely fashion. As such, the courts decided that the student was not entitled to compensatory services (*Wenger v. Canastota Central School District*, 1997, 1999). Likewise, a school board's timely action to correct deficiencies in a student's IEP led the federal trial court in New Jersey to deny compensatory services (*D.B. v. Ocean Township Board of Education*, 1997). Failure to take advantage of offered services may be a ground for denial of awards of compensatory services. In such a case, the Ninth Circuit uncovered evidence that school officials offered parents extra tutoring and summer school for their child, but they rejected the proposal (*Parents of Student W. v. Puyallup School District No. 3*, 1994). As such, the court affirmed the denial of the parents' request for compensatory services. Two years later, the federal trial court in Minnesota denied compensatory speech therapy services where parents withdrew their son from his educational program and rejected the services offered by school officials (*Moubry v. Independent School District No. 696*, 1996).

Attorney Costs and Fees

The IDEA contains one of the most comprehensive mechanisms that Congress ever created for dispute resolution. Litigation is expensive and many parents, after succeeding in their disputes with school boards, believe that they should be reimbursed for their costs in securing the rights of their children. Many parents sense that they achieve limited victories if they prevail in showing that school officials failed to provide the FAPE their children were entitled to receive under the IDEA but are left with large legal bills. Initially, most courts viewed awards of attorney fees as awards for damages (see, e.g., *Diamond v. McKenzie*, 1985).

In *Smith v. Robinson* (1984) the Supreme Court interpreted the IDEA as not permitting parents to recovery their legal expenses. Unhappy with this outcome, Congress amended the IDEA in 1986 by adding the Handicapped Children's Protection Act (HCPA) (20 U.S.C. § 1415(I)(3)) to its provisions. The HCPA permits courts to provide awards of reasonable attorney fees to parents who prevail against school boards in any actions or proceedings brought pursuant to the IDEA. Awards are based on the prevailing rates in the community in which cases arose. Courts have the authority to judge what is a reasonable amount of time spent preparing and arguing cases in terms of the issues litigated. Awards may be limited if school boards made settlement offers more than ten days before the proceedings began that were equal to or more favorable than the final relief that parents obtained. In addition, fee awards may be reduced if courts find that parents unreasonably protracted disputes, the hourly rates of attorneys were excessive, or the time spent and legal services furnished were excessive in light of the issues litigated. While attorney fees may be awarded for representation at administrative and judicial hearings, they are unavailable for representation at IEP meetings unless such sessions are convened in response to administrative or judicial orders (20 U.S.C. § 1415(i)(3)(D)(ii); 34 C.F.R. § 300.517(c)(2)(ii)).

Hearing officers cannot grant awards of attorney fees because this authority is reserved for the courts (*Mathern v. Campbell County Children's Center*, 1987). However, parents do not necessarily have to go to court to recover their legal expenses. Agreements may be worked out with school boards for payment of the parents' legal expenses. If parents are required to file court action to recover attorney fees, and they succeed, they may recover their costs in filing the fee petition as well (*Angela L. v. Pasadena Independent School District*, 1990). Parents do not need to exhaust administrative remedies prior to filing fee petitions since hearing officers cannot award attorney fees (*J.G. v. Board of Education of the Rochester City School District*, 1986, 1987; *Esther C. v. Ambach*, 1988; *Sidney K. v. Ambach*, 1988).

If Parents Prevail

One of the most often litigated issues under the IDEA's attorney fees provisions deals with whether parents were prevailing parties. While on its face the issue seems straightforward, unfortunately, it is not. Most special education disputes involve multiple issues and parents may have had only partial success. Courts generally define prevailing parents as those who succeeded on most of the issues litigated. Even so, in some cases where parents have not prevailed on all issues, the courts have granted partial awards.

Full Awards

For the most part, courts grant full awards when parents prevail on the major issues in the litigation, even if they did not succeed on some minor points. In most instances, the work performed litigating the minor issues is inseparable from that litigating the major issue, is insignificant compared to that required by the major issue, and/or is performed in conjunction with the work completed for the major issue (*Turton v. Crisp County School District*, 1988; *Angela L. v. Pasadena Independent School District*, 1990; *Phelan v. Bell*, 1993). Courts generally conclude that the parents are the prevailing party when they acquire the primary relief sought or prevail in the principal issue in their suit (*Barbara R. v. Tirozzi*, 1987; *Kristi W. v. Graham Independent School District*, 1987; *Neisz v. Portland Public School District*, 1988; *Mitten v. Muscogee County District*, 1989).

Parents may still receive full reimbursement of their legal expenses even when they do not prevail on all issues. Generally, courts grant full awards if the time spent litigating the various issues cannot be easily apportioned on an issue-by-issue basis. In an illustrative case, the Sixth Circuit awarded attorney fees to parents who did not receive the residential placement they requested but succeeded in obtaining additional services (*Krichinsky v. Knox County Schools*, 1992). In other cases, courts agreed that parents were entitled to full fee awards because the matters before the administrative hearings were intertwined, and could not have been viewed as a series of separate claims, and the parents received most of what they requested (*Moore v. Crestwood Local School District*, 1992; *Noyes v. Grossmont Union High School District*, 2004).

Partial Awards

Parents can receive partial awards of attorney fees even if they do not prevail on the most significant question in the litigation but do succeed on some of the issues. At the same time, parents may receive partial awards when they prevail on some of their claims, and the issues litigated are distinct enough so that the work done on each claim can be separated from the work done on all others (*Max M. v. Illinois State Board of Education*, 1988; *Burr v. Sobol*, 1990; *Koswenda v. Flossmoor School District No. 161*, 2002). Requested fee awards may be reduced for various other reasons. If a court thinks that a requested hourly rate or the number of hours billed was excessive (*Mr. D. v. Glocester School Committee*, 1989; *Hall v. Detroit Public Schools*, 1993; *Troy School District v. Boutsikaris*, 2003) or finds fault with the time sheets submitted by attorneys (*In re Conklin*, 1991; *Smith v. District of Columbia*, 2004), the court can make adjustments in requested fee awards. In one case, a federal trial court in Indiana reduced a requested fee amount in determining that the parents' counsel unnecessarily protracted the proceedings (*Howey v. Tippecanoe School Corporation*, 1990). Another court ruled that an attorney who was unfamiliar with special education laws could not bill for the time and research spent in learning the statutes (*King v. Floyd County Board of Education*, 1998).

Courts do not always reduce awards by evaluating the number of hours spent litigating each issue and reducing them by the amount of fees charged for unsuccessfully litigating certain issues. Sometimes, awards are adjusted in proportion to the parents' overall success and failure in the litigation. As such, when the federal trial court in New Jersey had difficulty apportioning legal costs issue-by-issue, it simply reduced the requested fee award by fifty percent because the parents had not achieved their primary objective, even though they were successful on several other significant issues (*Field v. Haddonfield Board of Education*, 1991).

If Parents Do Not Prevail

Parents cannot recover their legal expenses when school boards are the prevailing parties. It should go without saying that parents who do not succeed on any of their claims do not achieve prevailing party status (*Wheeler v. Towanda Area School District*, 1991). As discussed in the previous section, parents may receive limited reimbursement awards if they prevail on at least some of their claims. Parents cannot be awarded attorney fees if their legal relationships with their boards are unaltered following litigation, even if they received minor victories (*Salley v. St. Tammany Parish School Board*, 1995; *Board of Education of Downers Grove Grade School District No. 58 v. Steven L.*, 1996; *Metropolitan School District of Lawrence Township v. M.S.*, 2004). Parents also are not the prevailing party if the changes that occur are not a direct result of the litigation but are caused by other factors.

As noted, courts sometimes grant parents partial reimbursement of their legal expenses if they obtain some, but not all, of the relief that they sought. If the relief obtained is insignificant, courts may not grant even partial awards. As reflected by a case from the Seventh Circuit, parents were not entitled to an award of attorney fees, even though they obtained an order that conferred some benefits on their daughter since they did not succeed on most of their claims (*Hunger v. Leininger*, 1994). Additionally, a federal trial court in Wisconsin denied a fee request in writing that the relief the parents obtained was minimal in light of their overall objectives (*Linda T. ex rel. William A. v. Rice Lake Area School District*, 2004).

Courts may deny fee awards if they deem that parents unnecessarily protracted proceedings (*Fischer v. Rochester Community Schools*, 1991) or the problems they complained of could have been resolved without resort to administrative or judicial review (*Combs v. School Board of Rockingham County*, 1994). Parents may not receive fee awards if they request administrative hearings before the school boards have had full opportunities to develop appropriate IEPs (*Johnson v. Bismarck Public School District*, 1991; *Patricia E. v. Board of Education of Community High School District No. 155*, 1995; *Payne v. Board of Education, Cleveland City Schools*, 1996; *W.L.G. v. Houston County Board of Education*, 1997).

Catalyst Theory

In the past, courts awarded attorney fees based on the catalyst theory, even if an administrative hearing or judicial action never took place (see, e.g., *Doucet v. Chilton County Board of Education*, 1999; *Daniel S. v. Scranton School District*, 2000). Under the catalyst theory, courts can award fees if suits, or even threats of litigation, bring about change in a defendant's behavior, causing a termination in proceedings. However, recent litigation appears to have struck down the catalyst theory (Wenkart, 2002).

In a nonschool case, *Buckhannon Board & Care Home v. West Virginia Department of Health and Human Resources (Buckhannon)* (2001), the Supreme Court rejected the catalyst theory on the basis that a prevailing party must prevail before the courts in judgments on the merits or through consent decrees (Osborne, 2003). Subsequently, circuit courts denied fee requests by relying on the rationale in *Buckhannon*, explaining that the high Court's analysis governed claims filed pursuant to the IDEA (*J.C. v. Regional School District No. 10*, 2002; *John T. by Paul T. and Joan T. v. Delaware County Intermediate Unit*, 2003; *T.D. v. LaGrange School District No. 102*, 2003; *Doe v. Boston Public Schools*, 2004; Osborne, 2005).

Fees for Administrative Hearings

The IDEA permits parents to recover attorney fees if they prevail in "any action or proceeding" brought under its procedural safeguards (20 U.S.C. § 1415(i)(3)(B); 34 C.F.R. § 300.517(a)). The meaning of the phrase "any action or proceeding" has been in dispute. Many school boards claimed that it refers only to court actions and that attorney fees are not recoverable for work performed at the administrative hearing level. After some controversy, it is well settled that attorney fees are available for representation at administrative hearings even if disputes are settled without judicial action. In addition, it is well settled that parents can file suits solely for the purpose of recovering legal expenses (Osborne & DiMattia, 1991).

The District of Columbia Circuit resolved the leading, and most controversial, case on the topic in 1990 (*Moore v. District of Columbia*, 1990). Initially, a divided three-judge panel decreed that congressional language in the HCPA provided for awards of attorney fees only where the losing parties in administrative actions appealed to the courts and prevailed in judicial actions (*Moore v. District of Columbia*, 1989). According to the court, fees could not be awarded to parents who prevailed at the administrative level and brought judicial action only to obtain attorney fees. While this opinion was contrary to the majority of cases from the other circuits, the court granted a rehearing en banc (Osborne & DiMattia, 1991). On further review, the court vacated its earlier judgment, declaring that attorney fees were available for administrative proceedings. This time the court concluded that Congress, using the phrase "any action or proceeding," meant to authorize fees for parents who prevailed in civil actions or administrative proceedings. The court added that the legislative history of the HCPA supported its interpretation. Subsequently, courts unanimously agreed that parents who prevailed at the administrative level could recover their legal expenses (Osborne & DiMattia, 1991).

Settlement Offers

School boards can lessen their liability by attempting to reach settlements with parents before beginning administrative hearings. One section of the HCPA provides that fees are unavailable for legal representation that occurs after school boards make written settlement offers if the final relief that parents obtain is not more favorable than the settlement offer. School boards must make settlement offers at least ten days before the scheduled start of due process hearings (20 U.S.C. § 1415(i)(3)(D)(i); 34 C.F.R. § 300.517(c)(2)(i)).

In order to avoid paying fee awards, settlement offers from school boards must be deemed to be equal to or better than the final relief that parents obtained. Settlement offers need not be identical to final administrative orders in order to stop the time clock of the attorney from ticking. Parents are not entitled to awards of attorney fees when the final relief they obtain is substantially similar to (*Hyden v. Board of Education of Wilson County*, 1989) or less favorable than (*Mr. L. and Mrs. L. v. Woonsocket Education Department*, 1992) the offers made by school boards. On the other hand, parents can be reimbursed for their legal costs when they win more favorable terms than their boards offer (*Capistrano Unified School District v. Wartenberg*, 1995; *Virginia McC. v. Corrigan-Camden Independent School District*, 1995). Courts may be called on to consider whether settlement offers were, in fact, more favorable than the final results obtained through administrative proceedings. In such a case, a federal trial court in Ohio rejected a board's claim of a more favorable settlement offer because the offer did not include specific details (*Gross ex rel. Gross v. Perrysburg Exempted Village School District*, 2004).

Courts recognized that parents are entitled to collect attorney fees for legal work that was completed up to the time of settlement offers, even when hearings are canceled because parents accepted the offers (*E.P. v. Union County Regional High School District No. 1*, 1989; *Shelly C. v. Venus Independent School District*, 1989; *Barlow-Gresham Union High School District No. 2 v. Mitchell*, 1991). Yet, in the wake of *Buckhannon*, lower courts have denied fees when the parties reached settlement agreements before completing administrative hearings (*Brandon K. v. New Lenox School District*, 2001; *J.S. v. Ramapo Central School District*, 2001; *Jose Luis R. v. Joliet Township H.S. District 204*, 2002; *P.O. ex rel. L.T. and T.O. v. Greenwich Board of Education*, 2002; *Algeria v. District of Columbia*, 2004; *Smith v. District of Columbia*, 2004; *Smith ex rel. Smith v. Fitchburg Public Schools*, 2005). Still, attorney fees may be awarded for settlement agreements if hearing officers or courts sanction the agreements. Courts agreed that incorporating settlement agreements into orders or reading them into records gives them the judicial imprimatur called for by *Buckhannon* (*D.M. ex rel. G.M. and C.M. v. Board of Education, Center Moriches Union Free School District*, 2003; *Abraham v. District of Columbia*, 2004).

The issue of settlement offers is not completely resolved. At least one court maintained that parents who gained the relief they sought through mediation or a settlement agreement are entitled to attorney fees in spite of *Buckhannon*. In this dispute, a federal trial court in California reasoned that applying *Buckhannon* to settlement agreements under the IDEA would contravene the act's preference for early settlements (*Noyes v. Grossmont Union High School District*, 2004).

Fees to Attorneys From Public Agencies

Many parents use attorneys from public advocacy agencies in special education litigation. These agencies provide low-cost or free legal services via sliding scale fee arrangements. Courts agree that when parents who are represented by public agency attorneys prevail in special education actions, the attorneys are entitled to be reimbursed at the prevailing rate in their communities even if the fee is higher than the one that the agency would have charged the parents (*Eggers v. Bullitt County School District*, 1988; *Mitten v. Muscogee County School District*, 1989; *Yankton School District v. Schramm*, 1996).

Fees to Lay Advocates and Pro Se Parents

Parents often, especially in the early stages of disputes, rely on the aid of lay advocates to advise and represent them in meetings with school boards. Although the services of lay advocates may be beneficial in resolving disputes, because they are not attorneys, advocates cannot be reimbursed for legal representation (*Arons v. New Jersey State Board of Education*, 1988). If advocates work in conjunction with attorneys, it is possible that they may be reimbursed for their services as part of the attorneys' costs (*Heldman v. Sobol*, 1994). Even so, representation solely by lay advocates is not reimbursable (*Connors v. Mills*, 1998).

Most courts agree that parents who represent themselves may not be compensated under the IDEA even if they are members of the bar (*Rappaport v. Vance*, 1993; *Heldman v. Sobol*, 1994; *Miller v. West Lafayette Community School Corporation*, 1996; *Doe v. Board of Education of Baltimore County*, 1998; *Erickson v. Board of Education of Baltimore County*, 1998; *Woodside v. School District of Philadelphia Board of Education*, 2001). On the other hand, a federal trial court in Georgia decreed that nothing in the language of the IDEA prohibits an award of fees to an attorney-parent (*Matthew V. v. DeKalb County School System*, 2003).

Fees for Expert Witnesses

The IDEA permits parents to recover other costs of bringing special education suits along with attorney fees (Osborne, 2005). However, for years the courts did not agree over whether parents could recover the costs of expert witness fees. A variety of federal courts found that parents may include the costs of expert witnesses in their requests for attorney fee awards, reasoning that these expenses are often a necessary part of administrative hearings (*Chang v. Board of Education of Glen Ridge Township*, 1988; *Turton v. Crisp County School District*, 1988; *Aronow v. District of Columbia*, 1992; *P.L. by Mr. and Mrs. L. v. Norwalk Board of Education*, 1999; *Mr. J. v. Board of Education*, 2000; *Pazik v. Gateway Regional School District*, 2001; *Brillon v. Klein Independent School District*, 2003; *Murphy v. Arlington Central School District Board of Education*, 2005). A trial court in Georgia even held that parents were entitled to be reimbursed for the services of an expert who did not testify but who did contribute to the development of the case (*Turton v. Crisp County School District*, 1988). On the other hand, the federal trial court in New Jersey refused to reimburse parents for the full costs of an expert witness because it was of the opinion that even though the expert witness was helpful, the expert's presence was not necessary (*E.M. v. Millville Board of Education*, 1994).

Other courts denied requests for reimbursement of expert witnesses. The District of Columbia Circuit denied expert witness fees reasoning that the IDEA does not enable a prevailing party to shift expert witness fees (*Goldring v. District of Columbia*, 2005). On at least two occasions the Eighth Circuit denied expert witness fees in deciding that nothing in the plain language of the IDEA suggests that the courts are authorized to award fees for expert witnesses (*Neosho R-V School District v. Clark*, 2003; *Missouri Department of Elementary and Secondary Education v. Springfield R-12 School District*, 2004). Similarly, the Seventh Circuit declined to award expert witness fees absent specific authorization within the statute (*T.D. v. LaGrange School District No. 102*, 2003). Previously, a federal trial court in North Carolina denied a request for reimbursement of expert witness fees on the basis that the IDEA does not provide for an award of expert witness fees (*Eirschele v. Craven County Board of Education*, 1998).

As is typically the case, the Supreme Court intervened to resolve the difference between the Circuits and to ensure a more uniform interpretation of the IDEA. In *Arlington Central School District v. Murphy* (2006), the Supreme Court, reversing the Second Circuit's earlier order to the contrary, interpreted the IDEA as not permitting parents to be reimbursed for the services of expert witnesses or consultants who assisted them in their disputes with school boards (Osborne & Russo, 2006). Although recognizing that this created the anomalous situation whereby parents who prevailed in their disputes with their school boards could recover attorney fees, but not expenses to cover the costs associated with expert witnesses or consultants who helped them to win their cases, the Court concluded that since Congress was aware of this fact but refused to modify the IDEA accordingly, it saw no reason to rewrite the statute.

Fees for Representation in Complaint Resolution Procedures

The IDEA's regulations require states to adopt procedures to resolve complaints filed by organizations or individuals over alleged violations of the IDEA (34 C.F.R. §§ 300.151–300.153). Whether fees are available for representation in filing complaints through the IDEA's complaint resolution procedures is unsettled. The Ninth Circuit and the federal trial court in Vermont agreed that fees may be awarded for representation in the filing of complaints under a state's or the IDEA's complaint resolution procedures (*Upper Valley Association of Handicapped Citizens v. Blue Mountain Union School District No. 21*, 1997; *Lucht v. Molalla River School District*, 1999). Conversely, the federal trial court in Minnesota denied a fee award for an attorney who filed a complaint on behalf of a student with disabilities (*Megan C. v. Independent School District No. 625*, 1999). The court ascertained that the filing of a complaint was not an action or proceeding for purposes of recovering attorney fees under the IDEA. Noting that the IDEA does not authorize a complaint resolution procedure, the Second Circuit affirmed that fees are not reimbursable for representation at complaint resolution proceedings (*Vultaggio v. Board of Education, Smithtown Central School District*, 2003).

Fees for Representation at IEP Meetings

The IDEA specifically prohibits reimbursements of attorney fees for attendance at IEP meetings unless such sessions were convened as a result of administrative or judicial actions (20 U.S.C. § 1415(i)(3)(D)(ii); 34

C.F.R. § 300.517(c)(2)(ii)). Courts consistently denied fees for representation at IEP meetings (*E.C. ex rel. R.C. v. Board of Education of South Brunswick Township*, 2001). On the other hand, at least one court allowed reimbursement for the time an attorney spent scheduling an IEP meeting when that effort was the direct result of a court order (*Watkins v. Vance*, 2004).

Awards to Local School Boards

The IDEA allowed for recovery of legal expenses by prevailing parents but did not originally grant school boards the right to seek reimbursement for their legal expenses if they prevailed in litigation. Using their general powers of equity, courts have sometimes, albeit reluctantly, awarded attorney fees to boards in determining that parental claims were frivolous or unnecessarily prolonged the litigation. The First Circuit, for example, concluded that a board was entitled to reimbursement of legal expenses under Appellate Rule 38 in finding that the parents' suit was "completely devoid of merit and plagued by unnecessary delay" (*Caroline T. v. Hudson School District*, 1990, p. 757). The court commented that the parents engaged in tactics throughout the proceedings that led to undue delays and also failed to cooperate in negotiations to settle the dispute. In another case, a federal trial court in New York denied a prevailing board's request for attorney fees based on the claim that the parents brought the action in bad faith (*Hiller v. Board of Education of the Brunswick Central School District*, 1990). The court was convinced that since both parties proceeded in good faith, they should bear their own costs.

In a major change, the 2004 amendments included a provision that permits school boards to seek reimbursement of their legal expenses when parents file complaints that are later found to be frivolous, unreasonable, or without foundation; or when the litigation was continued after it clearly became frivolous, unreasonable, or without foundation (20 U.S.C. § 1415(i)(3)(B)(i)(II); 34 C.F.R. § 300.517(a)(ii)). Moreover, boards may obtain awards when parents' suits are filed for improper purposes, cause unnecessary delays, or needlessly increase the cost of litigation (20 U.S.C. § 1415(i)(3)(B)(i)(III); 34 C.F.R. § 300.517(a)(iii)). Under this section, awards are to be levied against the parents' attorney, not the parents themselves. In light of past judicial reluctance to award attorney fees to boards under their general powers of equity, even under circumstances similar to those described within the statute, it school boards remain reluctant to use this provision to recover some of the costs of litigation.

By the same token, school boards may not continue litigation that is clearly frivolous, unreasonable, or without foundation or engage in any tactics that unnecessarily prolong litigation or otherwise abuse the process. Under the Federal Rules of Civil Procedure, a federal trial court in California sanctioned a board and its attorney for raising frivolous objections, making misstatements, and mischaracterizing facts (*Moser v. Bret Harte Union High School District*, 2005).

⚖️

SPECIAL EDUCATION LAW IN PRACTICE

Legal Case No. 13—Unilateral Placements in Private Schools If Free Appropriate Public Education
Is Not Provided in Public Schools

FLORENCE COUNTY SCHOOL DISTRICT FOUR V. CARTER
United States Supreme Court, 1993
510 U.S. 7

Justice O'CONNOR delivered the opinion of the Court.

The Individuals with Disabilities Education Act (IDEA or Act), requires States to provide disabled children with a "free appropriate public education," . . . This case presents the question whether a court may order reimbursement for parents who unilaterally withdraw their child from a public school that provides an inappropriate education under IDEA and put the child in a private school that provides an education that is otherwise proper under IDEA, but does not meet all the requirements of § 1401(a)(18). We hold that the court may order such reimbursement, and therefore affirm the judgment of the Court of Appeals.

I

Respondent Shannon Carter was classified as learning disabled in 1985, while a ninth grade student in a school operated by petitioner Florence County School District Four. School officials met with Shannon's parents to formulate an individualized education program (IEP) for Shannon, as required under IDEA. The IEP provided that Shannon would stay in regular classes except for three periods of individualized instruction per week, and established specific goals in reading and mathematics of four months' progress for the entire school year. Shannon's parents were dissatisfied, and requested a hearing to challenge the appropriateness of the IEP. Both the local educational officer and the state educational agency hearing officer rejected Shannon's parents' claim and concluded that the IEP was adequate. In the meantime, Shannon's parents had placed her in Trident Academy, a private school specializing in educating children with disabilities. Shannon began at Trident in September 1985 and graduated in the spring of 1988.

Shannon's parents filed this suit in July 1986, claiming that the school district had breached its duty under IDEA to provide Shannon with a "free appropriate public education," § 1401(a)(18), and seeking reimbursement for tuition and other costs incurred at Trident. After a bench trial, the District Court ruled in the parents' favor. . . . The District Court concluded that Shannon's education was "appropriate" under IDEA, and that Shannon's parents were entitled to reimbursement of tuition and other costs.

The Court of Appeals for the Fourth Circuit affirmed. The court agreed that the IEP proposed by the school district was inappropriate under IDEA. . . . Accordingly, "when a public school system has defaulted on its obligations under the Act, a private school placement is 'proper under the Act' if the education provided by the private school is 'reasonably calculated to enable the child to receive educational benefits.'"

The court below recognized that its holding conflicted with *Tucker v. Bay Shore Union Free School Dist.*, in which the Court of Appeals for the Second Circuit held that parental placement in a private school cannot be proper under the Act unless the private school in question meets the standards of the state education agency. We granted certiorari to resolve this conflict among the Courts of Appeals.

II

In *School Comm. of Burlington v. Department of Ed. of Mass.*, we held that IDEA's grant of equitable authority empowers a court "to order school authorities to reimburse parents for their expenditures on private special education for a child if the court ultimately determines that such placement, rather than a proposed IEP, is proper under the Act." Congress intended that IDEA's promise of a "free appropriate public education" for disabled children would normally be met by an IEP's provision for education in the regular public schools or in private schools chosen jointly by school officials and parents. In cases where cooperation fails, however, "parents who disagree with the proposed IEP are faced with a choice: go along with the IEP to the detriment of their child if it turns out to be inappropriate or pay for what they consider to be the appropriate placement." For parents willing and able to make the latter choice, "it would be an empty victory to have a court tell them several years later that they were right but that these expenditures could not in a proper case be reimbursed by the school officials." Because such a result would be contrary to IDEA's guarantee of a "free appropriate public education," we held that "Congress meant to include retroactive reimbursement to parents as an available remedy in a proper case."

As this case comes to us, two issues are settled: (1) the school district's proposed IEP was inappropriate under IDEA, and (2) although Trident did not meet the § 1401(a)(18) requirements, it provided an education otherwise proper under IDEA. This case presents the narrow question whether Shannon's parents are barred from reimbursement because the private school in which Shannon enrolled did not meet the § 1401(a)(18) definition of a "free appropriate public education." We hold that they are not, because § 1401(a)(18)'s requirements cannot be read as applying to parental placements.

Section 1401(a)(18)(A) requires that the education be "provided at public expense, under public supervision and direction." Similarly, § 1401(a)(18)(D) requires schools to provide an IEP, which must be designed by "a representative of the local educational agency," and must be "establish[ed]," "revise[d]," and "review[ed]" by the agency, § 1414(a)(5). These requirements do not make sense in the context of a parental placement. In this case, as in all *Burlington* reimbursement cases, the parents' rejection of the school district's proposed IEP is the very reason for the parents' decision to put their child in a private school. In such cases, where the private placement has necessarily been made over the school district's objection, the private school education will not be under "public supervision and direction." Accordingly, to read the § 1401(a)(18) requirements as applying to parental placements would effectively eliminate the right of unilateral withdrawal recognized in *Burlington*. Moreover, IDEA was intended to ensure that children with disabilities receive an education that is both appropriate and free. To read the provisions of § 1401(a)(18) to bar reimbursement in the circumstances of this case would defeat this statutory purpose.

Nor do we believe that reimbursement is necessarily barred by a private school's failure to meet state education standards. Trident's deficiencies, according to the school district, were that it employed at least two faculty members who were not state-certified and that it did not develop IEP's. As we have noted, however, the § 1401(a)(18) requirements—including the requirement that the school meet the standards of the state educational agency do not apply to private parental placements. Indeed, the school district's emphasis on

state standards is somewhat ironic. As the Court of Appeals noted, "it hardly seems consistent with the Act's goals to forbid parents from educating their child at a school that provides an appropriate education simply because that school lacks the stamp of approval of the same public school system that failed to meet the child's needs in the first place." Accordingly, we disagree with the Second Circuit's theory that "a parent may not obtain reimbursement for a unilateral placement if that placement was in a school that was not on [the State's] approved list of private" schools. Parents' failure to select a program known to be approved by the State in favor of an unapproved option is not itself a bar to reimbursement.

Furthermore, although the absence of an approved list of private schools is not essential to our holding, we note that parents in the position of Shannon's have no way of knowing at the time they select a private school whether the school meets state standards. South Carolina keeps no publicly available list of approved private schools, but instead approves private school placements on a case-by-case basis. In fact, although public school officials had previously placed three children with disabilities at Trident . . . Trident had not received blanket approval from the State. South Carolina's case-by-case approval system meant that Shannon's parents needed the cooperation of state officials before they could know whether Trident was state-approved. As we recognized in *Burlington*, such cooperation is unlikely in cases where the school officials disagree with the need for the private placement.

III

The school district also claims that allowing reimbursement for parents such as Shannon's puts an unreasonable burden on financially strapped local educational authorities. The school district argues that requiring parents to choose a state-approved private school if they want reimbursement is the only meaningful way to allow States to control costs; otherwise States will have to reimburse dissatisfied parents for any private school that provides an education that is proper under the Act, no matter how expensive it may be.

There is no doubt that Congress has imposed a significant financial burden on States and school districts that participate in IDEA. Yet public educational authorities who want to avoid reimbursing parents for the private education of a disabled child can do one of two things: give the child a free appropriate public education in a public setting, or place the child in an appropriate private setting of the State's choice. This is IDEA's mandate, and school officials who conform to it need not worry about reimbursement claims.

Moreover, parents who, like Shannon's, "unilaterally change their child's placement during the pendency of review proceedings, without the consent of state or local school officials, do so at their own financial risk." They are entitled to reimbursement only if a federal court concludes both that the public placement violated IDEA and that the private school placement was proper under the Act.

Finally, we note that once a court holds that the public placement violated IDEA, it is authorized to "grant such relief as the court determines is appropriate." Under this provision, "equitable considerations are relevant in fashioning relief," and the court enjoys "broad discretion" in so doing. Courts fashioning discretionary equitable relief under IDEA must consider all relevant factors, including the appropriate and reasonable level of reimbursement that should be required. Total reimbursement will not be appropriate if the court determines that the cost of the private education was unreasonable.

Accordingly, we affirm the judgment of the Court of Appeals.

So ordered.

Questions for Discussion

1. Does the outcome of this case serve the best interest(s) of students with disabilities?
2. How far can, or should, courts go in extending this rationale? For example, what if parents wished to send their children to religiously affiliated charter schools? What if parents sought reimbursement for costs associated with homeschooling?

Summary of Important Legal Policies, Principles, and Practices

1. Generally, the courts have held that monetary, or punitive damages are unavailable under the IDEA 2004, unless school districts "egregiously" failed to legally comply with the IDEA's major requirements, including the FAPE provision.
2. The parents of students with disabilities who prevail in their student placement legal challenges can, under certain circumstances, be reimbursed for the costs of tuition as well as other expenses related with unilateral private student placements. The U.S. Supreme Court issued two important decisions relating to the issue of tuition reimbursement to parents who unilaterally placed their children in private schools. These two cases are *Burlington School Committee v. Department of Education* (1985) and *Florence County School District Four v. Carter* (1993).
3. Some courts have granted the remedy of awards in the form of compensatory educational services. These services were offered when school officials failed to provide FAPE to eligible students with disabilities and the student's parents were financially unable to obtain alternate special education services for their children.
4. Since litigation-related costs can be expensive, the courts have, under certain circumstances, provided attorney costs and fees. The attorneys' costs and fees remedy provision has been litigated, especially relating to what attorney costs and fees are recoverable. To date, the courts have not developed specific legal guidance on this issue.

Useful Online Resources

Wrightslaw: IDEA 2004: Rule 11 and Attorney Fees

This article discusses the "new" attorney fee statute in IDEA 2004 allows school districts to recover attorney costs and fees from parents. Website: www.wrightslaw.com/law/idea/attyfees.rule11.htm

Recommended Reading

Lin, T. (2003). Recovering attorney's fees under the Individuals with Disabilities Education Act. *Education Law Reporter, 180,* 1–24.

Zirkel, P. A. (2006). Compensatory education under the IDEA: The Third Circuit's partially misleading position. *Penn State Law Review, 110,* 879–902.

Zirkel, P. A. (2013, Spring). Adjudicative remedies for denials of FAPE under the IDEA. *Journal of the National Association of Administrative Law Judiciary, 33,* 215–241.

References

Abraham v. District of Columbia, 338 F. Supp.2d 113 (D.D.C. 2004).

Alamo Heights Independent School District v. State Board of Education, 790 F.2d 1153 (5th Cir. 1986).

Algeria v. District of Columbia, 391 F.3d 262 (D.C. Cir. 2004).

Anderson v. Thompson, 658 F.2d 1205 (7th Cir. 1981).

Angela L. v. Pasadena Independent School District, 918 F.2d 1188 (5th Cir. 1990).

Appellate Rule 38, Fed.R.App.P. 38.

Arlington Central School District Board of Education v. Murphy, 126 S. Ct. 2455 (2006), *reversing Murphy v. Arlington Central School District*, 402 F.3d 332 (2d Cir. 2005).

Aronow v. District of Columbia, 780 F. Supp. 46 (D.D.C. 1992), 791 F. Supp. 318 (D.D.C. 1992).

Arons v. New Jersey State Board of Education, 842 F.2d 58 (3d Cir. 1988).

Ash v. Lake Oswego School District, 766 F. Supp. 852 (D. Or. 1991), *aff'd*, 980 F.2d 585 (9th Cir. 1992).

Babb v. Knox County School System, 965 F.2d 104 (6th Cir. 1992).

Barbara R. v. Tirozzi, 665 F. Supp. 141 (D. Conn. 1987).

Barlow-Gresham Union High School District No. 2 v. Mitchell, 940 F.2d 1280 (9th Cir. 1991).

Barnett v. Fairfax County School Board, 927 F.2d 146 (4th Cir. 1991).

Bernardsville Board of Education v. J.H., 42 F.3d 149 (3d Cir. 1994).

Big Beaver Falls Area School District v. Jackson, 624 A.2d 806 (Pa. Commw. Ct. 1993).

Board of Education of the County of Cabell v. Dienelt, 843 F.2d 813 (4th Cir. 1988).

Board of Education of Downers Grove Grade School District No. 58 v. Steven L., 89 F.3d 464 (7th Cir. 1996).

Board of Education of the Hendrick Hudson Central School District v. Rowley, 458 U.S. 176 (1982).

Board of Education of Oak Park & River Forest High School District No. 200 v. Illinois State Board of Education, 21 F. Supp.2d 862 (N.D. Ill. 1988), *vacated and remanded on other grounds sub nom. Board of Education of Oak Park & River Forest High School District No. 200 v. Kelly E.*, 207 F.3d 931 (7th Cir. 2000).

Brandon K. v. New Lenox School District, 2001 WL 1491499 (N.D. Ill. 2001).

Brillon v. Klein Independent School District, 274 F. Supp.2d 864 (S.D. Tex. 2003).

Brown v. Wilson County School District, 747 F. Supp. 436 (M.D. Tenn. 1990).

Buckhannon Board & Care Home v. West Virginia Department of Health and Human Resources, 532 U.S. 598 (2001).

Bucks County Department of Mental Health/Mental Retardation v. Commonwealth of Pennsylvania, 379 F.3d 61 (3d Cir. 2004).

Burlington School Committee v. Department of Education, Commonwealth of Massachusetts, 471 U.S. 359 (1985).

Burr v. Sobol, 748 F. Supp. 97 (S.D.N.Y. 1990).

Capistrano Unified School District v. Wartenberg, 59 F.3d 884 (9th Cir. 1995).

Carlisle Area School District v. Scott P., 62 F.3d 520 (3d Cir. 1995).

Caroline T. v. Hudson School District, 915 F.2d 752 (1st Cir. 1990).

Chang v. Board of Education of Glen Ridge Township, 685 F. Supp. 96 (D.N.J. 1988).

Charlie F. v. Board of Education of Skokie School District 68, 98 F.3d 989 (7th Cir. 1996).

Cleveland Heights—University Heights City School District v. Boss, 144 F.3d 391 (6th Cir. 1998).

Cocores v. Portsmouth, NH School District, 779 F. Supp. 203 (D.N.H. 1991).

Combs v. School Board of Rockingham County, 15 F.3d 357 (4th Cir. 1994).

Conklin, In re, 946 F.2d 306 (4th Cir. 1991).

Connors v. Mills, 34 F. Supp.2d 795 (N.D.N.Y. 1998).

Cremeans v. Fairland Local School District Board of Education, 633 N.E.2d 570 (Ohio App. Ct. 1993).

Daniel S. v. Scranton School District, 230 F.3d 90 (3d Cir. 2000).

D.B. v. Ocean Township Board of Education, 985 F. Supp. 457 (D.N.J. 1997).

Deal ex rel. Deal v. Hamilton County Department of Education, 392 F.3d 840 (6th Cir. 2004).

Diamond v. McKenzie, 602 F. Supp. 632 (D.D.C. 1985).

DiBuo v. Board of Education of Worcester County, 309 F.3d 184 (4th Cir. 2002).

D.M. ex rel. G.M. and C.M. v. Board of Education, Center Moriches Union Free School District, 296 F. Supp.2d 400 (E.D.N.Y. 2003).

Doe v. Anrig, 651 F. Supp. 424 (D. Mass. 1987).

Doe v. Board of Education of Baltimore County, 165 F.3d 260 (4th Cir. 1998).

Doe v. Boston Public Schools, 358 F.3d 20 (1st Cir. 2004).

Doucet v. Chilton County Board of Education, 65 F. Supp.2d 1249 (M.D. Ala. 1999).

Drew P. v. Clarke County School District, 676 F. Supp. 1559 (M.D. Ga. 1987), *affirmed*, 877 F.2d 927 (11th Cir. 1989).

E.C. ex rel. R.C. v. Board of Education of South Brunswick Township, 792 A.2d 583 (N.J. Sup. Ct. 2001).

Eggers v. Bullitt County School District, 854 F.2d 892 (6th Cir. 1988).

Eirschele v. Craven County Board of Education, 7 F. Supp.2d 655 (E.D.N.C. 1998).

E.M. v. Millville Board of Education, 849 F. Supp. 312 (D.N.J. 1994).

E.P. v. Union County Regional High School District No. 1, 741 F. Supp. 1144 (D.N.J. 1989).

Erickson v. Board of Education of Baltimore County, 162 F.3d 289 (4th Cir. 1998).

Esther C. v. Ambach, 535 N.Y.S.2d 462 (N.Y. App. Div. 1988).

Eugene B. v. Great Neck Union Free School District, 635 F. Supp. 753 (E.D.N.Y. 1986).

Evans v. District No. 17 of Douglas County, 841 F.2d 824 (8th Cir. 1988).

Field v. Haddonfield Board of Education, 769 F. Supp. 1313 (D.N.J. 1991).

Fischer v. Rochester Community Schools, 780 F. Supp. 1142 (E.D. Mich. 1991).

Florence County School District Four v. Carter, 510 U.S. 7 (1993).

Forest Grove School District v. T.A., 557 U.S. 230 (2009).

Ft. Zumwalt School District v. Missouri State Board of Education, 865 F. Supp. 604 (E.D. Mo.1994).

Garland Independent School District v. Wilks, 657 F. Supp. 1163 (N.D. Tex. 1987).

Garner, B. A. (Ed.). (1999). *Black's law dictionary* (7th ed.). St. Paul, MN: West.

Garro v. State of Connecticut, 23 F.3d 734 (2d Cir. 1994).

Gary A. v. New Trier High School District No. 203, 796 F.2d 940 (7th Cir. 1986).

Gerasimou v. Ambach, 636 F. Supp. 1504 (E.D.N.Y. 1986).

Gerstmyer v. Howard County Public Schools, 850 F. Supp. 361 (D. Md. 1994).

Glendale Unified School District v. Almasi, 122 F. Supp.2d 1093 (C.D. Cal. 2000).

Goldring v. District of Columbia, 416 F.3d 70 (D.C. Cir. 2005).

Greenland School District v. Amy N., 358 F.3d 150 (1st Cir. 2004).

Gross ex rel. Gross v. Perrysburg Exempted Village School District, 306 F. Supp.2d 726 (N.D. Ohio 2004).

Hall v. Detroit Public Schools, 823 F. Supp. 1377 (E.D. Mich. 1993).

Heldman v. Sobol, 846 F.3d 285 (S.D.N.Y. 1994).

Hiller v. Board of Education of the Brunswick Central School District, 743 F. Supp. 958 (N.D.N.Y. 1990).

Howey v. Tippecanoe School Corporation, 734 F. Supp. 1485, (N.D. Ind. 1990).

Hudson v. Wilson, 828 F.2d 1059 (4th Cir. 1987).

Hunger v. Leininger, 15 F.3d 664 (7th Cir. 1994).

Hurry v. Jones, 734 F.2d 879 (1st Cir. 1984).

Hyden v. Board of Education of Wilson County, 714 F. Supp. 290 (M.D. Tenn. 1989).

Individuals with Disabilities Education Act, 20 U.S.C. §§ 1400–1482 (2005).

J.C. v. Regional School District No. 10, 278 F.3d 119 (2d Cir. 2002).

Jefferson County Board of Education v. Breen, 853 F.2d 853 (11th Cir. 1988).

J.G. v. Board of Education of the Rochester City School District, 648 F. Supp. 1452 (W.D.N.Y. 1986), *aff'd*, 830 F.2d 444 (2d Cir. 1987).

John T. by Paul T. and Joan T. v. Delaware County Intermediate Unit, 318 F.3d 545 (3d Cir. 2003).

Johnson v. Bismarck Public School District, 949 F.2d 1000 (8th Cir. 1991).

Johnson v. Lancaster-Lebanon Intermediate Unit 13, Lancaster City School District, 757 F. Supp. 606 (E.D. Pa. 1991).

Johnson v. Metro Davidson County School System, 108 F. Supp.2d 906 (M.D. Tenn. 2000).

Jose Luis R. v. Joliet Township H.S. District 204, 2002 WL 54544 (N.D. Ill. 2002).

J.S. v. Ramapo Central School District, 165 F. Supp.2d 570 (S.D.N.Y. 2001).

King v. Floyd County Board of Education, 5 F. Supp.2d 504 (E.D. Ky. 1998).

Koswenda v. Flossmoor School District No. 161, 227 F. Supp.2d 979 (N.D. Ill. 2002).

Krichinsky v. Knox County Schools, 963 F.2d 847 (6th Cir. 1992).

Kristi W. v. Graham Independent School District, 663 F. Supp. 86 (N.D. Tex. 1987).

Lascari v. Board of Education of the Ramapo Indian Hills Regional High School District, 560 A.2d 1180 (N.J. 1989).

Lester H. v. Gilhool, 916 F.2d 865 (3d Cir. 1990).

Linda T. ex rel. William A. v. Rice Lake Area School District, 337 F. Supp.2d 1135 (W.D. Wis. 2004).

L.K. ex rel. J.H. v. Board of Education for Transylvania County, 113 F. Supp.2d 856 (W.D.N.C. 2000).

Lucht v. Molalla River School District, 225 F.3d 1023 (9th Cir. 1999).

Malehorn v. Hill City School District, 987 F. Supp. 772 (D.S.D. 1997).

Manchester School District v. Christopher B., 807 F. Supp. 860 (D.N.H. 1992).

Mark H. v. Lemahieu, 513 F. 3d 922 (9th Cir. 2008).

Martin v. School Board of Prince George County, 348 S.E.2d 857 (Va. Ct. App. 1986).

Marvin H. v. Austin Independent School District, 714 F.2d 1348 (5th Cir. 1983).

Mathern v. Campbell County Children's Center, 674 F. Supp. 816 (D. Wyo. 1987).

Matthew V. v. DeKalb County School System, 244 F. Supp.2d 1331 (N.D. Ga. 2003).

Mayo v. Baltimore City Public Schools, 40 F. Supp.2d 331 (D. Md. 1999).

Max M. v. Illinois State Board of Education, 684 F. Supp. 514 (N.D. Ill. 1988), *aff'd*, 859 F.2d 1297 (7th Cir. 1988).

Max M. v. Thompson, 566 F. Supp. 1330 (N.D. Ill. 1983), 592 F. Supp. 1437 (N.D. Ill. 1984), *sub nom. Max M. v. Illinois State Board of Education*, 629 F. Supp. 1504 (N.D. Ill. 1986).

M.C. ex rel. J.C. v. Central Reg. School District, 81 F.3d 389 (3d Cir. 1996).

Megan C. v. Independent School District No. 625, 57 F. Supp.2d 776 (D. Minn. 1999).

Metropolitan School District of Lawrence Township v. M.S., 818 N.E.2d 978 (Ind. Ct. App. 2004).

Miener v. Missouri, 800 F.2d 749 (8th Cir. 1986).

Miller v. West Lafayette Community School Corporation, 665 N.E.2d 905 (Ind. 1996).

Missouri Department of Elementary and Secondary Education v. Springfield R-12 School District, 358 F.3d 992 (8th Cir. 2004).

Mitten v. Muscogee County District, 877 F.2d 932 (11th Cir. 1989).

Moore v. Crestwood Local School District, 804 F. Supp. 960 (N.D. Ohio 1992).

Moore v. District of Columbia, 886 F.2d 335 (D.C. Cir. 1989); 907 F.2d 165 (D.C. Cir. 1990).

Moser v. Bret Harte Union High School District, 366 F. Supp.2d 944 (E.D. Cal. 2005).

Moubry v. Independent School District No. 696, 951 F. Supp. 867 (D. Minn. 1996).

Mr. D. v. Glocester School Community, 711 F. Supp. 66 (D.R.I. 1989).

Mr. J. v. Board of Education, 98 F. Supp.2d 226 (D. Conn. 2000).

Mr. L. and Mrs. L. v. Woonsocket Education Department, 793 F. Supp. 41 (D.R.I. 1992).

M.S. ex rel. S.S. v. Board of Education of the City School District of the City of Yonkers, 231 F.3d 96 (2d Cir. 2000).

Ms. M. ex rel. K.M. v. Portland School Committee, 360 F.3d 267 (1st Cir. 2004).

Muller v. Committee on Special Education of the East Islip Union Free School District, 145 F.3d 95 (2d Cir. 1998).

Murphy v. Arlington Central School District Board of Education, 402 F.3d 332 (2d Cir. 2005).

Murphy v. Timberlane Regional School District, 973 F.2d 13 (1st Cir. 1992), *on remand*, 819 Supp. 1127 (D.N.H. 1993), *aff'd*, 22 F.3d 1186 (1st Cir. 1994a), *contempt finding*, 855 F. Supp. 498 (D.N.H. 1994b).

Muth v. Central Bucks School District, 839 F.2d 113 (3d Cir. 1988), *rev'd and remanded on other grounds sub nom. Dellmuth v. Muth*, 491 U.S. 223 (1989).

Nein v. Greater Clark County School Corporation, 95 F. Supp.2d 961 (S.D. Ind. 2000).

Neisz v. Portland Public School District, 684 F. Supp. 1530 (D. Or. 1988).

Neosho R-V School District v. Clark, 315 F.3d 1022 (8th Cir. 2003).

Noyes v. Grossmont Union High School District, 331 F. Supp.2d 1233 (S.D. Cal. 2004).

Osborne, A. G. (2003). Attorneys' fees under the IDEA after *Buckhannon*: Is the catalyst theory still viable? *Education Law Reporter, 175,* 397–407.

Osborne, A. G. (2005). Update on attorneys' fees under the IDEA. *Education Law Reporter, 193,* 1–12.

Osborne, A. G., & DiMattia, P. (1991). Attorney fees are available for administrative proceedings under the EHA. *Education Law Reporter, 66,* 909–920.

Osborne, A. G., & Russo, C. J. (2001). Are damages an available remedy when a school district fails to provide an appropriate education under IDEA? *Education Law Reporter, 152,* 1–14.

Osborne, A. G., & Russo, C. J. (2006). The Supreme Court rejects parental reimbursement for expert witness fees under the IDEA: *Arlington Central School District Board of Education v. Murphy. Education Law Reporter, 213,* 333–348.

Parents of Student W. v. Puyallup School District No. 3, 31 F.3d 1489 (9th Cir. 1994).

Patricia E. v. Board of Education of Community High School District No. 155, 894 F. Supp. 1161 (N.D. Ill. 1995).

Patricia P. v. Board of Education of Oak Park and River Forest High School District No. 200, 203 F.3d 462 (7th Cir. 2000).

Payne v. Board of Education, Cleveland City Schools, 88 F.3d 392 (6th Cir. 1996).

Pazik v. Gateway Regional School District, 130 F. Supp.2d 217 (D. Mass. 2001).

Phelan v. Bell, 8 F.3d 369 (6th Cir. 1993).

Pihl v. Massachusetts Department of Education, 9 F.3d 184 (1st Cir. 1993).

P.J. v. State of Connecticut State Board of Education, 788 F. Supp. 673 (D. Conn. 1992).

P.L. by Mr. and Mrs. L. v. Norwalk Board of Education, 64 F. Supp.2d 61 (D. Conn. 1999).

P.O. ex rel. L.T. and T.O. v. Greenwich Board of Education, 210 F. Supp.2d 76 (D. Conn. 2002).

Powell v. DeFore, 699 F.2d 1078 (11th Cir. 1983).

Puffer v. Raynolds, 761 F. Supp. 838 (D. Mass. 1988).

Rapid City School District v. Vahle, 922 F.2d 476 (8th Cir. 1990).

Rappaport v. Vance, 812 F. Supp. 609 (D. Md. 1993).

Ridgewood Board of Education v. N.E., 172 F.3d 238 (3d Cir. 1999).

Rehabilitation Act, Section 504, 29 U.S.C. § 794.

Russo, C. J. (2006). Negligence. In C. J. Russo (Ed.), *Key legal issues for schools: The ultimate resource for school business officials* (pp. 83–97). Lanham, MD: Rowman & Littlefield Education.

S-1 v. Spangler, 650 F. Supp. 1427 (M.D.N.C. 1986), *vacated and remanded due to mootness* 832 F.2d 294 (4th Cir. 1987), *on remand* (unpublished opinion), *aff'd sub nom. S-1 v.*

Salley v. St. Tammany Parish School Board, 57 F.3d 458 (5th Cir. 1995).

Schoenfield v. Parkway School District, 138 F.3d 379 (8th Cir. 1998).

Shelly C. v. Venus Independent School District, 878 F.2d 862 (5th Cir. 1989).

Sidney K. v. Ambach, 535 N.Y.S.2d 468 (N.Y. App. Div. 1988).

Smith ex rel Smith v. Fitchburg Public Schools, 401 F.3d 16 (1st Cir. 2005).

Smith v. District of Columbia, 117 Fed. Appx. (D.C. Cir. 2004).

Smith v. Robinson, 468 U.S. 992 (1984).

State of West Virginia ex rel. Justice v. Board of Education of the County of Monongalia, 539 S.E.2d 777 (W.Va. 2000).

Still v. DeBuono, 101 F.3d 888 (2d Cir. 1996).

Straube v. Florida Union Free School District, 778 F. Supp. 774 (S.D.N.Y. 1991), 801 F. Supp. 1164 (S.D.N.Y. 1992).

Suzawith v. Green Bay Area School District, 132 F. Supp.2d 718 (D. Wis. 2000).

Taylor v. Board of Education of Copake-Taconic Hills Central School District, 649 F. Supp. 1253 (N.D.N.Y. 1986).

T.D. v. LaGrange School District No. 102, 349 F.3d 469 (7th Cir. 2003).

Tice v. Botetourt County School District, 908 F.2d 1200 (4th Cir. 1990).

Timms v. Metropolitan School District, EHLR 554:361 (S.D. Ind. 1982), aff'd, 718 F.2d 212 (7th Cir. 1983), *amended*, 722 F.2d 1310 (7th Cir. 1983).

Todd D. v. Andrews, 933 F.2d 1576 (11th Cir. 1991).

Troy School District v. Boutsikaris, 250 F. Supp.2d 720 (E.D. Mich. 2003).

Tucker v. Calloway County Board of Education, 136 F.3d 495 (6th Cir. 1998).

Turton v. Crisp County School District, 688 F. Supp. 1535 (M.D. Ga. 1988).

Union School District v. Smith, 15 F.3d 1519 (9th Cir. 1994).

Upper Valley Association of Handicapped Citizens v. Blue Mountain Union School District No. 21, 973 F. Supp. 429 (D. Vt. 1997).

Valerie J. v. Derry Cooperative School District, 771 F. Supp. 483 (D.N.H. 1991).

Vander Malle v. Ambach, 667 F. Supp. 1015 (S.D.N.Y. 1987).

Virginia McC. v. Corrigan-Camden Independent School District, 909 F. Supp. 1023 (E.D. Tex. 1995).

Vultaggio v. Board of Education, Smithtown Central School District, 343 F.3d 598 (2nd Cir. 2003).

Warren G. v. Cumberland County School District, 190 F.3d 80 (3d Cir. 1999).

Watkins v. Vance, 328 F. Supp.2d 27 (D.D.C. 2004).

Wenger v. Canastota Central School District, 979 F. Supp. 147 (N.D.N.Y. 1997), *affirmed*, 181 F.3d 84, 136 Ed.Law Rep. 226 (2d Cir. 1999) (mem.).

Wenkart, R. D. (2002). Attorneys' fees under the IDEA and the demise of the catalyst theory. *Education Law Reporter, 165*, 439–445.

Wheeler v. Towanda Area School District, 950 F.2d 128 (3d Cir. 1991).

W.L.G. v. Houston County Board of Education, 975 F. Supp. 1317 (M.D. Ala. 1997).

Woodside v. School District of Philadelphia Board of Education, 248 F.3d 129 (3d Cir. 2001).

Yancy v. New Baltimore City Board of School Commissioners, 24 F. Supp.2d 512 (D. Md. 1998).

Yankton School District v. Schramm, 900 F. Supp. 1182 (D.S.D. 1995), aff'd, 93 F.3d 1369 (8th Cir. 1996).

Zirkel, P. A., & Hennessy, M. K. (2001). Compensatory educational services in special education cases: An update. *Education Law Reporter, 150*, 311–332.

Zirkel, P. A., & Osborne, A. G. (1987). Are damages available in special education suits? *Education Law Reporter, 42*, 497–508.

12

Parental Involvement in the Special Education Decision-Making Process

---

Key Concepts and Terms in This Chapter

- Parental Notification and Consent Requirements
- Rights of Noncustodial Parents
- Parental Rights During the IEP Process
- Rights of Students Reaching the Age of Majority
- Family Educational Rights and Privacy Act (FERPA)

The Significant Role of Parents in the Special Education Process Under the IDEA

Since the inception of the Education for all Handicapped Children Act (EAHCA) in 1975, parental participation has and continues to be a cornerstone of the federal law, now known as the Individuals with Disabilities Education Act (IDEA). In order to facilitate and promote the primary goal of the IDEA 2004, providing a free appropriate public education (FAPE) in the least restrictive environment (LRE) to all eligible students with disabilities, Congress included significant and numerous parental rights in the IDEA 2004 statute in order that parents could advocate and fully participate in the IDEA process on behalf of their children. The IDEA 2004 requires local education agencies (LEAs) to develop and monitor strict notice and participation requirements. These parental notice and participation provisions are integral components of the IDEA 2004 and govern many crucial aspects of the special education process, ranging from the identification of to post-high school transition of students with disabilities. These parental participation provisions expressly stated in the IDEA 2004 statute and regulations strongly encourage parents to become integral partners in the education of their children. Table 12.1 highlights the eight major entitlements parents are afforded to participate in the development of their child's individualized education program.

This chapter focuses on more specific legal rights afforded to parents and their children in the special education decision-making process, including the right to be notified of school district actions involving the provision of FAPEs. The chapter also includes an extensive discussion of student and parent rights with regard to student records.

The IDEA 2004 statute has expanded the definition of parent. According to the IDEA 2004, the term *parent* now means a natural, adoptive, or foster parent of a child (unless a foster parent is prohibited by state law from serving as a parent); a guardian (but not the state if the child is a ward of the state); an individual acting in the place of a natural or adoptive parent (including a grandparent, stepparent, or other relative) with whom the child lives, or an individual who is legally responsible for the child's welfare; or an individual assigned to be a surrogate parent (20 U.S.C. § 1402(23)).

Table 12.1 Eight Major Legal Entitlements Under the IDEA Allowing Parents to Participate in the IEP Process of Their Child

1. The right of parents to receive a complete explanation of all the procedural safeguards available under IDEA and the procedures in the state for presenting complaints
2. Confidentiality and the right of parents to inspect and review the educational records of their child
3. The right of parents to participate in meetings related to the identification, evaluation, and placement of their child, and the provision of FAPE (a free appropriate public education) to their child
4. The right of parents to obtain an independent educational evaluation (IEE) of their child
5. The right of parents to receive "prior written notice" on matters relating to the identification, evaluation, or placement of their child, and the provision of FAPE to their child
6. The right of parents to give or deny their consent before the school may take certain actions with respect to their child
7. The right of parents to disagree with decisions made by the school system on those issues
8. The right of parents and schools to use IDEAs mechanisms for resolving disputes, including the right to appeal determinations

Source: Center for Parent Information and Resources (CPIR), *Parent Rights Under the IDEA (2017)*, Retrieved from: www.parentcenterhub.org/parental-rights/

According to the IDEA, a parent can be defined as any of the following:

1. The child's biological or adoptive parent;
2. Foster parent, unless state law, regulations, or contractual obligations with a state or local entity prohibit a foster parent from acting as a parent;
3. A guardian generally authorized to act as the child's parent or authorized to make educational decisions for the child (but not the state if the child is a ward of the state);
4. An individual acting in the place of a biological or adoptive parent (including a grandparent, stepparent, or other relative) with whom the child lives, or an individual who is legally responsible for the child's welfare; and
5. A surrogate parent who is been appointed in accordance with 34 C.F.R. §300.30; and 34 C.F.R. § 300.519.

Surrogate Parents Under the IDEA

Since some children and youth with disabilities are either homeless or wards of the state, the IDEA 2004 places legal responsibility on individual states and local education agencies (LEAs) to appoint surrogate parents in a timely manner. More specifically, states are mandated to appoint a surrogate parent no more than thirty days after a determination by the local school district that a particular student is in need of a surrogate parent (34 C.F.R. §300.519(h)).

In one case, a sixteen-year-old special education student was tried as an adult and sentenced to two years of incarceration. Once incarcerated, the student's parents were neither notified nor or involved in meetings concerning his IEP. The Florida Department of Corrections claimed that because the student was incarcerated as an adult, he had the transferred right of an adult. A federal trial court disagreed, positing that the student's rights of majority did not transfer until he reached the age of majority under state law (*Paul Y. by Kathy Y. v. Singletary*, 1997).

Model Forms and Notices Addressing Parental Participation

When reauthorizing the most recent IDEA 2004, Congress mandated that the Secretary of Education of the U.S. Department of Education create model forms and develop guidance to simplify the IDEA's parental notice provisions and make them accessible online. Presently, these model forms are accessible online and include the following content:

1. A model individualized education plan (IEP) form (website: www2.ed.gov/policy/speced/guid/idea/modelform-iep.pdf);

2. A model notice of procedural safeguard documents for parents (website: www2.ed.gov/policy/speced/guid/idea/modelform-safeguards.pdf);
3. A model prior written notice document for parents (https://sites.ed.gov/idea/files/modelform2_Prior_Written_Notice.pdf);
4. Guidance on the required content of forms under the IDEA 2004 (https://sites.ed.gov/idea/files/modelform-compendium.pdf).

Required Prior Notice Requirements for Parents

Under the IDEA 2004, local education agencies are required to give parents basic notices, including prior written notice as well as notice of the IDEA 2004's procedural safeguards. School districts must provide a parent prior written notice when the school either proposes or change any of the following:

1. Identification of the student
2. Evaluation of the student
3. Educational placement of the student
4. Provision of FAPE to the child (34 C.F.R. §300.503)

Procedural Safeguard Requirements Involving Parents

The primary function of the IDEA 2004 procedural safeguard requirements is to make parents equal partners with school personnel in the education of their children. The IDEA 2004 requires that a local education agency provide a copy of the procedural safeguards notice to parents. More specifically, parents must be given a copy of the procedural safeguards notice at the following periods of the special education process, including

1. At the initial referral or parental request for an evaluation;
2. On the receipt of the first due process request or the first state complaint involving the parent-child during a school year;
3. When the school decides to make a disciplinary removal that constitutes a change of student placement based on a violation of a code of student conduct; and
4. Based on a request by a parent.

(34 C.F.R. § 300.504(a))

Student Records Under the IDEA

Another important way the IDEA 2004 affords parents access to and active participation in their child's special educational program is through direct access to their child's educational records. Basically, the IDEA 2004 requires individual states, local education agencies, and other agencies to meet two requirements based on the educational records of students with disabilities. First, the IDEA 2004 requires that school districts provide parents of children with disabilities an opportunity to inspect and review all educational records relating to the child's identification, evaluation, and educational placement as well as any records related to the student's provision of a free appropriate public education (FAPE) (34 C.F.R. § 300.501(a)). Second, the IDEA 2004 requires all school districts to ensure the confidentiality of any student's personally identifiable data, information, and records in accordance with the requirements of the Family Educational Rights and Privacy Act (FERPA) (20 U.S.C. § 1232g; 34 C.F.R. §300.123). Under the federal FERPA statute, "personally identifiable" is defined as information that contains the following:

1. The name of the child, the child's parents, or other family member;
2. The address of the child;
3. A personal identifier, such as the child's Social Security number or student number; and

4. A list of personal characteristics or other information that would make it possible to identify the child with reasonable certainty.

(34 C.F.R. 300.32)

Congress passed the Family Educational Rights and Privacy Act (FERPA) (20 U.S.C. § 1232g) in 1974, a year before it enacted the original version of the IDEA. FERPA outlines the rights of students and their parents with regard to educational records. FERPA has two main goals: to grant parents and eligible students access to their educational records and to limit the access of outsiders to those records. FERPA and the IDEA and its regulations apply with equal force to parents (20 U.S.C. 1232(g); 34 C.F.R. § 99.4) and eligible students with disabilities. Insofar as parents, rather than students, typically exercise the right to access records, this section focuses more on parental rights. Due to the fact that numerous records are kept pertaining to students in special education placements, a large part of the IDEA's regulations (34 C.F.R. §§ 300.611–300.627) deal with this important topic. The IDEA's regulations prohibit school authorities from disclosing any personally identifiable information about students with disabilities (34 C.F.R. § 300.622) while requiring school boards to protect the confidentiality of this information (34 C.F.R. § 300.623).

Student Records Covered Under FERPA

FERPA covers all "educational records" maintained by educational agencies or by persons acting on their behalf that contain personally identifiable information relating to students (20 U.S.C. § 1232g(a)(4)(A)). To the extent that "educational records" may include information about more than one student, parents (20 U.S.C. § 1232g(a)(1)(A)) who review the records of their children can examine only those portions of group data that are specific to their own children (20 U.S.C. § 1232g(a)(1)(A)).

Two cases highlight the importance of safeguarding student records in the context of special education. In the first, the federal trial court in Connecticut decided that school board officials violated parents' privacy rights when they released their names and that of their child to a local newspaper following a due process hearing (*Sean R. v. Board of Education of the Town of Woodbridge*, 1992). In the second case, the Eighth Circuit, noting that strong public policy favors protection of the privacy of minors where sensitive matters are concerned, affirmed that judicial proceedings under the IDEA can be closed to the public (*Webster Groves School District v. Pulitzer Publishing Co.*, 1990). The court also pointed out that the IDEA restricts the release of information concerning students with disabilities without parental permission. In an attempt to safeguard that information and prevent stigmatization of the student, the court emphasized that access to the courtroom could be restricted and the files sealed.

Many school boards record directory information which may include each child's

name, address, telephone listing, date and place of birth, major field of study, participation in officially recognized activities and sports, weight and height of members of athletic teams, degrees and awards received, and the most recent previous educational agency or institution attended by the student.

(20 U.S.C. § 1232g(a)(5)(A))

Before school officials can release directory information on current students, they must provide parents with public notice of the categories of records that are designated as directory and afford them a reasonable time to request that the material not be released without their consent (20 U.S.C. § 1232g(a)(5)(B); 34 C.F.R. § 99.37). Inasmuch as the disclosure provisions relating to directory information do not apply to former students, school officials can release such data without obtaining any prior approvals (34 C.F.R. § 99.37(b)).

FERPA requires school personnel to inform parents annually of their right to inspect and review, request amendment of, and consent to disclosure of educational records, along with the right to file a complaint with the federal Department of Education alleging failures to comply with the dictates of the statute (34 C.F.R. §§ 99.7, 300.612). Typically, parents receive a single notice by a means that is reasonably likely to inform them of their rights. This notice may be included in school newsletters, student handbooks, notes home, local access TV announcements, e-mails, or other methods or combination of means designed to ensure that they receive notice.

In spite of FERPA's comprehensiveness, the statute grants exceptions so that a variety of documents are not considered to be educational records subject to the statute's mandatory disclosure provisions (34 C.F.R.

§ 99.3(b)). Four exemptions in particular are relevant to special education. First, records generated by educational personnel that are in the sole possession of their makers and are not accessible by or revealed to any other persons except temporary substitutes are not subject to release (20 U.S.C. § 1232g (a)(4)(B)(1)). Second, records kept separately by the law enforcement units of educational agencies that are used only for their own purposes cannot be accessed by third parties (20 U.S.C. § 1232g(a)(4)(B)(2)). Third, records that are made in the ordinary course of events relating to individuals who work at, but who do not attend, educational institutions, and which refer exclusively to individuals in their capacity as employees, and are not available for any other purpose, are not subject to disclosure (20 U.S.C. § 1232g(a)(4)(B)(3)). Fourth, records relating to students who are eighteen years of age or older, or who attend postsecondary educational institutions, which are made by physicians, psychiatrists, psychologists, or other professionals or paraprofessionals for use in their treatment and are not available to others, except at the request of the students, cannot be released (20 U.S.C. § 1232g(a)(4)(B)(4)).

Legal Rights to Inspect and Review Student Records

As indicated previously, parents have the right to inspect and review records containing personally identifiable information relating to the education of their children (20 U.S.C. § 1232g(a)(1)(A), 34 C.F.R. § 300.613). In this respect, FERPA grants noncustodial parents the same right of access to educational records as custodial parents, absent court orders or applicable state laws to the contrary (34 C.F.R. § 99.4). Along with access rights, FERPA requires school officials to provide parents with reasonable interpretations and explanations of information contained in the records of their children (34 C.F.R. § 99.10(c)).

Under FERPA, parental permission or consent is transferred to eligible students who reach their eighteenth birthdays or who attend postsecondary institutions (20 U.S.C. § 1232g(d); 34 C.F.R. § 300.625(b)). In an important exception relating to special education, school officials can take the age and the type or severity of student disabilities into consideration when granting rights of access (34 C.F.R. §§ 300.574, 300.625(a)). Other restrictions of interest are that postsecondary institutions do not have to permit students to inspect financial records in their files that include information about the resources of their parents (20 U.S.C. § 1232g(a)(1)(B); 34 C.F.R. § 99.12(b)(1)) or letters of recommendations where they waived their rights of access (20 U.S.C. § 1232g(a)(1)(C); 34 C.F.R. § 99.37(b)(2)(3)). Further, school officials are not required to grant access to records pertaining to individuals who are not or never have been students at their institutions (20 U.S.C. § 1232g(a)(6)).

Exceptions

Parties generally can access school records, other than directory information, only if parents provide written consent (20 U.S.C. §§ 1232g(b)(1), 1232g(b)(2)(A)). However, FERPA contains nine major exceptions where parental permission is not required before officials can review educational records. The purpose of these exceptions is to assist in the smooth administration of schools, especially as personnel from different school systems interact with one another. First, school employees with legitimate educational interests can access student records (20 U.S.C. § 1232g(b)(1)(A)). Second, officials representing schools to which students apply for admission can access their records as long as parents receive proper notice that the information has been sent to the receiving institution (20 U.S.C. § 1232g(b)(1)(B)). Third, authorized representatives of the U.S. Comptroller General, the Secretary of the Department of Education, and state and local education officials who are authorized to do so by state law can view student records for law enforcement purposes (20 U.S.C. § 1232g(b)(1)(C)(E)). Fourth, persons who are responsible for evaluating eligibility for financial aid can review appropriate educational records of students (20 U.S.C. § 1232g(b)(1)(D)).

Fifth, members of organizations conducting studies on behalf of educational agencies or institutions developing predictive tests or administering aid programs and improving instruction can view records as long as doing so does not lead to the release of personal information about students (20 U.S.C. § 1232g(b)(1) (F)). Sixth, individuals acting in the course of their duties for accrediting organizations can review student records (20 U.S.C. § 1232g(b)(1)(G)). Seventh, parents of dependent children can access student records (20 U.S.C. § 1232g(b)(1)(H)). Eighth, persons who protect the health and safety of students or other persons can view records in emergency situations (20 U.S.C. § 1232g(b)(1)(I)). Ninth, written permission is unnecessary if student records are subpoenaed or otherwise obtained through judicial orders, except that the parents must be notified in advance of a school board's compliance (20 U.S.C. §§ 1232g(b)(1)(J), 1232g(b)(2)(B)). Prior to ordering the release of information, courts weigh the need for access against the privacy interests of students. FERPA adds that its provisions do not prohibit educational officials from disclosing information concerning registered sex offenders who are required to register by federal law. Of course, in any of these instances, school officials cannot release or quote any personally identifiable information relating to children without parental consent.

A third party seeking disclosure of student records must have written consent from parents specifying the record(s) to be released, the reason(s) for the proposed release, and to whom the information is being given (34 C.F.R. § 99.30). FERPA further stipulates that parents have the right to receive a copy of the materials to be released (20 U.S.C. § 1232g(b)(2)(A)). In addition, school officials must keep records of all individuals or groups, except exempted parties, who request or obtain access to students' records (20 U.S.C. § 1232g(b)(4)(A)). These records not only must explain the legitimate interests of those who are granted access to educational records but must also be kept with records of individuals students whose files were accessed (20 U.S.C. § 1232g(b)(4)(A); 34 C.F.R. § 300.614).

Educational agencies that maintain student records must comply with parental requests for review without unnecessary delay. Unless parents agree otherwise, they must be granted access no later than 45 days after making their requests (20 U.S.C. § 1232g(a)(1)(A); 34 C.F.R. § 99.10(b)). Of course, nothing prohibits school officials from granting parental requests for access to student records more quickly. Agencies that receive parental requests for access to records cannot charge fees to search for or to retrieve student records (34 C.F.R. §§ 99.11(b), 300.614(b)). Once materials are located, school officials may charge parents for copies if doing so does not effectively prevent them from exercising their rights to inspect and review the educational records of their children (34 C.F.R. §§ 99.11(a), 300.614(a)).

Amending Student Records

Parents who disagree with the content of educational records can ask school officials to amend the information (34 C.F.R. § 99.20(a), 300.618(a)). If officials refuse to amend records within a reasonable time (34 C.F.R. §§ 99.20(b)(c), 300.618(c)), parents are entitled to hearings at which hearing officers evaluate whether challenged material is accurate and appropriately contained within the educational records of students (34 C.F.R. § 99.21, § 300.619).

Hearing officers must both conduct hearings and render decisions over amending student records within a reasonable time (34 C.F.R. § 99.22). If hearing officers are convinced that contested material is inaccurate, misleading, or otherwise violate student rights to privacy, school officials must amend them accordingly and inform the parents in writing that this has been done (34 C.F.R. §§ 99.21(b)(1), 300.620(a)). Conversely, if hearing officers believe that materials in educational records are not inaccurate or misleading, or do not otherwise violate student rights to privacy, the challenged information need not be removed or amended (34 C.F.R. §§ 99.21(b)(2), 300.620(b)). Parents who remain concerned over the content of educational records relating to their children, even after hearing officers decide that they are acceptable, can add statements explaining their objections which must be kept with the contested information for as long as it is kept on file (34 C.F.R. §§ 99.21(c), 300.620(c)).

Destroying Student Special Education Records

Insofar as the amount of records in student files can multiply rapidly, it should not be surprising that the IDEA's regulations allow for the destruction of information that is no longer needed. While neither the IDEA nor its regulations define the term, the latter does stipulate that records can be destroyed when they are no longer needed to provide children with services (34 C.F.R. § 300.624(a)). The regulation adds not only that parents must be advised that records are going to be destroyed but also that school officials can keep a record of student names, addresses, phone numbers, grades, attendance records, classes attended, grade levels completed, and years completed, with a time limitation (34 C.F.R. § 300.624(b)).

Enforcement of FERPA

FERPA includes enforcement provisions for situations when parents are denied the opportunity to review the records of their children, or records are released impermissibly. In *Gonzaga University v. Doe* (2002), the Supreme Court confirmed that the sole remedy for aggrieved parties is to file written complaints detailing the specifics of an alleged violation with the federal Department of Education's Family Policy Compliance Office (FPCO) (34 C.F.R. §§ 99.63).

Complaints must be filed within 180 days of either alleged violations or the dates when the aggrieved party knew or reasonably should have known about violations (34 C.F.R. §§ 99.64). When the FPCO receives complaints, its staff must notify officials at the educational institutions in writing, detailing the substance of the alleged violations and asking them to respond before considering whether to proceed with investigations (34 C.F.R. § 99.65). If, after investigations are completed (34 C.F.R. § 99.66), the FPCO staff agree that violations occurred, the Department of Education can withhold further payments under its programs, issue orders to compel compliance, or ultimately terminate institutional eligibility to receive federal funding if officials refuse to comply within a reasonable time (34 C.F.R. § 99.67).

In the only other Supreme Court case involving FERPA, *Owasso Independent School District v. Falvo* (2002), the Court found that peer-grading, whereby teachers permit students to grade the papers of classmates, does not turn the materials in question into educational records covered by FERPA. The Court concluded that a school board did not violate the law by permitting teachers to use the practice over the objection of a mother whose children attended schools in the district (Russo & Mawdsley, 2002).

Parental Due Process Rights

Although a majority of the due process rights addressed in the IDEA 2004 statute and regulations are focused on providing special education and related services to eligible students with disabilities, the U.S. Supreme Court's decision in *Winkelman v. Parma City School District* (2007) held that parents have distinct legal rights that are independent of and in addition to those of their children with disabilities served under the IDEA 2004. The Supreme Court ruling in *Winkelman (2007)* empowers today's parents of students with disabilities with substantive rights to appear *pro se* in federal court to challenge the appropriateness of their child's Individualized Education Plan (IEP) (McNeal, 2010). In this case, the parents, Mr. and Mrs. Winkelman were ready to send their six-year-old son, Jacob, to one of their neighborhood elementary schools, Pleasant Valley Elementary, for the upcoming school year. The Winkelman's were already aware that their son had autism spectrum disorder (ASD) and were ready to work collaboratively with the local school district setting up his Individualized Education Plan (IEP). However, when school officials developed the IEP, the Winkelmans found the IEP document to be inadequate and felt the school did not follow the proper procedures under IDEA. As a result, the Winkelmans filed a formal complaint alleging the school district had failed to provide their son, Jacob, with the required free and appropriate public education (FAPE) under the IDEA. Both the local and state special education hearing officer ruled against the Winkelmans and in favor of the Parma City School District claiming that Jacob was, in fact, receiving a free and appropriate public education. The Winkelmans then appealed this decision with the United States District Court for the Northern District of Ohio. While waiting for the decision of the district court, the Winkelmans enrolled Jacob in a private school, because they believed Pleasant Valley Elementary wasn't well suited to meet the needs of their son and his disability. The Winkelmans' suit in the United States District court sought the reversal of the administrative decision, reimbursement for private school expenses, and reimbursement for attorney's fees. The United States District Court once again ruled against the Winkelman's and in favor of Parma City School District. After this ruling, the Winkelman's once again appealed the decision with the federal U.S. Court of Appeals for the Sixth Circuit. At this point, the Winkelmans chose to appear in court *pro se* or without an attorney. Based on the Winkelman's decision to appear in court without an attorney, the Sixth Circuit dismissed the case until the Winkelmans found an attorney to represent them. After petitioning the Sixth Circuit, the case went on the U.S. Supreme Court. Two major legal questions surrounded this Supreme Court case; one being if the Winkelmans could, as parents, represent their child in court or if they needed to have a separate legal counsel. The second legal question before the Supreme Court was if their rights, as parents, and their child's rights were considered the same under the IDEA 2004.

The main legal question addressed in *Winkelman* is whether the nonlawyer parents of a disabled child can appear *pro se* in federal court either on their own behalf or on behalf of the child in a lawsuit under the Individuals with Disabilities Education Act (IDEA). The U.S. Supreme Court ruled that parents are now allowed to bring a *pro se* court action involving any procedural or substantive claim arising under the IDEA 2004. The Supreme Court in *Winkelman* rejected the view of some circuit courts that, under the statute, parents are "guardians" of their children's right to an appropriate education, rather than "real parties in interest" themselves.

Parental Participation in the IEP Process

Individualized education plans, or IEPs are written documents including statements of students' current academic achievement and functional performance, annual goals, how teams will measure progress toward those goals, the specific educational services to be provided, the extent to which children can participate in the general education program, accommodations the pupils will need on state assessments, and the date of initiation and duration of services (20 U.S.C. § 1414(d)). School personnel, acting in conjunction with parents, must develop IEPs before providing students with disabilities with special education and related services. IEPs must be in effect at the beginning of each school year (34 C.F.R. § 300.323).

According to the IDEA, IEPs must be developed by teams that include a student's parents, a regular education teacher (if the child is or will be participating in regular education), a special education teacher or provider, a school board representative, and an individual who can interpret evaluation results (20 U.S.C. § 1414(d)(1)(B)). The school board representative must be someone who is qualified to either provide or supervise special education, knows the general education curriculum, and knows the availability of school board resources. Failure to include a district representative can be fatal to a school board, as it can be taken as an indication that the parents were denied full opportunity to discuss all options (*Pitchford ex rel M. v. Salem-Keizer School District No. 24J*, 2001). At the same time, the requirement that the IEP team include persons knowledgeable about placement options does not mandate the presence of an expert in the parents' preferred methodology (*Dong v. Board of Education of the Rochester Community Schools*, 1999).

In light of the IDEA's emphasis on inclusion, the need for the participation of a regular education teacher on IEP teams cannot be overemphasized. Courts have invalidated IEPs when regular education teachers were not included on teams and students either were or would be participating in general education curricula (*Arlington Central School District v. D.K. and K.K.*, 2002; *Deal ex rel. Deal v. Hamilton County Department of Education*, 2004; *M.L. v. Federal Way School District*, 2005). When participation in general education is not an issue, it is unnecessary for regular education teachers to be part of IEP teams (*Cone ex rel. Cone v. Randolph County Schools*, 2004). Other persons may be present at the request of either the parents or school boards, and students may attend if appropriate. Individual members of IEP teams may be excused from attending meetings with the consent of the parents, but they must file written reports (20 U.S.C. § 1414(d)(1)(C)).

IEP Meetings

IEP meetings are designed to provide parents with the best opportunity to participate in the development of appropriate educational programs for their children. The purpose of IEP meetings is to share evaluation results, develop IEPs, and make placement decisions. While parents may have attended meetings where they provided school officials with information about and discussed the educational status of their children, most decisions regarding placements are made at IEP conferences. The IDEA's regulations specify that school personnel must take steps to ensure that at least one of a student's parents is present at IEP meetings (34 C.F.R. § 300.322). IEP meetings must occur within thirty calendar days of a determination that children need special education and related services (34 C.F.R. § 300.323(c)(1)). Failure to meet this timeline may result in IEPs being invalidated (*Knable v. Bexley City School District*, 2001). For students who attend private schools, a representative of the private schools must be present at IEP meetings (34 C.F.R. § 300.325).

Parental input into the IEP process cannot be minimized. One of the IDEA's unique features is that it provides for parental participation. Parents cannot simply be given token opportunities for participation. As such, parental input into the IEP process must be genuine. In one instance, the Ninth Circuit affirmed that an IEP that was developed without input from a student's parents and his teacher in a religiously affiliated school was invalid (*W.G. and B.G. v. Board of Trustees of Target Range School District No. 23*, 1992). The court emphasized that procedural violations that infringe on parents' opportunity to participate in the formulation of their child's IEP resulted in a denial of a free appropriate public education (FAPE). Similarly, the federal trial court in the District of Columbia wrote that the failure of public school officials to attend an IEP meeting that took place at a private school in which the student was enrolled rendered the proposed placement invalid (*Smith v. Henson*, 1992). Additionally, informal contacts between parents and school officials do not fully meet the IDEA's parental participation requirements. To this end, a state court in Pennsylvania proclaimed that impromptu meetings between a student's mother and school officials did not satisfy the IDEA's requirement of affording her the opportunity to participate in the development of an IEP (*Big Beaver Falls Area School District v. Jackson*, 1992).

Parental participation is meaningless if parents do not understand what is going on at IEP (or other) meetings. Accordingly, school officials must take necessary steps to ensure that parents do understand the proceedings. This may require officials to provide interpreters if the parents' primary mode of communication is not standard English (*Rothschild v. Grottenthaler*, 1990). Officials must take other steps to ensure that parents fully understand the proceedings. In two separate cases, the federal district court in Connecticut ruled that parents have the right to tape-record IEP meetings. In the first dispute, the student's mother had limited English proficiency and requested permission to tape-record the proceedings so that she could better understand and follow what was said at the meeting (*E.H. and H.H. v. Tirozzi*, 1990). In this case, since the court interpreted the IDEA's intent of parental participation as meaning more than mere presence at the IEP conference, the court decided that tape recordings would have allowed the parents to become active and meaningful participants in planning for the education of their children.

In 2013, the Ninth U.S. Circuit Court of Appeals ruled in *Doug C. v. State of Hawaii Department of Education* (2013), an important legal decision illustrating the invaluable role of parental participation at IEP meetings, especially if the designated IEP team is considering changes to the existing IEP of the student. In this case, the Ninth Circuit ruled that the parent's right to participate in the IEP meeting was more important than the Hawaii Department of Education's need to meet an existing IEP annual review deadline (Chapman, 2015). A parent, Doug C. had e-mailed the special education coordinator of his school district the day of his son's IEP meeting indicating he could not attend the meeting because he was sick. The parent offered to reschedule the IEP meeting for the following week, which was a few days past the annual IEP review date set by the Hawaii Department of Education. In response, the district special education coordinator attempted to convince the parent to participate in his son's IEP meeting the same morning by phone, but the parent indicated he was not well and wanted to participate in person. The special education coordinator decided to go ahead with the IEP meeting without a parent present. At the meeting, the IEP team decided to change the student's existing placement from a private special education facility to a public high school workshop readiness program. The parent rejected that IEP because it was created without his participation and the father requested a due process hearing. Initially, the special education hearing officer and the District Court ruled in favor of the school district. Doug C. appealed to the ninth U.S. circuit Court of Appeals. The Ninth Circuit ruled in favor of the parent, Doug C. rejecting the argument that the IEP meeting needed to be held by the state's annual IEP review deadline. The Ninth Circuit maintained the state education officials could have continued to provide the student with special education and related services after the state's review date had passed. The court indicated that the importance of parental participation in their child's IEP was more important than the state's IEP review date deadline. Based on the Ninth Circuit's decision, the case was sent back to the District Court for consideration of the parent's right to tuition reimbursement for the placement of his son in a private program for students with disabilities. The *Doug C.* legal decision firmly reinforces the importance of parental participation in the IEP process, especially if school officials are considering adjusting or changing a student's existing IEP.

⚖️

SPECIAL EDUCATION LAW IN PRACTICE

Legal Case No. 14—Right of Non-Attorney Parents to Proceed *Pro Se* in IDEA Lawsuits

WINKELMAN EX REL. WINKELMAN V. PARMA CITY SCHOOL DISTRICT
550 U.S. 516 (2007)

Justice KENNEDY delivered the opinion of the Court.

Some four years ago, Mr. and Mrs. Winkelman, parents of five children, became involved in lengthy administrative and legal proceedings. They had sought review related to concerns they had over whether their youngest child, 6-year-old Jacob, would progress well at Pleasant Valley Elementary School, which is part of the Parma City School District in Parma, Ohio.

Jacob has autism spectrum disorder and is covered by the Individuals with Disabilities Education Act (Act or IDEA), . . . His parents worked with the school district to develop an individualized education program (IEP), as required by the Act. All concede that Jacob's parents had the statutory right to contribute to this process and, when agreement could not be reached, to participate in administrative proceedings including what the Act refers to as an "impartial due process hearing."

The disagreement at the center of the current dispute concerns the procedures to be followed when parents and their child, dissatisfied with the outcome of the due process hearing, seek further review in a United States District Court. The question is whether parents, either on their own behalf or as representatives of the child, may proceed in court unrepresented by counsel though they are not trained or licensed as attorneys. Resolution of this issue requires us to examine and explain the provisions of IDEA to determine if it accords to parents rights of their own that can be vindicated in court proceedings, or alternatively, whether the Act allows them, in their status as parents, to represent their child in court proceedings.

I

. . .

The school district proposed an IEP for the 2003–2004 school year that would have placed Jacob at a public elementary school. Regarding this IEP as deficient under IDEA, Jacob's nonlawyer parents availed themselves of the administrative review

provided by IDEA. They filed a complaint alleging respondent had failed to provide Jacob with a free appropriate public education; they appealed the hearing officer's rejection of the claims in this complaint to a state-level review officer; and after losing that appeal they filed, on their own behalf and on behalf of Jacob, a complaint in the United States District Court for the Northern District of Ohio . . . . [T]hey challenged the administrative decision, alleging, among other matters: that Jacob had not been provided with a free appropriate public education; that his IEP was inadequate; and that the school district had failed to follow procedures mandated by IDEA. Pending the resolution of these challenges, the Winkelmans had enrolled Jacob in a private school at their own expense. They had also obtained counsel to assist them with certain aspects of the proceedings, although they filed their federal complaint, and later their appeal, without the aid of an attorney. The Winkelmans' complaint sought reversal of the administrative decision, reimbursement for private-school expenditures and attorney's fees already incurred, and, it appears, declaratory relief.

The District Court granted respondent's motion for judgment on the pleadings, finding it had provided Jacob with a free appropriate public education. Petitioners, proceeding without counsel, filed an appeal with the Court of Appeals for the Sixth Circuit. Relying on its recent decision in *Cavanaugh v. Cardinal Local School Dist.*, the Court of Appeals entered an order dismissing the Winkelmans' appeal unless they obtained counsel to represent Jacob. In *Cavanaugh* the Court of Appeals had rejected the proposition that IDEA allows nonlawyer parents raising IDEA claims to proceed *pro se* in federal court. The court ruled that the right to a free appropriate public education "belongs to the child alone," not to both the parents and the child. It followed, the court held, that "any right on which the [parents] could proceed on their own behalf would be derivative" of the child's right, so that parents bringing IDEA claims were not appearing on their own behalf. As for the parents' alternative argument, the court held, nonlawyer parents cannot litigate IDEA claims on behalf of their child because IDEA does not abrogate the common-law rule prohibiting nonlawyer parents from representing minor children. As the court in *Cavanaugh* acknowledged, its decision brought the Sixth Circuit in direct conflict with the First Circuit, which had concluded, under a theory of "statutory joint rights," that the Act accords to parents the right to assert IDEA claims on their own behalf. See *Maroni v. Pemi-Baker Regional School Dist.*

Petitioners sought review in this Court. In light of the disagreement among the Courts of Appeals as to whether a nonlawyer parent of a child with a disability may prosecute IDEA actions *pro se* in federal court, we granted certiorari.

II

Our resolution of this case turns upon the significance of IDEA's interlocking statutory provisions. Petitioners' primary theory is that the Act makes parents real parties in interest to IDEA actions, not "mer[e] guardians of their children's rights." If correct, this allows Mr. and Mrs. Winkelman back into court, for there is no question that a party may represent his or her own interests in federal court without the aid of counsel. Petitioners cannot cite a specific provision in IDEA mandating in direct and explicit terms that parents have the status of real parties in interest. They instead base their argument on a comprehensive reading of IDEA. Taken as a whole, they contend, the Act leads to the necessary conclusion that parents have independent, enforceable rights. Respondent, accusing petitioners of "knit[ting] together various provisions pulled from the crevices of the statute" to support these claims, reads the text of IDEA to mean that any redressable rights under the Act belong only to children.

We agree that the text of IDEA resolves the question presented. We recognize, in addition, that a proper interpretation of the Act requires a consideration of the entire statutory scheme. Turning to the current version of IDEA, which the parties agree governs this case, we begin with an overview of the relevant statutory provisions.

A

The goals of IDEA include "ensur[ing] that all children with disabilities have available to them a free appropriate public education" and "ensur[ing] that the rights of children with disabilities and parents of such children are protected." To this end, the Act includes provisions governing four areas of particular relevance to the Winkelmans' claim: procedures

to be followed when developing a child's IEP; criteria governing the sufficiency of an education provided to a child; mechanisms for review that must be made available when there are objections to the IEP or to other aspects of IDEA proceedings; and the requirement in certain circumstances that States reimburse parents for various expenses. . . .

IDEA requires school districts to develop an IEP for each child with a disability, with parents playing "a significant role" in this process. . . . Parents serve as members of the team that develops the IEP. . . . IDEA accords parents additional protections that apply throughout the IEP process. . . . The statute also sets up general procedural safeguards that protect the informed involvement of parents in the development of an education for their child. . . .

. . .

When a party objects to the adequacy of the education provided, the construction of the IEP, or some related matter, IDEA provides procedural recourse: It requires that a State provide "[a]n opportunity for any party to present a complaint . . . with respect to any matter relating to the identification, evaluation, or educational placement of the child, or the provision of a free appropriate public education to such child." By presenting a complaint a party is able to pursue a process of review that, as relevant, begins with a preliminary meeting "where the parents of the child discuss their complaint" and the local educational agency "is provided the opportunity to [reach a resolution]." If the agency "has not resolved the complaint to the satisfaction of the parents within 30 days," the parents may request an "impartial due process hearing," which must be conducted either by the local educational agency or by the state educational agency, and where a hearing officer will resolve issues raised in the complaint.

. . .

. . . Once the state educational agency has reached its decision, an aggrieved party may commence suit in federal court: "Any party aggrieved by the findings and decision made [by the hearing officer] shall have the right to bring a civil action with respect to the complaint."

IDEA, finally, provides for at least two means of cost recovery that inform our analysis. First, in certain circumstances it allows a court or hearing officer to require a state agency "to reimburse the parents [of a child with a disability] for the cost of [private school] enrollment if the court or hearing officer finds that the agency had not made a free appropriate public education available to the child." Second, it sets forth rules governing when and to what extent a court may award attorney's fees. Included in this section is a provision allowing an award "to a prevailing party who is the parent of a child with a disability."

B

Petitioners construe these various provisions to accord parents independent, enforceable rights under IDEA. We agree. The parents enjoy enforceable rights at the administrative stage, and it would be inconsistent with the statutory scheme to bar them from continuing to assert these rights in federal court.

The statute sets forth procedures for resolving disputes in a manner that, in the Act's express terms, contemplates parents will be the parties bringing the administrative complaints . . . . Claims raised in these complaints are then resolved at impartial due process hearings, where, again, the statute makes clear that parents will be participating as parties. . . . The statute then grants "[a]ny party aggrieved by the findings and decision made [by the hearing officer] . . . the right to bring a civil action with respect to the complaint."

Nothing in these interlocking provisions excludes a parent who has exercised his or her own rights from statutory protection the moment the administrative proceedings end. Put another way, the Act does not *sub silentio* or by implication bar parents from seeking to vindicate the rights accorded to them once the time comes to file a civil action. Through its provisions for expansive review and extensive parental involvement, the statute leads to just the opposite result.

Respondent, resisting this line of analysis, asks us to read these provisions as contemplating parental involvement only to the extent parents represent their child's interests. In respondent's view IDEA accords parents nothing more than "collateral tools related to the child's underlying substantive rights-not freestanding or independently enforceable rights."

This interpretation, though, is foreclosed by provisions of the statute. IDEA defines one of its purposes as seeking "to ensure that the rights of children with disabilities and parents of such children are protected." The word "rights" in the quoted language refers to the rights of parents as well as the rights of the child; otherwise the grammatical structure would make no sense.

Further provisions confirm this view. IDEA mandates that educational agencies establish procedures "to ensure that children with disabilities and their parents are guaranteed procedural safeguards with respect to the provision of a free appropriate public education." It presumes parents have rights of their own when it defines how States might provide for the transfer of the "rights accorded to parents" by IDEA, and it prohibits the raising of certain challenges "[n]otwithstanding any other individual right of action that a parent or student may maintain under [the relevant provisions of IDEA]," To adopt respondent's reading of the statute would require an interpretation of these statutory provisions (and others) far too strained to be correct.

Defending its countertextual reading of the statute, respondent cites a decision by a Court of Appeals concluding that the Act's "references to parents are best understood as accommodations to the fact of the child's incapacity." This, according to respondent, requires us to interpret all references to parents' rights as referring in implicit terms to the child's rights-which, under this view, are the only enforceable rights accorded by IDEA. Even if we were inclined to ignore the plain text of the statute in considering this theory, we disagree that the sole purpose driving IDEA's involvement of parents is to facilitate vindication of a child's rights. It is not a novel proposition to say that parents have a recognized legal interest in the education and upbringing of their child. . . . There is no necessary bar or obstacle in the law, then, to finding an intention by Congress to grant parents a stake in the entitlements created by IDEA. Without question a parent of a child with a disability has a particular and personal interest in fulfilling "our national policy of ensuring equality of opportunity, full participation, independent living, and economic self-sufficiency for individuals with disabilities."

We therefore find no reason to read into the plain language of the statute an implicit rejection of the notion that Congress would accord parents independent, enforceable rights concerning the education of their children. We instead interpret the statute's references to parents' rights to mean what they say: that IDEA includes provisions conveying rights to parents as well as to children.

A variation on respondent's argument has persuaded some Courts of Appeals. The argument is that while a parent can be a "party aggrieved" for aspects of the hearing officer's findings and decision, he or she cannot be a "party aggrieved" with respect to all IDEA-based challenges. Under this view the causes of action available to a parent might relate, for example, to various procedural mandates, and reimbursement demands. The argument supporting this conclusion proceeds as follows: Because a "party aggrieved" is, by definition, entitled to a remedy, and parents are, under IDEA, only entitled to certain procedures and reimbursements as remedies, a parent cannot be a "party aggrieved" with regard to any claim not implicating these limited matters.

This argument is contradicted by the statutory provisions we have recited. True, there are provisions in IDEA stating parents are entitled to certain procedural protections and reimbursements; but the statute prevents us from placing too much weight on the implications to be drawn when other entitlements are accorded in less clear language. We find little support for the inference that parents are excluded by implication whenever a child is mentioned, and vice versa. . . . Without more, then, the language in IDEA confirming that parents enjoy particular procedural and reimbursement-related rights does not resolve whether they are also entitled to enforce IDEA's other mandates, including the one most fundamental to the Act: the provision of a free appropriate public education to a child with a disability.

We consider the statutory structure. The IEP proceedings entitle parents to participate not only in the implementation of IDEA's procedures but also in the substantive formulation of their child's educational program. Among other things, IDEA requires the IEP Team, which includes the parents as members, to take into account any "concerns" parents have "for enhancing the education of their child" when it formulates the IEP. The IEP, in turn, sets the boundaries of the central entitlement provided by IDEA: It defines a "'free appropriate public education'" for that parent's child.

The statute also empowers parents to bring challenges based on a broad range of issues. The parent may seek a hearing on "any matter relating to the identification, evaluation, or educational placement of the child, or the provision of a free appropriate public education to such child." To resolve these challenges a hearing officer must make a decision based on whether the child "received a free appropriate public education." When this hearing has been conducted by a local educational agency rather than a state educational agency, "any party aggrieved by the findings and decision rendered in such a hearing may appeal such findings and decision" to the state educational agency. Judicial review follows, authorized by a broadly worded provision phrased in the same terms used to describe the prior stage of review: "[a]ny party aggrieved" may bring "a civil action."

These provisions confirm that IDEA, through its text and structure, creates in parents an independent stake not only in the procedures and costs implicated by this process but also in the substantive decisions to be made. We therefore conclude that IDEA does not differentiate, through isolated references to various procedures and remedies, between the rights accorded to children and the rights accorded to parents. As a consequence, a parent may be a "party aggrieved" for purposes of [IDEA] with regard to "any matter" implicating these rights. The status of parents as parties is not limited to matters that relate to procedure and cost recovery. To find otherwise would be inconsistent with the collaborative framework and expansive system of review established by the Act. . . .

Our conclusion is confirmed by noting the incongruous results that would follow were we to accept the proposition that parents' IDEA rights are limited to certain nonsubstantive matters. The statute's procedural and reimbursement-related rights are intertwined with the substantive adequacy of the education provided to a child, and it is difficult to disentangle the provisions in order to conclude that some rights adhere to both parent and child while others do not. Were we nevertheless to recognize a distinction of this sort it would impose upon parties a confusing and onerous legal regime, one worsened by the absence of any express guidance in IDEA concerning how a court might in practice differentiate between these matters. It is, in addition, out of accord with the statute's design to interpret the Act to require that parents prove the substantive inadequacy of their child's education as a predicate for obtaining, for example, reimbursement under [IDEA], yet to prevent them from obtaining a judgment mandating that the school district provide their child with an educational program demonstrated to be an appropriate one. The adequacy of the educational program is, after all, the central issue in the litigation. The provisions of IDEA do not set forth these distinctions, and we decline to infer them.

The bifurcated regime suggested by the courts that have employed it, moreover, leaves some parents without a remedy. The statute requires, in express terms, that States provide a child with a free appropriate public education "at public expense," including specially designed instruction "at no cost to parents." Parents may seek to enforce this mandate through the federal courts, we conclude, because among the rights they enjoy is the right to a free appropriate public education for their child. Under the countervailing view, which would make a parent's ability to enforce IDEA dependant on certain procedural and reimbursement-related rights, a parent whose disabled child has not received a free appropriate public education would have recourse in the federal courts only under two circumstances: when the parent happens to have some claim related to the procedures employed; and when he or she is able to incur, and has in fact incurred, expenses creating a right to reimbursement. Otherwise the adequacy of the child's education would not be regarded as relevant to any cause of action the parent might bring; and, as a result, only the child could vindicate the right accorded by IDEA to a free appropriate public education.

The potential for injustice in this result is apparent. What is more, we find nothing in the statute to indicate that when Congress required States to provide adequate instruction to a child "at no cost to parents," it intended that only some parents would be able to enforce that mandate. The statute instead takes pains to "ensure that the rights of children with disabilities and parents of such children are protected." . . .

We conclude IDEA grants parents independent, enforceable rights. These rights, which are not limited to certain procedural and reimbursement-related matters, encompass the entitlement to a free appropriate public education for the parents' child.

C

Respondent contends, though, that even under the reasoning we have now explained petitioners cannot prevail without overcoming a further difficulty. Citing our opinion in *Arlington Central School Dist. Bd. of Ed. v. Murphy*, respondent argues that statutes passed pursuant to the Spending Clause, such as IDEA, must provide "'clear notice'" before they can burden a State with some new condition, obligation, or liability. Respondent contends that because IDEA is, at best, ambiguous as to whether it accords parents independent rights, it has failed to provide clear notice of this condition to the States.

Respondent's reliance on *Arlington* is misplaced. In *Arlington* we addressed whether IDEA required States to reimburse experts' fees to prevailing parties in IDEA actions. "[W]hen Congress attaches conditions to a State's acceptance of federal funds," we explained, "the conditions must be set out 'unambiguously.'" The question to be answered in *Arlington*, therefore, was whether IDEA "furnishes clear notice regarding the liability at issue." We found it did not.

The instant case presents a different issue, one that does not invoke the same rule. Our determination that IDEA grants to parents independent, enforceable rights does not impose any substantive condition or obligation on States they would not otherwise be required by law to observe. The basic measure of monetary recovery, moreover, is not expanded by recognizing that some rights repose in both the parent and the child. . . .

Respondent argues our ruling will, as a practical matter, increase costs borne by the States as they are forced to defend against suits unconstrained by attorneys trained in the law and the rules of ethics. Effects such as these do not suffice to invoke the concerns under the Spending Clause. . . .

III

The Court of Appeals erred when it dismissed the Winkelmans' appeal for lack of counsel. Parents enjoy rights under IDEA; and they are, as a result, entitled to prosecute IDEA claims on their own behalf. The decision by Congress to grant parents these rights was consistent with the purpose of IDEA and fully in accord with our social and legal traditions. It is beyond dispute that the relationship between a parent and child is sufficient to support a legally cognizable interest in the education of one's child; and, what is more, Congress has found that "the education of children with disabilities can be made more effective by . . . strengthening the role and responsibility of parents and ensuring that families of such children have meaningful opportunities to participate in the education of their children at school and at home."

In light of our holding we need not reach petitioners' alternative argument, which concerns whether IDEA entitles parents to litigate their child's claims *pro se*.

The judgment of the Court of Appeals is reversed, and the case is remanded for further proceedings consistent with this opinion.

- It is so ordered.
- Justice SCALIA, with whom Justice THOMAS joins, concurring in the judgment in part and dissenting in part.

I would hold that parents have the right to proceed *pro se* under the Individuals with Disabilities Education Act (IDEA), when they seek reimbursement for private school expenses or redress for violations of their own procedural rights, but not when they seek a judicial determination that their child's free appropriate public education (or FAPE) is substantively inadequate.

Whether parents may bring suits under the IDEA without a lawyer depends upon the interaction between the IDEA and the general *pro se* provision in the Judiciary Act of 1789. The latter . . . provides that "[i]n all courts of the United States *the parties* may plead and conduct their own cases personally or by counsel." The IDEA's right-to-sue provision, provides that "[a]ny *party aggrieved* by the findings and decision [of a hearing officer] shall have the right to bring a civil action with respect to the [administrative] complaint." Thus, when parents are "parties aggrieved" under the IDEA, they are "parties" within the meaning of [the Judiciary Act], entitled to sue on their own behalf.

As both parties agree, "party aggrieved" means "[a] party entitled to a remedy; espy., a party whose personal, pecuniary, or property rights have been adversely affected by another person's actions or by a court's decree or judgment." This case thus turns on the rights that the IDEA accords to parents, and the concomitant remedies made available to them. Only with respect to such rights and remedies are parents properly viewed as "parties aggrieved," capable of filing their own cases in federal court.

A review of the statutory text makes clear that, as relevant here, the IDEA grants parents only two types of rights. First, under certain circumstances "a court or a hearing officer may require the [school district] to reimburse *the parents*" for private school expenditures "if the court or hearing officer finds that the [school district] had not made a free appropriate public education available to the child." Second, parents are accorded a variety of procedural protections, both during the development of their child's individualized education program (IEP). It is clear that parents may object to procedural violations at the administrative due process hearing, and that a hearing officer may provide relief to parents for certain procedural infractions. Because the rights to reimbursement and to the various procedural protections are accorded to parents themselves, they are "parties aggrieved" when those rights are infringed, and may accordingly proceed *pro se* when seeking to vindicate them.

The Court goes further, however, concluding that parents may proceed *pro se* not only when they seek reimbursement or assert procedural violations, but also when they challenge the substantive adequacy of their child's FAPE—so that parents may act without a lawyer *in every IDEA case*. In my view, this sweeps far more broadly than the text allows. Out of this sprawling statute the Court cannot identify even *a single* provision stating that parents have the substantive right to a FAPE. The reason for this is readily understandable: The right to a free appropriate public education obviously inheres in the child, for it is he who receives the education. As the IDEA

instructs, participating States must provide a "free appropriate public education . . . to all children with disabilities. . . . " The statute is replete with references to the fact that a FAPE belongs to the child. . . . The parents of a disabled child no doubt have an *interest* in seeing their child receive a proper education. But there is a difference between an *interest* and a statutory *right*. The text of the IDEA makes clear that parents have no *right* to the education itself.

The Court concedes, as it must, that while the IDEA gives parents the right to reimbursement and procedural protection in explicit terms, it does not do so for the supposed right to the education itself. The obvious inference to be drawn from the statute's clear and explicit conferral of discrete types of rights upon parents and children, respectively, is that it does not by accident confer the parent-designated rights upon children, or the children-designated rights upon parents. The Court believes, however, that "the statute prevents us from placing too much weight on [this] implicatio[n]." That conclusion is in error. Nothing in "the statute," undermines the obvious "implication" of Congress's scheme. What the Court relies upon for its conclusion that parents have a substantive right to a FAPE is not the "statutory structure," but rather the myriad *procedural* guarantees accorded to parents in the administrative process. But allowing parents, by means of these guarantees, to help shape the contours of their child's education is simply not the same as giving *them* the right to that education. Nor can the Court sensibly rely on the provisions governing due process hearings and administrative appeals, the various provisions that refer to the "parent's complaint," or the fact that the right-to-sue provision, refers to the administrative complaint, which in turn allows parents to challenge "any matter" relating to the provision of a FAPE. These provisions prove nothing except what all parties concede: that parents *may* represent their child *pro se* at the administrative level . . . . Parents thus have the power, at the administrative stage, to litigate *all* of the various rights under the statute since at that stage they are acting not only on their *own* behalf, but on behalf of *their child* as well. This tells us nothing whatever about *whose* rights they are. The Court's spraying statutory sections about like buckshot cannot create a substantive parental right to education where none exists.

Harkening back to its earlier discussion of the IDEA's "text and structure" (by which it means the statute's procedural protections), the Court announces the startling proposition that, in fact, the "IDEA does not differentiate . . . between the rights accorded to children and the rights accorded to parents." If that were so, the Court could have spared us its painful effort to craft a distinctive parental right out of scattered procedural provisions. But of course it is not so. The IDEA quite clearly differentiates between the rights accorded to parents and their children. As even petitioners' *amici* agree, "Congress specifically indicated that parents have rights under the Act that are separate from and independent of their children's rights." Does the Court seriously contend that a child has a right to reimbursement, when the statute most definitively provides that if "*the parents* of a child with a disability" enroll that child in private school, "a court . . . may require the [school district] to reimburse *the parents* for the cost of that enrollment"? Does the Court believe that a child has a procedural right under [IDEA], which gives *parents* the power to excuse an IEP team member from attending an IEP meeting? The IDEA does not remotely envision communal "family" rights.

The Court believes that because parents must prove the substantive inadequacy of a FAPE before obtaining reimbursement, and because the suitability of a FAPE may also be at issue when procedural violations are alleged, it is "out of accord with the statute's design" to "prevent [parents] from obtaining a judgment mandating that the school district provide their child" with a FAPE. . That is a total non sequitur. That Congress has required parents to demonstrate the inadequacy of their child's FAPE in order to vindicate their own rights says nothing about whether parents possess an underlying right to education. The Court insists that the right to a FAPE is the right "most fundamental to the Act." Undoubtedly so, but that sheds no light upon whom the right belongs to, and hence upon who can sue in their own right. Congress has used the phrase "party aggrieved," and it is this Court's job to apply that language, not to run from it.

The Court further believes that a distinction between parental and child rights will prove difficult to administer. I fail to see why that is so. Before today, the majority of Federal Courts of Appeals to have considered the issue have allowed parents to sue *pro se* with respect to some claims, but not with respect to the denial of a FAPE. . . . The Court points to no evidence suggesting that this majority rule has caused any confusion in practice. Nor do I see how it could, since the statute makes clear and easily administrable distinctions between parents' and children's legal entitlements.

Finally, the Court charges that the approach taken by the majority of Courts of Appeals would perpetuate an "injustice," since parents who do not seek reimbursement or allege procedural violations would be "without a remedy." That, of course, is not true. They will have the same remedy as all parents who sue to vindicate their children's rights: the power to bring suit, represented by counsel. But even indulging the Court's perception that it is unfair to allow some but not all IDEA parents to proceed *pro se*, that complaint is properly addressed to Congress, which structured the rights as it has, and limited suit to "party aggrieved." And there are good reasons for it to have done so. *Pro se* cases impose unique burdens on lower courts-and on defendants, in this case the schools and school districts that must hire their own lawyers. Since *pro se* complaints are prosecuted essentially for free, without screening by knowledgeable attorneys, they are much more likely to be unmeritorious. And for courts to figure them out without the assistance of plaintiff's counsel is much more difficult and time-consuming. In both categories of *pro se* parental suit permitted under a proper interpretation of the statute, one or the other of these burdens is reduced. Actions seeking reimbursement are less likely to be frivolous, since not many parents will be willing to lay out the money for private education without some solid reason to believe the FAPE was inadequate. And actions alleging procedural violations can ordinarily be disposed of without the intensive record-review that characterizes suits challenging the suitability of a FAPE.

* * *

Petitioners sought reimbursement, alleged procedural violations, and requested a declaration that their child's FAPE was substantively inadequate. I agree with the Court that they may proceed *pro se* with respect to the first two claims, but I disagree that they may do so with respect to the third.

Questions for Discussion

1. In his dissent, Justice Scalia expressed his concern that allowing parents who are not attorneys to initiate litigation can be costly to school systems. What additional costs could a school district incur by the ruling?

2. The Court failed to address what should take place if the interests of parents differ from those of their children. For example, if students in secondary schools disagree with their parents as to the content of their IEPs, it is possible that students and their parents, as well as their school boards, might all resort to litigation, creating the anomalous situation of having three different lawyers present. What if a noncustodial parent disagrees with the custodial parents and the student, then a fourth lawyer could be added to the mix?

3. Two related arguments against allowing parents to proceed on behalf of their children in IDEA cases is that their children, the real beneficiaries of the IDEA, should be represented by competent counsel and that their entitlements should not be compromised by the failure of their parents to obtain competent counsel. Conversely, others might argue that a child's entitlement would be compromised even further if parents were unable to file suit due to their inability to obtain counsel. Which side do you think has the better argument?

⚖️

SPECIAL EDUCATION LAW IN PRACTICE

Legal Case No. 15—Importance of Parental Participation in the IEP Process in the Change
of Current Educational Placement

DOUG C. V. HAWAII DEPARTMENT OF EDUCATION
9TH Circuit, 2013
720 F.3d 1038 (2013)

PAEZ, Circuit Judge:

Plaintiff Doug C., individually and on behalf of his son, Spencer C., appeals the district court's judgment finding that the defendant, the Hawaii Department of Education, did not deny Spencer a free appropriate public education ("FAPE"), and thus did not violate the Individuals with Disabilities Education Act ("IDEA"), by holding an annual individualized education program ("IEP") meeting without the participation of a parent. Parental participation in the IEP and educational placement process is central to the IDEA's goal of protecting disabled students' rights and providing each disabled student with a FAPE. We conclude that the Department violated the IDEA's explicit parental participation requirements. The Department held Spencer's annual IEP meeting without parental participation even though Doug C. did not "affirmatively refuse[ ] to attend," but rather actively sought to reschedule the meeting in order to participate. By denying Doug C. the opportunity to participate in the IEP process, the Department denied Spencer a FAPE. We have jurisdiction under, and we reverse.

The IEP meeting in question changed Spencer's placement from Horizons Academy, a private special education facility, to the Workplace Readiness Program at Maui High School. Pending the outcome of these administrative and judicial review proceedings, Doug C. continued Spencer's placement at Horizons Academy at his own expense. We remand to the district court for further proceedings regarding Doug C.'s entitlement to reimbursement of Spencer's private school tuition. Because we conclude that the Department denied Spencer a FAPE, Doug C. is entitled to reimbursement if he can establish that "the private school placement was proper under the Act."

I

Spencer is an 18-year-old student in the Maui District of the Hawaii Department of Education. He was diagnosed with autism age two. As a result of his condition, the Department determined that Spencer is eligible to receive special education and other related services, and his educational rights are protected by the IDEA. Beginning in fifth grade, Spencer's IEP placed him at a private special education facility, Horizons Academy, at the expense of the Department of Education. The Department held Spencer's annual IEP meeting on November 9, 2010 despite Doug C.'s inability to attend the meeting that day. At that meeting, the Department changed Spencer's educational placement, moving him to a program at Maui High School, his local public school.

The central issue in this case is whether the Department's efforts to include Doug C. in the November IEP meeting are sufficient to meet the requirements of the IDEA. A close review of the events leading up to the IEP meeting is therefore critical. The IEP team and Doug C. first discussed the annual IEP meeting date during a student support meeting in September 2010. Kaleo Waiau, a special education coordinator at Maui High School, testified that Doug C. and members of the education team all agreed that the IEP meeting would be held on October 28. Doug C. testified that he thought that they had only agreed, tentatively, to meet sometime in late October. In any event, Waiau called Doug C. on October 22 to confirm the October 28 meeting. Doug C. stated that he was unavailable that day, and they settled instead on either November 4 or 5 (the testimony on which is inconsistent). Doug C. testified that the November date was also tentative, subject to checking his calendar and confirming. The following day, Doug C. called Waiau to let him know that he was not available on that day, and they settled firmly on November 9 instead.

On the morning of November 9, Doug C. e-mailed Waiau at 7:27 a.m. He explained that he was sick and therefore unable to attend the IEP meeting. He suggested rescheduling the meeting for the following week, on either November 16 or 17. The annual review deadline for Spencer's IEP was Saturday, November 13. According to Waiau, some of the members of the IEP team were not available on Friday, November 12. Therefore, Waiau offered to reschedule for either Wednesday, November 10, or Thursday, November 11, accommodating the other members' schedules while still holding the meeting before the deadline. Doug C. responded that he could possibly participate on either of those days, but could not definitively commit to either day since he was ill and could not guarantee that he would recover in time. Waiau also suggested that Doug C. participate by phone or the Internet. But Doug C. explained that (1) he wanted to be physically present at his son's IEP meeting and (2) he did not feel physically well enough to participate meaningfully through any means that day.

Waiau decided to go forward with the meeting on November 9 as scheduled. He testified that he had already asked "13 people on three separate occasions to change their schedules and cancel other commitments" to schedule the meeting. Therefore, without a firm commitment from Doug C. for one of the two dates he proposed, Waiau refused to reschedule the meeting. Waiau and the IEP team held the meeting without the participation of Doug C. The only Horizons Academy staff member on Spencer's IEP team also did not attend.

With these key participants absent, the IEP team changed Spencer's placement from Horizons Academy to the Workplace Readiness Program at Maui High School. After the meeting, Waiau sent Doug C. the new, completed IEP for his review. The team held a follow-up IEP meeting on December 7 with Doug C. and a staff member from Horizons. At the follow-up meeting, the team reviewed the already completed IEP "line by line." Waiau testified that Doug C. provided no substantive input, while Doug C. explained that he rejected the IEP in its entirety because he was excluded from the development process. No changes were made to the IEP during the December 7 meeting.

The day before the follow-up IEP meeting, Doug C. filed a request for a due process hearing as provided for by the IDEA. He argued, *inter alia*, that the lack of parental participation in the IEP meeting denied Spencer a FAPE. After a hearing, the administrative hearing officer issued a decision finding that the Department did not deny Spencer a FAPE and dismissed his claims for relief. The district court affirmed, holding that plaintiffs "failed to show that Defendant did not fulfill its statutory duty to ensure that Doug was afforded an opportunity to participate at the November 9, 2010 IEP meeting." Doug C. timely appealed.

III

A

Parental participation in the IEP and educational placement process is critical to the organization of the IDEA. Indeed, the Supreme Court has stressed that the IDEA's structure relies upon parental participation to ensure the substantive success of the IDEA in providing quality education to disabled students:

[W]e think that the importance Congress attached to these procedural safeguards cannot be gainsaid. It seems to us no exaggeration to say that Congress placed every bit as much emphasis upon compliance with procedures giving parents and guardians a large measure of participation at every stage of the administrative process as it did upon the measurement of the resulting IEP against a substantive standard. We think that the congressional emphasis upon full participation of concerned parties throughout the development of the IEP . . . demonstrates the legislative conviction that adequate compliance with the procedures prescribed would in most cases assure much if not all of what Congress wished in the way of substantive content in an IEP.

Echoing the Supreme Court, we have held that parental participation safeguards are "[a]mong the most important procedural safeguards" in the IDEA and that "[p]rocedural violations that interfere with parental participation in the IEP formulation process undermine the very essence of the IDEA." We have explained that parental participation is key to the operation of the IDEA for two reasons: "Parents not only represent the best interests of their child in the IEP development process, they also provide information about the child critical to developing a comprehensive IEP and which only they are in a position to know."

In accordance with the foregoing, the regulatory framework of the IDEA places an affirmative duty on agencies to include parents in the IEP process. The public agency "responsible for providing education to children with disabilities," is required to "take steps to ensure that one or both of the parents of a child with a disability are present at each IEP meeting or are afforded an opportunity to participate" including providing ample notice and "scheduling the meeting at a mutually agreed on time and place." Moreover, if a parent cannot attend, the agency must offer other methods of participation such as video or teleconferencing. Most importantly, a meeting may *only* be conducted without a parent if "the public agency is *unable* to convince the parents that they should attend." And in that circumstance, the agency must keep a detailed record of its attempts to include the parent.

B

Doug C. did not "affirmatively refuse[ ] to attend the meeting," nor could it be said that the Department was "unable to convince" him to attend. To the contrary, Doug C. vigorously objected to the Department holding an IEP meeting without him and asked the Department to reschedule the meeting for the following week. In response to the Department's offer to reschedule for either of the following two days, he agreed to try to attend but, understandably, could not firmly commit to a meeting date only one or two days later while he was sick. Despite the foregoing, the Department went forward with the IEP meeting without him, over his repeated objections, and, at that meeting, decided to change Spencer's educational placement for the first time in six years.

The fact that it may have been frustrating to schedule meetings with or difficult to work with Doug C. (as the Department repeatedly suggests) does not excuse the Department's failure to include him in Spencer's IEP meeting when he expressed a willingness to participate. We have consistently held that an agency cannot eschew its affirmative duties under the IDEA by blaming the parents. An agency cannot blame a parent for its failure to ensure meaningful procedural compliance with the IDEA because the IDEA's protections are designed to benefit the student, not the parent. Because the Department's obligation is owed to the child, any alleged obstinance of Doug C. does not excuse the Department's failure to fulfill its affirmative obligation to include Doug C. in the IEP meeting when he expressed a willingness (indeed eagerness) to participate, albeit at a later date.

The Department's central argument is that it could not accommodate Doug C.'s request to reschedule because of the impending annual IEP deadline on November 13. Even assuming that the annual deadline should somehow trump parental participation, the Department's argument fails on the facts of this case. Waiau, the coordinator of the IEP meeting, testified that he refused to reschedule the meeting for the Wednesday or Thursday *before* the deadline because Doug C. could not firmly commit to either of those dates because of his illness, even though Doug C. testified that he said that he

likely could attend. Waiau explained that he did not wish to disrupt the other IEP's members' schedules without a firm commitment.

This argument may seem reasonable but quickly unravels because, under the IDEA, the attendance of Doug C., Spencer's parent, must take priority over other members' attendance for the reasons discussed above. Indeed, a parent can consent to the absence of other team members at the meeting. By refusing to reschedule the meeting for Wednesday or Thursday, Waiau improperly prioritized the schedules of the other members of the team over the attendance of Doug C. Moreover, Waiau also testified that he did not offer Doug C. the option of meeting on the Friday *before* the annual review deadline because other members of the IEP team were not available to meet that day. Once again, the Department improperly prioritized its own representatives' schedules and attendance over the attendance of the parent.

Even if the Department's theory of the case was supported by the facts, the Department's argument that it absolutely could not reschedule the IEP meeting for a date even a few days after the annual deadline in order to include Doug C. is untenable. Waiau's testimony suggests, and the Department's counsel represented at oral argument, that if the annual deadline passed without a new IEP, services would "lapse." The district court took a similar position. We reject this argument because it is premised on the erroneous assumption that the Department is authorized (let alone *required*) to cease providing services to a student if his annual IEP review is overdue. The IDEA mandates annual review of a student's IEP. However, the Department cites no authority, nor could it, for the proposition that it cannot provide any services to a student whose annual review is overdue.

The more difficult question is what a public agency must do when confronted with the difficult situation of being unable to meet two distinct procedural requirements of the IDEA, in this case parental participation and timely annual review of the IEP. In considering this question, we must keep in mind the purposes of the IDEA: to provide disabled students a free appropriate public education and to protect the educational rights of those students. It is also useful to consider our standard for determining when a procedural error is actionable under the IDEA. We have repeatedly held that "procedural inadequacies that result in the loss of educational opportunity or seriously infringe the parents' opportunity to participate in the IEP formulation process, clearly result in the denial of a FAPE."

When confronted with the situation of complying with one procedural requirement of the IDEA or another, we hold that the agency must make a reasonable determination of which course of action promotes the purposes of the IDEA and is least likely to result in the denial of a FAPE. In reviewing an agency's action in such a scenario, we will allow the agency reasonable latitude in making that determination.

In this case, the Department was allegedly confronted with two options: including Doug C. in the meeting and missing the IEP annual deadline by several days or proceeding with the IEP meeting without Doug C. but meeting the annual deadline. As discussed, the Supreme Court and this court have both repeatedly stressed the vital importance of parental participation in the IEP creation process.

C

We recognize that not every procedural violation results in the denial of a FAPE, but procedural errors "that result in the loss of educational opportunity, or seriously infringe the parents' opportunity to participate in the IEP formulation process." The failure to include Doug C. In the IEP meeting clearly infringed on his ability to participate in the IEP formulation process. That reason alone is cause to conclude that Spencer was denied a FAPE.

The procedural violation here also denied Spencer a FAPE for the separate reason that it resulted in the denial of an educational opportunity. A procedural error results in the denial of an educational opportunity where, absent the error, there is a "strong likelihood" that alternative educational possibilities for the student "would have been better considered." Thus, an IEP team's failure to properly consider an alternative educational plan can result in a lost educational opportunity even if the student cannot definitively demonstrate that his placement would have been different but for the procedural error. *See id.* Here, there is a strong likelihood that the benefits of placement at Horizons Academy, Doug C's preferred placement for his son, would have been more thoroughly considered if Doug C. had been present at the meeting. It is particularly likely that the merits of continuing Spencer's placement at Horizons Academy were not adequately considered in light of the fact that the IEP team member from the Academy was also absent.

Therefore, both because (1) Doug C's opportunity to participate was seriously infringed and (2) the procedural violation denied Spencer an educational opportunity by causing the merits of his placement at Horizon Academy to receive insufficient consideration, the Department denied Spencer a FAPE.

We note that a parent's decision to place his child in a private school is "proper" so long as the school the parent selects "provides educational instruction specially designed to meet the unique needs of a handicapped child, supported by such services as are necessary to permit the child to benefit from instruction." This standard is met even if the private school provides "some, but not all" of the students educational needs; the placement need not "maximize the[ ] child's potential." Where, as here, the private school selected by the parent is the same school that the child has previously attended for several years under IEPs that have been approved by all parties, we think it highly unlikely that the placement does not represent a "proper" placement. Nonetheless, we remand to permit the district court to consider the question. The district court may remand this issue to the state hearing officer to decide in the first instance.

REVERSED and REMANDED.

Questions for Discussion

1. The *Doug C.* decision makes clear that parental participation is a crucial component of a student's IEP process and that school-based IEP teams should prioritize involving parents in positive, collaborative efforts to develop a student's special education programs and placements. At what point does a parent's continued refusals allow the school-based IEP team to proceed with a meeting without the parent(s) present? For example, do you think school officials need to document all instances of the parent refusing to attend their child's IEP meeting?

2. In one instance, the district special education coordinator requested that the parent attend his son's IEP meeting via video conferencing instead of being physically present at the meeting. What do you think are some of the advantages of parents attending their child's IEP meeting through technology-based options, such as video conference? Are there any disadvantages of this option? Explain.

3. In some instances, the parent(s) may attend their child's IEP meeting but is not an active participant in the IEP process. What can school officials do to encourage greater and more collaborative discussions with parents at their child's IEP meeting?

Summary of Important Legal Policies, Principles, and Practices

1. When enacting the IDEA, Congress intended making parents equal partners in the development of a free appropriate public education (FAPE) for students with disabilities.
2. The IDEA 2004 provides both students with disabilities and their parents specific procedural rights, including parental notification.
3. Another method of providing parents heightened participation in the special education process under the IDEA is though access to student records. The IDEA 2004 prohibits school officials disclosing any personally identifiable information regarding students with disabilities while requiring school districts to protect the confidentiality of this information.
4. The Family Educational Rights and Privacy Act, also known as FERPA clarifies the legal rights of students with disabilities and their parents with regard to educational records. Both the IDEA 2004 and FERPA deny ineligible students access to their educational records and limit this access to outsiders.
5. The IDEA 2004 encourages parental participation in the Individualized Education Plan (IEP) process. The federal law strongly encourages students, parents, and school officials to work collaboratively developing special education and related services appearing on the IEP document.

Useful Online Resources

Center for Parent Information and Resources (CPIR)
Questions and Answers About IDEA: Parent Participation
The Center for Parent Information and Resources (CPIR) was created to assist designated parent with centers across the country serving students with disabilities. CPIR creates useful information for the parents of students with disabilities: www.parentcenterhub.org/qa2/

Recommended Reading

Burke, M. M. (2013). Improving parental involvement: Training special education advocates. *Journal of Disability Policy Studies, 23*, 225–234.

Goldman, S. E., & Burke, M. M. (2017). The effectiveness of interventions to increase parent involvement in special education: A systematic literature review and meta-analysis. *Exceptionality, 25*, 97–115.

Herseim, J. V. (2016). *Fostering meaningful parent-school partnerships at every IEP team meeting*. Palm Beach Gardens, FL: LRP Publications.

Machado, I. (2014). *IDEA and joint custody: Your school district's obligations to each parent*. Palm Beach Gardens, FL: LRP Publications.

Turnbull, H. R., Shogren, K. A., & Turnbull, A. P. (2011). Evolution of the parent movement: Past, present, and future. In J. M. Kauffman & D. P. Hallahan (Eds.), *Handbook of special education* (pp. 639–653). New York, NY: Routledge.

Vanegas, S. B., & Abdelrahim, R. (2016). Characterizing the systems of support for families of children with disabilities: A review of the literature. *Journal of Family Social Work, 19*(4), 286–327.

Yell, M. L., Katsiyannis, A., & Losinski, M. (2015). *Doug C. v. State of Hawaii Department of Education*: Parental participation in IEP development. *Intervention in School and Clinic, 51*(2), 118–121.

References

Arlington Central School District v. D.K. and K.K., 2002 WL 31521158 (S.D.N.Y. 2002).

Big Beaver Falls Area School District v. Jackson, 615 A.2d 910 (Pa. Commw. Ct. 1992).

Chapman, R. (2015). *The everyday guide to special education law: A handbook for parents, teachers, and other professionals*. Denver, CO: Mighty Press.

Cone ex rel. Cone v. Randolph County Schools, 302 F. Supp.2d 500 (M.D.N.C. 2004).

Deal ex rel. Deal v. Hamilton County Department of Education, 392 F.3d 840 (6th Cir. 2004).

Dong v. Board of Education of the Rochester Community Schools, 197 F.3d 703 (6th Cir. 1999).

Doug C. v. State of Hawaii Board of Education, 720 F.3d 1038 (9th Cir. 2013).

E.H. and H.H. v. Tirozzi, 735 F. Supp. 53 (D. Conn. 1990).

Family Educational Rights and Privacy Act (FERPA), 20 U.S.C. § 1232g (1974).

Gonzaga University v. Doe, 536 U.S. 273 (2002).

Individuals with Disabilities Education Act, 20 U.S.C. §§ 1400–1482 (2005).

Knable v. Bexley City School District, 238 F.3d 755 (6th Cir. 2001).

McNeal, L. (2010). Access granted: The Winkelman case ushers in a new era in parental advocacy. *Brigham Young University Education Law Review*, *1*(5), 129–147.

M.L. v. Federal Way School District, 394 F.3d 634 (9th Cir. 2005).

Owasso Independent School District v. Falvo, 534 U.S. 426 (2002).

Paul Y. by Kathy Y. v. Singletary, 979 F. Supp. 1422 (S.D. Fla. 1997).

Pitchford ex rel. M. v. Salem-Keizer School District No. 24J, 155 F. Supp.2d 1213 (D. Or. 2001).

Rothschild v. Grottenthaler, 907 F.2d 286 (2d Cir. 1990).

Sean R. v. Board of Education of the Town of Woodbridge, 794 F. Supp. 467 (D. Conn. 1992).

Smith v. Henson, 786 F. Supp. 43 (D.D.C. 1992).

Russo, C. J., & Mawdsley, R. D. (2002). *Owasso Independent School District v. Falvo*: The Supreme Court upholds peer-grading. *School Business Affairs*, *68*(5), 34–36.

Webster Groves School District v. Pulitzer Publishing Co., 898 F.2d 1371 (8th Cir. 1990).

Winkelman v. Parma City School District, 150 Fed. Appx. 406 (6th Cir. 2005), *cert. granted*, 127 S. Ct. 467 (2006), 127 S. Ct. 1994 (2007).

W.G. and B.G. v. Board of Trustees of Target Range School District No. 23, 960 F.2d 1479 (9th Cir. 1992).

III
Federal Antidiscrimination Statues
Impacting Students With Disabilities

13
Eligibility and Legal Protections Under Section 504 and the ADA

Key Concepts and Terms in This Chapter

- Definition and Eligibility Requirements Under Section 504
- Otherwise Qualified
- Definition and Eligibility Requirements Under the Americans with Disabilities Act (ADA)
- Reasonable Student Accommodations Under Section 504

Overview of Section 504

Prior to the enactment of the Education for All Handicapped Children Act (EHCA), Congress passed Section 504 of the Rehabilitation Act of 1973 (Section 504), which was the first major federal legislation in the U.S. specifically designed to protect individuals (both children and adults) with disabilities from discrimination. More specifically, Congress passed Section 504 with the explicit intent of legally protecting persons with disabilities from their employers and service providers who receive financial support from the federal government (29 U.S.C. § 794). In practice, various federal, state, and local agencies and programs receiving federal funding cannot discriminate against any "qualified person" with disabilities in any of the agency's activities, including employment practices. However, employers, agencies, and private groups or organizations that do not receive federal funding are not legally covered under Section 504 (Chapman, 2015). Thus, there is a gap in Section 504 coverage for those employers, agencies, or private groups that do not receive federal funding. Individuals working with those employers, agencies, or private groups are not legally protected from discrimination under Section 504. In order to address this gap in coverage, Congress enacted the Americans with Disabilities Act (ADA) in 1990, which also legally protects "qualified persons" with disabilities from discrimination but extends beyond the legal reach of employers, programs, agencies, and facilities that receive federal funding (42 U.S.C. §12101–12213). Unlike Section 504, the ADA does not legally require that a specific employer, agency, or other entity receive federal funding in order to be covered under the ADA.

As noted earlier, in addition to the Individuals with Disabilities Education Act (IDEA), the legal rights of students with disabilities are protected under two other significant pieces of federal antidiscrimination statutes. The first federal antidiscrimination statute, Section 504 of the Rehabilitation Act of 1973 (Section 504) traces its origins back to 1918, a time when the U.S. government sought to provide rehabilitation services for military veterans returning from World War I. According to Section 504, which is actually codified as part of federal labor law, rather than education law states,

> [n]o otherwise qualified individual with a disability . . . shall, solely by reason of her or his disability, be excluded from participation in, be denied the benefits of, or be subjected to discrimination under any program or activity receiving Federal financial assistance.

> (29 U.S.C. § 794)

Section 504 effectively prohibits recipients of federal financial assistance, public and nonpublic, from discriminating against individuals with disabilities in the provision of services or employment.

The second statute, the Americans with Disabilities Act (ADA), was enacted in 1990 "to provide a comprehensive national mandate for the elimination of discrimination against individuals with disabilities" (42 U.S.C. § 12101(b)(2)). Basically, Section 504's definition of disability cross-references the definition of disability found under the ADA (Colker, 2018). Congress expanded the scope of Section 504's coverage by passing the ADA to provide protection to individuals with disabilities throughout society (*Vande Zande v. State of Wisconsin Department of Administration*, 1994). While the ADA effectively extends the legal protections of Section 504 to the private sector, to date, it has not had a major effect on the delivery of a free appropriate public education (FAPE) under the IDEA. Instead, the ADA's greatest impact has been on the employment of individuals with disabilities. Moreover, while the ADA, like Section 504, prohibits discrimination against individuals on the basis of their disabilities, it does not require the delivery of a FAPE (Wenkart, 1993). The IDEA still remains the major statute that guarantees a student's right to receive a free appropriate public education. In light of the broad range of protections that Section 504 and the ADA provide, this chapter examines the key provisions of these statutes. In 2008, Congress amended the ADA to expand the definition of disability to include individuals who suffer from epilepsy, diabetes, cancer, multiple sclerosis, and other ailments (ADA Amendments of 2008). The 2008 ADA Amendments also expanded the definition of major life activities by adding eating, sleeping, walking, standing, lifting, bending, speaking, breathing, learning, reading, concentrating, thinking, communicating, and the operation of major bodily functions to its list of covered activities (42 U.S.C. §§ 12102(2)(A)-(B)). Both state and local governmental entities, including private and private schools are legally required to correct any existing policy(ies) or practice(s) that is inconsistent with the ADAs requirement of non-discrimination on the basis of an individual's disability. In school environments, for example, the ADA requires all newly constructed and altered buildings with public accommodation to be designed and constructed in such a way that they are both readily accessible to and usable by persons with disabilities.

It is important to keep in mind that while Section 504 covers not only children but also employees, parents, and others who visit schools, like the ADA, it does so without any age restrictions. Even so, this book focuses on the rights of students. Section 504 defines an individual with a disability as one "who (i) has a physical or mental impairment which substantially limits one or more of such person's major life activities, (ii) has a record of such an impairment, or (iii) is regarded as having such an impairment (29 U.S.C.A. § 706(7)(B))." The regulations define physical or mental impairments as including the following:

(A) any physiological disorder or condition, cosmetic disfigurement, or anatomical loss affecting one or more of the following body systems: neurological; musculoskeletal; special sense organs; respiratory, including speech organs; cardiovascular; reproductive, digestive, genito-urinary; hemic and lymphatic; skin; and endocrine; or
(B) any mental or psychological disorder, such as mental retardation, organic brain syndrome, emotional or mental illness, and specific learning disorders.

(45 C.F.R. § 84.3(j)(2)(i), 34 C.F.R. § 104.3(j)(2)(i))

In order to have records of impairment, individuals must have histories of, or been identified as having, mental or physical impairments that substantially limit one or more major life activities. As defined in one of Section 504's regulations, individuals who are regarded as having impairments are those who have

(A) a physical or mental impairment that does not substantially limit major life activities but that is treated by a recipient as constituting such a limitation; (B) a physical or mental impairment that substantially limits major life activities only as a result of the attitudes of others toward such impairment; or (C) none of the impairments . . . but is treated by a recipient as having such an impairment.

(45 C.F.R. § 84.3(j)(2)(iv), 34 C.F.R. § 104.3(j)(2)(iv))

"'Major life activities' means functions such as caring for one's self, performing manual tasks, walking, seeing, hearing, speaking, breathing, learning, and working" (45 C.F.R. § 84.3(j)(2)(i)). Once students are identified as having disabilities, the next step is to evaluate whether they are "otherwise qualified." In order to be "otherwise qualified," students must be "(i) of an age during which nonhandicapped persons are provided such services, (ii) of any age during which it is mandatory under state law to provide such services to handicapped persons, or (iii) [a student] to whom a state is required to provide a free appropriate public education [under the IDEA] (45 C.F.R. § 84.3(k)(2)." Students who are "otherwise qualified," meaning that they are eligible to participate in programs or activities despite the existence of impairments, must be permitted to participate in programs or activities as long as it is possible to do so by means of a "reasonable accommodation" (34 C.F.R. § 104.39).

Once identified, qualified students are entitled to an appropriate public education, regardless of the nature or severity of their impairments. In order to guarantee eligible children an appropriate education, Section 504's regulations include due process requirements for evaluation and placement similar to those under the IDEA (34 C.F.R. § 104.36). In making modifications for students, as discussed in greater detail later in this chapter, educators must provide aid, benefits, and/or services that are comparable to those available to children who do not have impairments.

Students with severe disabilities may sometimes require special education classes or other services that are not offered in the general education environment. Whenever students must be removed from regular classes to receive programming, the services have to be provided in facilities that are comparable to those provided for the education of peers who do not have impairments. For example, a federal trial court in Pennsylvania found that the commonwealth's Secretary of Education violated Section 504 by failing to ensure that the educational facilities for students with disabilities were comparable to those of peers who did not have disabilities (*Hendricks v. Gilhool*, 1989). The court emphasized that the facilities did not have to be precisely equivalent, but observed that in this instance they were substantially unequal. The court ruled that officials violated Section 504 when they relocated special education classes to lesser facilities to accommodate classes for students without disabilities.

In addition to Section 504, the ADA provides a comprehensive federal mandate to eliminate discrimination against people with disabilities and to provide "clear, strong, consistent and enforceable standards" (42 U.S.C.A. § 12101(b)(2)) to this end. The ADA's broad definition of a disability is comparable with the one in Section 504: "(a) a physical or mental impairment that substantially limits one or more of the major life activities; (b) a record of such an impairment; or (c) being regarded as having such an impairment" (§ 12102(2)). Further, as under Section 504, "major life activities" includes "caring for one's self, performing manual tasks, walking, seeing, hearing, speaking, breathing, learning, and working" (34 C.F.R. § 36.104). The ADA, like Section 504, does not require individuals to have certificates from doctors or psychologists in order to be covered by it, but can ask for proof (Kaesberg & Murray, 1994).

According to the Supreme Court, persons are otherwise qualified for purposes of Section 504 if they are capable of meeting all of a program's requirements in spite of their disabilities (*School Board of Nassau County, Florida v. Arline*, 1987; *Southeastern Community College v. Davis*, 1979). If persons are otherwise qualified, recipients of federal funds are expected to make reasonable accommodations to allow them to participate in programs or activities unless doing so would create undue hardships on the programs (34 C.F.R. § 104.12(a)). As with Section 504, under the ADA otherwise qualified individuals with disabilities must be provided with reasonable accommodations so that they may participate in programs provided by public entities (42 U.S.C. § 12111(9)). Public entities include state and local governments, agencies, and other instrumentalities of a government (42 U.S.C. § 12131(1)). Insofar as schools are public entities under the ADA, they are prohibited from discriminating against individuals with disabilities in much the same way as under Section 504 (42 U.S.C. § 12132). While the ADA includes extensive requirements to provide access to public transportation for the disabled, public school transportation is specifically exempted from these provisions (42 U.S.C. § 12141).

Section 504 offers a degree of protection against discrimination to students who have disabilities but are not eligible to receive services under the IDEA. Under the IDEA students must fall into one of the categories of disabilities outlined within the statute and must require special education services as a result of that disability, to receive services (20 U.S.C. § 1401(a)(1)(A)). However, the protections of Section 504 reach a much wider population. Figure 13.1 illustrates that Section 504's definition of disability is broader compared to the IDEA's definition. Section 504 eligibility extends to wider audience of individuals with disabilities.

One of the best examples of the broader reach of Section 504 involves students with infectious diseases. Under the IDEA, students with infectious diseases are entitled to special education services only if their academic performance is adversely affected by their illnesses (34 C.F.R. § 300.8). Yet, pursuant to Section 504, students with infectious diseases such as HIV/AIDS cannot be discriminated against or excluded from schools unless there is a high risk of transmission of their diseases (*Doe v. Belleville Public School District*, 1987; *Doe v. Dolton Elementary School District*, 1988; *Martinez v. School Board of Hillsborough County*, 1988, 1989; *New York State Association for Retarded Children v. Carey*, 1979; *Ray v. School District of DeSoto County*, 1987; *Thomas v. Atascadero Unified School District*, 1987). A case from a federal trial court in

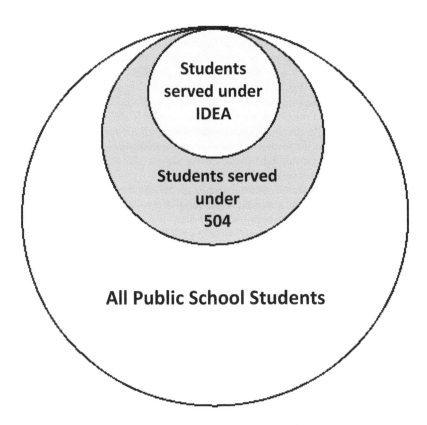

Figure 13.1 Section 504 Compared to IDEA Student Coverage

Illinois is illustrative (*Doe v. Dolton Elementary School District*, 1988). Where officials excluded a student from attending regular classes and all extracurricular activities after he was diagnosed as having AIDS, the court decided that he was entitled to the protection of Section 504 because he was regarded as having a physical impairment that substantially interfered with his life activities. The court added that because there was no significant risk that the student would have transmitted AIDS in the classroom setting, the school officials who sought to exclude him violated his rights under Section 504.

The majority of public school students with disabilities are covered by the IDEA, Section 504, and the ADA. For this reason, plaintiffs frequently file suits alleging violations of all three statutes. Generally, courts agree that compliance with the IDEA regarding the provision of a FAPE establishes compliance with Section 504 and the ADA (*Barnett v. Fairfax County School Board*, 1989, 1991; *Cordrey v. Euckert*, 1990; *Doe v. Alabama State Department of Education*, 1990). Still, the IDEA's requirements for a FAPE are more stringent than those under Section 504 (*Colin K. v. Schmidt*, 1983; *Darlene L. v. Illinois Board of Education*, 1983).

When considering differences between the IDEA and Section 504, the federal trial court in Massachusetts went so far as to explain that school officials did not violate the latter when they offered special education services to a student with learning disabilities in a manner that was not procedurally correct (*Puffer v. Raynolds*, 1988). The court reasoned that since the officials offered the services, he was neither discriminated against nor denied the services. Further, the court pointed out that the procedural errors had to be addressed via the IDEA's due process mechanism. Similarly, the Fourth Circuit was of the opinion that a school board did not violate Section 504 by refusing to provide special education services in a student's neighborhood school when the needed services were available in a centralized location (*Barnett v. Fairfax County School Board*, 1991). The court maintained that officials had not discriminated against the student because he was not denied services.

When school systems provide services to students under Section 504 or the ADA, they must be appropriate. In one such case, a federal trial court in New Hampshire posited that a student, who alleged that he had not been provided with educational services that adequately addressed his learning disability, presented a claim under Section 504 (*I.D. v. Westmoreland School District*, 1992).

Some students who do not qualify for special education services under the IDEA may be eligible for accommodation plans under Section 504 that are discussed later in this chapter. Even so, the different statutes have distinct purposes so that the services that students are entitled to receive may vary under each. A case from the District of Columbia is illustrative. The federal trial court upheld the school board's finding that a student with attention deficit hyperactivity disorder (ADHD) was not eligible for services under IDEA because his educational performance was not adversely affected by his ADHD (*Lyons v. Smith*, 1993). On the other hand, the court was convinced that a hearing officer could have ordered the board to provide special education services to the student who was designated as otherwise qualified under Section 504 in appropriate circumstances. The court did emphasize that Section 504 does not require affirmative efforts to overcome the student's disability, but simply is designed to prevent discrimination on the basis of the disability. Consequently, in some situations, boards may need to provide special education services to students with disabilities in order to eliminate discrimination.

Concerns also arise as to whether students with disabilities who are incarcerated are entitled to receive special education services (*Green v. Johnson*, 1982). In such a situation, a federal trial court in Illinois indicated that Section 504 is applicable to correctional facilities (*Donnell C. v. Illinois State Board of Education*, 1993). Insofar as correctional facilities receive federal funds to provide educational services to inmates, the court said that they fall within the scope of Section 504.

The major thrust of the ADA has been to extend the protections of Section 504 to the private sector while clarifying other issues by codifying judicial interpretations of the latter. Due to the similarities between the two statutes, compliance with Section 504 generally translates to compliance with the ADA (*Vande Zande v. State of Wisconsin Department of Administration*, 1994). While most suits are filed on the basis of both Section 504 and the ADA, students generally receive no greater relief under the ADA than under Section 504. Of course, in rare situations where the ADA has adopted stricter standards, school boards are required to meet those greater requirements. As such, when school officials make diligent good faith efforts to comply with Section 504, they should not run into difficulty with the ADA (Miles, Russo, & Gordon, 1991).

Unlike the IDEA 2004, which requires school officials to identify, assess, and serve students with disabilities, Section 504 and the ADA are federal antidiscrimination statutes to the extent that they prohibit school officials and others from offering unequal opportunities to qualified individuals. In a case illustrating this principle, the federal trial court in Arizona emphasized that a student did not need to prove that an act of discrimination was intentional in order to present an actionable claim under Section 504 (*Begay v. Hodel*, 1990). According to the court, the failure of school officials to correct a situation that resulted in a denial of access suggested an impermissible disparate impact sufficient to present such a claim under Section 504. When officials failed to correct architectural barriers in the student's high school which, in turn, forced her to attend a school several miles away, causing her to have to commute over poor roads, thereby aggravating her condition and forcing her to withdraw from school, the court concluded that they violated her rights.

The Second Circuit noted that Section 504 does not require that all students with disabilities receive identical benefits (*P.C. v. McLaughlin*, 1990). Recognizing that courts must allow for professional judgment, the court indicated that a student would have to show that more suitable arrangements were available but were not offered in order to substantiate a discrimination claim under Section 504.

School officials cannot discriminate against students with disabilities on the basis of the means by which they address their impairments. In a case from California, a federal trial court was of the view that as long as the means by which a student addressed her circumstances were reasonable, school officials could not discriminate against her on the basis of how she chose to address her condition (*Sullivan v. Vallejo City Unified School District*, 1990).

As reflected in any number of cases discussed in previous chapters, courts declined to intervene in situations where parents disagreed with the methodologies used in specific placements as long as school officials could demonstrate that their selected approaches were appropriate. In a case from Nebraska, the federal trial court agreed that the ADA does not provide parents with any additional clout regarding the choice of methodology (*Petersen v. Hastings Public Schools*, 1993). The court asserted that since the methodology selected by school officials to instruct students with hearing impairments was no less effective than the one preferred by their parents, it met the requirements of the ADA.

In a non-education dispute with implications for schools, a federal trial court in Pennsylvania held that although a public entity was not prohibited from providing benefits, services, or advantages to individuals with disabilities or to a particular class of individuals with disabilities beyond those required by the ADA, it could not discriminate in the provision of affirmative services (*Easley v. Snider*, 1993). The court wrote that providing services to persons with physical disabilities while not providing the same to individuals with physical and mental disabilities constituted discrimination since there was no rational reason for excluding those physically disabled individuals who also had mental disabilities from the benefits of the program.

In yet another non-education case of significance, a federal trial court in Florida acknowledged that the elimination of all recreation programs for individuals with disabilities violated the ADA where similar programs were still offered to those who did not have disabilities (*Concerned Parents to Save Dreher Park Center v. City of West Palm Beach*, 1994). City officials eliminated the programs due to fiscal constraints, but the court wrote that any benefits provided to persons who did not have disabilities had to have been made available on an equal basis to those with disabilities. Therefore, the court thought that since city officials chose to provide recreation services to people who were not disabled, the ADA required them to provide equal opportunities for persons with disabilities.

Otherwise *Qualifed* Students With Disabilities Under Section 504

In *Southeastern Community College v. Davis* (*Davis*) (1979), the U.S. Supreme Court's initial case interpreting Section 504 within an educational context, the Court ruled that in order to be considered otherwise qualified, students with disabilities must be able to participate in programs or activities in spite of their impairments as long as they can do so with reasonable accommodations. Although *Davis* was set in the context of higher education, its implications for elementary and secondary schools are identical. Under Section 504, students must meet all of the usual qualifications for participation. The student who filed suit unsuccessfully challenged her being denied admission to a nursing program because she was hearing impaired and relied on lip-reading to understand speech. In upholding the actions of officials who denied the student's application due to safety considerations, the Court reasoned that Section 504 did not require educational institutions to disregard the disabilities of applicants or to make substantial modifications in their programs to allow participation. The Court emphasized that legitimate physical qualifications could be essential to participation in programs.

A federal trial court in Kentucky applied the principles from *Davis* in declaring that a blind student who had multiple disabilities in addition to a visual impairment and was denied admission to the state's school for the blind was not otherwise qualified. The court asserted that since the student did not meet the school's admission criteria that applicants demonstrate the ability for academic and vocational learning, self-care, and independent functioning, he was not entitled to attend (*Eva N. v. Brock*, 1990). While the court agreed that school officials did not have to admit the student, the IDEA still obligated them to provide the student with a FAPE. The Supreme Court of Ohio later upheld the denial of a blind student's application to attend medical school on the ground that the accommodations that she sought were not reasonable because they would have required fundamental alterations to the essential nature of the program and/or since they imposed undue financial or administrative burdens on the school (*Ohio Civil Rights Commission v. Case Western Reserve University*, 1996). Conversely, a federal trial court in Tennessee decreed that a student who suffered from an autoimmune disease was otherwise qualified to attend a private school because she had the necessary academic qualifications (*Thomas v. Davidson Academy*, 1994).

In the area of sports participation, the Seventh Circuit affirmed that when a coach refused to select a student for his high school's basketball team, this did not violate his rights under Section 504 (*Doe v. Eagle-Union Community School Corporation*, 2001a). The court recognized that even though the student had a Section 504 alternative learning plan, he was not selected for the team because the coach did not believe that he was otherwise qualified insofar as he lacked the requisite skill level. The Supreme Court refused to hear a further appeal in the case (*Doe v. Eagle-Union Community School Corporation*, 2001b).

Parents who have disabilities also may exert rights under Section 504 to in order to obtain services that allow them to better participate in the educational programs of their children. In such a case, the Second Circuit affirmed part of a judgment that ordered a school board to provide hearing-impaired parents with the services of a sign-language interpreter so that they could participate in school related functions (*Rothschild v. Grottenthaler*, 1990). The court was convinced that as parents of students attending the school, they were otherwise qualified to participate in parent-oriented activities but would have been unable to do so without accommodations.

Reasonable Student Accommodations Under Section 504 and the ADA

Section 504 and the ADA do not legally require that school districts disregard completely the disabilities of those who wish to participate in their programs and activities. School districts must allow student participation when doing so would only require them to make reasonable accommodations. School officials are not required to make substantial modifications or fundamental alterations to existing educational programs and activities (*Southeastern Community College v. Davis*, 1979). The requirement to provide reasonable accommodations to allow individuals with disabilities to participate does not carry with it the duty that local school districts must lower their standards. Reasonable student accommodations do require adaptations to allow access, but do not require officials to eliminate essential prerequisites to student participation.

Similar to the IDEA 2004, once identified, qualified students are entitled to a free appropriate public education (FAPE), regardless of the nature or severity of their impairments. To guarantee that an appropriate education is made available, Section 504's regulations include due process requirements for student evaluation and placement similar to those under the IDEA 2004 (34 C.F.R. § 104.36). In making accommodations for students, educators must provide aid, benefits, and/or services that are comparable to those available to children who do not have impairments. Accordingly, qualified students must receive comparable materials, teacher quality, length of school term, and daily hours of instruction. Moreover, programs for qualified children should not be separate from those available to students who are not impaired, unless such segregation is necessary for these students to be successful. While school officials are not prohibited from offering separate programs for students with impairments, these students cannot be required to attend such classes unless they cannot be served adequately in other settings (34 C.F.R. § 104.4(b)(3)). If such programs are offered separately, facilities must, of course, be comparable (34 C.F.R. § 104.34(c)).

Reasonable accommodations may involve minor adjustments such as providing a hearing interpreter for a student (*Barnes v. Converse College*, 1977), permitting a child to be accompanied by a service dog (*Sullivan v. Vallejo City Unified School District*, 1990), modifying a behavior policy to accommodate a student with an autoimmune disease who was disruptive (*Thomas v. Davidson Academy*, 1994), and/or using nonverbal signals to make a student aware of inappropriate sensory stimulation and giving the student preferred seating in the school lunchroom to minimize environmental influences that might have disrupted the student's ability to concentrate on the task at hand (*Molly L. ex rel. B.L. v. Lower Merion School District*, 2002). At the same time, school officials do not have to grant all requests for accommodations. For example, in addition to the cases discussed below under the defenses to Section 504, a federal trial court in Missouri ruled that school officials did not have to establish a "scent-free" environment for a child with severe asthma because she was not otherwise qualified to participate in its educational program (*Hunt v. St. Peter School*, 1997). The court added that the school's voluntary "scent-free" policy met Section 504's "minor adjustment" standard. Additionally, a federal trial court in Pennsylvania rejected claims that school officials violated the Section 504 rights of a student who was classified as other health impaired in refusing to provide him with video teleconferencing equipment so that he could participate in classroom activities when he was absent (*Eric H. ex rel. John H. v. Methacton School District*, 2003). In agreeing with the board's determination that the presence of the equipment in the classroom was disruptive to students in the class, the court noted that officials did not violate Section 504 because the student was not denied benefits that would have been provided to children who were not disabled.

On the other hand, where a student in New York was unable to attend school due to a chronic illness, the Second Circuit ruled that the refusals of educational officials to provide her with reasonable accommodations, such as not requiring her to climb stairs if she felt too sick and allowing her to lie down on a couch if she needed to rest, presented actionable claims under both Section 504 and the ADA (*Weixel v. Board of Education of the City of New York*, 2002). Further, when school officials forced a student with asthma to perform physical exercise as a punishment, thereby triggering an attack of his illness, a federal trial court in Tennessee, in rejecting the school board's request for summary judgment, concluded that educators violated his rights under the ADA (*Moss v. Shelby County*, 2005). The court held that school officials should have modified their standard punishment to accommodate the student's asthma.

Academic modifications might include permitting children more time to complete examinations or assignments, using peer tutors, distributing outlines in advance, employing specialized curricular materials, and/or permitting students to use laptop computers to record answers on examinations. In modifying facilities, school officials do not have to make every classroom and/or area of buildings accessible; it may be enough to bring services to children, such as offering keyboards for musical instruction in accessible class-rooms rather than revamping entire music rooms for students who wish to take piano classes.

In a related concern, Section 504's only regulation directly addressing private schools stipulates that officials in such schools may not exclude students on the basis of their conditions if they can, with minor adjustments, be provided with appropriate educations (34 C.F.R. § 104.39(a)). This regulation also states that private schools "may not charge more for the provision of an appropriate education to handicapped persons than to nonhandicapped persons except to the extent that any additional charge is justified by a substantial increase in cost to the recipient (34 C.F.R. § 104.39(b))." As such, private schools may be able to charge additional costs to parents of children with impairments.

In a case from Texas that made its way to the Supreme Court, the justices interpreted the delivery of basic school health services to a student with physical impairments that would have allowed her to be present in a classroom as a reasonable accommodation (*Tatro v. State of Texas*, 1980, 1981, 1983, 1984). Insofar as the student needed to be catheterized approximately every four hours, a service that a school nurse, health aide, or other trained layperson were all capable of carrying out, courts agreed that when school officials refused to provide such a service, they violated Section 504 rights.

In recent years, parents have filed suits under the IDEA seeking programs in fully inclusive settings for their children with severe disabilities. In ordering inclusive placements for many of these students, courts also are turning to Section 504 for guidance. In one case, the federal trial court in New Jersey commented that excluding a student from the regular education classroom without first investigating and providing reasonable accommodations violated Section 504 (*Oberti v. Board of Education of the Borough of Clementon School District*, 1992, 1993). The court explained that a segregated special education placement may be the program of choice only when it is necessary for the child to receive educational benefit.

Returning to sports and extracurricular activities, disputes often arise over whether school boards and athletic associations can be required to waive nonessential eligibility requirements. On the one hand, at least two courts directed athletic associations to waive age limitation requirements to allow students who repeated grades due to their learning disabilities to participate in sports (*Hoot v. Milan Area Schools*, 1994; *University Interscholastic League v. Buchanan*, 1993). The courts agreed that where the association allowed waivers of other rules, a waiver of the rule prohibiting students over the age of nineteen from participating in sports was a reasonable accommodation. Further, the Sixth Circuit affirmed that in preventing a transfer student from participating in sports when he changed schools solely due to his need to receive special education services, officials violated his rights under Section 504 (*Crocker v. Tennessee Secondary School Athletic Association*, 1990). In an admittedly different factual context, the Sixth Circuit subsequently decided that a high school athletic association's eight semester eligibility rule did not violate either Section 504 or the ADA and that a student's claim that it violated his rights was without merit (*McPherson v. Michigan High School Athletic Association*, 1997). Previously, the Eighth Circuit held that since a student who challenged an athletic association's age restrictions was not otherwise qualified under either the ADA or Section 504 because he exceeded the age limit, he was not entitled to relief (*Pottgen v. Missouri State High School Activities Association*, 1994).

In a non–age-related case involving sports, a federal trial court in Illinois rejected the claims of a student athlete who was suspended from his football and lacrosse teams for disciplinary infractions (*Long v. Board of Education, District 128*, 2001). The court posited that waiving the athletic code of conduct would have been an unreasonable accommodation under Section 504 and the ADA because it would have sent the message to others that student athletes could thwart the enforcement of team rules by threatening legal actions, thereby making it difficult for school officials to maintain effective control over their athletic programs.

Most jurisdictions have instituted requirements that students pass comprehensive state-administered tests in order to graduate with a standard high school diploma. This requirement has become more prevalent following the passage of the No Child Left Behind Act. Under Section 504 and the ADA, school boards may be required to modify test-taking situations to allow students with disabilities to complete their examinations. Even so, school officials are not required to alter the content of the tests themselves (*Brookhart v. Illinois State Board of Education*, 1983). While altering the content of tests to accommodate the inability of individuals to learn amounts to a substantial modification, modifying the manner in which examinations are administered to accommodate student disabilities is probably reasonable. In other words, allowing a visually impaired student to take a Braille version of a test is a reasonable accommodation, but changing the content of an examination to make it easier would likely not be required.

A significant number of disputes over testing accommodations that were litigated in the context of post-secondary institutions apply to situations in elementary and secondary schools. These cases help to illustrate the point that accommodations in how tests are administered are required, but alterations to their contents are not. In one such case, a federal trial court in New York ordered additional accommodations for a visually impaired law school graduate who was sitting for the bar examination. Although the Board of Bar Examiners granted some, but not all, of the graduate's requested accommodations, since her physician testified that they were necessary, the court ordered that they be made on the ground that the purpose of the ADA was to guarantee that those with disabilities are not disadvantaged but are put on an equal footing with others (*D'Amico v. New York State Board of Law Examiners*, 1993). Conversely, another case from New York involving a law school graduate reveals that applicants are not entitled to accommodations just because they may have failed an examination in the past without accommodations (*Pazer v. New York State Board of Law Examiners*, 1994). The court was convinced that requested accommodations were not necessary for a student who claimed to have a learning disability since the testimony of an acknowledged expert on dyslexia proved to be credible and persuasive in establishing that he did not have such a condition.

As discussed later in the chapter under defenses, accommodations that are unduly costly, create an excessive monitoring burden, or expose other individuals to excessive risk are not required. In an illustrative case, the Eighth Circuit decided that inoculating staff members against the hepatitis B virus so that a carrier of that disease could attend a learning center program went beyond the requirements of Section 504 (*Kohl v. Woodhaven Learning Center*, 1989). Similarly, a federal trial court in Kentucky ruled that a school for the blind could not be required to hire additional staff or modify the mission of the institution to accept a student who did not meet the minimum qualifications for admission to the school (*Eva N. v. Brock*, 1990).

Student Admissions Evaluations

Insofar as some public schools may require students with disabilities to take admissions examinations and/or be interviewed prior to being accepted and/or placed, in order to evaluate whether applicants are otherwise qualified, provisions in Section 504 address this situation. The regulations cover four areas: pre-placement evaluation, evaluation, placement, and reevaluation (34 C.F.R. § 104.35).

As to pre-placement evaluations, the regulations require school officials to evaluate all children who, due to their conditions, need or are believed to need special education or related services. These evaluations are to be completed before officials take any actions with respect to the initial placements of children in regular or special education, as well as prior to making any later significant changes in placement.

Section 504's evaluation provisions require school officials to follow procedures similar to those under the IDEA. These provisions require officials to validate tests and other evaluation materials for the specific purposes for which they are used and to ensure that they are administered by trained personnel in conformance with the instructions provided by their producers. These materials must also be tailored to assess specific areas of educational need and cannot be designed to provide a single general intelligence quotient. Further, these materials must be selected and administered in a way that best ensures that when tests are administered to students with impaired sensory, manual, or speaking skills, the results accurately reflect their aptitude or achievement level or whatever other factor the test purports to measure, rather than reflecting their impaired sensory, manual, or speaking skills, except where those skills are the factors that the tests purport to measure.

When school officials apply placement procedures to students under Section 504, their interpretations of data must consider information from a variety of sources, including aptitude and achievement tests, teacher recommendations, physical condition, social and cultural background, and adaptive behaviors that have been documented and carefully considered. In addition, not only must any such decisions be made by groups of persons, including knowledgeable individuals, but all children must be periodically reevaluated in a manner consistent with the dictates of the IDEA 2004.

Under Section 504, schools relying on examinations or interviews may be required to provide reasonable accommodations to applicants with impairments. While school officials are not required to alter the content of examinations or interviews, they may have to make accommodations in how tests are administered or interviews are conducted. Put another way, school officials would not be required to make examinations easier so that students who simply lacked the requisite knowledge could pass, but they would have to alter the conditions under which examinations are administered, or interviews are conducted, so that students with impairments who have the requisite knowledge and skills to pass or express themselves fully could do so despite their conditions.

The accommodations that educators provide for examinations may be as simple as providing quiet rooms without distractions, essentially private rooms away from others, for students who suffer from attention deficit hyperactivity disorder or procuring the services of a reader or Braille versions of examination for applicants who are blind. Moreover, students with physical disabilities may require special arrangements such as scribes to record answers to questions, and/or to be permitted to use computers to record answers on examinations. In like fashion, whether as part of examinations or admissions interviews, students who are hearing impaired might be entitled to the services of sign-language interpreters to communicate directions that are normally given orally. At the same time, school officials may be required to provide students with learning disabilities with extra time to complete examinations or may have to make computers available to children who are more comfortable with them than with traditional paper-and-pencil tests.

Prior to receiving accommodations, students must prove that they have conditions such as learning disabilities (*Argen v. New York State Board of Law Examiners*, 1994) and that the extra time to take examinations is necessary due to their impairments. The purpose of providing the extra time is to allow students who might have difficulty processing information sufficient opportunity to show that they are capable of answering the questions.

In a major difference from the IDEA, which requires school officials to identify, assess, and serve students with disabilities, under Section 504, students and/or their parents are responsible for making school officials aware of the fact that they need testing, or interviewing, accommodations. To this end, administrators should require proof that students have impairments in need of accommodation in order to demonstrate knowledge and skills on examinations. Students, through their parents, should also suggest which accommodations would be most appropriate. In considering whether students are entitled to accommodations, school officials must make individualized inquiries. School officials may be liable for violating Section 504 if they refuse to make testing accommodations or make modifications only for students with specified impairments.

Section 504 Service Plans

As noted, students who qualify under the Section 504 definition are entitled to reasonable accommodations so that they may access school programs. Making accommodations may involve alterations to physical plants, such as building wheelchair ramps or removing architectural barriers, so that students may physically enter and get around school buildings. School officials must also allow students to bring service animals into classrooms (*Sullivan v. Vallejo City Unified School District*, 1990), but they are not required to provide accommodations that go beyond what would be considered reasonable. Accommodations that are excessively expensive, that expose the school's staff to excessive risk, or that require substantial modifications to the missions or purposes of programs are not required.

Neither Section 504 nor its regulations mandate the creation of written agreements with regard to student accommodations or specify the content of such documents. Even so, school officials in many districts meet with parents to formalize the accommodations and services that they will provide to eligible students. These written agreements are euphemistically referred to as Section 504 service plans. In practical terms, school officials should be sure to include the following components in each written Section 504 service plan:

1. **Demographic data:** student's name, date of birth, school identification number, grade, school, teacher, parents' names, address, telephone numbers, and the like
2. **Team members:** a listing of all team members who contributed to the development of the service plan, and their respective roles
3. **Impairment:** a detailed description of the student's impairment and its severity, along with an explanation of how it impedes the child's educational progress
4. **Accommodations and services:** a detailed description of the accommodations and services to be offered under the plan, including the frequency and location of services, where they will be provided, and by whom they will be provided

In addition, officials should attach the evaluative reports or assessments that helped to determine the nature of a student's impairment and the need for accommodations and services.

Legal Defenses Under Section 504

Even if students appear to be "otherwise qualified," school officials can rely on one of three defenses to avoid being charged with non-compliance of Section 504. This represents a major difference between Section 504 and the IDEA, since no such defenses are applicable under the IDEA 2004. Another major difference between the two federal laws is that the federal government provides public schools with direct federal financial assistance to help fund programs under the IDEA but offers no financial incentives to aid institutions, public and nonpublic, as they seek to comply with the dictates of Section 504. Interestingly, these defenses emerged largely as a result of two Supreme Court cases not involving students in elementary and secondary schools.

In *Southeastern Community College v. Davis* (*Davis*) (1979), the Court held that officials at a community college did not violate the rights of an unsuccessful applicant to a nursing program. The Court explained that since officials denied the applicant entry on the basis that her hearing impairment would have made it unsafe for her to participate, she was not otherwise qualified to do so. On the other hand, in the Court's first case on Section 504 in a school setting, *School Board of Nassau County, Florida v. Arline* (1987), it affirmed that educational officials violated a teacher's rights by discharging her due to recurrences of tuberculosis. In determining that the teacher was otherwise qualified for the job, the Court created a four-part test for use in cases involving contagious diseases. The elements that the Court relied on in ordering the teacher's reinstatement were the nature of the risk, its duration, its severity, and the probabilities that the disease would be transmitted and cause varying degrees of harm. On remand, a federal trial court in Florida agreed that since the teacher was otherwise qualified, she was entitled to return to her job (*Arline v. School Board of Nassau County*, 1988).

The first defense under Section 504 is that officials can be excused from making accommodations that result in "a fundamental alteration in the nature of [a] program" (*Southeastern Community College v. Davis*, 1979, p. 410). The second defense permits school officials to avoid compliance if modifications impose an "undue financial burden" (*Davis*, p. 412) on an institution or entity as a whole. The third defense is that an otherwise qualified student with a disability can be excluded from a program if the student's presence creates a substantial risk of injury to himself, herself, or others (*School Board of Nassau County, Florida v. Arline*, 1987). As such, a student with a severe visual impairment could be excluded from using a scalpel in a biology laboratory. However, in order to comply with Section 504, school officials would probably have to offer a reasonable accommodation such as providing a computer-assisted program to achieve an instructional goal similar to the one that would have been achieved in a laboratory class.

Finally, Section 504, which is enforced by the Office of Civil Rights, requires each recipient of federal financial aid to file an assurance of compliance; provide notice to students and their parents that their programs are nondiscriminatory; engage in remedial actions where violations are proven; take voluntary steps to overcome the effects of conditions that resulted in limiting the participation of students with disabilities in their programs; conduct a self-evaluation; designate a staff member, typically at the central office level, as compliance coordinator; and adopt grievance procedures (34 C.F.R. § 104.5).

Effect of Mitigating Measures

Prior to the ADA Amendments of 2008 individuals were denied protection if their conditions could be controlled by medications or other measures. Even so, the amendment includes an exception so that officials of various institutions can consider the mitigating effects of ordinary eyeglasses or contact lenses in determining whether visual impairments substantially limit major life activities. According to a Dear Colleague Letter issued by the U.S. Department of Education's Office for Civil Rights in 2012, "Congress intended to ensure a broad scope of protection…and to convey that the question of whether an individual's impairment is a disability under the ADA and Section 504 should not demand extensive analysis" (Ali, 2012; 42 U.S.C. § 12102(4)(A)). This expansion upon the definition of a disability was an effort to return to the original intent of the law, which Congress believed had been inaccurately narrowed through the Supreme Court's interpretation as evidenced in case law (See, e.g. *Sutton v. United Air Lines, Inc.*, 1999; *Toyota Motor Manufacturing v. Williams*, 2002).

As indicated earlier, individuals are not considered to have disabilities for purposes of Section 504 and the ADA if their major life activities are not substantially limited by the condition. Although prior case law found that short-term conditions, or those that can be mitigated, were not considered to be impairments under Section 504, (See, e.g. *Albertson's, Inc. v. Kirkingburg*, 1999; *Murphy v. United Parcel Service*, 1999; *Sutton v. United Air Lines*, 1999) the ADA Amendments Act of 2008 clarified that the term *substantially limits* should be broadly interpreted and the determination made "without regard to the ameliorative effects of mitigating measures" (42 U.S.C. § 12102(4)(E)(i)(I)-(IV)). The only exceptions are eyeglasses and contact lenses. It remains to be decided on a case-by-case basis whether particular temporary impairments constitute disabilities. For example, impairments that are episodic or in remission may be considered to be disabilities if they substantially limit major life activities when active (42 U.S.C. § 12102 (4)(D)). However, Congress determined that an individual is not regarded as having a disability if the impairment is minor or lasts 6 months or less (42 U.S.C. § 12102(3)(B)).

One question that has not been answered is whether persons who choose not to use available mitigating measures or devices would qualify as individuals with disabilities under the ADA and Section 504. For example, even though many students are prescribed medication for attention deficit hyperactivity disorder, for various reasons many parents choose not to have their children take the psychotropic medications that are usually prescribed. In such situations, where student impairments can be fully mitigated through use of medications, it is unclear whether students would qualify as disabled under the statutes if their parents were unwilling to administer the medications. Interestingly, the IDEA prohibits states, and school systems, from requiring children to take medications as a condition of attending school, being evaluated, or receiving services (20 U.S.C. § 1412(a)(25)). Even so, it is unclear whether courts will interpret the ADA and Section 504 as not allowing school personnel to consider whether a student could take measures to mitigate impairments in making such evaluations.

⚖️

SPECIAL EDUCATION LAW IN PRACTICE
Legal Case No. 16—Legal Defenses Under Section 504

SCHOOL BOARD OF NASSAU COUNTY, FLORIDA V. ARLINE
Supreme Court of the United States, 1987
480 U.S. 273

Justice BRENNAN delivered the opinion of the Court.

Section 504 of the Rehabilitation Act of 1973 prohibits a federally funded state program from discriminating against a handicapped individual solely by reason of his or her handicap. This case presents the questions whether a person afflicted with tuberculosis, a contagious disease, may be considered a "handicapped individual" within the meaning of § 504 of the Act, and, if so, whether such an individual is "otherwise qualified" to teach elementary school.

I

From 1966 until 1979, respondent Gene Arline taught elementary school in Nassau County, Florida. She was discharged in 1979 after suffering a third relapse of tuberculosis within two years. After she was denied relief in state administrative proceedings, she brought suit in federal court, alleging that the school board's decision to dismiss her because of her tuberculosis violated § 504 of the Act.

. . . Arline was hospitalized for tuberculosis in 1957. For the next 20 years, Arline's disease was in remission. Then, in 1977, a culture revealed that tuberculosis was again active in her system; cultures taken in March 1978 and in November 1978 were also positive.

The superintendent of schools for Nassau County, Craig Marsh, then testified as to the school board's response to Arline's medical reports. After both her second relapse, in the spring of 1978, and her third relapse in November 1978, the school board suspended Arline with pay for the remainder of the school year. At the end of the 1978–1979 school year, the school board held a hearing, after which it discharged Arline, "not because she had done anything wrong," but because of the "continued reoccurence [sic] of tuberculosis." In her trial memorandum, Arline argued that it was "not disputed that the [school board dismissed her] solely on the basis of her illness. Since the illness in this case qualifies the Plaintiff as a 'handicapped person'" it is clear that she was dismissed solely as a result of

her handicap in violation of Section 504." The District Court held, however, that although there was "[n]o question that she suffers a handicap," Arline was nevertheless not "a handicapped person under the terms of that statute." The court found it "difficult . . . to conceive that Congress intended contagious diseases to be included within the definition of a handicapped person." The court then went on to state that, "even assuming" that a person with a contagious disease could be deemed a handicapped person, Arline was not "qualified" to teach elementary school.

The Court of Appeals reversed, holding that "persons with contagious diseases are within the coverage of section 504," and that Arline's condition "falls . . . neatly within the statutory and regulatory framework" of the Act. The court remanded the case "for further findings as to whether the risks of infection precluded Mrs. Arline from being 'otherwise qualified' for her job and, if so, whether it was possible to make some reasonable accommodation for her in that teaching position" or in some other position. We granted certiorari and now affirm.

II

In enacting and amending the Act, Congress enlisted all programs receiving federal funds in an effort "to share with handicapped Americans the opportunities for an education, transportation, housing, health care, and jobs that other Americans take for granted." To that end, Congress not only increased federal support for vocational rehabilitation, but also addressed the broader problem of discrimination against the handicapped by including § 504, an antidiscrimination provision patterned after Title VI of the Civil Rights Act of 1964. Section 504 of the Rehabilitation Act reads in pertinent part:

No otherwise qualified handicapped individual in the United States, as defined in section 706(7) of this title, shall, solely by reason of his handicap, be excluded from participation in, be denied the benefits of, or be subjected to discrimination under any program or activity receiving Federal financial assistance. . . .

29 U.S.C. § 794

In 1974, Congress expanded the definition of "handicapped individual" for use in Section 504 to read as follows:

[A]ny person who (i) has a physical or mental impairment which substantially limits one or more of such person's major life activities, (ii) has a record of such an impairment, or (iii) is regarded as having such an impairment.

29 U.S.C. § 706(7)(B)

The amended definition reflected Congress' concern with protecting the handicapped against discrimination stemming not only from simple prejudice, but also from "archaic attitudes and laws" and from "the fact that the American people are simply unfamiliar with and insensitive to the difficulties confront [ing] individuals with handicaps." To combat the effects of erroneous but nevertheless prevalent perceptions about the handicapped, Congress expanded the definition of "handicapped individual" so as to preclude discrimination against "[a] person who has a record of, or is regarded as having, an impairment [but who] may at present have no actual incapacity at all."

In determining whether a particular individual is handicapped as defined by the Act, the regulations promulgated by the Department of Health and Human Services are of significant assistance. As we have previously recognized, these regulations were drafted with the oversight and approval of Congress; they provide "an important source of guidance on the meaning of § 504." The regulations are particularly significant here because they define two critical terms used in the statutory definition of handicapped individual. "Physical impairment" is defined as follows:

[A]ny physiological disorder or condition, cosmetic disfigurement, or anatomical loss affecting one or more of the following body systems: neurological; musculoskeletal; special sense organs; respiratory, including speech organs; cardiovascular; reproductive, digestive, genito-urinary; hemic and lymphatic; skin; and endocrine.

In addition, the regulations define "major life activities" as "functions such as caring for one's self, performing manual tasks, walking, seeing, hearing, speaking, breathing, learning, and working."

III

Within this statutory and regulatory framework, then, we must consider whether Arline can be considered a handicapped individual. According to . . . testimony . . . Arline suffered tuberculosis "in an acute form in such a degree that it affected her respiratory system," and was hospitalized for this condition. Arline thus had a physical impairment as that term is defined by the regulations, since she had a "physiological disorder or condition . . . affecting [her] . . . respiratory [system]." This impairment was serious enough to require hospitalization, a fact more than sufficient to establish that one or more of her major life activities were substantially limited by her impairment. Thus, Arline's hospitalization for tuberculosis in 1957 suffices to establish that she has a "record of . . . impairment" within the meaning of 29 U.S.C. § 706(7)(B)(ii), and is therefore a handicapped individual.

Petitioners concede that a contagious disease may constitute a handicapping condition to the extent that it leaves a person with "diminished physical or mental capabilities," Brief for Petitioners 15, and concede that Arline's hospitalization for tuberculosis in 1957 demonstrates that she has a record of a physical impairment. Petitioners maintain, however, that Arline's record of impairment is irrelevant in this case, since the school board dismissed Arline not because of her diminished physical capabilities, but because of the threat that her relapses of tuberculosis posed to the health of others.

We do not agree with petitioners that, in defining a handicapped individual under § 504, the contagious effects of a disease can be meaningfully distinguished from the disease's physical effects on a claimant in a case such as this. Arline's contagiousness and her physical impairment each resulted from the same underlying condition, tuberculosis. It would be unfair to allow an employer to seize upon the distinction between the effects of a disease on others and the effects of a disease on a patient and use that distinction to justify discriminatory treatment.

Nothing in the legislative history of § 504 suggests that Congress intended such a result. That history demonstrates that Congress was as concerned about the effect of an impairment on others as it was about its effect on the individual. . . .

Allowing discrimination based on the contagious effects of a physical impairment would be inconsistent with the basic purpose of § 504, which is to ensure that handicapped individuals are not denied jobs or other benefits because of the prejudiced attitudes or the ignorance of others. By amending the definition of "handicapped individual" to include not only those who are actually physically impaired, but also those who are regarded as impaired and who, as a result, are substantially limited in a major life activity, Congress acknowledged that society's accumulated myths and fears about disability and disease are as handicapping as are the physical limitations that flow from actual impairment. Few aspects of a handicap give rise to the same level of public fear and misapprehension as contagiousness. Even those who suffer or have recovered from such noninfectious diseases as epilepsy or cancer have faced discrimination based on the irrational fear that they might be contagious. The Act is carefully structured to replace such reflexive reactions to actual or perceived handicaps with actions based on reasoned and medically sound judgments: the definition of "handicapped individual" is broad, but only those individuals who are both handicapped and otherwise qualified are eligible for relief. The fact that some persons who have contagious diseases may pose a serious health threat to others under certain circumstances does not justify excluding from the coverage of the Act all persons with actual or perceived contagious diseases. Such exclusion would mean that those accused of being contagious would never have the opportunity to have their condition evaluated in light of medical evidence and a determination made as to whether they were "otherwise qualified." Rather, they would be vulnerable to discrimination on the basis of mythology—precisely the type of injury Congress sought to prevent. We conclude that the fact that a person with a record of a physical impairment is also contagious does not suffice to remove that person from coverage under § 504.

IV

The remaining question is whether Arline is otherwise qualified for the job of elementary schoolteacher. To answer this question in most cases, the district court will need to conduct an individualized inquiry and make appropriate findings of fact. Such an inquiry is essential if § 504 is to achieve its goal of protecting handicapped individuals from deprivations based on prejudice, stereotypes, or unfounded fear, while giving appropriate weight to such legitimate concerns of grantees as avoiding exposing others to significant health and safety risks. The basic factors to be considered in conducting this inquiry are well established. In the context of the employment of a person handicapped with a contagious disease, we agree with amicus American Medical Association that this inquiry should include . . . "[findings of]

facts, based on reasonable medical judgments given the state of medical knowledge, about (a) the nature of the risk (how the disease is transmitted), (b) the duration of the risk (how long is the carrier infectious), (c) the severity of the risk (what is the potential harm to third parties) and (d) the probabilities the disease will be transmitted and will cause varying degrees of harm."

In making these findings, courts normally should defer to the reasonable medical judgments of public health officials. The next step in the "otherwise-qualified" inquiry is for the court to evaluate, in light of these medical findings, whether the employer could reasonably accommodate the employee under the established standards for that inquiry.

Because of the paucity of factual findings by the District Court, we, like the Court of Appeals, are unable at this stage of the proceedings to resolve whether Arline is "otherwise qualified" for her job. . . .

We hold that a person suffering from the contagious disease of tuberculosis can be a handicapped person within the meaning of § 504 of the Rehabilitation Act of 1973, and that respondent Arline is such a person. We remand the case to the District Court to determine whether Arline is otherwise qualified for her position. The judgment of the Court of Appeals is Affirmed.

Questions for Discussion

1. Was this decision wise? Was it safe for the school community?

2. What are *Arline*'s implications for students with contagious diseases such as HIV/AIDS or hepatitis B? How would a school board's response be different for students with more contagious diseases based on the increased risk of infection? Under what circumstances could students with contagious diseases be excluded from inclusive programs in public schools?

3. Both the *Southeast Community College* and *Arline* legal decisions demonstrate that in order to be otherwise qualified, individuals with disabilities must be able to meet all of a program's requirements in spite of their impairments. Even so, Section 504 and the ADA require officials to make reasonable accommodations so that individuals may, in fact, meet programmatic requirements. In addition to those discussed in the text, what are some other reasonable accommodations that are typically provided in school settings?

⚖

Summary of Important Legal Policies, Principles, and Practices

1. Section 504 of the Rehabilitation Act of 1973 requires school districts to provide a free appropriate public education (FAPE) to qualified students with disabilities. Section 504's primary focus is the guaranteeing of equal access to educational facilities and services for students with disabilities.
2. Since Section 504 encompasses more than the sector of public education, the federal statute's definition of a person with a disability is much broader compared to the IDEA 2004's more narrowly defined definition of a student with a disability. Under Section 504, a person has a disability if that individual has a physical or mental impairment that substantially limits one or more of that person's major life activities.
3. Similar to Section 504, the Americans with Disabilities Act (ADA) prohibits discrimination against qualified persons with disabilities. The definition of a person with a disability under the ADA is basically the same as the one provided under Section 504. However, unlike Section 504, the ADA does not legally require that individual employers, agencies, or organizations receive federal funding in order to be covered.

Useful Online Resources

Office of Civil Rights (OCR), U.S. Department of Education
Parent and Educator Resource Guide to Section 504 in Public Elementary and Secondary Schools
A useful online resource that provides specific legal guidance to both parents and school officials regarding the rights of students with disabilities under Section 504 at www2.ed.gov/about/offices/list/ocr/docs/504-resource-guide-201612.pdf

Wrightslaw
Discrimination: Section 504 and the ADA
An excellent online resource detailing Section 504 and the ADA regulations as well as legal guidance from a variety of resources at www.wrightslaw.com/info/sec504.index.htm

Recommended Reading

Colker, R. (2018). *Federal disability law in a nutshell* (6th ed.). St. Paul, MN: West Academic.

Dieterich, C. A., & Chan, P. (2017). Legal implications for accommodating students with disabilities in teacher preparation field placements. *Teacher Education and Special Education*, 40(3), 194–211. doi:10.1177/0888406417700959

Ferrreri, F. (2018). *What do I do when . . . the answer book on Section 504* (5th ed.). Palm Beach Gardens, FL: LRP Publications.

Russo, C. J., & Osborne, A. G. (2009). *Section 504 and the ADA*. Thousand Oaks, CA: Corwin.

Sepiol, C. (2015). *Section 504: A legal guide for educators: Practical applications for essential compliance*. Eau Claire, WI: PESI Publishing & Media.

Zirkel, P. A. (2019). Are school personnel liable for money damages under the IDEA or Section 504 and the ADA? *Exceptionality*, 27(2), 77–80.

References

Albertson's, Inc. v. Kirkingburg, 527 U.S. 555 (1999).

Ali, R. (Jan. 19, 2012). *Dear Colleague Letter*, U.S. Department of Education, available at http://www2.ed.gov/about/offices/list/ocr/letters/colleague-201109.html.

Americans with Disabilities Act, 42 U.S.C.A. §§ 12101 *et seq.* (2005).

ADA Amendments Act of 2008, PL 110-325, 122 Stat. 3553 (2008).

Argen v. New York State Board of Law Examiners, 860 F. Supp. 84, (W.D.N.Y. 1994).

Arline v. School Board of Nassau County, 692 F. Supp. 1286 (M.D. Fla. 1988).

Barnes v. Converse College, 436 F. Supp. 635 (D.S.C. 1977).

Barnett v. Fairfax County School Board, 721 F. Supp. 757 (E.D. Va. 1989), *aff'd*, 927 F.2d 146 (4th Cir. 1991).

Begay v. Hodel, 730 F. Supp. 1001 (D. Ariz. 1990).

Brookhart v. Illinois State Board of Education, 697 F.2d 179 (7th Cir. 1983).

Chapman, R. (2015). *The everyday guide to special education law: A handbook for parents, teachers, and other professionals*. Denver, CO: Mighty Press.

Colin K. v. Schmidt, 715 F.2d 1 (1st Cir. 1983).

Colker, R. (2018). *Federal disability law in a nutshell* (6th ed.). St. Paul, MN: West Academic.

Concerned Parents to Save Dreher Park Center v. City of West Palm Beach, 846 F. Supp. 986 (S.D. Fla. 1994).

Cordrey v. Euckert, 917 F.2d 1460 (6th Cir. 1990).

Crocker v. Tennessee Secondary School Athletic Association, 735 F. Supp. (M.D. Tenn. 1990), *aff'd without published opinion sub nom: Metropolitan Government of Nashville and Davidson County v. Crocker*, 908 F.2d 973 (6th Cir. 1990).

D'Amico v. New York State Board of Law Examiners, 813 F. Supp. 217 (W.D.N.Y. 1993).

Darlene L. v. Illinois Board of Education, 568 F. Supp. 1340 (N.D. Ill. 1983).

Doe v. Alabama State Department of Education, 915 F.2d 651 (11th Cir. 1990).

Doe v. Belleville Public School District, 672 F. Supp. 342 (S.D. Ill. 1987).

Doe v. Dolton Elementary School District, 694 F. Supp. 440 (N.D. Ill. 1988).

Doe v. Eagle-Union Community School Corporation, 2 Fed Appx. 567 (7th Cir. 2001a), 534 U.S. 1042 (2001b).

Donnell C. v. Illinois State Board of Education, 829 F. Supp. 1016 (N.D. Ill. 1993).

Easley v. Snider, 841 F. Supp. 668 (E.D. Pa. 1993).

Eric H. ex rel. John H. v. Methacton School District, 265 F. Supp.2d 513 (E.D. Pa. 2003).

Eva N. v. Brock, 741 F. Supp. 626 (E.D. Ky. 1990).

Green v. Johnson, 513 F. Supp. 965 (D. Mass. 1982).

Hendricks v. Gilhool, 709 F. Supp. 1362 (E.D. Pa. 1989).

Hoot v. Milan Area Schools, 853 F. Supp. 243 (E.D. Mich. 1994).

Hunt v. St. Peter School, 963 F. Supp. 843 (W.D. Mo. 1997).

I.D. v. Westmoreland School District, 788 F. Supp. 634 (D.N.H. 1992).

Individuals with Disabilities Education Act, 20 U.S.C.A. §§ 1400–1482 (2005).

Kaesberg, M. A., & Murray, K. T. (1994). Americans with Disabilities Act. *Education Law Reporter, 90*, 11–20.

Kohl v. Woodhaven Learning Center, 865 F.2d 930 (8th Cir. 1989).

Long v. Board of Education, District 128, 167 F. Supp.2d 988 (N.D. Ill. 2001).

Lyons v. Smith, 829 F. Supp. 414 (D.D.C. 1993).

Martinez v. School Board of Hillsborough County, 861 F.2d 1502 (11th Cir. 1988), *on remand*, 711 F. Supp. 1066 (M.D. Fla. 1989).

McPherson v. Michigan High School Athletic Association, 119 F.3d 453 (6th Cir. 1997).

Miles, A. S., Russo, C. J., & Gordon, W. M. (1991). The reasonable accommodations provisions of the Americans with Disabilities Act. *Education Law Reporter, 69*, 1–8.

Molly L. ex rel. B.L. v. Lower Merion School District, 194 F. Supp.2d 422 (E.D. Pa. 2002).

Moss v. Shelby County, 401 F. Supp2d 850 (W.D. Tenn. 2005).

Murphy v. United Parcel Service, 527 U.S. 516 (1999).

New York State Association for Retarded Children v. Carey, 612 F.2d 644 (2d Cir. 1979).

No Child Left Behind Act, 20 U.S.C. §§ 6301–7941 (2002).

Oberti v. Board of Education of the Borough of Clementon School District, 801 F. Supp. 1393 (D.N.J. 1992), *aff'd*, 995 F.2d 1204 (3d Cir. 1993).

Ohio Civil Rights Commission v. Case Western Reserve University, 666 N.E.2d 1376 (Ohio 1996).

Pazer v. New York State Board of Law Examiners, 849 F. Supp. 284 (S.D.N.Y. 1994).

P.C. v. McLaughlin, 913 F.2d 1033 (2d Cir. 1990).

Petersen v. Hastings Public Schools, 831 F. Supp. 742 (D. Neb. 1993).

Pottgen v. Missouri State High School Activities Association, 40 F.3d 926 (8th Cir. 1994).

Puffer v. Raynolds, 761 F. Supp. 838 (D. Mass. 1988).

Ray v. School District of DeSoto County, 666 F. Supp. 1524 (M.D. Fla. 1987).

Rehabilitation Act, Section 504, 29 U.S.C.A. § 794 (2005).

Rothschild v. Grottenthaler, 907 F.2d 286 (2d Cir. 1990).

School Board of Nassau County, Florida v. Arline, 480 U.S. 273 (1987).

Southeastern Community College v. Davis, 442 U.S. 397 (1979).

Sullivan v. Vallejo City Unified School District, 731 F. Supp. 947 (E.D. Cal. 1990).

Sutton v. United Air Lines, 527 U.S. 471 (1999).

Tatro v. State of Texas, 625 F.2d 557 (5th Cir. 1980), *on remand*, 516 F. Supp. 968 (N.D. Tex. 1981), *aff'd*, 703 F.2d 823 (5th Cir. 1983), *aff'd sub nom. Irving Independent School District v. Tatro*, 468 U.S. 883 (1984).

Thomas v. Atascadero Unified School District, 662 F. Supp. 376 (C.D. Cal. 1987).

Thomas v. Davidson Academy, 846 F. Supp. 611 (M.D. Tenn. 1994).

Toyota Motor Manufacturing v. Williams, 534 U.S. 184 (2002).

University Interscholastic League v. Buchanan, 848 S.W.2d 298 (Tex. App. Ct. 1993).

Vande Zande v. State of Wisconsin Department of Administration, 851 F. Supp. 353 (W.D. Wis. 1994).

Weixel v. Board of Educ. of the City of New York, 287 F.3d 138 (2d Cir. 2002).

Wenkart, R. D. (1993). The Americans with Disabilities Act and its impact on public education. *Education Law Reporter, 82*, 291–302.

Epilogue

As you reach the conclusion of our book, we hope your level of special education legal literacy has increased compared to when you started reading. The law is constantly subject to changes and ongoing modifications and the laws impacting students with disabilities are no different. So, this book fully recognizes that individuals who work closely with students with disabilities must not only address their present levels of special education legal literacy, but also develop realistic and workable strategies to accurately and confidently keep up to date with ongoing legal developments in special education. Thus, it is necessary for all of us to recognize the value of maintaining our special education legal literacy by monitoring updates or more significant changes to the legal principles, policies, and practices impacting students with disabilities. Given ongoing advancements in technology, especially the availability of open-access online resources, anyone with reliable Internet access can locate valuable special education legal resources online, usually at little or no cost. The biggest challenge, however, is knowing where to look and recognizing whether a particular online resource is credible or not. Hopefully, this book points you in the right "online" direction.

We welcome your comments and insights on the book. We realize the challenging task associated with translating complex special education jargon and legalese into useful and meaningful guidance for today's educational practitioners. As such, we encourage you to contact us with your comments and experiences using the book. Please feel free to contact us.

Kevin Brady
University of Arkansas
kpbrady@uark.edu

Charlie Russo
University of Dayton
crusso1@udayton.edu

Cynthia Dieterich
Baldwin Wallace University
cdieteri@bw.edu

Allan Osborne
Former principal
Snug Harbor Community School
allan_osborne@verizon.net

Nicole Snyder
Chair, Special Education Law Practice
McKenna Snyder LLC
Attorneys At Law
nsnyder@mckennalawllc.com

Appendices

Appendix A
Summary Table of Contents of IDEA 2004 Statute

Part A—General Provisions (Subchapter I)

Section	Topics Covered
1400	Short Title; Table of Contents; Findings; Purposes
1401	Definitions
1402	Office of Special Education Programs
1403	Abrogation of State Sovereign Immunity
1404	Acquisition of Equipment; Construction or Alteration of Facilities
1405	Employment of Individuals with Disabilities
1406	Requirements for Prescribing Regulations
1407	State Administration
1408	Paperwork Reduction
1409	Freely Associated States

Part B—Assistance for Education of All Children With Disabilities (Subchapter II)

1411	Authorization; Allotment; Use of Funds; Authorization of Appropriations
1412	State Eligibility
1413	Local Educational Agency Eligibility
1414	Evaluations, Eligibility Determinations, Individualized Education Programs, and Educational Placements
1415	Procedural safeguards
1416	Monitoring, Technical Assistance, and Enforcement
1417	Administration
1418	Program information
1419	Preschool grants

Part C—Infants and Toddlers With Disabilities (Subchapter III)

1431	Findings and Policy
1432	Definitions
1433	General Authority
1434	Eligibility
1435	Requirements for Statewide System
1436	Individualized Family Service Plan
1437	State Application and Assurances
1438	Uses of Funds
1439	Procedural Safeguards

Part D—National Activities to Improve Education of Children With Disabilities (Subchapter IV)

Subpart 1—State Personnel Developmental Grants

Subpart 2—Personnel Preparation, Technical Assistance, Model Demonstration Projects, and Dissemination of Information

Subpart 3—Supports to Improve Results for Children With Disabilities

Subpart 4—General Provisions

Appendix B

Summary Table of Contents of IDEA 2004 Regulations

Part 300—Assistance to States for the Education of Children With Disabilities

Subpart A—General

Purposes and Applicability

Sec. 300.1 Purposes.
300.2 Applicability of this part to State and local agencies.

Definitions Used in This Part

300.4 Act.
300.5 Assistive technology device.
300.6 Assistive technology service.
300.7 Charter school.
300.8 Child with a disability.
300.9 Consent.
300.10 Core academic subjects.
300.11 Day; business day; school day.
300.12 Educational service agency.
300.13 Elementary school.
300.14 Equipment.
300.15 Evaluation.
300.16 Excess costs.
300.17 Free appropriate public education.
300.18 Highly qualified special education teachers.
300.19 Homeless children.
300.20 Include.
300.21 Indian and Indian tribe.
300.22 Individualized education program.
300.23 Individualized education program team.
300.24 Individualized family service plan.
300.25 Infant or toddler with a disability.
300.26 Institution of higher education.
300.27 Limited English proficient.
300.28 Local educational agency.
300.29 Native language.

300.30 Parent.
300.31 Parent training and information center.
300.32 Personally identifiable.
300.33 Public agency.
300.34 Related services.
300.35 Scientifically based research.
300.36 Secondary school.
300.37 Services plan.
300.38 Secretary.
300.39 Special education.
300.40 State.
300.41 State educational agency.
300.42 Supplementary aids and services.
300.43 Transition services.
300.44 Universal design.
300.45 Ward of the State.

Subpart B—State Eligibility

General

300.100 Eligibility for assistance.

FAPE Requirements

300.101 Free appropriate public education (FAPE).
300.102 Limitation—exception to FAPE for certain ages.

Other FAPE Requirements

300.103 FAPE—methods and payments.
300.104 Residential placement.
300.105 Assistive technology.
300.106 Extended school year services.
300.107 Nonacademic services.
300.108 Physical education.
300.109 Full educational opportunity goal (FEOG).
300.110 Program options.

Subpart G—Authorization, Allotment, Use of Funds, Authorization of Appropriations

Allotments, Grants, and Use of Funds

300.700 Grants to States.
300.701 Outlying areas, freely associated States, and the Secretary of the Interior.
300.702 Technical assistance.
300.703 Allocations to States.
300.704 State-level activities.
300.705 Subgrants to LEAs.
300.706 [Reserved]

Secretary of the Interior

300.707 Use of amounts by Secretary of the Interior.
300.708 Submission of information.
300.709 Public participation.
300.710 Use of funds under Part B of the Act.
300.711 Early intervening services.
300.712 Payments for education and services for Indian children with disabilities aged three through five.
300.713 Plan for coordination of services.
300.714 Establishment of advisory board.
300.715 Annual reports.
300.716 Applicable regulations.

Definitions that Apply to This Subpart

300.717 Definitions applicable to allotments, grants, and use of funds.

Acquisition of Equipment and Construction or Alteration of Facilities

300.718 Acquisition of equipment and construction or alteration of facilities.

Subpart H—Preschool Grants for Children With Disabilities

300.800 In general.
300.801–300.802 [Reserved]
300.803 Definition of State.
300.804 Eligibility.
300.805 [Reserved]
300.806 Eligibility for financial assistance.
300.807 Allocations to States.
300.808 Increase in funds.
300.809 Limitations.
300.810 Decrease in funds.
300.811 [Reserved]
300.812 Reservation for State activities.
300.813 State administration.
300.814 Other State-level activities.
300.815 Subgrants to LEAs.
300.816 Allocations to LEAs.
300.817 Reallocation of LEA funds.
300.818 Part C of the Act inapplicable.

Appendices

Appendix A to Part 300—Excess Costs Calculation
Appendix B to Part 300—Proportionate Share Calculation
Appendix C to Part 300—National Instructional Materials
Accessibility Standard (NIMAS)
Appendix D to Part 300—Maintenance of Effort and Early
Intervening Services
Appendix E to Part 300—Index for IDEA—Part B Regulations (34 CFR part 300)

Source: Wrightslaw (n.d.). Regulations for IDEA 2004 as published by the U.S. Department of Education. Retrieved from www.wrightslaw.com/idea/law/table.idea.regs.pdf

Appendix C
Comparison of IDEA, Section 504, and ADA

	IDEA	SECTION 504	ADA
Nature of Statute	Funding grant and civil rights statute	Civil rights statute	Civil rights statute
Statutory Reach	States and school districts accepting money under the statute	Public and private schools (preschool through grade 12) and higher education institutions accepting federal money	Public sector and parts of private sectory (e.g., secular private schools and daycare centers)
Protected Groups	Students with IDEA disabilities	Students, parents, and employees with Section 504 disabilities	Service recipients (e.g., students, parents) and employees with ADA disabilities
Definition of Disability	13 specific disabilities, if the disability adversely affects the child's education to the extent that special education and related services are needed (developmental delay allowed for younger children)	Functional definition (mental or physical impairment that substantially limits a major life activity, record of such, or regarded as having such an impairment)	Functional definition (essentially the same as Section 504)
Age Ranges	Part B: 3 through 21 Part C: Birth through 21	(Birth to death, depending on program or activity)	Same as Section 504
Program Requirements	Free appropriate public education (FAPE) in the Least Restrictive Environment (LRE) with an Individualized Education Program (IEP)	Nondiscrimination (FAPE) for school age children Reasonable modifications (programs and services) Reasonable accommodations (employment) Accessible facilities	Same as Section 504 ADA Accessibility Guidelines
Enforcement	Administrative complaint mechanisms Private right of action in court	Administrative complaint mechanisms Inferred private right of action in court	Administrative complaint mechanisms Private right of action in court
Implementing Agencies	OSEP within ED	OCR within ED Equal Employment Opportunity Commission (EEOC)	OCR EEOC Department of Justice (for Title III)

Appendix D
Chronological Listing of Leading Federal Level Cases Involving Special Education

Court Case	Year	Impact
Board of Education Hendrick Hudson School District. v. Amy Rowley	1982	First special education case. U.S. Supreme Court defines FAPE. See Endrew F case in 2017 for updated ruling on FAPE.
Abrahamson v. Hershman	1983	If a student with a disability requires residential placement then the school district must provide it.
Dept of Ed., State of Hawaii v. Katherine D	1984	"Congressional preference for educating handicapped children in classrooms with their peers is made unmistakably clear." Please note that the term handicapped children is outdated and we now use the term child with a disability.
Irving Independent School District v. Tatro	1984	Court's first attempt to define the distinction between "school health services" and "medical services." Related services include health services that do not require a licensed physician.
Smith v. Robinson	1984	School must pay for necessary residential placements
School Committee of Town of Burlington, Mass. v. Massachusetts Department of Education	1985	Parents cannot be forced to waive their right to reimbursement if they place their child in an alternative school from the one recommended in the IEP. Parents who unilaterally change their child's placement do so at their own financial risk, but they may be reimbursed if the placement is deemed to ban appropriate available option.
Timothy W. v. Rochester. N.H., School District	1988	Zero rejection—a core principal of IDEA, must be adhered to.
Honig v. Doe	1988	School discipline case. U.S. Supreme Court clarified procedural issues designed to protect children with disabilities. Schools cannot expel students for behaviors related to their disabilities.
Danny R. R. v. State Board of Ed.	1989	Least Restrictive Environment—FAPE means student has right to be educated with their nondisabled peers to the maximum extent possible.
Zobrest v. Catalina School District	1993	District may pay for student services if needed even when the student with a disability attends a Catholic school without violating separation of church and state.
Florence County School Dist. Four v. Carter	1993	If schools do not provide FAPE and a private school does, the parents are entitled to reimbursement, even if the placement is not a state-approved special education school.

(Continued)

(Continued)

Court Case	Year	Impact
Oberti v. Board of Education	1993	The presumption is that the student with a disability will be included with supplementary aids and services because it is "a fundamental value of the right to public education for children with disabilities." If placement outside the classroom is necessary, the school district must then include the child in as many school programs with children who do not have disabilities "to the maximum extent appropriate."
Sacramento City School District v. Rachel H	1994	Landmark victory regarding the right of students with disabilities to be educated alongside their nondisabled peers.
Cedar Rapids Community School Dist. v. Garret F.	1999	The exception for "medical services" from IDEA's related services provision only if services must be provided by a physician.
Buckhannon v. West Virginia Dept. of Health and Human Resources,	2001	Absent some sort of resolution on the merits, or a judicial determination altering the legal position of the parties, attorney's fees are not warranted.
Shapiro v. Paradise Valley Unified School District	2004	The failure of the district to provide critical information is a denial of the parent's right to participate.
Zachary Deal v. Hamilton Bd. of Ed	2004	The district's predetermined methodology violated the IDEA because it failed to consider the individual educational needs of the student prior to determining "appropriate" services.
Schaffer v. Weast,	2005	Supreme Court held that the burden of proof in a due process hearing that challenges an IEP is placed upon the party seeking relief. However—this does NOT require that states who place the burden on the schools to change that.
Arlington Cent. School Dist. Bd. of Educ. v. Murphy	2006	IDEA does not authorize the payment of the experts' fees of the prevailing parents.
Winkelman v. Parma City School Dist.	2007	Supreme Court resolved the issue as to whether a nonlawyer parent of a child with a disability may prosecute IDEA actions pro se in federal court. Court said that the parents enjoy enforceable rights at the administrative stage, and it would be inconsistent with the statutory scheme to bar them from continuing to assert these rights in federal court.
Forest Grove v. T.D.	2009	IDEA authorizes reimbursement for private special-education services when a public school fails to provide a FAPE and the private school placement is appropriate, regardless of whether the child previously received services through the public school. You do NOT have to try the public school before you get reimbursed for private school!
Doug C. v. Hawaii	2013	If a parent was not included in the IEP meeting, then procedural process under IDEA was violated, and the IEP is invalid.
F. H. v. Memphis City Schools	2014	A settlement agreement written between school and parent, if not honored by school, is a breach of contract that is enforceable by the courts.
Fry v. Napoleon Comm. Sch. District	2017	"We hold that exhaustion is not necessary when the gravamen of the plaintiff's suit is something other than the denial of the IDEA's core guarantee—what the Act calls a 'free appropriate public education.'"
Endrew F. v. Douglas County School District RE-1	2017	Supreme Court rejects the "de minimis" standard of FAPE! "A student offered an educational program providing 'merely more than de minimis' progress from year to year can hardly be said to have been offered an education at all."

Source: Treimanis A. (n.d.). Important special education cases. Retrieved from http://spedlawyers.com/important-special-education-cases/

Parent Consent

Date: _____

To: _____
    Parent(s)/guardian(s)/adult student

We are requesting your consent for the action checked
below regarding

                          _____
                                 Student's name

The attached written notice explains the action to be taken.

> We ask consent to take the following action:
>
> ☐ Initial evaluation of your child.
> ☐ Initial provision of special education and related services.
> ☐ Reevaluation of your child (using additional assessments).
> ☐ Other:

By giving consent, you are acknowledging that (1) you have been fully informed of all information relevant to the activity for which consent is sought; (2) you understand that the granting of consent is voluntary on your part and may be revoked at any time; (3) if you revoke consent, the revocation is not retroactive, which means that it does not negate any activity that has already taken place; and (4) if you refuse to give consent, the district may request mediation or a due process hearing to override your failure to give consent for evaluations or reevaluations. The district does not need your consent for a reevaluation if the district has made reasonable efforts to obtain your consent for tests administered for the reevaluation and you have failed to respond to these requests.

    The district may not ask an Administrative Law Judge to override your denial of consent if this is for the initial provision of special education and related services. However, if you do not provide consent for the initial provision of special education and related services, the district will not be considered to be in violation of the requirement to make a free, appropriate, public education (FAPE) available to your child.

☐ **I give** my consent.
☐ **I do not** give my consent.   Reason (optional): _____

                                        _____

                                        _____

_____
   Parent/guardian/adult student signature   *Date*

Source: Washington State Department of Education

Appendix F
Review of Referral for Special Education Evaluation

> **PURPOSE:** The purpose of this form is to review information regarding a student who has already been referred and to make a decision whether to evaluate the student for special education services.

Review of Referral for Special Education Evaluation

Student name: _____ Date district received referral: _____

Student ID #: _____ Birth date: _____ Grade: _____ Age: _____

Home School: _____ Gender: _____

Race/Ethnicity: _____ Primary Language in Home: _____

Parent/Guardian Name(s): _____ email address: _____

Address: _____ City/State/Zip: _____

Home Phone: _____ Work Phone: _____

Is a surrogate parent needed?   ☐ Yes   ☐ No   If yes, follow procedures for appointing a surrogate.

Person who made referral: _____ Position/Role: _____

Article I.

REASON FOR REFERRAL *(check all that apply)*:	
Instructional Concerns	**Behavioral Concerns**
☐ Pre-literacy skills	☐ Attention and concentration
☐ Basic reading skills	☐ Noncompliance with teacher directives
☐ Pre-numeracy skills	☐ Following directions
☐ Basic math skills	☐ Easily frustrated
☐ Written language skills	☐ Extreme mood swings
☐ Cognitive learning strategies	☐ Social/peer interaction skills
☐ Communication skills	☐ Adaptive behavior skills
☐ Other:	☐ Other:
☐ Other:	☐ Other:
☐ Other:	☐ Other:
☐ No instructional concerns noted	☐ No behavioral concerns noted

Review of Medical Information/Records *(describe any medical concerns currently impacting the student. Consider whether the student has any medical diagnoses, if the student is currently taking any medication at school and/or at home, is the student currently using any assistive technology devices, does the student wear glasses, does the student wear a hearing aid, etc.):*

Pre-referral Interventions *(describe any current or past supplemental programs/services or interventions provided to the child, such as Title 1, early intervention services, preschool, individualized interventions, etc. Describe any scientific research-based interventions implemented and the results.):*

Educational History *(describe the student's educational history, including appropriate instruction in reading and math and the student's response, school attendance/absences, whether the student has ever repeated a grade, the student's English proficiency level and how it was determined, current performance levels in academic and/or functional areas (primarily those areas of concern), any home/environmental factors that might affect the student's performance in school, whether the student has been previously referred for special education services, etc.):*

Other Relevant Information *(describe any other relevant information from the parent, school, other agencies, etc.):*

Referral Team Recommendations

- Special education evaluation recommended (*parent receives Prior Written Notice and Consent for Evaluation*).
- Special education evaluation not recommended at this time (*parent receives Prior Written Notice*).

<table>
<tr><td>Other Referral Team Recommendations:</td></tr>
<tr><td> </td></tr>
</table>

Referral Team Members (including parent(s)):	
Name	Position/Title

Procedural Safeguards notice must be provided to parent upon initial referral.

Appendix G
Preschool Referral

Student: Student Name   DOB: 00 / 00 / 2000

Previous Early Intervention Services (EI)

Is this student currently transitioning from Part C-Infant/Toddler Program?   yes   no

Date transition meeting from Part C-Infant Toddler Program was held: 00 / 00 / 2000

Who referred the child for EI services?

Age at which child started receiving EI services/child service coordination:

Age at which child stopped receiving EI services/child service coordination:

Frequency of EI services:

The student:

Has a current Individualized Family Service Plan (IFSP). Intervention goals include: (circle all that apply)

Cognitive	Adaptive
Communication	Fine Motor
Social/Emotional	Gross Motor
Behavior	Family Issues

Other:

Receives EI special instruction: (circle all that apply)

Speech/Language	Therapy
Occupational	Therapy
Physical	Therapy
Developmental	Instruction

Describe the progress the child has made on his/her IFSP goals:

Student: <u>Student Name</u>   DOB: 00 / 00 / 20__

Reason(s) for Referral/Areas of Concern

Learning/Behavioral

☐ difficulty remembering facts, details
☐ asks for help too quickly
☐ short attention span for age
☐ quickly abandons playing with toys
☐ difficulty following directions
☐ destructive
☐ physically aggressive with others
☐ appears withdrawn
☐ temper tantrums (describe)
☐ fights and/or bites

☐ takes inappropriate risks
☐ talks about hurting self or others
☐ repeats same behavior over and
  over (explain)

☐ fearful
☐ repeats same problem solving strategy,
  even when unsuccessful
☐ will not attempt difficult tasks
☐ difficulty making transitions from one
  activity to another
☐ fearful of new situations
☐ cries easily
☐ consistent inappropriate emotional reactions to situations/people
☐ plays poorly with others (explain)
☐ provokes/aggravates others/defiant
☐ requires constant supervision
☐ talks excessively, attention seeking

☐ other:

Communication

☐ difficulty using spoken language
☐ nonverbal
☐ unable to communicate basic wants/needs
☐ is not understood by familiar listener
☐ speech is choppy, stuttering
☐ has a vocabulary of less than 50 words
☐ difficulty eating certain foods (list foods)

☐ difficulty understanding language of others
☐ is not understood by unfamiliar listener
☐ voice constantly sounds hoarse
☐ slow, labored speech
☐ drools constantly
☐ frequently chokes on liquids, food
☐ frequent middle ear infections

Physical/Sensory

☐ lacks age appropriate self-care (feeding, dressing/undressing, toileting, bathing)
☐ impaired vision (explain) date of last opthamological exam:
☐ impaired hearing (explain)
☐ date of last audiological exam: 00 / 00 / 2000   date of last otological exam: 00 / 00 / 2000
☐ lacks age appropriate gross motor skills
☐ lacks age appropriate visual–motor skill
☐ falls down easily, hurts him/herself frequently
☐ lacks physical mobility at home/school
☐ has seizures/epilepsy
☐ cochlear implant: date of implantation: 00 / 00 / 2000
☐ overreacts to typical sights, sounds, tastes, textures
☐ primary mode of communication (circle): signing, cueing, auditory-oral/verbal

_____   ____ / ____ /
(Parent Signature)   (Date)

_____ SCHOOL SYSTEM

INDIVIDUALIZED EDUCATION PROGRAM (IEP)

IEP Meeting Date:	Purpose of IEP Meeting: Initial ☐ Annual Review ☐ Amendment ☐
Student Name:	Date of Birth: GTID#
Eligibility Category(s):	Most Recent Eligibility Date(s):
School:	Grade: School Year:
Parent(s):	
Address:	Email:
Phone (home): (work):	(cell phone):

Team Members in Attendance

REQUIRED MEMBERS	ADDITIONAL MEMBERS
Parent:	Name/Title:
Parent:	Name/Title:
Local Education Agency Representative (LEA):	Name/Title:
Special Education Teacher:	Name/Title:
Regular Education Teacher:	Name/Title:
Student (age 18 or if transition is being discussed):	Name/Title:
Agency representative (responsible for transition services):	Name/Title:

I. Present Levels of Academic Achievement and Functional Performance

Results of initial or most recent evaluation and results of state and district assessments:
Description of academic, developmental and/or functional strengths:
Description of academic, developmental and/or functional needs:
Parental concerns regarding their child's education:
Impact of the disability on involvement and progress in the general education curriculum (for preschool, how the disability affects participation in appropriate activities):

II. Consideration of Special Factors

a) **Does the student have behavior which impedes his/her learning or the learning of others?** ☐ Yes ☐ No
If yes, consider the appropriateness of developing a Behavior Intervention Plan.
Behavior Intervention Plan developed? ☐ Yes ☐ No
Refer to Behavior Intervention Plan for additional information.

b) **Does the student have Limited English proficiency?** ☐ Yes ☐ No
If yes, consider the language needs as related to the IEP and describe below.

c) **Does the student have blindness/visual impairment?** ☐ Yes ☐ No
If yes, provide for instruction in Braille and the use of Braille, unless the IEP Team determines that instruction in Braille is not appropriate for the student after an evaluation of the student's reading and writing skills, needs, and appropriate reading and writing media, including evaluation of future needs for instruction in Braille or the use of Braille. Describe below.

d) **Does the student have communication needs?** ☐ Yes ☐ No
If yes, consider the communication needs and describe below.

e) **Is the student deaf or hard of hearing?** ☐ Yes ☐ No
If yes, consider and describe the student's language and communication needs, opportunities for direct communication with peers and professional personnel in the student's language and communication

mode, academic level and full range of needs, including opportunities for direct instruction in the student's language and communication mode. Describe communication needs below.

f) **Does the student need assistive technology devices or services?** ☐ Yes ☐ No
If yes, describe the type of assistive technology and how it is used. If no, describe how the student's needs are being met in deficit areas.

g) **Does the student require alternative format for instructional materials?** ☐ Yes ☐ No
If yes, specify format(s) of materials required below.

☐ **Braille**   ☐ **Large type**   ☐ **Auditory**   ☐ **Electronic text**

_____
_____
_____
_____
_____
_____

III. Transition Service Plan

A transition service plan must be completed no later than entry into 9th grade or by age 16, whichever comes first, or younger, if determined appropriate by the IEP team and updated annually. If transition service plan is developed, attach to the IEP.

IV. Measurable Annual Goals

Measurable Annual Goals: Academic and/or functional goals designed to meet the child's needs that result from the disability to enable the child to be involved in and make progress in the general education curriculum or to meet each of the child's other educational needs that result from the disability.	Criteria for Mastery	Method of Evaluation	Progress at Reporting Period			
			1 (date)	2 (date)	3 (date)	4 (date)
1.						
2.						
3.						
4.						

Report of Student Progress

When will the parents be informed of the child's progress toward meeting the annual goals?

V. Measurable Annual Goals and Short-Term Objectives/Benchmarks

Academic and/or functional goals designed to meet the child's needs that result from the disability to enable the child to be involved in and make progress in the general education curriculum or to meet each of the child's other educational needs that result from the disability.

MEASURABLE ANNUAL GOAL:_____

Short-term objectives/benchmarks: Measurable, intermediate steps or targeted sub-skills to enable student to reach annual goals.	Criteria for Mastery	Method of Evaluation	Progress at Reporting Period			
			1 (date)	2 (date)	3 (date)	4 (date)

Report of Student Progress

When will the parents be informed of the child's progress toward meeting the annual goals?

VI. Student Supports

To advance appropriately toward attaining annual goals; to be involved and progress in the general curriculum; to be educated and participate with other children in academic, nonacademic, and extracurricular activities, the following accommodations, supplemental aids and services and/or supports for school personnel will be provided:

Instructional Accommodations

Classroom Testing Accommodations

Supplemental Aids and Services

Supports for School Personnel

VII. Assessment Determination for District and Statewide Assessments for Grades K–12

a) The student will participate in the following regular required assessments (Each state mandated test and subtest must be considered individually and documented below).

Specific Testing Accommodations (Accommodations used for assessment must be consistent with accommodations used for classroom instruction/testing and specified in the IEP. Some accommodations used for instruction may not be allowed for statewide assessment. Refer to the GaDOE Student Assessment Handbook for the only allowable accommodations. Conditional accommodations are only allowable for students who meet eligibility criteria.) All subtests must be considered individually. If the CRCT-M is considered, the Participation Guidelines for the CRCT-M must be completed and attached.

Test	Subtest	Setting	Timing/ Scheduling	Presentation	Response	None, Standard or Conditional

b) **The student will participate in the Georgia Alternate Assessment (GAA)** ☐ Yes ☐ No
   If yes, provide a statement of why the child cannot participate in regular required assessment.

_____

_____

_____

VIII. Special Education: Instruction/Related Services in General Education Classroom/ Early Childhood Setting

Options Considered ✓		Frequency	Initiation of Services (mm/dd/yy)	Anticipated Duration (mm/dd/yy)	Provider Title	Content/ Specialty Area(s)
	Consultative					
	Collaborative					
	Co-teaching					
	Supportive Services					
	Related Services					

IX. Special Education: Instruction/Related Services Outside of the General Education Classroom

Options Considered ✓		Frequency	Initiation of Services (mm/dd/yy)	Anticipated Duration (mm/dd/yy)	Provider Title	Content/ Specialty Area(s)
	Separate Class					
	Separate School					
	Home Instruction					
	Residential					
	Hospital/Homebound					
	Supportive Services					
	Related Services					

X. The Explanation of the Extent, if Any, to Which the Child Will Not Participate With Peers Without Disabilities in the Regular Class and/or in Nonacademic and Extracurricular Activities

_____

_____

_____

_____

_____

_____

_____

_____

XI. Extended School Year

a) **Are extended school year services necessary?** ☐ Yes ☐ No
   If yes, complete the section below.

b) **Goals to be extended or modified:**

_____

_____

_____

_____

_____

_____

_____

Services	Frequency	Initiation of Services (mm/dd/yy)	Anticipated Duration (mm/dd/yy)	Provider Title	Location

XII. Documentation of Notice of IEP Meeting

	Date	Method of Notification	By Whom
1st Notification		☐ Invitation ☐ Phone Call ☐ In Person ☐ Reminder notice ☐ Other:	
2nd Notification		☐ Invitation ☐ Phone Call ☐ In Person ☐ Reminder notice ☐ Other:	1.
3rd Notification		☐ Invitation ☐ Phone Call ☐ In Person ☐ Reminder notice ☐ Other:	2.

XIII. Parent Participation in the IEP Process

The Following Documents Were Provided to Parent(s)

- Parental Rights in Special Education
- Individualized Education Program (IEP)
- Eligibility Report(s)
- Evaluation
- Other: _____

_____

_____

_____

_____

If Parent Did Not Attend the Meeting, Complete Below

On _____ the documents were: ☐ Mailed ☐ Given in Person ☐ Sent via Student ☐
Other _____

Source: Georgia Department of Education (2011)

Appendix I
Transition Plan

Name:	Projected date of Graduation:	Date of Initial Transition Program Development: _____ Update: _____

Preferences, Strengths, Interests, and Course of Study based on Present Levels of Performance and Age Appropriate Transition Assessments (Areas for consideration include course of study, postsecondary education, vocational training, employment, continuing education, adult services and community participation)

Desired Measurable Postsecondary/Outcome Completion Goals (These goals are to be achieved *after* graduation and there must be a completion goal for Education/Training and Employment)

Education/Training—

Employment—

Independent Living (as appropriate)—

Based on age appropriate transition assessments, in the spaces below, include measurable Transition IEP Goals and Transition Activities/Services appropriate for the child's postsecondary preferences, strengths, and needs. Note: There must be at least a measurable Transition IEP Goal to help the child reach each of the desired Measurable Postsecondary/Outcome Completion Goals.

Education/Training (Goals based on academics, functional academics, life centered competencies or career/technical or agricultural training needs and job training.)

Transition IEP Goal(s)	Transition Activities/Services	Person/Agency Involved	Date of Completion/Achieved Outcome

Development of Employment (Goals based on occupational awareness, employment related knowledge and skills and specific career pathway knowledge and skills.)

Transition IEP Goal(s)	Transition Activities/Services	Person/Agency Involved	Date of Completion/Achieved Outcome

Community Participation (Goals based on knowledge and demonstration of skills needed to participate in the community (e.g., tax forms, voter registration, building permits, social interactions, consumer activities, accessing and using various transportation modes.))

Transition IEP Goal(s)	Transition Activities/Services	Person/Agency Involved	Date of Completion/Achieved Outcome

Adult Living Skills & Post School Options (Goals based on skills for self-determination, interpersonal interactions, communication, health /fitness and the knowledge needed to successfully participate in Adult Lifestyles and other Post School Activities (e.g., skills needed to manage a household, maintain a budget and other responsibilities of an adult.))

Transition IEP Goal(s)	Transition Activities/Services	Person/Agency Involved	Date of Completion/Achieved Outcome

Related Services (Goals based on Related Services that may be required now to help a child benefit from regular and special education and transition services (e.g., speech/language, occupational therapy, counseling, vocational rehabilitation training or the planning for related services that the individual may need access to as an adult.))

Transition IEP Goal(s)	Transition Activities/Services	Person/Agency Involved	Date of Completion/Achieved Outcome

Daily Living Skills (Goals based on adaptive behaviors related to personal care and well-being to decrease dependence on others.)

Transition IEP Goal(s)	Transition Activities/Services	Person/Agency Involved	Date of Completion/Achieved Outcome

TRANSFER OF RIGHTS (Required by age 17): _____ was informed on _____
of his/her rights, if any, that will transfer at age 18.

Name   Date

RIGHTS WERE TRANSFERRED (Required by age 18): _____ was informed on _____
of his/her rights.

Name   Date

Appendix J
Private School Placement Form

Services Plan (SP)

For Parentally Placed Private School Students

School District: _____

Purpose of SP Meeting:	Initial ☐	Annual Review ☐	Amendment ☐	
Student Name:	Date of Birth:	Grade:	School Year:	
Eligibility Category(s):	Most Recent Eligibility Date(s):			
Private School:				
Parent(s):				
Address:	Email:			
Phone (home):	(work):	(cell phone):		

Team Members in Attendance

Special Education Teacher:	Parent/Guardian:
Regular Education Teacher:	Student:
School System Representative:	Name/Title:
Private School Representative:	Name/Title:

Special Education Services

Special Education Service(s)/Related Services	Minutes or Segments	Initiation of Service(s)	Duration of Service(s)	Provider Title(s)	Location	
					Regular Education	Special Education

Present Levels of Academic Achievement and Functional Performance

Results of initial or most recent evaluation and results of state and district assessments:

Description of academic, developmental, and/or functional strengths:

Description of academic, developmental, and/or functional needs:

Parental concerns regarding their child's education:

Impact of the disability on involvement and progress in the general education curriculum:

Consideration of Special Factors

Does the student have behavior which impedes his/her learning or the learning of others?	☐ Yes	☐ No
Does the student have Limited English proficiency?	☐ Yes	☐ No
Is the student blind or visually impaired?	☐ Yes	☐ No
Does the student have communication needs?	☐ Yes	☐ No
Is the student deaf or hard of hearing?	☐ Yes	☐ No
Does the student need assistive technology devices or services?	☐ Yes	☐ No

If yes to any of the above, describe below.

_____

_____

TRANSITION PLAN—If transition services are to be provided to the student (no later than entry into 9th grade or by age 16, whichever comes first) attach transition plan to the SP.

Student Supports

To advance appropriately toward attaining annual goals; to be involved and progress in the general curriculum; to be educated and participate with other nondisabled students, the following accommodations, supplemental aids and services, and/or supports for school personnel will be provided.

Instructional Accommodations

Classroom Testing Accommodations

Supplemental Aids and Services

Supports for School Personnel

Annual Goals

Annual Goal: The annual goals are developed to address deficits as described in the present levels of academic achievement and functional performance.	Criteria for Mastery	Method of Evaluation	Progress at Reporting Period			
			1 (Date)	2 (Date)	3 (Date)	4 (Date)

Report of Student Progress

When will the parents be informed of the student's progress toward meeting the annual goals? _____

TRANSFER OF RIGHTS (Required by age 17): _____ was informed on _____ of his/her rights, if any, that will transfer at age 18.

(Name)   (Date)

RIGHTS WERE TRANSFERRED (Required by age 18): _____ was informed on _____ of his/her rights.

(Name)   (Date)

Glossary of Legal Terms

Administrative appeal a quasi-judicial proceeding before an independent hearing officer or administrative law judge.

Administrative law judge an individual presiding at an administrative due process hearing who has the power to administer oaths, hear testimony, rule out questions of evidence, and make determinations of fact. The role of an administrative law judge in IDEA proceedings is identical to that of an independent hearing officer.

Affirm to uphold the opinion of a lower court on appeal.

Allegation an unsupported assertion made in a legal proceeding by a party who expects to prove it in court.

Alternative dispute resolution procedures for settling disputes by means other than litigation; e.g., by arbitration or mediation. Such procedures are usually less costly and faster.

Appeal a party's request to a higher court to review a decision by a lower court. In cases where the right exists, the appeal must be made according to certain procedures and limitations.

Appellant the party bringing a court appeal.

Appellate court any state or federal court empowered to review and amend the judgments of a lower court over which it has jurisdiction.

Case law a primary source of law or legal authority formed by the body of reported court cases.

Certiorari (abbreviated as cert.) a petition for a superior court to review the decision of a lower court. Review may be granted or denied at the discretion of the superior court.

C.F.R. (abbreviation for Code of Federal Regulations) the repository regulations promulgated by various federal agencies to implement laws passed by Congress.

Citation in legal writing, a notation that directs the reader to a specific source of authority, such as a court case, statute, regulation, or journal article.

Civil action a lawsuit, as opposed to a criminal prosecution, commenced in order to recover a private or civil right, or to obtain a remedy for the violation of such a right.

Civil rights or civil liberties personal, natural rights guaranteed and protected by the Constitution or state constitutions, e.g., freedom of speech and the press, freedom from discrimination.

Class action a lawsuit commenced by one or more members of an ascertainable class who sue on behalf of themselves and others having the same complaint and seeking the same remedy.

Code a written collection of laws or regulations arranged according to an elaborate subject-matter classification scheme (e.g., the U.S. Code and Code of Federal Regulations).

Common law law deriving its authority not from legislative enactments, but from ancient and continuing custom or from the judgments and decrees of courts enforcing those customs.

Compensatory damages a judicial award intended to compensate plaintiff for an actual loss.

Complaint the original pleading that initiates a lawsuit and that sets forth a claim for relief.

Consent decree a judgment entered by consent of the parties whereby the defendant agrees to stop alleged illegal activity without admitting guilt or wrongdoing.

Damages the monetary compensation awarded by a court to the prevailing party in a lawsuit for injury, loss, or other harm done to their rights, their property, or their person through the illegal or wrongful conduct of another.

Declaratory relief a judgment or opinion of the court that merely sets forth the rights of the parties without ordering anything to be done.

Defendant the defending party in a civil action who must answer the complaint; the plaintiff's opponent.

De novo a trial *de novo* refers to a situation where a court hears evidence and testimony that may have been previously heard by a lower court or administrative body.

Dissenting opinion a court opinion, written by a judge or minority of the judges sitting on a court, setting forth views that contradict and often criticize the judgment and reasoning of the majority opinion. Only the majority opinion has the force of law.

Due process of law a phrase from the Fifth and Fourteenth Amendments of the United States Constitution that generally refers to the reasonable, fair, and equitable application and administration of the law. Procedural due process refers to constitutionally guaranteed rights to fair notice, fair hearing, and other fair procedures in any legal proceedings that might jeopardize one's life, liberty, or property.

Enjoin to command, especially a court's command or order forbidding certain action; the word also can be used to mean require certain action.

Et. seq. this is generally used in a citation to indicate "and the sections that follow."

Ex parte an action initiated at the request of one party and without notice to the other party.

Finding a conclusion or decision upon a question of fact reached as a result of a judicial examination or an investigation by a court or jury.

Good faith a term referring to a party's honest intent. A good faith undertaking is one devoid of any fraud or any motive to take unfair advantage. **Bad faith** is the opposite.

Hearing a proceeding with definite issues of fact or law to be resolved, in which witnesses are heard, the parties confront each other, and an impartial officer presides.

Holding part of the court's decision that applies the law to the facts of the case.

Independent hearing officer an impartial third-party decision-maker who conducts an administrative hearing and renders a decision on the merits of the dispute.

Injunction an equitable remedy, or court order, forbidding a party from taking a considered action, restraining the party from continuing an action, or requiring a party to take some action.

In re indicating that there are no adversarial parties in a judicial proceeding, this refers to the fact that a court is considering only a res ("thing"), not a person.

Judgment the decision of a court that has the authority to resolve the dispute.

Jurisdiction legal right by which a court exercises its authority; this also refers to the geographic area within which a court has the authority to rule.

Moot when a real, or live, controversy no longer exists; a legal suit becomes moot if, for example, there is no longer any dispute because a student with a disability turns 21 years old.

On remand this occurs when a higher court returns a case to a lower court with directions that it take further action.

P.L. an abbreviation for Public Law; a public law is a statute passed by Congress. The IDEA was initially referred to as P.L, 94–142, the 142nd piece of legislation introduced during the 94th Congress.

Plaintiff the party bringing suit in a court of law by the filing of the complaint.

Precedent any decided case that may be used as authority in deciding subsequent similar cases.

Preponderance of the evidence level of legal proof required in a civil suit; evidence that has the greater weight or is more convincing. Conversely, a criminal case requires proof beyond a reasonable doubt.

Pro se this refers to a person who represents himself or herself in a court of law.

Privacy, right of the right to live without unwarranted interference by the public in matters with which the public is not necessarily concerned; the right of a person to be free from unwarranted publicity. The term encompasses a number of rights recognized as inherent in the concept of "ordered liberty." This right is not absolute.

Punitive damages compensation awarded to a plaintiff that is over and above the actual loss suffered; these damages are designed to punish the defendant for wrongful action and to act as an incentive to prevent similar action in the future.

Reevaluation a complete and thorough reassessment of a student. Generally, all of the original assessments will be repeated, but additional assessments must be completed if necessary; the IDEA 2004 requires educators to reevaluate each child with a disability at least every three years.

Remand to return a legal case to a lower court, usually with specific instructions for further action.

Res judicata meaning "a thing decided." A rule that a final judgment of a court is conclusive and acts to prevent subsequent action on the same legal claim.

Settlement agreement an out-of-court agreement made by the parties to a lawsuit to settle the case by resolving the major issues that initiated the litigation.

Standing an individual's right to bring a suit to court: in order to have standing an individual must be directly affected by, and have a real interest in, the issues litigated.

Stare decisis meaning "let the decision stand." This refers to following a legal precedent.

State-level review officer an impartial person (or panel of usually three or more persons) who reviews the decisions of an independent hearing officer from an administrative due process proceeding under the IDEA. The IDEA provides that if administrative due process hearings are held at the local school district level, provisions must be made for an appeal at the state level.

Statute of limitations specifies the period of time within which a legal suit must be filed.

U.S.C. (abbreviation for United States Code) the official compilation of statutes enacted by Congress.

Vacate set aside a lower court's decision in an appeal.

Index

Note: Page numbers in italic indicate a figure and page numbers in bold indicate a table on the corresponding page.

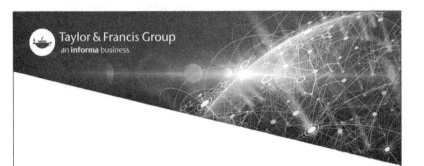